16.9.66

THE PARADOX OF PLEASURE
AND RELATIVITY
THE PSYCHOLOGICAL CAUSAL LAW

THE PARADOX OF PLEASURE
AND RELATIVITY

THE PSYCHOLOGICAL CAUSAL LAW

by

D. G. GARAN, Ph.D., J.U.D., LL.D.

PHILOSOPHICAL LIBRARY
New York

Copyright, 1963, by

Philosophical Library, Inc.

15 East 40th Street, New York, N.Y.

All rights reserved

Library of Congress Catalog Card Number: 63-15602

Printed in the United States of America

CONTENTS

I. **The Paradox of Psychological Causation** 1

II. **Pleasure and Relativity** 25

Inner Selection. Conditioning. Measurement of Pleasure. Relativity of Sensations. Relativity of Cognition. Equivalence of Emotions. Fixation. Contrast. Opposite Causation. Unlimited Intellectual Potential. Conclusions.

III. **The Imitation of Scientism** 64

Experimentalism. Behaviorism. Gestalt Psychology. Field Theory. Hormic Theories. Other Schools.

IV. **The Paradox of Neuroses and Psychoses** 99

Anxiety. Obsessive-Compulsive Reactions. Phobic Reactions. Neurotic Depressive Reactions. Complex of Guilt. Compulsive Shyness. Complex of Inferiority. Projection. Conversion Hysterias. Amnesia and Fugue. Multiple Personality. Psychoses. Treatment of Neuroses and Psychoses. Drug Treatment. Shock Treatment. Analysis. Conclusion.

V. **The Ghost World of Freudians** 142

The Id. The Superego. The Censor. The Subconscious. Instincts. Oedipus Complex. Cannibalistic

v

Drive. Castration Complex. Sexual Drives. Sublimation. Resistance, Distortions and Symbolism. Dream Interpretation. Self-Punishment. Defense. Repression. Success of Psychoanalysis. Freud. Adler. Jung. Rank. Jones.

VI. The Paradox of Adjustment **176**

Education. Abstract Learning. Juvenile Delinquency. Sexual Maladjustment. Overweight. Smoking and Drinking. Use of Drugs. Headaches. Sleeplessness. Work. Shelving of Worries. Play. Physical Care. Daydreaming. Social Adjustment. Old Age. Suicide. Conclusions.

VII. Everyday Value Delusions **222**

Happiness. Beauty. Harmony. Reason and Truth. Purpose of Life. Love. Hope and Faith. Freedom. Sense of Humor. Disvalues. Pain. Death. Conclusions.

VIII. Cultural Value Delusions **259**

Morals. Religion. Philosophy. Aesthetics. Literature. Cultural Inertia. Conclusions.

IX. The Relativity of Knowledge (From Philosophy to Physics) **312**

Philosophical Method. Philosophical Schools. Conclusion. Relativity of Knowledge in Physics. Ether and Field. The Mysteries of Atom. The Particle-Wave Dilemma. The Mystery of Gravitation. Electromagnetism. Cosmogonic Creation. Conclusion.

X. The Paradox of Disease and Cure **372**

Heart Disease. Hypertension. Arteriosclerosis. Dia-
betes. Arthritis. Gastric Disorders. Cancer. Some
Other Paradoxes. Infectious Diseases. Longevity.
Rejuvenation. Inheritance.

XI. The Paradox in Economics, Politics and History **437**

Economics. Business Cycles. Politics. Democracy.
Communism. Totalitarianism. Aristocracy. Theory
of History. Cyclic Theories. Spengler. Toynbee. Conclusions.

Index **495**

FOREWORD

The central concept of this book is so new that most readers will find it unacceptable or even ridiculous. That is why it is new. If the causal principle of human reactions, to which this concept amounts, did not seem so utterly impossible to man, it would have been discovered the first time man reflected about it. For as a natural principle it can be only simple. All basic principles of sciences are simple, but were not discovered for so long because they seemed impossible and often ridiculous in human terms.

Since this central concept leads to the understanding for the first time of the causal laws of all human reactions, including feeling and thought, the explanations in this book extend to varied fields, from physiology to the nature of the philosophical method. These explanations are as unexpected as the central concept is. They originate from a point of view that represents almost the reverse of what the humanistic and generally accepted "scientific" view has been. In psychology, psychiatry, psychoanalysis, adjustment, education and learning, a unified causal explanation is given. It has never been possible before because its underlying, seemingly paradoxical logic is contrary to everything psychologists presently consider as true and scientific.

In medicine, the mysterious causes of the increasing modern diseases become explainable, as the paradoxical causal logic of physiologic reactions becomes understood. In the field of thought, the relativity of knowledge explains the inherent contradictions and fallacies of philosophy and all humanistic speculations. What is more important, the dilemmas of modern physics become explainable, as the universal one-sidedness of man's knowledge of physical reality is revealed in the light of the relativity of knowledge. Equally unexpected causal explanations are offered in the fields of the social sciences, particularly, economics, politics and the study of history.

Naturally, the greatest change of causal insights is offered by the book in those fields that deal with values, which means all the humanities. But the approach of this book is furthest away from any rationalism or ideological radicalism. Actually, it reveals that the reactionary and superstitious cultural tradition harbors deeper wisdoms, which prove best what the book explains. The book offers a scientific vindication of the restrictive cultural tradition against all rationalism and modern "scientism," whereas the humanistic theorists have been able to offer only value beliefs and prejudiced rationalizations, clearly untenable in the age of the sciences. Of course, the book is indifferent to all values, for its aim is to explain their causal sources scientifically. This irreverence, together with the seeming impossiblity of the central concept, may be irritating to the reader. But whatever his feelings, it is hoped they will not obscure the simple truth this book tries to explain.

If it be any consolation, the reader of this book is spared the complex or mystifying sophistications so characteristic of modern treatises on psychology. The book does not need to go beyond the simplest, down-to-earth explanations, to have plenty to say — and still leave out much. Modern psychology, and with it all human sciences, are at a stage of knowledge where it is exactly the simplest basic principles that are missing throughout their enormous elaborations in every area. This has to be admitted, however deep the respect that we have for the erudition and genius of scientists and psychologists.

D. G.

x

THE PARADOX OF PLEASURE
AND RELATIVITY
THE PSYCHOLOGICAL CAUSAL LAW

I

THE PARADOX OF PSYCHOLOGICAL CAUSATION

The laws of psychological causation have still not been discovered, as every psychologist well knows. There are a dozen dissenting schools in modern psychology. Each school may present dozens of controversial theories, which are in fact so different that each would imply different causal principles. But there is no understanding of the basic causal law or principle by which psychological mechanisms work, though it has to be simple as all principles of nature are. The consequences of such absence of understanding of what makes man tick are apparent. Whereas in other fields science has increased its power and efficiency a thousandfold, in the sciences about man we still continue living by inertial cultural traditions based on superstitions and taboos. Moreover, insofar as psychological theories have tried to change tradition, they have produced confusion, if not direct harm, rather than progress.

One can easily imagine what enormous difference it would make if we knew how to engineer our feelings, motivations or mental capacities. If we were able to change man's mind, everything else would change automatically. Essentially, not much is needed to lay the foundation for such engineering. All sciences, vast as they may be, have grown out of the simplest causal insights. From the realization that plants grow from seeds, in agriculture, or that water has to be raised higher by damming it up, in irrigation engineering, to the discovery of the law of selective evolution in the natural sciences — the causal insights have been elementarily simple. But they have been sufficient to bring about tremendous progress in the end. If we could have a similar simple understanding of causal

1

connections between psychological events, we would have the simple beginnings of an engineering of human motivation. In our age of scientism there would be no lack of resources or determination to bring it to full bloom at once.

Why do we lack such simple insight into psychological causation? It cannot be for the reason that psychological phenomena are inaccessible, as, for instance, physical phenomena are in the submicroscopic world of atoms where physical science faces its dilemmas. Nothing is closer or more accessible to man than the workings of his own mind. Can it be the complexity of psychological events? This is usually suspected as the reason. To be sure, psychological processes are inconceivably complex. But so are all natural processes. Millions of millions of factors and events are necessary to produce a species. But the law of selective evolution, which is simplicity itself, enables us to understand and predict the evolution of species, or even to control it, as in the case of biocultures and mass breeding. In every natural process the elements are innumerable and complex, but the underlying principles under which they work are simple and become easily applicable as soon as science succeeds in explaining them. *Nature does not know complex principles. Its method of working can be only elementarily simple. Since psychological reactions are natural processes, their underlying principles or causal laws must also be elementarily simple.*

The reason why man does not know these laws must be something else. It must be something very grave, since the understanding of these laws would entail consequences more important for man than anything else in the world.

At this point we had better state the simple down-to-earth truths on which the laws of psychological causation rest, even if these truths may appear unsubstantiated at this stage of our discussion. Psychological life, like living in general, consists of the emergence of needs and the finding of corresponding satisfactions. Psychologists readily admit that the need-satisfaction mechanism is at the basis of all behavior. The purpose of this mechanism is to maintain the normalcy of the organism, to keep it capable of persisting. This persistence for persistence's sake is self-explanatory.

2

Any form of life that is incapable of persisting is not there any more. The whole business of living is this maintenance of normalcy — or existing for the sake of existence. Nobody would contest this as regards animals, but one may have doubts as regards man. We cannot go into a discussion of this now, but a simple reflection that all human values collapse when their basis, physical existence, is threatened may be sufficient here.

The most important point is that an *organism has a strictly predetermined identity in its statics as well as its dynamics.* It has to remain the same or grow at essentially the same rate. It cannot become something more or accumulate excessive growth. Therefore needs and satisfactions can mean only oscillations of quantitatively equal "downs" and "ups" relative to the unchanging level of normalcy. Since all psychological, even intellectual, experiences are only elaborations of more fundamental needs and satisfactions, all our psychological experiences are subject to the same rule.

From these basic insights the simple truths of psychological causation follow. They mean that *any motivation as satisfaction can be created only by creation of an equal opposite need, and any feeling of value can arise only from an equal opposite feeling of what we shall call disvalue. In other words, all psychological reactions have their causal source in their opposites.* Satisfaction as the restoration of normalcy after a disturbance can exist only to the extent that there was a disturbance; and a disturbance has meaning only to the extent that there was previous normalcy.

What makes the truths of relative causation humanly unacceptable is that they reveal the relativity or the inherent limitation of psychological life, which makes every human endeavor appear futile. There can be a positive experience, value, or advance only after an equal negative experience or retreat, as *there can be only a disturbance of normalcy and an equal return back to it, never anything more.* Man strives for positive experience alone, but such experience is impossible without an equal opposite experience. Insofar as man has no needs, but the fullest satisfaction, as for instance in his normal breathing, he feels no satisfaction nor anything. Value without its opposite is logically as well as emotion-

3

ally nonsensical. There is not one value in the world that does not have its opposite.

The quantitative as well as qualitative equivalence between satisfaction and need will be explained in detail later, but even a superficial observation is sufficient to show that the equivalence is always there. The pleasure of drinking is proportional to previous suffering from thirst. Enjoyment of rest can mean nothing without the previous painfulness of exertion. The more difficult a task is, the greater the satisfaction upon its completion.

To be sure, in practice the analysis can become involved. There is the special instance where satisfaction can come without previous need. Then the opposite feeling comes afterward. We would call it overenjoyment, or *overadjustment*. Drug addiction, or any clearly excessive enjoyment that ends with an aftermath, is the best example. Schematically we can picture the process as an overdrawal of those resources that constitute normal reserves. These then are restored by an opposite process as soon as the excessive stimulation ceases. In reality, the overadjustment consists mostly of excessive releases in the rate of metabolism rather than in energy resources. The return to normalcy, therefore, means a slowing down in that rate, with all the feelings resembling slow dying that it entails. By the way, such restoration is often started by deeper mechanisms immediately, even while the overstimulation is going on.

Also, there can be releases that afford no immediate pleasure because the extra resources they set free may be stored up against an emergency. Or there can be a simple removal of normal requirements by use of sedatives, in which case excess reserves become available without intensification of metabolism, though the normal requirements have to be met later. Furthermore, the all-important *conditioning* by which restrictions and reserves are established always comes into play. Biological conditioning has become a part of the normalcy of higher animals, and cultural conditioning constitutes a great part of human normalcy. Release from conditioned restrictions is the main source of overenjoyments or overadjustments, as we shall see later.

In the meantime, it is sufficient to realize that whatever over-

4

expenditure of normal reserves or release from normal restrictions is used as source of pleasure, the opposite process of restoration or restriction, accompanied by equal opposite emotions, has to take place afterward. A simple observation of the inevitability of aftermaths following every overstimulation shows that this is true. Another reflection may help. More than anything else man has searched for means that would give him a pleasure gain. Pleasure is the source not only of happiness but of all motivation. If a man has pleasure, he has will power, character, or any psychological capacity he wants. Still, nobody has found the means for increase of pleasure or happiness. We know intuitively that any such means would inevitably defeat itself. Though many drugs and techniques are known that can produce pleasure, reasonable people know that such happiness can never last and can bring only more trouble in the end. Lucky formulas for happiness usually belong in fairy tales — and in books by modern promoters of happiness, emotional richness, or positive thinking.

Whatever the conditions, *there can be no satisfaction or pleasure without previous or subsequent equally great need or displeasure.* One may visualize the process by thinking of a trip in a plane which starts from and returns to the same level but during the flight may ascend or descend. However complex the ascents and descents of the flight, the totals of moving up and down will be always equal. In living experience as well, the movements "down" and "up" in regard to the normal level are always equal. And they are the only ones that count in terms of experiences. Only changes are experienced, as modern psychologists have finally found out. No value experience results from continuation on the same level, even if this level be one of highest satisfaction or pain. A person continuously and unremittingly satiated to the highest limit with water or food would feel no satisfaction about it. Likewise, a person born with a defect which if suddenly inflicted on somebody else would make him cringe in pain feels nothing about it. It has to be kept in mind that all experiences are ultimately value experiences and derive from physiological functions.

At this point we may return to the question, why the simple truths of psychological causation are not known to man. It is because

5

man cannot accept the relativity of psychological causation and continue to have normal motivation or even to exist. If man accepted the fact that pleasure depends upon previous displeasure, he might as well abandon seeking for satisfaction of his needs. If he believed that the feeling of security is more enjoyable after a feeling of insecurity, he would end by not caring for his safety. Or if he accepted the fact that enjoyment of well-being depends upon previous privations, he might as well live in misery. Apparently, if such an attitude prevailed among a strain of people, they would soon perish in the struggle with the constant adversities of nature. Or they would be overcome physically as well as spiritually by those who believe in pleasure gain and strive incessantly for their satisfactions.

The idea of relative causation is completely incompatible with normal existence. Accordingly, we have a natural protection against relativistic attitudes, the same as we have against unhealthy foods. A harmful food is unpalatable, or tastes and smells bad. In causal terms the food is not uneatable because it smells bad, but smells bad because it is uneatable. For the same reason the idea of relative causation is boring and ridiculous. The nature and cultural conditioning of man are using here the strongest deterrents, boredom and ridiculousness, against the idea of relativity. This makes man keep away from the idea as from a smelling gutter at the side of the thoroughfare of normal life. Only a freak could have an interest in exploring it. Any idea of the relativity of values is discarded even before it amounts to a thought.

But have not people noticed, at least in passing, this most important truth? The truth of relative causation is as well known as the truth that by every act of life we are approaching our death — and as much ignored. We all know that the use of special means for the release of pleasure leads nowhere, and that any endeavor to reach happiness directly must fail. But we cannot help seeking for means of pleasure release at every moment of our lives. We would do nothing else but that, if it were not for cultural conditioning and restrictions. Civilized man accepts these readily because he knows deeply the ultimate uselessness of the search for pleasure.

6

The idea of relativity is equally known in theoretical thinking. Of course, the serious men of deep thoughts would never dwell on the boring and ridiculous practical aspects of relative causation. Consequently, the idea has never been worked out into the practically important discovery that it is. Serious thinkers are opposed to any strain of thought that is irreverent to values. The case of the school of the Sophists is interesting. The Sophists were relativists. Protagoras said that man is the measure of all things. Denial of any truths by Gorgias emerged as a consequence of the relativistic approach. How the other Sophists — Callicles, Euthydemus, Polus, or Trasymachus — expressed their attitudes we know only from the dialogues of Plato, who certainly chose only the loftiest subjects. Sophism represented the last word — though a nonsensical word — in philosophy. It came after everything that could be said was said. Though the Sophists were far less naïve than other philosophers in distinguishing truths from value delusions, they made themselves ridiculous, and nobody has wanted to be associated with sophism since.

But in its nobler and practically more remote aspects, relative causation has been recognized in Western philosophy from Plato to Spencer. Plato observed that a state that follows a pleasure is painful, while a state that follows pain is pleasurable. Plato termed them neutral states, for he wanted to remain logical and not call pleasurable something which objectively could not be so called.

The Neoplatonists recognized evil as necessary for discerning good. The Stoics were aware of psychological relativity in their arguments about the nature and futility of happiness. St. Augustine held the same view as the Neoplatonists about the role of evil. Even St. Thomas spoke of the need for comparison. Hobbes dealt with psychological relativity itself, and held that happiness can exist only during the process of attaining a value not after the attainment of it. Spinoza, equally, held that joy arises only during the transition from an experience of lesser value to that of a greater value. Leibniz held ideas similar to the Neoplatonists and Augustine in regard to the necessity of evil.

In the philosophies of Spencer and Hamilton we find the relativity idea fully developed with regard to the more abstract human reactions. Hegelianism, which is probably the highest attainment in philosophy, rests on the doctrine of opposites — thesis and antithesis — which amounts to recognition of the main principle of relative causation in regard to cognition. We may also mention that the most modern schools of philosophy — pragmatism, phenomenalism, conventionalism, positivism — are relativistic in their approach. In this respect the modern schools correspond to those of the period of the Greek Sophists, except that the modernists are more technically specific and "scientifically" sophisticated. In their main theme — the nature of knowledge — these schools recognize that the goal-success, question-answer, or need-satisfaction limitation applies to all knowledge.

The most significant confirmation of relative causation is found in our practical life and cultural tradition. Man cannot accept the causal truth of relativity consciously. But when he has to develop his motivations — by following unconsciously evolved, often superstitiously explained, cultural traditions — he has to use methods that comply accurately with the causal law. Culture has become a system of restrictions under which new needs are evolved. This sounds like a truism, but has a deeper meaning. In order to increase the possibility of satisfaction or pleasure, need or restriction has to be increased. This is the only way to produce more motivation — actually, more pleasure, which is the source of all motivation. The paradox of psychological causation lies in the fact that *pleasure is the source of all motivation, but it can be increased only by first increasing its opposite — displeasure or restriction.*

In the light of this paradox it becomes clear why all cultural, educational, moral and religious systems are restrictive. Restriction of enjoyment of the natural drives, especially of sexual pleasures, has been the main purpose of all cultural traditions. Sexual satisfactions are the source of feelings of the highest beauty, and of the richest psychological releases. But they are under the strictest taboos in all cultures. To take another example, personal freedom and the pursuit of one's own interests or judgments are the highest values. But bending the will of the growing individual, keeping him hermetically closured in the atmosphere of his family or cultural group, and teaching him deference to authority, constitute the basis of education in all cultures.

8

We never fully realize how thorough our cultural restrictions and prejudices are because we live in their atmosphere. Einstein has said, in connection with the question of a person's judgment about himself, that fish do not know the water they live in. The more pervading a cultural restriction or conditioning is, the less it is noticed. In any event, cultural adjustment means a constant restriction of our own nature, of our natural inclinations and drives, though at the same time the release or satisfaction of these drives is the only source of motivation. Apparently, the cultural tradition embodies compliance with the paradoxical causal truth that release or satisfaction can arise only after restriction or need.

As regards the recognition of relative causation in the *sciences*, its paradoxical, completely different logic precludes any such possibility. Here we may say more about the principal difference between the logic of relative causation and the logic of the physical sciences, which is the only logic that the modern scientist knows. *In relative causation an addition of value gives less value, and taking away from it gives more, as negative value or disvalue produces positive value, and vice versa.* Adding more satisfaction either precludes the possibility of further satisfaction, or amounts to oversatisfaction, which is bound to lead to the opposite feeling of displeasure. Only the accumulation of need, or displeasure, can give satisfaction or pleasure without further reversal.

In the simpler cases of overenjoyments, like intoxication, drug addiction, or other overstimulation, everybody can easily observe that they lead to exactly opposite effects or displeasure. And in the case of simpler satisfactions, like eating, drinking, or rest, it is clear to everybody that only previous need or displeasure can be the cause of satisfaction or pleasure. But all situations are not so simple, and common-sense insights are discarded by the scientist proceeding under the only scientific logic he knows, in his often complex work. It must be clear, however, that the scientist who does not take into account the reversed logic of relative causation is bound to arrive at conclusions that are just the reverse of what is actually true.

To illustrate the point, let us imagine an experiment where a smoker is given nicotine-containing pills. Every time he takes a pill his desire for smoking decreases. The experimenter might conclude that these pills are good for getting out of the habit of smoking. In fact, they would increase the desire for smoking, as can be easily understood. This example is very close to real-life situations in which a complex or disease caused by overadjustment is often "cured" by means that increase rather than diminish the overadjustment. We shall show cases of this nature throughout this book.

The important thing is that *the reversed logic of relative causation applies to every aspect and every phase of human adjustment.* Its recognition would mean completely new insights in all fields of human psychology and physiology — education, adjustment, psychiatry, all humanistic and social sciences, even medicine — as well as in the understanding of human knowledge in general, from philosophical doctrines to man's understanding of physical reality.

We may mention one more confusing effect of the scientifically logical or experimental approach. You can observe easily for yourself that when you are hungry and start eating, the food tastes perfect — all of it. But as you become satiated, you start finding that there is something or other wrong with it. Finally, you may stop eating just because the food is too salty, or too gluey, or something else. In fact, *satisfaction* is the true reason for your starting to loathe the food, not dissatisfaction with any particular characteristic of it. For, if that characteristic were not present, some other would be found. This should appear clear enough to everybody. But psychologists lose this insight in dealing with more complex problems, because it means accepting the above logic that dissatisfaction results from satisfaction. What happens in this example applies to every instance of need-satisfaction — and, consequently, to all human behavior.

In practice, the paradox of relative causation is more involved because the opposite reaction starts accumulating from the moment the experience begins. The simplest way to picture the process is to think of a spring that swings up and down. At the end of its swing down, for instance, there may be one final bit of resistance, one tiny unit of force, that seems to stop the movement and make the spring go upward. But, in fact, the force for the upward movement has been accumulating from the moment the spring started to go down. It is helpful to keep in mind that any reaction or experience means only regaining a balance or identity of organism after disturbance or change. In the physical world a change or interference produces permanent corresponding effects. A thing retains the position, size, movement or value given to it by an interference. But in the organic world, *as far as living reactions are concerned*, the effect is a *reversed* one, as an organism tends to regain its previous balance.

Because of the imperceptible but constant reversal that accompanies any value experience, experimental logic and methods become inapplicable in psychology. What good is the usual experiment, if at every moment you have to account for an invisible parallel process that cancels out every effect you observe from the experiment? An experiment that would follow paradoxical relative logic could be devised, but it would go against everything psychologists now consider scientific. As it is, the psychologist turns to the usual methods and logic of the physical experimental sciences every time he wants to be scientific. In his experiments or case observations he makes his conclusions on the basis of the immediate effects without suspecting that the reversal of these effects is building up at the same time.

For instance, on the all-important issue of motivation, the psychologist always finds that increased release leads to better motivation. Actually, increased release leads to loss or exhaustion of motivation; and exactly its opposite, the restriction of release or accumulation of needs can provide for new satisfactions or better motivation — just as cultural tradition and practice confirm. The fallacy here is important and has not failed to show its effects. The "scientific" efforts of modern psychology have been enormous, but only a host of contradictory and abstruse theories, often bordering upon mystification, have resulted.

Here the importance of recognizing the law of relative causation, which we have been explaining, becomes evident. This law is certainly unacceptable to the healthy mind and can only appear ridiculous to anybody. There would be no point in dwelling on it if it were not for the fact that it offers *the only causal explanation* of human adjustment that we can have. As such this law can serve as the basis for a science in all fields of human adjustment and thought. Such a science has not started yet, just as chemistry did not start with alchemy but with a principle completely opposed to it, namely, that of the permanence or equivalence of matter. *The law of relative causation represents such a principle of equivalence in psychology and all adjustment. In its light the endeavors of modern psychology based on complex formulas, manipulative skills and accidental happenings are purely alchemistic.*

The fact that the truth of relative causation seems ridiculous explains why it has never been "discovered." What is more, its ridiculousness may rather point to its fundamental scientific value and importance. All fundamental scientific theories have at first appeared ridiculous. Is not the idea of a round, spinning earth, with people hanging down on the other side and everybody in danger of skidding off, ridiculous? The theory of gravitation is equally funny; it rather fits jokes about a drunken man being pulled to the ground. The theory of evolution supplied its opponents with the best joke — about the ancestors of evolutionists; Bishop Wilberforce will be remembered for having used the joke at the presentation of Darwin's theory. The theory of the permanence of matter is equally funny and may serve for a joke. There is the sad operatic one about Parisian students reassuring their landlord that matter is never lost. Newton's law of force and counterforce may not appear too serious either if you start picturing how a table pushes back at you when you try to push it. Einstein's Theory of Relativity is perhaps the best example of the unbelievable in scientific discoveries. Whitehead has said that all great ideas have at first appeared unbelievable.

This is understandable if we consider that man's outlook is a *value outlook* and that the *origin of value notions is paradoxical*, due to the dependence of value upon disvalue or satisfaction upon need. Man values, and therefore sees as important, what he needs. But a thing needed always means that which is lacking. Consequently, *man sees as most significant in the world what is actually lacking in it, or as a general law what is rather an exception*

12

in it. On the other hand, those realities that are so general as to be
omnipresent are not even noticed by man.

For instance, there is little order in this world, as there are millions of possible disorderly events to be found for every orderly one. However, we see the world as full of order, because due to the extreme scarcity of order man invests the highest effort in searching for it and values it above everything else. Finally, his main preoccupation becomes looking for order or laws in nature. Consequently, we see the world under the aspect of orderliness, and soon assume order as its essence. The same applies to such value beliefs as the existence of Providence, love or harmony in the world. Because man is not provided for and has to live amidst constant needs, he values Providence above everything else and sees it as the law governing the world. Equally, because man as an intricate organism lives under constant danger of harm, in a world inherently destructive to organization, he sees love and security in all their forms as the higher essences. Harmony has its prominent meaning for man only because it is the striking exception to the same general chaos in the universe. On the other hand, the values that are really "provided" for plentifully, like the gravitation that keeps everything in place or the forces that hold matter together, mean nothing to man. If explained, they remain queer abstractions, seem even ridiculous, as in the case of gravitation.

To take another example, evolution from the animal seems preposterous to man because he *is* so close to the ape. Being so close to the animal, man needs and values everything that takes him further away from it. He therefore sees the essence of being human in his difference from the animal. Equally, the truth of a moving, round and universally insignificant earth was resisted by man because he struggles for stability, permanent certainty and greatness, which he and his world lack most. To understand the universe, and his world in it, causally, man would have had to reverse his value certainties — to see how insignificant, unstable and accidental rather than central his world is. If he had done so, he would have seen what the true place of earth is in the universe the first time he looked at the curved horizon, rising sun or distant stars.

It can be said that man would, in all cases, get closer to causal truths if he reversed those truths that seem to him most convincing and that constitute the great discoveries of humanist thinkers. Each step of fundamental scientific advance has meant a conflict with the most firmly held human truths. From the heliocentric theory to selective evolution and Einstein's Theory of Relativity, the rejection of the values of man, and the recognition of their relativity, have been the road signs of progress. The truth of relative causation, as an absolute reversal of the value outlook itself, is the last step. As such it will, naturally, be resisted by man with the utmost conviction of its ridiculousness.

The value outlook is the greatest obstacle to science — to establishment of what is causally true. Modern science is still dominated by the humanistic tradition. This is supported at present by the fact that through an intuitive wisdom men prefer to hold to tradition rather than follow the fallacies of modern "scientism." But it should be clear that any humanistic approach means a value outlook, and as such is an inherent hindrance to science.

The fallacies of the value outlook are so deeply rooted in man that even physical reality is seen by him in a helplessly one-sided way. Hence, the dilemmas of modern physicists, who see that reality in the same one-sided way. The value delusion here consists in man's naïveté of viewing only matter as real while dismissing as nothingness its causal opposite — just because it is absolutely omnipresent. Physicists have always recognized that there must be a universal medium, which they have called the ether, without which the workings of the universe are inexplainable. Einstein recognized the universal field to be as concrete as matter. But it has all remained a mystery because no material effects — resistance, drag or density — of the "ether" or field could be discerned despite thorough efforts by physicists. In simple words, the universal medium cannot be felt in any way. If the physicists abandoned the one-sided human value outlook, they would recognize that the opposite of matter is as real as matter, and that such opposite, as a medium which is absolutely everywhere and participates in absolutely every effect of matter and energy, can never

14

be recognized or felt in any way and still be a million times denser than any substance. Such "ether" or field could then explain all the dilemmas of physics, as we shall see later.

Practically more important are the fallacies of the value outlook which govern in the human sciences. There the theorist sees positive values — satisfactions, positive feelings and releases — as the essence or causal nature of everything. In fact, they derive from the negative backgrounds of needs, feelings of disvalue and restrictions. These are the true causal sources of positive values. But the theorist either does not connect them with values because they are so different from values, or sees them as undesirable hindrances in the attainment of values. Naturally, this leads to theories which emphasize as causally important just the reverse of what is important in every case of human motivation and adjustment. We will come across this problem of *negative background causation* repeatedly.

In short, the fact that the idea of relativity seems so contrary to everything man believes in as to appear ridiculous may be the best guarantee that it is one of the remaining important hidden truths. Another guarantee is the simplicity in observation and reasoning by which this idea can be "discovered." There is so little ingenuity in our "discovery" that we may fear the label of simplism. We do not claim discoveries. But we do claim freedom from universal value attitudes, and that is what really matters here. The greatest discoveries have been made upon the simplest observations — a swinging chandelier, a falling apple, or the survival of the stronger animal — of things which were always there but were never "seen."

Revolutionary discoveries in science are products not so much of greater knowledge as of audacity in abandoning old approaches. The ancients had all the knowledge they needed to understand the heliocentric system. They could see that ships disappeared behind the curved horizon, that the earth faced the sun and starts in circular fashion, and so on. The Greeks and Egyptians had theories on almost every aspect of the heliocentric system. A unified theory was offered by Aristarchus of Samos. But nothing happened. Nobody was crazy enough to say "no" to the existing certainties.

15

Equally, selective evolution could have been understood with one-tenth of the knowledge that people had. But this theory, which explains the greatest miracles of nature, remained closed to the human mind striving desperately to understand them. It simply went against the deepest value beliefs. Some thinkers, e.g., Anaximander and Empedocles, touched the idea so closely that one can only wonder how they ever missed it.

Of course, discoveries increase as science advances. But it is more the reliance on abstract thought even if it contradicts value beliefs than knowledge as such which increases discoveries. The idea of relative causation has to be the last "discovery" to be accepted because it is the ultimate in denial of value beliefs.

And there are reasons not to be excited about such a discovery even if it is accepted.

It is true that the understanding of relative causation would enable the scientist to deal with human psychology in a causally understood way for the first time. This means the possibility of a science, like an engineering, of human motivation. All that is needed is the imposition of more restrictions so that more releases become possible. This is being done all the time through cultural conditioning—but in a blind intuitive way. Science, built on causal understanding, could make it all a thousandfold more efficient. The complexity of psychological life would be as little an obstacle here as is the complexity of biological life in prediction or control of selection. Once restriction is imposed or needs accumulated, there is a source of motivation that can be used indiscriminately for *any* motivation. A person with a background of painful labor finds satisfactory *any* kind of easier work. Nor would there be any loss in human happiness. There is never any loss, or gain, in the pleasure economy. Reaching a higher level of restrictions is painful, but once reached it enables the person to live with incomparably richer motivations. And in the whole even the initial painfulness is fully compensated.

But an endeavor to increase motivation by self-restriction amounts practically to trying to lift oneself by one's own boot straps. There can be no motivation without pleasure. The motivation to restrict oneself can be a future pleasure. We usually work hard in the certainty of enjoying the fruits of our work later; in fact, the enjoyment is used up by anticipation while the hard work goes on. But a self-restriction without anticipated or immediate pleasure is as impossible as a stream that would flow uphill. If it were possible, the road to hell would not be paved with good intentions. Every one of us knows that if he could impose on himself more effort or restriction, he could attain everything. The trouble is that we simply cannot do it. Even if one manages to produce an extra bit of will power and imposes on himself a hardship, the opposite reaction of relaxation of the same will power has to follow, because the relative reversals apply to every value experience.

Restrictions have to come from outside, and by way of conditioning, which imposes on us restrictions while utilizing our needs for growth, security or competition. But the forms and intensity of conditioning are determined by long tradition, evolving blindly and reaching its effects only after it becomes part of the over-all cultural atmosphere. Here we encounter the main difficulty. Relative causation applies to every cultural evaluation. If a parent or educator imposes on the child a restriction greater than is generally considered normal, the opposite reaction by the child, or parent himself, will inevitably follow. We have to keep in mind that what is recognized as rationally right or wrong matters little. The deciding factor is the value standard. This, however, can be attained only by comparison with other values, held by other persons, which in their turn can be determined only by comparison with still other values, and so on. Thus the general cultural level depends on each and all individuals in the society. We rest on each other here as grains of sand do in reaching their level in a heap. Of course, the over-all atmosphere we live in is not known to us.

What the use of scientific understanding of psychological causation can help to achieve is a gradual change in the general cultural trends. All sciences have started with a tiny change at the beginning, leading to cumulative effects and stupendous progress in the end. In trying to build a science of motivation the initial progress would be even tinier, for reasons we have just explained. At first there would be an understanding — only by the reason, however — that restriction and acceptance of displeasures is the key to enrichment of motivation. This would help at least to get rid of the innumerable theories of modern psychologists and humanists advocating releases and positive value experiences as sources of motivation. Secondly there would be a readiness — again only rational at first — to accept restrictions, as it became understood that, in the end, no pleasure loss is caused by restrictions. This would constitute sufficient beginnings of a science, considering that in our age of sciences and planning the purely rational elements may prevail to a certain extent.

But it may be questioned whether the relativistic attitude toward values would not weaken motivation. It is true that a relativistic attitude implies indifference to values. However, it is not the depth of a value feeling, but its elaboration and transformation into useful, hard and naturally less interesting activities, that make adjustment richer and more intellectually controlled. Savages and mentally unstable people have deeper emotions in every respect than a civilized person, because they yield more fully to the physiological releases which are the source of all emotions. Not the depth of an emotion but the contents of its elaborations is what matters. The more restricted or shallower an emotion is, the more elaboration can be placed on it in the total. In motivation it does not help much if the person wishes something passionately, but it helps if he is able to restrict other wishes and to maintain discipline over himself.

As regards the amount of emotions, every man has to live through a certain total of reactions, whatever he does. He can live faster and exhaust the potential of his reactions sooner; or he can live slower and have every reaction conditioned into more extensive ideational experiences. This may reflect even on the length of person's life. A person with a sober relativistic outlook would act as more mature and intellectual people do. He would be more ready to accept the restrictions of conditioning and learning, therefore more capable in all respects.

From what we have said it may be clear already that the causal understanding of psychology, as revealed in the law of relative causation, would lead to a complete change of insights in every field of human sciences, even the theory of the physical sciences. This law of relative causation implies not only a different, but an exactly reversed causal logic, to be applied in understanding all human behavior, from biological reactions to the nature of philosophical thought. In outline, the acceptance of the law of relative causation would entail the following changes:

First of all, psychology would become a science. The psychologist would be able to understand, predict and help control the properly psychological phenomena — motivation, emotion and intellectual potential — which make man tick the way he does. At present psychology amounts either to an extension of physiology, or to a causally unconnected gathering of social data, as far as it remains scientific. Its scientism amounts to a misunderstood imitation of the physical sciences. Beyond that, psychology is dominated by abstruse contradictions and an alchemistic approach, even mystifications of a ghost world. This is best illustrated by psychoanalysis, the most popular of all theories. The effort of modern psychology is enormous, and its theories unbelievably multiple, each implying a different world of basic principles. Apparently psychology has not yet found its scientific basis — the simple natural principles of psychological causation. It is still struggling through its alchemistic stage of recondite formulas, occult forces and gratuitous gains.

Further, the seemingly paradoxical causation in the fields of adjustment, education and psychological abnormalities would be understood for the first time. This would offer the possibility of making these fields scientific, even if practical success would be tiny at the beginning. At least the misleading and harmful modern theories on education and adjustment would be discarded. The theories that advocate "progressive" education, freedom from repressions, greater license in adjustment, and more enjoyment or release in all its forms would be exposed as the fallacies that they are. With them would go the alchemistic nonsense now constituting nine-tenths of psychological theorization, especially in psychoanalysis and the popular writings by promoters of happiness and better adjustment. Understanding of the simple though seemingly paradoxical natural basic cause of mental abnormalities would enable

19

psychiatrists at least to stop the alarming increase of mental illnesses. This disquieting problem of modern life reveals the paradox that relative causation explains: as modern man becomes able to attain increased satisfactions at the deepest levels, the powers of his psychic life are lost.

As to our humanistic systems of value beliefs, and the whole subject matter of the humanities that now constitute a great part of our higher education, the recognition of the value delusions would become inevitable. All these beliefs and disciplines are based on value principles, but in fact every value owes its existence to an equal disvalue. If one really wants to promote a psychological value, he has to promote its opposite, the disvalue, first. All this does not mean that humanistic education could ever lose its importance. Conditioning is the source of culture, but conditioning means restriction under promise of greater release. It is a long, inherently deceitful process that requires an atmosphere of overwhelming spiritual superiority as well as beliefs in supranatural redemption and justification. All cultures have evolved similar restrictive and superstitious morals and religions. They embody an intuitive understanding of relative causation. Supporting such blind understanding with a clear scientific one can only help.

The delusions of the value outlook and of an anthropomorphic world of gods and heavens would, however, become untenable. A humble serenity and rational detachment belong to the greater maturity of the humanity of the future. The history of man is an evolution from an emotional way of life — brutish, nasty and short because filled with its own tragic misunderstandings — toward a scientific life where man can plan its duration as well as its efficiency. The realization that no gain in pleasure release is possible whatever man does would enable him to plan his releases, even to decide how much of the ultimate fear of death he wants to leave for the last moment. The restriction of releases means a slower and therefore longer life. It would also mean a richer and more efficient life, for reasons we have explained.

Further, the process of human thinking, as a process of evaluations, would reveal its equally paradoxical nature. What men have always considered as the highest forms of thinking lead in fact to the lowest kind of knowledge, the same as striving for pure satisfaction leads to impossibility of satisfaction. Only new needs can give new satisfaction. Philosophy, which represents an endeavor towards pure knowledge, is the emptiest of all systems of knowledge. It amounts to an intellectual "neurotic" complex — striving for satisfaction without previous accumulation of need. Only our delusory attitude toward values keeps the philosophical interest alive in us.

In the theory of the sciences the concept of relativity would open insights into background causation. Modern science has reached in many fields, especially in the theory of physics and in psychology, a limit where the simplest phenomena resist further explanation to the point of mystery. There is no need for the mystifications and abstruseness that scientists resort to now. But the scientists should be able to look beyond physical phenomena, or positive values, and see the far more important causal background reality. Such reality is at present either not noticed, because it is so absolutely essential as to be omnipresent, or is not connected causally with values because as their opposite it appears completely different and unrelated to them.

In the social sciences, new causal understanding would change the theory in every field. Social adjustment rests on psychology with all its paradoxical causal logic, which the present social scientists and humanists do not even suspect. The irrationality of wars, persecutions, witch hunts or economic depressions, as well as the mysterious cyclic declines of peoples in history, would become causally understood. The new insights would affect, however, only the theory or "scientism" in these fields, particularly in the political sciences, economics and the study of history. Nothing much can be changed in practical social adjustment, for the reasons we have explained. But here as well, a theoretical causal understanding could help to establish new trends, or at least to expose the theoretical fallacies that stand in their way.

Finally, the understanding of the relativity of human reactions would radically change the approach, even the logic itself, of modern physiology. As we saw, increasing a satisfaction leads to exhaustion of further satisfaction; a negative feeling results which

21

is felt as a disease. Such disease can be "cured" by opening further releases. The result is a deeper overadjustment and abnormalcy, that worsens in a vicious-circle way upon every improvement — the same as in all complexes and neuroses. It should be understood that doctor deals only with *reactions* of the patient or of his separate organs and tissues, even while he makes the most extensive analyses. His only guide is the improvement in these *reactions*. The paradox of deeper deterioration through more improvement therefore applies to all medication. Moreover, such deterioration can never be detected by the experimental methods, built on the logic of direct cause-effect relationship. This explains why medicine is still only an art, not a science.

Of course, in those cases where medicine deals with causal factors other than reactions it has made truly scientific and spectacular progress, as for instance in the treatment of infectious diseases or in surgery. This only shows what can be done when causal understanding is present. In the last fifty years deaths from infectious diseases have decreased tenfold. At the same time the functional and malignant diseases have more than doubled, and doctors have to admit that they do not know their causes.

We will try to go into more detail in all these fields in this book. Of course, one cannot expect us to deal comprehensively with any one of them; it could not be done in any one book. On the other hand, we can easily deal with the fundamental principles or laws on which these sciences rest. Dealing with any science means dealing with nature, and there are no complex principles in nature. If any theory is complex or abstruse *in principle*, as we often find at present in the human sciences, it is the best indication that such theory is wrong. The technical complexity and vastness of the sciences is due to the endless *quantitative* effects which man cannot grasp in a simple way. We can easily leave out the quantitative technical aspects.

The reason why we have to go through all these fields of the sciences is that we have to check how general and true the law of relative causation is. Of course, there is the plain interest of seeing how far-reaching an idea can be. But we are aware that it is more important to check whether it stands up under the test of all existing scientific knowledge and thus proves its reality. In such a checking we can take, understandably, only the outstanding theories in every field and analyze them very briefly. This may give the impression that we are resorting to the cheap method of tearing down in a cursory way the best that there is in every field. Unfortunately, we cannot do differently. But we wish to emphasize that by discussing in a seemingly critical way the best scientific theories we do not intend to doubt their technical superiority or to compete with the erudition of their authors. We are interested only in one aspect: the application, or rather the lack of application, of the seemingly paradoxical logic that governs the causation of human adjustment and values.

We believe that understanding simple down-to-earth truths is at present more important in the fields of the human sciences than any recondite elaborations. These sciences are at the stage of scientism that the physical sciences were ages ago. And history tells us that at such a stage high learning tends to perpetuate humanistic delusions, stifling the common sense which is always closer to the simple truths on which a true science can be built. Coming down from lofty sophistications to the simplest earthly truths is how the sciences have advanced. We side with the practical wisdom embodied in cultural traditions. But we also have to expose human value delusions, for that is the only way to explain how the simple psychological causal truths have remained hidden to man. We are fully aware that showing every important belief of man to be a delusion and, consequently, everybody to be a dupe is not a gracious or respectable way of writing. But we have no choice.

We are not using in this book any experimental material of our own. This may appear as a great defect to modern reader used to the identification of scientism with experimentalism. We showed how misleading an experiment in living adjustment can be if its causal logic is not understood. Nobody can be against experiment as a verification of an idea in practice. In the physical sciences experiment is necessary to establish what exactly is going on in a process and how. If physicists could see how atoms act, they would never construct their involved experiments on the structure and effects of matter. It would be downright silly to do so. But in psychology experimentalists are trying to do exactly that. There is nothing more accessible to man, in every minutest detail and aspect, than his own experiences. Observation of one's own experiences is the most perfect experiment in the world. Only the naïve belief of psychologists that they should do as the physical scientists do in order to make psychology scientific has made experiment so important in psychology. We shall discuss the problem of experimentalism and introspectionism later. But whatever the function of experiment in psychology, it cannot be essential for our discussion in this book. We are discussing here only the very basic causal principles of psychology. As such they have to be evident absolutely everywhere, in the tiniest detail of experience as well as in the most general properties of life.

It is not any lack of observable material that has prevented psychologists from discovering the causal truths of human behavior, but the absolute unacceptability of such truths to man. If they were acceptable, they would have been discovered the first time man became conscious of his own experiences.

II

PLEASURE AND RELATIVITY

Pleasure as the driving force in the universal mechanism of need-satisfaction is the source of all motivation. But modern psychology has nothing to say about it. Of course, it would not matter if other words or concepts were used. But the fact is that psychology does not know what to do with the simple but universal truth that happiness or pleasure in its various forms is the goal and source of all human motivation. Psychology thus ignores the very mechanism that makes man tick psychologically. The deeper reason for this unbelievable omission is that, unless man understands the paradox of relative causation, pleasure neither appears to be the cause of motivation nor can be meaningfully related to the rest of experiences. For due to that paradox an increase in pleasure leads to the lowering of motivation in the end; while restrictions of pleasure increase the motivational potential.

Our life activities can be traced directly back to the motive of pleasure or happiness in some nine cases out of every ten. We constantly calculate in terms of pleasure what we shall eat, drink, smoke, enjoy, learn, read or do; how we shall work, rest, play, enjoy art, arrange our home or activities, marry or compete for status. Of course, in many cases we accept displeasure in seeking for a future pleasure, or deny ourselves lower pleasures for sake of more worthy ones. Also, a person may suffer hardships for the sake of security, superiority, or higher, even abstract, goals. But pleasure as the motive in these cases will become clear after we discuss the biological and cultural conditioning. First, let us consider the nature of pleasure.

Pleasure is the principle by which living beings find adjustments that enable them to survive. Everybody can easily see that we are guided in eating the right food by the pleasantness of our taste; or that sexual satisfactions are so highly pleasant because they play so highly important a role in racial survival. The word "pleasure" is often used to designate the animal drives in ourselves. These drives are miraculously purposeful in the animal, though they may have become objectionable in highly conditioned civilized behavior. Of all the million things that an animal could do, it does only that which we know is pleasant. If the psychologist wants to remain a scientist, accepting natural principles and the animal drives as the basis for later evolved human adjustment, he has to admit that the whole human motivation is built on the pleasure mechanism. We will see later that pleasure or any emotion is not less real than its underlying physiological processes; it is rather their organically integrated unified expression.

In terms of adjustment pleasure is not just a feeling, but a universal mechanism that is at the basis of all adjustment and all subordinate mechanisms. Though the animal does not know or feel pleasure — it does not even know the fact of its own existence — it does only what is pleasant; the same applies to every cell in its body. Following pleasure, therefore, is tantamount to following the driving force of existence. *Living existence, in all its forms, and pleasure can be viewed as one and the same thing, under two aspects.* Thus we find here reaffirmation of the self-explanatory principle of existence for the sake of existence, with pleasure as the universal driving force realizing itself through the mechanism of need-satisfaction; it is clear that what lies behind the need as well as the satisfaction is the striving for pleasure. From point of view of living adjustment, *pleasure is the goal and self-realization of everything for which and by which living beings exist.*

The process by which pleasure thus realizes itself is also self-explanatory and self-creating. Pleasure means in its fundamental forms an energy flow. But every energy flow has the property of establishing and strengthening its pathways by its own operation. This is known to apply even to the most highly refined organic processes — psychological reactions. The law of effect, established by Thorndike, and known since the time of Pavlov, is based on the self-widening of pleasurable pathways.

Pleasure flow is the flow of the life energy itself; what exactly this energy consists of does not matter here (we shall try to explain the mechanics of living process later). But energy flow left unopposed loses itself in formless dissipation. The more opposition there is, the more complex forms such energy flow acquires. *Higher adjustment means the realization of the pleasure flow under an increasing multiplicity of obstacles.* These obstacles represent the difficulties encountered by the animal in its evolution and embodied in its adjustment. The life energy in the amoeba and man is the same, except that in man it realizes itself under myriads of complexities evolved to overcome difficulties. This evolution means the universal method of living adjustment — conditioning or learning. A stream, encountering an obstacle, becomes more circuitous and complex while overcoming it. The result is greater resourcefulness, more-sidedness, and extended or, actually, delayed life process. Thus the opposition to satisfaction is what enriches adjustment, whether it be during its evolution or in its already attained state. Basically, every need — the source of satisfaction or motivation — is only a non-satisfaction due to obstacles; it is a hindrance or disturbance in the normal flow of the life energy or pleasure.

The method by which the higher conditioning as the embodiment of difficulties prevails is also self-explanatory. Since such conditioning means greater resourcefulness, those species survive better which have more of it — which have encountered more obstacles or restrictions. Through millions of years of such selective preference for restrictions, finally, restrictive mechanisms inside an organism evolve, which create "obstacles" even when these are not physically there. Human foresight discerning obstacles in advance, and the need for learning, are the highest attainments in this respect. A step below are the "curiosity" of higher mammals and all the complex, essentially superfluous forms of higher living adjustment. It is important to understand that selection turns the advantage of the more circuitous adjustment auto-

27

matically into a creative force that shapes everything according to this advantage.

INNER SELECTION

We do not need to go into an explanation of the principle of selective evolution. Though this principle is the greatest discovery ever made by man, it is simplicity itself. However, the usual theory of selection, which sees evolution as the survival or extinction of whole organisms only, is a crude, even impossible theory. If all individuals of a species, except one, were to perish with each tiny improvement, no species would last for long. For in gradual natural evolution there are myriads of tiny improvements before even a slight adaptive change results.

Actually, evolution works mainly through what we would call *inner selection*. By internal selection even the tiniest mechanisms inside organism survive, or become extinct, depending from their efficiency. The above principle of self-strengthening energy flow makes such selective adaptation self-operative. Any mechanism, on the side of either release or restriction, that does not perform efficiently is superseded by those that do; and any one that performs better self-increases automatically. Thus the evolutionary adaptation works from below, under the universally persisting and self-explanatory pleasure principle which governs the adjustment of whole organisms as well as that of every tiniest mechanisms inside every organism. Only this self-realization of selection through every one of the myriads of details of an organism can explain the miraculous richness and imperceptible gradualness of evolutionary adaptation.

Of course, another principle, that of cooperative subordination all through an organism, must be working before such selective organic self-improvement can take place; otherwise every cell or mechanism would expand on its own and the organism would disintegrate. The evolution of such subordination goes on through millions of years and its products are unimaginably complex, as in every natural evolution. But, as in all evolution, the *principle* that makes myriads of factors conform, from the simplest begin-

28

nings up, as if under a never-relenting shaping force, is simple. This principle is the same endless trial-and-error selection on the basis of *advantage* gained by the *union* of more processes, cells or mechanisms. Only those processes can persist, under universal competition and the striving for more release, which offer closer cooperation. The mechanisms that evolve to maintain the restrictive subordinating controls over other mechanisms, in order to gain this decisive advantage, work and self-select in the same way at all levels; those which are more efficient, in their already specified function, expand and eliminate those that are not.

CONDITIONING

Under evolutionary conditioning or learning, enforced by obstacles to direct satisfaction, simple pleasures become complex processes. Eating becomes hunting. Absorption of food becomes complex digestion and the accumulation of reserves. Resting becomes a need for security extending to numerous dangers and factors in the environment. Such conditionings or restrictions become a normalcy and are no longer felt. Most of the restrictions become so ingrown that they cannot be relaxed by any means. Some restrictions, however, can be relaxed by special means; for example, by narcotic drugs. Naturally, such relaxation gives great release or pleasure. But since biological normalcy automatically re-establishes itself as soon as the interference can be overcome, aftermaths and intensified restrictions follow. Man tries to derive greater pleasure in hundreds of ingenious ways. Consequently there are hundreds of disorders and "diseases" caused by overadjustment. They have remained mysteries because they follow a paradoxical logic: they become worse as more improvement — in the form of further overadjustment — is lived through.

Cultural conditioning means, equally, creating more restrictions and needs so that richer satisfactions become possible. Here as well the more direct natural pleasures are restricted and made more complex and refined. The most interesting thing here is that the restriction of pleasure is achieved by the operation of the pleasure flow itself, just as a more circuitous or refined stream is formed by the operation of the stream itself. This is the same in all conditioning. There is never any other motivation than the pleasure available. Conditioning therefore is a contradictory process. In the simplest cases we easily see that this is so. The child is restricted in his more direct natural pleasures under promise of other, less direct enjoyments, or by being shown more complex forms of satisfaction. Pleasure flow thus finds its more circuitous release. Gradually, it may be curbed so that it turns against the original natural pleasure.

The more advanced means of conditioning are extremely subtle. That is why cultural and moral tradition is so involved and education such a difficult art. At every step in conditioning an indirect and limited pleasure is substituted for an immediate natural pleasure — all in the name of pleasure. Worthier future pleasures, rewards and redemptions, of increasingly indirect nature, are the main ingredients of cultural and moral education. It can be said that conditioning always involves deceit, perpetuated with sincere belief by the educator himself in rationalized explanations. This hidden deceit has been a source of endless contradictions and rationalizations in humanistic theory.

Cultural conditioning is little understood, or even noticed, because it is omnipresent. We live in it as in an atmosphere. If it were only occasional, it would be noticed; but then it would be less effective. We notice brain-washing only where the conditioning is used to make people adopt some extraordinary behavior — where, in fact, the conditioning is less thorough. Civilized man believes that he lives according to reason — and he can always prove it. Actually, reason is only an instrument for the attainment of conditioned value goals. We all know that reasoning is the most precise way of finding out what is right. Accordingly, we like to base our behavior on reason. People and societies have held thousands of conflicting value beliefs, and nobody has lacked arguments yet to prove that his views are derived from nothing but reason. Even a child contradicting his parents or a nagging wife accusing her husband offers the best of reasons. If man lived by reason, a savage, who often has as good brain as we have, would produce a Constitution, a Christian dogma or a research program, all of which we believe to be products of reason.

The basic natural needs and satisfactions that serve as the basis for conditioning are little understood or noticed for the same reason, namely, their omnipresence.

The highest need is the *need for growth*. The whole behavior of the child is dominated by it. Because the child instinctively wants to be a grownup more than anything else, he imitates at every instance the people around him and grows up to be the same as they are. As part of the need for growth can be considered the ever continuous needs of the individual to exercise his capacities, to do things, or to interact with his environment. Woodworth has drawn attention to these capacities and tendencies under his Behavior-Primacy theory of motivation. Actually, it is not any activity for the sake of activity that motivates behavior, but the pleasure drive or natural need, which is not noticed because of its omnipresence. By offering only definite, limited outlets for the exercise of this need, bearing on various capacities, conditioning is imperceptibly imposed.

The second highest need is the *need for survival or security*. The greatest fear of the child is to be abandoned by its parents. The feeling of love arises from this need for security (just as the heavenly feeling of romantic love arises from the equally natural and deep need of reproduction). The need for security is superior to the need of food, rest, or even sexual needs, as experiments with animals have shown — if any experiment is needed. The first thing one notices about an animal in its natural state is its alertness. It does not do anything before ascertaining that everything is safe. It is not difficult to see how the animal's curiosity and man's need for knowledge have grown out of this need.

In cultural conditioning, the love for the parent is the pivotal mechanism. Of course, the more refined and perfect the feeling of security offered to the child, the more intense and varied becomes his need of it, due to the relativity of values. The love becomes a kind of neurotic complex, with beneficial results. The child becomes a neurotic perfectionist in trying to conserve love. The highest degree is reached when the child does what the parents approve even when they are not present or cannot be expected to know about it. Then the conditioning has become an inner conscience. Respect for authority, love of neighbor and unquestioned clinging to cultural values are the main results of this conditioning.

The next higher need is the *need for superiority*. Competition is an essential part of living. Selective survival depends on the capacity and eagerness to compete. Even plants have to "know" how to compete for sun. Consequently, only those living beings survive which obey the principle of competition. In human society the competition centers on moral and cultural worth, where it becomes a source of another "neurotic" perfectionism. Its strength depends on how universally every activity in society is already covered by cultural occupations and how thorough is the conditioning. Striving for knowledge, power and moral excellence, as well as a curious social conformity, are the end results. This need for superiority often intergrows with the need for security. The thirst for power and position, which has mystified psychologists and philosophers, has an unexciting explanation. At every moment man feels that the greatest dangers as well as benefits come from other men. He cannot rest in safety unless he is above other men. Here the feeling which accumulates at every moment, as if drop by drop all the time, counts more than any spectacular event or grand reasoning.

It has to be kept in mind that the pleasure potential inherent in all these general needs is higher than that attaching to subordinate physiological functions. If the security of a person is jeopardized, other satisfactions like eating or drinking have not much value for him. Or if he suffers a death-like anxiety under thwarted growth, he would rather suffer any other pain. Also in his drive to compete the person may be ready to suffer any pain. It is only natural that this be so. The more basic functions govern the subordinate ones because the latter have grown out of them. By the way, needs can be classified under different headings. But the basic needs can be only few, while their branching off into subordinate needs is endless.

What we said may be sufficient to show that the most general needs as well as their conditioning are noticed least, because they

32

are so general as to be omnipresent. Unsuspecting observers may find no substance in this talk about the conditioning of any needs. But it is exactly the generality of conditioning, like the quality of an unnoticeable atmosphere, which is its strength. Value attitudes which are not even mentioned in a healthy society are the strongest ones, as can be observed in regard to our taboos on sex. Psychologists looking for events that they can register in the manner of the experimental sciences do not find much. Most psychologists know that some kind of conditioning must be the method by which natural drives are transformed into civilized behavior. They try to attach the conditioning to such clearly describable functions as alimentation and sex, or reactions like fear, rage and love. In fact, these functions cannot be conditioned, except for producing gross abnormalities like those of Pavlov's dogs.

But modern psychology is still at the stage where explanations are sought in salient or unusual events, while what is general and really important causally is overlooked. Some of these explanations are amazing. Serious psychologists explain that, for instance, social cooperation is conditioned by the manner in which the mother holds the child during feeding. Others state that any motivation could be evolved by conditioning such reactions as the child's fear of noise or shock. Still others hold that the talent of writing, for instance, may be developed because the act of passing fluid from a pen represents a sublimation of the sexual act.

In any event, conditioning — the main source of cultural behavior — is completely ignored in our humanistic theories built on the assumption that cultural behavior comes from human nature. In fact, the human being in his natural state is a miserable animal. In the rare cases where children have been found who have grown up in nature outside human society, they have behaved like animals. The two Kamala girls who were discovered living with wolves in the jungles of Mindapore even ran on all fours. It took eight years before the girl who lived longer learned the first human response of kindness toward her foster mother.

Further, the humanistic theorists have a difficult task explaining away cultural contradictions that arise from the deceit inherent in conditioning. Any rationalist, free educator or social reformer can point out the hypocrisies of cultural life and can produce programs that really give the liberties and natural enjoyments proclaimed in humanistic theories. Of course, such programs collapse before they do real harm. Humanity has long learned to protect itself against rationalism in practice. But in theoretical thinking the misunderstandings as well as the rationalizations and superstitions have survived, and have even become more ingrained under the ingenuity and zeal of modern thinkers.

The nature of learning is best evident from the organ through which it is effected. The brain is primarily a system of restrictions. The role of the forebrain, the newest addition to it, for instance, is negative more than anything else. Remove it partly or isolate it by lobotomy, and man feels only relief or an upsurge of energy, without an apparent loss of capacities. The later effects, however, are a reduction of adjustment toward the more primitive levels of the animal. Apparently, the higher adjustment is attained by restriction more than by anything else. Medicine is familiar with the general phenomenon of improvement of releases in cases of paralysis of the brain by disease or operation. Yacorzynski describes in his book, *Medical Psychology*, a couple of typical cases.

We may say a few words here about drug addiction. It offers one example where overadjustment is recognized easily, because nobody holds any natural delusions in this matter. The explanations usually given are physiological. According to one explanation, the Nissl's granules, which cover nerve endings, are destroyed by the drug, but by way of compensation start increasing so vigorously that when drug is discontinued they cause oversensitivity and tension. This explanation accords with relative causation — the endeavor of the body to maintain or return to normalcy. Generally, the present attitude is that the abnormalities produced by drug addiction could be removed by the use of some other drug or treatment, in less painful ways. Surely, the abnormalities can be removed. In fact, they are being removed by the body itself, in its endeavor to regain normalcy. That is exactly what constitutes the addict's suffering, and is so desperately resisted by him. The only treatment that could help him to maintain the good feeling would be one that helps to sustain the abnormality, or intoxication. Trying to get out of drug addiction without suffering just as much as was previously enjoyed is like trying to eat one's cake and have it too. Practice has shown this to be so. Incidentally, even placebos may cause aftereffects, as Dr. Henry K. Beecher has shown. This confirms the fact that drug aftereffects do not occur because of some specific chemical residue left in the blood.

We may add here a general observation about physiological explanations of psychological phenomena. Of course, such phenomena are only organically integrated unified expressions of physiological processes. But these processes take place by millions of infinitesimal elements at every tiniest spot and shortest instant, whereas man can deal consciously only with something "one" at a time. Man is inherently uncapable of understanding how physiological processes become an experience. Even where he gains a picture in terms of physiological wholes, it is only partial because of the infinitesimal causal relationships between them. And a partial picture of a causal constellation is worse than none.

MEASUREMENT OF PLEASURE

The impossibility of measuring pleasure, in any usual way, has been one reason why psychologists have considered the use of the pleasure concept impossible. Pleasure cannot be measured in physical units, or tied down to absolute physical terms. This may present an obstacle for modern psychologists trying to deal in terms of the physical sciences. But in the properly psychological world of motivations and values, pleasure is neither unmeasurable nor a vague concept. Pleasure is the most pursued and most noticed value. Everybody follows it like a golden thread at every moment of his life. Pleasure is like money. If you have it, you can have everything else. All other things are evaluated in terms of pleasure. This means that pleasure would be the best yardstick, provided it could be related quantitatively to other psychological values; measuring never means anything else than precise relating.

35

The law of relative causation makes such precise relating possible, since it shows that pleasure and displeasure, the two values that govern all motivation, will come out precisely equal. Anyway, the precision of this rule, together with one's precise knowledge of his pleasurable experiences, make it possible for him to ascertain in every case how much he has or lacks in terms of psychological potential, better than with any possible method of measuring in psychology. Nothing more is needed in practice. If one knows that he has to meet every pleasure expenditure with an equal accumulation of needs or displeasure, in order not to get into emotional debt, he has a workable rule for managing his motivation economy. The psychologist trying to help a person could do so by applying the same rule, and by analyzing under it the past experiences of the person, for which he can have no direct measurements anyway.

Moreover, the understanding of the *relative* nature of psychological and corresponding physiological reactions may enable psychologists to work out methods for measuring pleasure even in physical terms. For instance, a *relative* change in the rate of metabolism may serve as the basis for correct measuring. Psychologists have tried to measure the hedonic tone or pleasure from various reactions: degree of hormonal activity, innervation of the parasympathetic system, visceral activity, galvanic skin response, even the posture of the body. Without regard to the relative meaning of these reactions the measurements were bound to fail. Even a child knows that an accelerated heartbeat may be evoked by pleasant surprise as well as by danger. A release of energy may mean a pleasant feeling, but if at the same time the energy has to be used or reserved for an emergency, there is no surplus available for pleasure. Above all, the previous state of the organism may mean a difference between pleasure and displeasure under the same circumstances. Bread and butter for lunch may be exciting for a hungry man but not for a well-fed man.

The previous *value* background as well as the *purpose* of the organism determine the psychological value of every function. But in modern psychology such concepts are shunned as unscientific. Dealing with nothing but external data is the scientific ambition of modern psychology and has given rise to behaviorism, operationism and instrumentalism as preferred methods. Imagine what would happen if a bank used a similar method and evaluated its operations from external data alone. It would close all paying windows and retain only receiving ones as a matter of better profit policy. The operations of the organism are much more intricately but also more purposefully related than banking operations.

Also, the clinging by psychologists to *ideationally logical* analyses of mental phenomena makes causal relating or measuring of emotions unfeasible. All psychological analyses, including those using ink blots, abstract or ambiguous pictures, game sets, dream work or free association, are aimed at discovering logical causal connections between thought contents and emotions. In fact, thought contents are accidental and therefore misleading as to the emotional meaning of experience. For instance, everybody knows that any idea, arising from an accidental occurrence, may befall an irritated person and that he will attribute to it everything in his plight, becoming preoccupied with it to the deepest "subconscious" levels. If logical thought coincided with emotion, a neurotic could be cured by the change of his ideas through a good argument. Psychologists know how impossible this is, and have resorted to deliberate abstruseness in analysis — from ink blots to dream symbolism. This adds obscurity and latitude in interpretation. What was ascertained directly is now ascertained through added paraphernalia that merely increase the margin of confusion. A child looking at an ink blot may see two butterflies flying into each other, or two armies colliding, depending upon what he heard or read that day, even if he tends to see a conflict. What is more, he will tend to see more conflict or threat the more his past was overprotected or free of conflict.

"Subconscious" expressions are even more misleading. Dreams depend upon accidental stimulations, as all thought associations do. A bell-like sound may make one dream that he is in church. Further, he may dream either of a wedding or a funeral, depending from what he saw on the Late Show. As to the free association, it evokes what is emotionally more salient, which means unusual and, therefore, causally least essential. This applies to all ideational contents, whatever the analysis used in revealing them, and makes all analyses, searching for ideational logical connections, utterly misleading. Incidentally, the irrationality recognized by theories of the subconscious is explained as a result of subconscious motivations. These, however, are assumed to be logical in themselves, and the whole analysis aims at discovering their logic.

Returning to the measurement of pleasure, we may ask whether the possibility of exact measuring here is so important. If we know that the only goal is to accumulate every possible bit of pleasure potential, and that there is never too much of it, exact measurement is a waste of effort. It appears important to the modern psychologist because he hopes to promote positive emotions by acquiring greater know-how and precision in manipulating them. Actually no skill or know-how is wanting here and no manipulation can help. We all know what to do to become perfect beings. But we are unable to do it because we lack the motivation, which ultimately means the satisfaction or pleasure potential, to be acquired in the paradoxical way of accumulating its opposite — hard, unpleasant needs. Everything works perfectly when the satisfaction potential or interest is there, and no know-how, manipulations or measurements can help if it is missing. Here, as everywhere else the modern psychologist resembles an alchemist searching for elaborate formulas with painfully precise ingredients, whereas the real solutions lie somewhere else completely.

In the end, it is not any technical difficulty, or the impossibility of precise measuring, that makes pleasure as the source of motivation unacceptable. All such difficulties could be overcome if the causal understanding were there. The real difficulty is the paradox of the pleasure economy. How can one accept the fact that pleasure supplies motivation if he sees that people who live primarily for pleasure have the least will power, character and motivation? No psychologist, however formally scientific, could miss this common truth. On the other hand, every experiment and case study shows that the availability of pleasure or release means availability of motivation. Hedonist theories failed. Freud postulated the pleasure principle, but could not explain why neurotics, who seek pleasure more than other people, should suffer from displeasure most. He noticed that a person living through the highest success succumbs to neurosis; or that a neurotic encountering real trouble suddenly recovers. Freud sought explanations in the vengeance of the Superego.

These unsolvable problems will remain as long as the logic of psychological causation is not understood. This logic means that every value and motivation derives from its opposite, as satisfaction derives from need. This amounts to the paradox of getting more value by decreasing it, or losing it by the very fact of accumulating it. Such logic is absurd and ridiculous under every formally scientific or experimental approach. And the learned psychologist would be the last person to accept it.

RELATIVITY OF SENSATIONS

First, we would like to mention an important, generally recognized law in psychology, perhaps the only one that deserves the name of a law — *the Weber-Fechner law*. This law confirms the relativity of sensations in mathematical form. According to this law, increase of sensation requires a logarithmical increase of stimulation. This means that, assuming a stimulation constant of 10, in order to double the sensation the stimulus has to be increased a hundred times; to triple it, a thousand times, and so on. The interpretation of this law is interesting. Wundt found that it rests on the general relativity of evaluations. He stipulated, however, that sensation values should be commensurable. Our causal explanation of all values as forms of pleasure shows all experiences to be commensurable.

The Weber-Fechner law means that value increment becomes lower as more value is added. The Weber-Fechner law is often explained by a function established by Bernouilli, by whose mathematics Fechner was influenced. Bernouilli explained his function by the example of lucky card player: his winnings decrease, in terms of relative value, as he goes on winning. It is safe to say that the underlying principle of the Weber-Fechner law is the decrease of value in direct proportion to the previous accumulation of the same value, just as relative causation requires. Any sensation extinguishes itself by its own operation, as only its opposite can sustain it. The difficulty of perceiving this truth in usual, fairly involved reactions is due to the elasticity and interdependence of organic functions.

No sensation is isolated from the rest of the body. When the skin on the fingertips freezes and loses sensitivity, after an initial strong sensation, we witness relativity of evaluations at work. But the relativity can never reach its logical conclusion here, because the skin is supported from below by other tissues, blood, secretions and the whole organism. We could make relativity attain its equalizing or self-effacing effects there too. But by that time the whole body with all its needs and satisfactions, evolved during the whole lifetime, would have become involved and the zero balance of existence, death, reached. This explains some discrepancies observed in the application of the Weber-Fechner formula to more involved or extreme sensations.

Another source of discrepancies is the impossibility of separating the functions and mechanisms of evaluation from those of the mere receiving of data for evaluation. Actually, the curious thing is that even the purely receptory parts of organs, like the light-sensitive fluids in eye, are subject to some relativity of reactions, as we shall see in discussing afterimages and some illusions. If we recall that relativity is due to the persistence of identity or equilibrium of organic formations, it is easily understandable that relativity should apply to almost every permanent tissue or function in the body.

The dependence of sensation upon previous experience or state is indirectly confirmed by the generally recognized observation in psychology that *only changes are experienced*. A sensation that persists unchanged for some time is not felt any more. But psychologists have never drawn the implied conclusion, namely, that permanent states, however valuable in absolute terms, have no value. The above intricacies probably are one reason for this omission. The main reason, however, is that psychologists have never tied in with the above observation the rule of the permanent identity of organism. If this were done, the law of relative causation would be an inevitable conclusion. Under the permanent identity of organism all changes, and therefore all experiences, can consist only of equal "ups" and "downs" within permanent limits.

Modern psychology has chosen, instead, the concept of *adaptation* in explaining the relative aspects of sensations in those cases where they are too evident. It is assumed that a mechanism ceases to react because it has discontinued its function, which has been taken over by other mechanisms. It is not noticed that adaptation explains only one phase in the whole process. A toe compressed in a narrow shoe aches for a while, then ceases to evoke any sensation. The next experience is relief after the shoe is removed. Apparently the sensation of abnormality had reached its limit when the pain experience ceased. The only possible experience then became the return to normalcy, with the accompanying relief. But in terms of adaptation there would be no reason for experiencing the relief. Thus, under the principle of adaptation the causal sequence is broken off where it becomes most interesting, namely, where the mysterious opposite effects start appearing.

As regards purely psychological experiences the above intricacies do not apply and the relativity rule is complete. The confusion with the mere receiving of sensations and the dependence on deeper physiological connections are excluded from the system of psychological evaluation. Perceiving, or receiving images on the retina, has no value before it is evaluated. You can "see" thousands of things, while thinking about something else, and never know that you saw them. Further, no physical state has any influence on our thoughts before it is evaluated through the psychological system itself. Nor can this system have direct repercussions on the physical self. The most grandiose thought can change nothing in your body. In brief, the psychological system is completely self-contained, like a complete organism in itself. Actually, it is a complete reflection of the physical organism as a whole.

41

This means that a value in the psychological system is evaluated completely and finally against its own past background. A psychological satisfaction heightened to its limit exhausts itself. The same applies to psychological need. A displeasure or conscious pain if extended is not felt any more, and becomes rather a mere expectancy of relief or satisfaction. This accords with the newest experiments in psychology, according to which further feeling of pain ceases after it reaches certain limits.

Any continuous feeling must decrease in a logarithmical curve according to the Weber-Fechner formula. At the end of such a curve even the highest stimulus fails to evoke appreciable sensation. Schematically this means that a person who has a progressively increasing success finally feels that he does not have much success. To keep his feeling of further success alive, the progressivity itself of the rate of success would have to be increased. Finally, there would be no success high enough in the whole world to keep the feeling of success alive in the most successful man.

RELATIVITY IN COGNITION

First, we wish to mention that the relativity of evaluations is often explained, especially by philosophers, as being due to the method of *comparison* by which the mind works. It is true that we make our conclusions by way of comparison. But what make sense in comparison are still values — satisfactions or dissatisfactions. Comparison means nothing more than matching innumerable needs against innumerable possibilities of satisfaction, with positive or negative results. In essence a mental comparison is no different from tasting a food. There the body matches each quality or value in the food with its existing needs. In the case of mental comparison the backgrounds that serve in the matching or evaluation are the products of ungraspably complex previous evaluations. Though the products of our thought are endlessly rich, they need nothing more than value and disvalue, derived from various sensations, to acquire this richness. In a television picture we need only black and white dots, forming changing backgrounds, to obtain all the possible visual experiences.

The important thing is that in any thought, whether of tiny details or general integrated wholes, satisfactions and dissatisfactions must result or there is no thought. This has important consequences for the understanding of any intellectual interest, motivation or evaluation, as well as for learning. They all depend on the previous accumulations of needs or negative backgrounds. But these are never suspected as having anything to do with the interests of learning. On the contrary, modern psychologists and progressive educators see the accumulation of needs, which is the difficult and unpleasant part in learning or education, as the part to be eliminated, because it seems to stand in the way of the pleasures of learning and positive interests. This explains many important misunderstandings in the modern theory of education. Equally, in philosophy or any speculative thought, striving for knowledge directly, without enlargement of needs in the form of widened factual premises or backgrounds, leads to exhaustion rather than enrichment of knowledge.

Though comparison is not the final explanation of relativity, it is a useful concept. It makes easier the understanding of relativity when one has to deal with whole backgrounds — without going into analysis of individual needs and satisfactions. Actually, such analysis would be impossible in most cases. Man can have a most involved experience consisting of millions of reactions, but he can think of it only as a generalized whole. In his conscious reactions man acts as a unified organism taking a stand in regard to any situation, or evaluating it, as a "one." Hence the need for generalization. Conscious thought consists of endlessly added generalizations, or "ones." That is why no man can think of more than one thing at once. Multiplicity is inherently incomprehensible to man.

By the way, this quality of mind has interesting implications. For instance, scientists wonder at the unusual intelligence of birds, insects, fish or other animals who find their way home over enormous distance or perform other complex tasks by instinct. Actually, what seems here insurmountably difficult for the mind dealing in one-by-one fashion is automatically easy in instinctive reactions proceeding on millions of fronts at once. That is why instinctive adjustment may seem extremely involved, as if miraculously superior to human capacities. Bergson built one of his main theses on this superiority of instinct over the intellect, which has to dismember everything into separate elements in order to grasp it.

Actually, there is nothing wonderous in instinctive adjustment. Man is equally unimaginably "intelligent" when he finds a food tasty or a woman beautiful. To match scientifically every need in the body with every element in a food that is found tasty in a few seconds would take years — if it could be done at all. Far more involved would be an analysis of the process by which a thing is found beautiful. Scientists try to reduce the "intelligence" of birds flying south or salmon going upstream to man's one-term intelligence. They try to find out what that one term is — magnetic lines, contours of land or temperature difference in water — that the birds or salmon use. Vast research has accumulated and controversial conclusions reached. It is not realized that there may be hundreds of such terms or stimulations, inner and external, which the bird responds to; and that there is no more, nor less, ability involved in it than in finding a food tasty.

Returning to the nature of human intellectual experiences, it is evident from everyday observations that value process is at their basis. Receiving sensations, even systemized sensations, does not in itself give an intellectual experience. One may read a half-page and still not know what he has read. The same applies to experiences involving other sensations. This can be easily observed in the case of absent-mindedness, intoxication, extreme stress, fear or some other overpowering parallel sensation. Also, the innumerable inner reactions are not felt as long as they are satisfied through their own mechanisms and leave no excessive needs to be dealt with by the organism as a whole.

The nature of consciousness itself can be best understood in terms of pleasure or value mechanisms. It is evident that consciousness comes with an additional system of restrictions resulting from the superimposition, on the lower brain, of the higher layer or cortex. We mentioned before the purely restrictive nature of the higher brain. In general, the brain exhibits throughout a series of superimposed restrictive systems, each one controlling the lower ones and through them the whole organism; and receiving organic reactions, with their need and satisfaction or value tone, through them. The important thing is that due to the additional restrictions there is an accumulation of the potential of satisfactions or pleasure to be derived from reactions coming from below. Since pleasure is the universal source of all life, an additional, inner life becomes self-operative under this potential.

Organic reactions, coming from below, become a source of further additional reactions — of further pleasure releases on their own, as in all life. Naturally, every lack or decrease in such releases becomes equally an additional source of stress and pain. There can be no pleasure gain, here as in all life. Only an additional, as if amplified, play of satisfaction and needs coming from below is attained. Consciousness, clearly, is a system of reactions about reactions or of experiences about experiences. This explains why there can be no understanding of the consciousness itself or of any of its ultimate terms. A still higher, additional level of evaluations would be necessary for that. Though we cannot understand consciousness in itself, we can think of it as resulting from a different higher type of pleasure economy with extra accumulations or "investments" as well as "losses," whereas the unconscious adjustment could be compared to a more direct or a hand-to-mouth pleasure economy.

Consciousness has a self-sustaining force and coherence that makes even a cautious thinker believe in the soul. The sense of *value* or *meaning* is the great miracle of consciousness. The pleasure principle provides the explanation. From the simplest performance of a cell to the highest experience, pleasure pervades every effort and gives to it a unifying value meaning. There can be nothing higher or different for man, because pleasure is everything for which and by which he exists.

EQUIVALENCE OF EMOTIONS

Now let us try to see, in plain practical terms, whether there is no way of beating the relativity rule and obtaining more pleasure. Why cannot one just keep up pleasant thoughts and discard unpleasant ones, as advised by advocates of positive thinking in the vein of Norman Vincent Peale. Everybody knows that a bright disposition, optimism or sense of superiority are sources of better motivation and success.

Such feelings can be derived from intoxication, but there the consequences are too evident. The production of better intoxicants has not often been offered as solution. Aldous Huxley in his *Brave New World Revisited* discusses the wondrous effects of new drugs and thinks that the happiness drug or "soma" is a possibility. Freud also believed that such drug is possible. If that is the case, men better abandon everything else and concentrate on producing that drug. For, if men reached an unlimited source of pleasure, they could do absolutely everything, even transform themselves into saints and geniuses in no time.

"Positive thinking" can work as little as Huxley's "soma," but the impossibility is not so evident.

Let us imagine that Mr. Jones decides one day to abandon his feelings of anxiety or inferiority and to start with new positive feelings. Let us assume that his anxiety is caused by his failure in his business and that he feels inferior in regard to his neighbor. Could he now start thinking about different things and thus create positive emotions? Even common sense tells us that he cannot. If this were possible, one could as well find an inexhaustible source of joy in thinking how grandly he would do as king of China; or a feeling of superiority in thinking how superior he is to the Papuans.

The causal reason for such an impossibility is that in our adjustive world there is a *strict correlation between every outside fact and the inside value attributed to it*. This is what makes possible the miraculous purposefulness of adjustment and motivation so that precise responses are evoked by definite external values or goals. There is no possibility of attributing a higher value to any one thing or goal without disturbing this miraculous adjustive normalcy of the person. The deeper reason for this is that there can be no value or satisfaction without need. Availability of positive feelings is the wonder by which one can achieve everything. But such feelings can appear only where there was a previous need. In simple words, a person must first want painfully a thing in order to derive joy from it. No other thing can do. A person simply cannot have any other positive emotions or values than those for which he has accumulated needs.

But accumulation of needs is painful, and that is the whole problem. A person does not accumulate any needs, or wants directed at any goals, unless he is forced through the conditioning of his basic needs of survival and competition to do so. "Positive thinking," aiming at an increase in satisfactions by the mere intention to have them is nonsensical, and can lead only to deeper emotional negativism.

Mr. Jones continues living in his emotional immobility or negativism as long as he does not accumulate new needs, as long as he succeeds in resisting this unpleasant process, by which natural normalcy seeks to establish itself. If Mr. Jones had already accumulated new needs, these could serve as source of new interests and satisfactions, or of positive thinking. Instead, Mr. Jones persists in the endeavor of obtaining positive feelings in an easy way — just as the "positive thinkers" advise. That is, he turns to his old overexhausted sources of satisfaction — his business success and superiority over his neighbor. He may disguise this search for further release under the embellishments suggested by the "positive thinkers," and may get some immediate feeling of relief. But in whatever way the rosy outlook is created, the return to reality becomes necessary if Mr. Jones is to retain his adjustive normalcy or coherent and consequential way of thinking. This means an opposite process, with opposite, negative emotions — and that is his whole trouble. Everybody can understand that Mr. Jones would not be so disturbed now if he had not entertained such high hopes about his business before. Nor would he feel inferior to his neighbor if he had not indulged in thoughts of superiority over him. One does not feel inferiority in regard to the millionnaires or geniuses one reads about in newspapers.

The only way Mr. Jones could continue keeping his rosy outlook without reversals would be by abdicating the strict correlation of values, i.e., his adjustive normalcy, forever. This means mental disorder or emotional instability. These serve to distort facts so as to suit the desired feelings. Everybody can easily observe this as the main characteristic of mentally unstable people. By the way, even a mentally disturbed person lives through equal "ups" and "downs." He gains some extra release by abandoning his higher needs, but following that he reaches the biological level where constant normalcy equally maintains itself. The "ups" of a mentally disturbed person are short and explosive, as when he erupts in laughing. These alternate with long "downs." Apparently, the background of restrictions, which makes the release possible, is accumulated but slowly, and is avidly used up at the first opportunity, in uncontrolled mirth.

The whole effort of intelligent adjustment and cultural life focuses on keeping the strictest possible correspondence between outside facts or goals and inside values or needs, so that everything works out correctly in terms of motivation. This correspondence becomes so extensive and refined that it is often ungraspable by the reason, and can be maintained only by virtue of long tradition and intuition. For instance, a culturally wise person does not care for the admiration that can be easily aroused by wearing flashy clothes or gilded uniforms. Instead, he prefers the inconspicuous admiration earned by important work. Also, the emotionally better conditioned or more intelligent person remains true to his values, however difficult they become to live up to. The changing of value relationships from moment to moment is the surest sign of emotional immaturity.

The advocates of "positive thinking" or of more happiness do not need to urge us toward easy emotional enrichment, which is attainable only through misplacement of values. Every one of us already does the utmost possible to get more positive feelings, by trying to fake reality as much as the stark facts permit. But every one of us also has learned since childhood that optimism unwar-

48

ranted by facts leads only to disappointment. An intelligent person has an intuitive understanding of the effects of relative causation.

In fact, all our troubles stem from the difficulty of resisting the temptations of easy emotional enrichment. One may need an extra motivation in his work, and may derive it from the enjoyment of his own superiority and the perfection of his work, or of things in general. Then, afterward, if this is not recognized by others or is not warranted by reality, he blames and hates everybody and everything. Of course, it all takes place on the level of automatic emotional reactions rather than through any clear reasoning. By simply being forced to return to inescapable reality the person lives through reactions opposite to the overenjoyed sense of his superiority, perfection or goodness. Hence the feelings of inferiority, dissatisfaction and guilt. Any other pleasurable feeling may be overenjoyed in the same way, with the same consequences.

In some cases one has no choice but to overspend. A public star, executive or social personality may have to bring up so much self-assurance and superiority, just to do his job, that this can never be justified by the true values of reality, especially as progressive increase in the overstimulation is necessary just to sustain the feeling. Then the person may resort to intoxication, narcotic or moral, to ward off reality. But the more he does so, the harder it becomes to ignore the widening rift between the aspired feeling and emotional or factual normalcy. The inevitable reversal becomes a dreaded precipice. Thus the smarter man, who knows the best techniques in controlling emotions and has the least reason to feel inferior or insecure, may succumb to the complex of inferiority and anxiety sooner than anybody else. If he gets good advice and works hard at it, he may avoid the opposite feelings further by tapping new physiological releases. The result may be an ulcer or other physiological disorder.

Conditioning is the only way to produce more motivation without causing opposite negative emotions. It means, however, restriction of satisfactions, which is sometimes unbearable for a person incapable of bearing restrictive delays in his pleasure releases.

Conditioning is the clue to understanding the character and emotional difficulties of a person. An intelligent person with little conditioning may decide correctly to strive for the right goals. But since he has accumulated no pleasure potential or real interests in the past, he has to live constantly in emotional debt. He pays it by depression after enthusiasm, and exhaustion after effort. He gets into bad temper often. Anger is an effort to squeeze out more release, by way of a forcible feeling of superiority or security. However, since reality does not warrant the feeling, anger leads only to an immediate emotional difficulty. On the other hand, a well-conditioned but less intelligent person may have all his interests tied up by conditioning to the last limit. Consequently, he may lack originality or spontaneity and be dull or pedantic.

The tasks that a person tries to accomplish on one side, and the degree of his conditioning combined with his intellectual capacities on the other, determine how much bad temper, depression, feeling of anxiety or inferiority result in each case. No amount of good advice, know-how or manipulating skill can help. The practical psychologist knows this very well. The secret of better adjustment is simple but hard to attain; one cannot get something for nothing, here as everywhere else. The endless technically abstruse analyses, explanations and advices of modern psychologists amount to an alchemistic sophistry.

But what about purely spiritual interests that do not seem to depend upon factual values? The promoters of better emotions can prove by hundreds of cases how new interests or happiness can be derived from insignificant things. We agree, that any one thing can provide the greatest interest or happiness to one person, and be a source of negative emotions for another. But the cause here is not a wish or compliance with a lucky formula; it is the hard, day-by-day, background formation through conditioning. By nature we have only crude biological needs. These have to be restricted and their satisfaction permitted only through definite cultural outlets which then acquire the satisfaction value. The pleasure of higher interests derives from an exactly equal restriction or displeasure in the past. The naïve humanistic observer may see, however, only the later higher satisfactions. He may never connect them with the restrictions of the past, which were unpleasant, boring and definitely resisted by the person. The two seem completely different in their "essence."

There can be no doubt that the refined spiritual life is more valuable in terms of any human progress one can think of. But the teachings of philosophers that the life of reason is a happier one is just a virtuous rationalization. The equivalence between higher pleasures and previous conditioned restrictions is inevitable. The higher satisfactions equally exhaust themselves, though the person retains his spiritual occupations as a second nature, with its own normalcy in which the play of equal "ups" and "downs" continues. The person with higher spiritual interests is more easily dissatisfied with existing achievements than other people. The real argument for more intellectual life is not any pleasure gain, but equivalence of emotions. By working hard and suffering restrictions during higher learning one loses nothing in terms of emotional values, but becomes able to live on a higher level of intellectual capacities.

If one tries to disengage himself from the deceiving material world in other ways, like living in the future or past, the relativity rule still applies. It is true that the future can be enjoyed by anticipation. But even a child knows that expecting too much brings disappointment. It is also true that memory can provide almost the same pleasure as living in reality. But an event over-enjoyed either immediately or during subsequent recall becomes a source of unpleasant feelings. On the other hand, events that were underenjoyed, that were valued as more negative than they actually were, are remembered with pleasure. Everybody can easily observe the paradox that people like to talk about their past calamities more readily than about their past enjoyments, though pleasantness as such is what everbody wants to recall.

Still one may say that if he had million dollars he would live happily to the end of his days. It is possible that one who spends half his life worrying about success enjoys the other half when the success comes, to the extent that the opposite feelings equalize themselves. But as to a state of complete satisfaction, such a state would be most unbearable. It would mean complete immobility, with no interests, no goals, and not the slightest diversity in sight. Of course, no person can stand such a state. Therefore the person who has everything soon uses it for the attainment of all kinds of overadjustments. Then complexes and neuroses become inevitable. This is the reason why mental difficulties, even suicides, are more frequent among people who have everything. Nor can a gradual addition of continuous success ensure uninterrupted happiness. As we saw, a cumulatively progressive increase in the rate of success would be necessary for that, and soon no success in the world would be great enough to give satisfaction.

Finally, one may ask whether there really is no difference whether one lives this way or that, dies old or young. It can be argued that dying young is a definite loss. But it can also be argued that it means a gain, since the worst part of life, old age, is avoided and only the good part lived. The truth is that exactly as much as is physiologically gained through growth or development is also taken away by death, whether it be early or preceded by the decline of aging. Variations in the steepness of ascent or descent cannot change the final equivalence of opposite emotions. If the descent is made more gradually, there is less negativity at each moment but it lasts longer, and vice versa. Here we may recall the example of a plane that starts and lands at the same zero level.

Some lives may seem more harmonious than others. The philosopher may live in an undisturbed, seemingly higher world. In truth, he looks with more resignation on the "ups" and "downs" of life. He wins less and loses less. Russell in his book, *Conquest of Happiness*, considers such a life the closest to a happy one. Apparently, Russell also recognizes that there can be no question of loss or gain but only of taking life with less or greater excitement. Of course, some people like to assert that they have discovered the secret of happiness. Some of them are the "experts" on happiness who would hate to admit defeat. Others are people who have incurred so much unhappiness in the past that anything different may seem to them a happy discovery.

Now we may consider some specific laws that result from the principle of relative causation.

FIXATION

By fixation we mean the attribution of value to a thing to an extent unreasonable by any objective standards, just because this thing happens to be used more often. The cause of fixation is the vicious-circle effect by which an object is valued more because it has been more often used and consequently is used still more often. A small initial preference for an object therefore may increase its value beyond any reasonable explanation. This may apply to any object, occupation or cultural institution, since they all mean searching for pleasure releases in some form, which becomes preferable to the extent that it has been used before. Avoidance of a displeasure may also be a form of pleasure release. Fixation explains the origin and nature of taboos, the unquestioned authority of traditions, the sacredness of beliefs, and the cultural inertia of which we are often unsuspecting victims.

The deeper reason for fixation is the fact that satisfaction or pleasure can appear only to the extent there is a previously accumulated need. Apart from the primary natural satisfactions, nothing is pleasant unless there is a previously established background for its enjoyment. Since the establishment of such a background is unpleasant, a person tries to resort every time to the background already established, even if it is becoming exhausted. As this is done, the same background is further enriched; the given need-satisfaction pathways are deepened and become "natural," to the exclusion of all others. Things for which no such background has been evolved have no value. You would not care much about becoming President of a country that is completely strange to you.

The previous background alone determines whether a thing has value, and how much. Of course, the more direct natural needs are common to all men. But even a slightly modified natural satisfaction is subject to fixation. Take ball games, in regard to which we have undoubtedly become unsuspecting fixation victims. The popularity of such games rests on the enjoyment of physical force and skill, which are primitive natural enjoyments. But for a person not used to the game it means merely chasing a small ball around a big field. The enjoyment of a game increases as the person develops definite forms or channels of evaluation along which the natural enjoyment potential and the satisfaction offered by the game can meet. Then, as more of such a background is evolved, the game is enjoyed more intensively — which leads to still further enrichment of the background.

The quality of mind that deepens fixations is the tendency of man to enjoy things in an easy way, without investments in new interests. A less resourceful mind aims at the nearest pleasure source available, and that means the things enjoyed previously. Even rats have been observed to stick to one food for long stretches, though eventually the needs of the organism force them to change. The general result of fixation is that a form of adjustment which happens to be there perpetuates itself with an irrational, inertial force that deepens itself in a vicious-circle way. Fortunately, fixation is counteracted by the urge of the more resourceful mind to use its more varied capacities. The less capacities people have, the more they become victims of cultural inertia.

Fixations are more prevalent than we realize. At your breakfast table you cannot enjoy the meal if you have to sit at a different place. The same applies to your newspaper or subject of conversation. Fixations extend to every detail of our lives and cultural values. It is useful to reflect here on the crazy things for which people have been ready to sacrifice their lives in different cultures — insignia, robes, titles, social musts, sacred occupations, honors and positions that often offer more trouble than comfort. We are no exception. Due to fixations we live under a cultural inertia that extends to every field of life, whether it be ambitions, social values, ball games, the car craze, fashions, the sacredness of art, humanistic dogmas or the "scientific" approach.

CONTRAST

Another interesting law is that of contrast. Everybody has noticed that a green insect is not seen in the grass, that a noise is not heard amidst similar noises, that an odor in the air is not noticed if it persists for long, and so on. We do not see what we "see," but only what offers contrast. The universality of contrast rests on the relativity rule that there can be no value without disvalue, or satisfaction without need. The latter are to be viewed here in their wider meaning of disturbance of normalcy and its restoration, in regard to all possible mechanisms, functions and their combinations, however tiny or involved they may be. When you pass from cold to warm, or when your eye passes from one color to another, there is the same disturbance and restoration. As has finally been recognized in psychology, only change can give sensation.

The universality of contrast offers interesting insights. One of them shows that things are known by what they are *not*, rather than by what they are. Any one thing can be known, not in itself, but only through differentiation against something else. Any differentiation means *contrasting* as to *opposite* values, at whatever point and to whatever extent the opposition is found. Gray is opposed to white only in one-half of it. Of course, what we know as "things" are actually unified wholes of values, or rather of other wholes, reaching further and further back. But whether we know separate values or their wholes, we know them by value differentiation or contrast — under the universal rule of value-disvalue. Everything in the world of mind has its ultimate cause in its opposite — in what it is not in terms of values.

The philosopher who tries to discover the essence of things in their inherent values is taking the most delusory course. Actually, in all theoretical thinking the same delusion prevails under what we called the *value outlook*. Positive values and feelings are seen as originating from sources of a similar positive nature, whereas just the reverse is true. This applies to the most sublime as well as the most earthly concepts. A person living through sublime feelings of harmony or peace sees some higher spiritual world as their source, whereas their real source is his previous deprivations, needs and harassments. Man viewing the earthly physical reality around him never sees anything in its contrasting opposite, "nothingness," though this alone makes physical matter as reality possible. If everything were matter, we could never know matter, and it would be nonexisting for man.

The law of contrast also offers explanations in other directions. For instance, the mysterious complexity of art, which may seem to reveal the existence of some trascendental harmony, can be reduced to the simplest terms in the light of contrast. Let us take music and look at its simplest aspect, rhythm. There are complex harmonies in various rhythms. Where do they come from? Rhythm appears clearly to rest on enjoyment of repetition, which means order. As we have said before, man finds this order so valuable or striking because there is so little of it in nature. The aestheticians who extol the prevalency of rhythms in nature are suffering from the same delusion of value outlook — they are noticing what is exceptional and are missing what is omnipresent. Anyway, the question arises: if repetition is the source of enjoyment, why is the repetition in music so interrupted and complicated that it constitutes rather a denial of true repetition? The requirement of contrast is the reason.

Any one thing to be experienced must have its opposite. In a closed-value system this opposition must be built in. To experience repetition more deeply, it has to be contrasted with something different. The one-to-one beat acquires strength where it is made to emerge against the background of a half-beat — which has to be rhythmical in its own turn to be enjoyable. Once the half-beat is assimilated as a true rhythm or true repetition, it may be further strengthened by addition of a one-fourth beat, and so on. Finally, a beat may be left out completely to offer greater contrast; or a parallel system of rhythms may be brought in to enrich the background of differentiations. By that time one may have a complex system, having its own complex but also miraculously harmonious laws. A theorist of aesthetics may then find this as an undeniable proof that there must be some transcendental, highly intelligent reason behind art.

The same applies to all aesthetic phenomena—from the existence of the octave to the apparent absurdity of abstract modern art.

OPPOSITE CAUSATION

The most interesting phenomenon of relative causation is the appearance of the emotional opposite in the case of emotional exaggeration. Logically speaking, such an opposite is a pure phantom, which has no reason to exist and emerges as if from nowhere. The cause of opposite effects is the necessity of the organism, or any mechanism in it, to return to normalcy after an exaggeration. Such a return means a process exactly opposite to the previous exaggeration—and exactly opposite experiences. Actually, everything in psychology derives from its opposite even if there is no exaggeration. In this sense opposite causation lies at the basis of all relative causation. All the other phenomena of relative causation—contrast, comparison, negative background causation, and the general correspondence between needs and satisfactions—tie in with opposite causation and can be brought out more strikingly in its context.

The simplest example of opposite causation is the afterimage. After you have looked for a while at a *bright* cross-like figure, you will see a *dark* cross upon closing your eyes. Or after you have read *red* print for some time you will see gray print as *green* for a while (red and green are value oposites, that can cancel out each other, because they represent two opposite sides in the same process). The opposite effects of afterimages are short-lasting because only a thin layer of a peripheral receiving mechanism is involved here. Afterimages have always been found intriguing by psychologists (Russian textbooks, which avoid all speculative diversions, admit some in regard to afterimages). There is every reason to be intrigued. But psychologists do not realize that they are viewing here only a thin edge of a world of most important phenomena in psychological life. *Emotional* aftereffects are the source of almost every psychological difficulty and mystery. For instance, the emotional as well as ideational phantoms of neurotics are due to such emotional aftereffects.

Theoretically, we could say that a person experiences the world not as it is but as it appears to him, like an opposite phantom against the specific background of his previous experiences or needs. In an experiment a subject wearing glasses which made things appear curved in one direction found everything curved in the opposite direction after he discontinued wearing the glasses. Practically, the "phantoms" of all normal persons are "normal" or similar, because of the similarity of physiological needs and satisfactions as well as the similarity of environment. As far as a person has his own peculiar but *constant* phantoms in his mental organization, they can never be known to others or to himself, because that person and others use the same words and conventional expressions of communication.

For instance, let us assume that a person sees horses in a form that others see giraffes, due to his peculiar background of comparisons. But he will still call his giraffe-like horses just "horses"; and when he draws them the drawings will come out like normal horses because his peculiar way of seeing form will equally apply to his drawings. For instance, El Greco could not have drawn his figures elongated because of a peculiarity in his vision, as some psychologists have suggested. If he really had seen everything more elongated, he would have seen the lines on the canvas also more elongated and accordingly would have drawn them that much shorter.

The same applies to every evaluation, perceptive or emotional. A person who permanently feels something one hundred percent more hostile than everybody else will deal with it as normal. He will deal with it as friendly when it appears to him a little less hostile, though in terms of others his inner evaluations still would mean hostility, not friendliness. Thus the permanent "phantoms" of a person cannot be discovered by others, and are not experienced as anything special by the person himself.

But "phantoms" do appear every time there has been an unusual change or exaggeration in the emotional background. The clearest, often observable instance is the aftermath of every intoxication. The drug addict suffers negative emotions as strong as was his enjoyment from intoxication though there is no *present* reason for such emotions to arise. We shall discuss later all kinds of phantom emotions that cause neuroses and psychoses. We shall also see, in discussing Gestalt theory, how the phantoms of perception, or illusions, arise because of peculiarities or "exaggerations" in the background of perception.

At present we want to make it clear that value is determined by the background against which, or side by side with which, it is evaluated. There are no permanent values inherent in an object. They depend upon differentiation from other values. If you suddenly found yourself in a world in which everything, including yourself, was twice as big as usual, you would not notice any difference. Alice in Wonderland noticed the shrinking and expansion of the things around her only when she did not shrink or expand with them. Such scaling up or down of values can be easily seen in the case of colors as well.

If one morning the sun rose green, shedding only green light, then objectively grass would be blackish gray, red roses whitish gray, the sky deep green, yellow sand light green, and so on. But everybody would find colors as usual. If this seems odd, think of what happens when you put on green glasses. After a while you see all colors, though in fact you see only differences or shades of green. In the case of sound, a melody can be sung in a different key, therefore with completely different notes, and still be recognized as the same.

The uniform scaling of values up and down is, however, only the simplest, most evident instance of the dependence of value upon background. In practice, more important because universally prevailing is the interdependence of nonuniform, endlessly varied values. There the effect is that any value acquires its magnitude and meaning from opposite values or value backgrounds. From the simple interdependence of the enjoyment of food and hunger to the most complex mental phantoms, this rule applies. People most often feel *fear, guilt* and *hate* without reason and against their will. Why? The reason is that most often people overenjoy the feelings of *security* and *personal worth,* and of *love* in its primitive form of self-love. The perennial problem of negative feelings in all their forms is there because the excessive enjoyment of positive feelings is always there. Normal people live with the same opposite causation, but they first accumulate needs and then experience the opposite satisfactions.

Everything works through opposites in the psychological world of values. If we knew all the factors involved, we could predict even the ideational contents of a person's thoughts. The ideas of the alcoholic about terrifying cold insects creeping through his veins are the opposites of the reassuring warm, solid and pleasant flow of blood during intoxication. The notions of reassuring endurance, undisturbed peace and harmonious unity in our sublimest experiences are the opposites of the threatening harassment, disturbing clamor and disruptive incongruity of the everyday struggle. The ideas of threat, hate, injustice and deception which plague the paranoiac, who as a rule feels persecuted by his best friend, are the opposites of his previous exaggerated feelings of security, love, fairness and sincerity enjoyed during the friendship.

In looking for ideational opposites one should, however, keep in mind that in themselves ideational contents are reactions through previously established reaction pathways, which, naturally, do not reverse. The opposite effects can appear only at the evaluation end of the process of experience. And as we said, there must be an exaggeration of values if an opposite phantom is to appear. Otherwise only the usual opposite effects of need-satisfaction and contrast result. This has to be kept in mind also in thinking of ordinary perception. The perceptive mechanisms also remain constant. Only in case of very strong excesses that may affect the mechanisms of perception themselves, does the opposite appear, as in the case of visual afterimages.

Opposite causation applies to every psychological experience — even if in usual cases it does not amount to more than the normal succession of needs and satisfactions. The opposite "phantoms" constitute the unexplainable emotional negativism, in all its forms, which is the cause of all psychological difficulties and disorders. But opposite causation has not even been noticed in modern psychology. The reason is that the paradoxical logic implied by it is contrary to everything that is considered scientific, logical or experimentally provable. As we saw before, according to that paradoxical logic less is obtained by addition and more by subtraction. The deeper reason is, of course, the fact that man cannot accept the truth of relativity. No man can live with the reasoning that the worse it gets, the more improvement he can expect — though this is undeniably true, as one can see by thinking about thirst and drinking, or any need and satisfaction.

Psychologists know that all experiences ultimately rest on the need-satisfaction mechanism. They also know of the permanency of organic identity. This is all that is needed to see the inevitability of the relativity rule and opposite causation. But no serious scientist would ever permit such an idea to linger long enough in his mind to become a thought. It is simply too ridiculous for that. However, the understanding of the relativity rule and opposite causation means the difference between the present impasse and a causal understanding in every field of human science. The examples are too many to be mentioned here. They will be given throughout this book.

UNLIMITED INTELLECTUAL POTENTIAL

Because of the relativity of values, a reaction can be made to acquire any value, by a change in the background. The tiniest release can become the most valuable one, able to set all our mechanisms in motion, provided there is a restriction of other releases so that the permitted release becomes the only outlet for satisfaction, and the dominant value. In psychology you can do as much with an "ounce" of release as with a "ton," depending upon the background restriction. Intellectual experiences need exactly the tiniest releases. But they become operative to the extent that the grosser natural pleasure releases are restricted. The natural releases are dangerous here because of their incomparably greater pleasure potential. If man could follow them freely, he would never bother with intellectual occupations or learning.

The imposition of restrictions is what cultural tradition and

61

conditioning strive for. The background of a lack of releases then makes all-important even remotely natural releases — refined, slight releases attaching to the more cultural and intellectual interests that the cultural tradition offers as the only channels of satisfaction. What is thus, unconsciously, achieved is a gradual channeling of the whole release potential, surging from the strong, gross, natural drives into myriads of weaker, more refined, intellectual reactions. These, of course, seem less efficient, and the whole process appears like a hindrance of motivation if analyzed in "scientific" terms. Modern psychologists and educators can prove that freer releases and more permissive, pleasanter methods of education give better results. Fortunately, the free education either discredits itself or changes imperceptibly into a restrictive one in practice.

We have to admit that acceptance of restrictions is the hardest thing for man to achieve and cannot be brought about by mere theoretical understanding or good intentions. But a theory could help, in our age of sciences, to shape general attitudes and methods so that they became a pressure brought on the individual from outside by way of cultural conditioning.

CONCLUSIONS

The laws of psychological causation are simple, as all natural laws are. But the understanding of these laws would be sufficient to turn psychology into a science. All sciences have started after abstruse, complex sophistications were replaced by simple laws. One can think here of alchemy, astrology, pre-Galilean physics or the pre-Darwinian natural sciences. Modern psychology, and with it all human sciences, are clearly at a similar stage of scientism. There are hundreds of most complex theories in psychology, all of them alchemistic; and the popularly dominating ones, like the psychoanalytic theories, belong clearly in the domain of occultism and mystery. Our human sciences rest on equally sophisticated, metaphysical tenets, like those of spiritual values, intrinsic rights and liberties, human nature and conscience.

The general truth is that real scientism has always appeared too simple and uninteresting to man. The alchemist found such truths as the permanence of matter beneath his learned interest because they offered no interesting "scientific" possibilities. On the other hand, he saw really interesting possibilities in the philosophical learning that dominated then. The truth is that only in the light of an inherently irrelevant learning do miraculous, really interesting or "scientific" possibilities appear feasible, whereas relevant scientific insights have always come out closer to the hard truth that you cannot get something for nothing.

Modern psychology is dominated by equally alchemistic endeavors to create more positive emotions without negative ones. Such endeavors appear fully feasible in the light of the physical sciences and their logic, which are inherently irrelevant and untrue for psychological causation with its seemingly paradoxical reversed logic. Psychology can be turned into a science by the acceptance of the logic of relativity or the equivalence of emotions just as alchemy was turned into chemistry by acceptance of the law of the equivalence of matter.

The great opportunities of psychology lie not in alchemistic possibilities but in the simple realization that by accepting restrictive suffering man loses nothing in terms of happiness, but in fact rises to a higher level of motivational potential. Only by the enrichment of needs or non-satisfactions can the potential of satisfactions be increased. Cultural tradition harbors, intuitively, this wisdom. But modern scientism, proceeding by the logic of direct increase in releases, makes the traditional restrictions appear stupid. The results are starting to show — from the increase in mental disorders and juvenile delinquency to the scourge of puzzling diseases that deepen with modern improvements. Much of the progress that would have been attainable under the miraculous possibilities of technological advance has been stymied by the fallacies of modern psychology.

III

THE IMITATION OF SCIENTISM

Modern psychology clings to the only logic and methods that modern man knows as scientific, namely, those of the physical sciences. But, as we saw, such logic and methods lead to conclusions exactly opposite to the simple truths of psychological causation. On these truths psychology could be built as a science, but the very advance of modern psychology means moving away from them. One has only to think of the truly enormous amount of learning, research and theorization in modern psychology. Such elaboration and complexity are incongruous in view of the simplicity of the causal truth to be found out. But they perpetuate and deepen that same "scientism" with such tremendous inertial weight that nobody can oppose it, whereas only a complete turnabout could help. Modern psychology lacks neither effort nor originality — but only within the framework of this scientism. Alchemy or Ptolemaic astronomy showed an equally spectacular amount of elaboration and originality — within the framework of the "scientism" of their times.

Experimentalism has been the main characteristic and the key to success of modern science. But in psychology experiment, as evolved by the physical sciences, does not cover the final or rather the continuous parallel effect that ultimately *reverses* the observable effect; and it leaves out the *opposite* background from which the observable effect derives its magnitude and meaning. Consequently the conclusions that such experiments lead to are contrary to the true cause-effect relationship. This is what happens in experiments or experimental case observations on emotions, values and motivations, which are the only matters that are relevant in psychology. Psychologists understand this and the experimental psychologists, who have preferred to remain scientific rather than yield to pointless theorizations, do not attempt further experiments in these matters. But experimental case observations in these matters are still the stuff on which modern psychology builds. And there the paradox of opposite causation invariably shows. To take the most glaring instance, observation shows that anxiety is caused by threatening circumstances. But men who live under constant threats are the least troubled by anxiety, whereas those who are guarded against any threat, as modern men in general are, suffer from anxiety to the point of complexes.

We shall see later how this paradox vitiates all psychological theories and observations. At present we may try to show, by some examples, what experiments, in the technical sense of the word, led to when applied to the properly psychological matters of evaluation and motivation.

To test the process of evaluation, Herring presented fourteen children with honey, chocolate, salt, egg white and vinegar. Each child came daily and tasted one, and only one, substance for weeks. The results showed some variation in values. But no definite change could be established. A simple common-sense reflection shows the incongruity inherent in such an experiment. How could tasting a substance for a few minutes have any influence on the tastes of anybody? A person's taste depends on his whole physiological and psychological background, determined not only by the innumerable past experiences in his own life, but also by his whole genetic background as far back as the origins of the human species. In other words, the determining factors here are inherent organic motivations or purposes, to which we will return in a moment.

Crawford and Washburn made similar experiments on the evaluation of colors. Even though their conclusions brought out the law of contrast, the same incongruity between the lifelong background and a few-hour experiment applies here. Beebe-Center made experiments with olfactory stimuli; Washburn, Child and Able had subjects listen to different styles of music. Valentine made a similar experiment on musical evaluations. Experiments on evaluation by

Waver, Zener, Volkmann, Bacon, Rood, Wasmann, Peckhams and Blatz can be mentioned in the same connection.

These experiments did not produce any consistent conclusions, but rather demarcated dead-end alleys for future research. The reason is clear if we consider that, apart from the paradoxical logic of opposite causation, any evaluation is determined by the past background far beyond the experiment. Thus the precondition of every experiment—that all variables except the one observed should be excluded and all factors accounted for—can never be fulfilled in an experiment on truly psychological phenomena. In fact, completely divergent conclusions may be reached in such experiments, or the experiment can be adjusted to support any view held by the experimenter.

For instance, on the important question of the role of reward and punishment in motivation two opposite views have been reached from experiments with animals. A chick punished by confinement upon reaching its food did not stop running for it. The experimenters could conclude that punishment did not change motivation. But other experimenters using different animals, such as rats, or different punishment, such as electric shock or noise, could prove that punishment changed motivation. Everybody can see that the past background of the animal makes the whole difference. This background can never be accounted for in an experiment. How, for instance, could the fright inspired in a mouse by a cat be measured or accounted for? The peculiarities of the whole biological history of the animal, as well as its training or experiences during its lifetime, determine what happens during the experiment, not the factors of the experiment alone. This should be too evident to be discussed, but psychologists have used hundreds of experiments of this kind to prove or disprove their theories.

Another source of error in psychological experiments — apart from paradoxical logic — is the absence in the subjects of real-life motivation during the tests. This means the difference between farce and life. The seriousness or compulsion of the needs of real life is what makes us tick the way we do. Without it life is like a game played without an opponent. For instance, experiments on the recall of pleasantness and unpleasantness show that pleasant experiences are more readily recalled. Such experiments have been conducted by Colgrove, Meltzer, O'Kelly, Stanger, Steckle, Tait, Thomson and Wohlgemuth. Naturally, the subjects when told during the test to recall whatever they wanted to recalled only pleasant memories. Everybody is ready to live in the most pleasant memories and happiest anticipations at the slightest permission to do so. In real life people do not do this because they know they have to remain realistic and to keep away from gratuitous enjoyments if they are to avoid emotional aftermaths.

By the way, some of the experimenters found that unpleasant events were recalled as often as pleasant ones. Actually, the experimenters here missed the point they were out to prove. The *unpleasant* events might have been recalled because they meant *pleasant* memories. As we saw, the most pleasant event leaves only a bitter memory if it was overenjoyed; and a calamity, which is usually avoided in reality as well as in memory, is recalled with pleasure if more anxiety was invested in it than there was real cause for in the light of later evaluation. We all like to recall our "tragedies" of early youth. But as scientists the experimenters could not accept the possibility that something unmpleasant can be pleasant — of all things, because of its unpleasantness in the past. Also, such a value phenomenon as overenjoyment or the innumerable emotional past factors accompanying it can never be dealt with in an experiment.

The difference between the seriousness of real life and the farce of experiment is shown best in the very important and very misleading experiments on the influence of pleasantness or unpleasantness on motivation and learning. Many experiments have been conducted to show that success in solving tasks is increased by the pleasantness of the task. We can easily understand why. The only motivation that a person can have in the laboratory is the pleasantness, or at least the absence of unpleasantness, in performing the given tasks. If a person has some specific interest, it means a hidden causal factor which will distort the results. In one experiment subjects who were unemployed workers and were paid by the hour did not get bored from drawing the same lines, though everybody else did.

In the laboratory there is not and should not be any motivation aroused by possible consequences. In real life just the reverse is true. We work harder if we find that we are doing badly. There may be a paralyzing pause after a setback. But this pause amounts to an accumulation of motivational energy for the difficulty ahead; actually, it means the accumulation of needs and therefore of pleasure potential. The famous psychologist William James noticed this "warming up" as a curious stalemate before starting a new task, though he speculated that it is only an obstacle and that the unsuspected energy which follows lies in us like an undiscovered treasure. Anyway, in long-range real-life situations only the imposition of needs or restrictions can produce motivation, whereas in the laboratory the satisfaction or release is its main source. Cultural and educational conditioning consists of imposing new needs so that new satisfactions follow automatically. In brief, experiment leads to conclusions that are exactly opposite to what is causally true in real life, in regard to the most important psychological factor — the source of motivation.

The main difficulty of experimentalism in psychology is that a psychological experience derives its causal meaning from *values* and *purposes*, but these can never be grasped in terms of their experimentally analyzable components. Theoretically, every experience can be reduced to biochemical reactions or at least to physiological stimuli-responses. But in these terms even the simplest psychological reaction becomes an unfathomable mystery. Take as an example the most primordial reactions of the reproductive drive. Even a moron could predict precisely, by one look at a beautiful woman what reactions and motives she will evoke in other men. But all the scientists in the world could not reach even an approximate guess, if they proceeded in terms of biochemistry or physiological elements without regard to values or purposes. Ordinary psychological reactions and evaluations, such as a simple motive of security or superiority, are incomparably more complex, but are fairly well understood, predicted or controlled by ordinary men analyzing them in terms of values and purposes.

Man understands easily *values* and *purposes* because he exists by them. In themselves they may be complexity itself, and would be ungraspable to a Martian not living by them. We have to deal in terms of values and purposes, which means satisfactions and needs, because they are the only expressions of the ungraspably complex natural processes that we can understand. *Values are not less real or mechanistic than the underlying biochemical processes. They are the unified wholes of these processes.* But dealing with values means gaining a unique advantage. For they have been perfected, through a million-year evolution, just for the purpose of their operative usefulness. A true operationalist in psychology would deal with nothing else but values. Man can replace this system of values by his own system of analytic data as little as he can replace a living organism by its physical components. Perfected guidance by value feelings applies to everything in behavior, because everything has evolved and is organized under the guidance of values. From the tiniest mechanism to the organism as a whole the capacity to evaluate determines whether they continue existing or are eliminated.

Even the strictest experimentalist thinks in terms of values and purposes when he plans his experiment or interprets its results. The subtlety of psychological life makes such procedure the most important prerequisite in constructing a meaningful experiment. The experimenting psychologist does not notice this part of his work, which involves introspection, because the sense-making planning and interpretation are taken for granted and nobody pays attention to them. But every time the modern scientist tries to produce a more scientific experiment, he gets closer to eliminating those elements which make sense in psychology. This is the reason why the advance of scientism in psychology has led to an increase in complex elaborations which explain nothing, and conflicting theories which add to the confusion.

The impossibility of the exact communication of truly psychological experiences is a greater obstacle to experimentation than is realized. It is clear to everybody that one can never know exactly how another person experiences what he reports as his experience. Past backgrounds determine what and how we experience anything. The person himself could connect them causally by introspection and thus understand a given psychological process. But the experimenter can never do this: he obtains only external data, never the causal backgrounds which determine the meaning of such data.

With that we come to the question of *introspection*. Earlier schools started with the self-evident method of looking at psychological events directly. This is the only reasonable thing to do. If a reporter had to find out what is going on during an involved business conference he would not prefer leaving the conference room and getting his information from the noises coming out of the room. Why should the psychologist refuse to look at the psychological phenomena directly, limiting himself to secondary data whose causal connections with the phenomena he never knows. Of course, the earlier schools produced more contradiction than clarification by the use of introspection. They understood the paradoxical logic of psychological causation as little as anybody else, but they attempted solutions of primary importance. Consequently their mistakes were glaring. The psychologist holding to strict modern experimentalism cannot commit important errors because he does not deal with psychologically really relevant problems.

The rejection of introspection in favor of experiment is the most conspicuous example of the blind imitation of the physical sciences. The physical sciences owe their success to the experimental approach. The physicist has to concentrate on the external experimental data alone because he never can get inside the matter and see *directly* what is happening, as the psychologist can in regard to the mind. The psychologist can observe to the last detail and for any period he wants every causal process and event inside his mind. He has here the most perfect experiment in the world going on right before him. Thus he has everything given that the physicist can only infer in a painfully cumbersome, indirect way. Still the psychologist wants to introduce the difficulties that face the physicist.

The reason why the psychologist gains nothing from this ideal experiment available to him is that he cannot accept the paradoxical logic by which it works. This logic is contrary to everything he lives by, and is therefore clearly ridiculous to him. Only an indifferent decadent attitude, bordering upon that of a freak, could normally lead to the recognition of that logic. The learned psychologist would be the last person to adopt such an attitude in his own field, where he aspires to the highest respect and seriousness.

It is often argued that psychological experiences are too complex to be dealt with in their entirety. Actually, this very complexity makes such dealing imperative. Everything in a psychological experience is so unimaginably complex but also so miraculously integrated that dealing with integrated wholes is the only possible way. Separate elements of an experience represent it as little as pieces of a body represent the living organism. Value concepts enable us to deal with the integrated wholes of every experience in a way streamlined to perfection. Every complexity disappears; and there is nothing inherently difficult in tracing the causal connections. As long as you can distinguish that Monday is less pleasant than Tuesday, or that coffee is sweeter after custard pie than after ice cream, you have everything you need to understand psychological causation. Nor is it true that a mind observing itself changes by the very act of observing, as Koehler has argued. The simple emotions are all that matter, and emotions cannot be changed by thought, however much we often try. If that could be done, men would attain the highest skill in doing it, and everybody would become a forever happy, perfect being.

Finally, the objection that the results of introspection cannot be verified is relevant only as to the objectivity of the observer. If a psychologist wants, consciously or unconsciously, to deceive himself or others, he can do that equally well with the experimental method. Think of the present innumerable conflicting theories, rooted in beliefs but "proved" by experimental observation.

Actually, there is no reason for a controversy to exist between experimentalism and introspectionism. In a correctly understood system of psychology experimental methods would have to be used for recording psychological events and relationships in their multiple and constant aspects; but introspection would have to supply the insights and interpretation. Of course, the first precondition for the usefulness of either method is an understanding of the basic law of psychological causation.

Because there is no such understanding at present, modern

psychology has, on the one hand, arrived at scores of conflicting and unbelievably complex theories — fully supported by experimental observations. On the other hand, those psychologists who have realized the futility of baseless theorizing have limited themselves to mere experimentation that does not involve, and does not seek to solve, any basic causal problems of psychology. The experiments are conducted mainly on animal behavior, physiological reflexes or permanent capacities. These cause no confusion because they involve no background causation. But it is exactly background causation that determines the human evaluations and goals, on which all behavior rests. Thus the only serious branch of psychology, experimental psychology, ends where psychology as such starts. This is the price paid for "scientism."

As regards various practical endeavors in psychology — educational, abnormal, clinical, industrial, vocational or child psychology — they are a part, not of a science, but of an art evolved by practice and depending on the good common sense of the psychologist rather than on theoretical understanding. Theory cannot help practical psychologists because there is no single area of agreement between the scores of theories and doctrines. The difference between any two theories, postulating their varied principles, forces and mechanisms, is greater than, for instance, the difference between the pre-Galilean and modern physics. Under such conditions there is not enough common ground for even a discussion. That is why the schools of modern psychology mostly ignore rather than discuss their differences. Every psychologist proceeds in his own way, as if everything were clear and certain.

Before we begin discussing the main theories, we may say a few words about social polls or surveys, which represent a wide area of application of the experimental method.

Surveys that gather facts can be accurate and useful — as factual information. But as soon as the properly psychological problems of evaluation and motives are brought in, the paradoxical causal logic applies. The famous Kinsey reports are mostly factual. Thus far they can raise no questions, but thus far they also have little to do with psychology. Kinsey was a zoologist, and his report on the sexual behavior of bees is not different in its nature from his report on the sexual behavior of human males or females. Even if some fact, like the increase of premarital intercourse in cities, may seem to have psychological bearing, in truth it does not, because it is not causally worked into any psychological context. If, for instance, one wants to draw conclusions from this fact about the moral attitude of youth, he may be misled. The increase in temptation may have been much greater than the yielding to sin. Therefore, in fact, there may have been moral improvement.

Most psychologists are aware of the contradictions inherent in value judgments and limit themselves to facts in their questions. But does that really help? First, facts also are noticed and reported depending upon value backgrounds. The woman who has scores of dresses may say that she has nothing to wear — and really mean it. The more important psychologically or emotionally a matter is, the more distorted will be the facts. In the often surveyed area of sexual behavior, for instance, a person with a background of sexual overenjoyment will experience lack of sexual fervor more often than others. Or a person with the strictest sexual standards will experience strongly, and assess as important, aberrations that remain unnoticed by a person living constantly with them.

Second, even assuming that facts are recorded correctly, they can mean completely different things depending upon value backgrounds. Value feelings, which determine behavior, are what should be recorded and measured if any human behavior is to be understood or predicted. Of course, this can be done only under the application of the seemingly paradoxical causal logic of value feelings. Under our existing understanding, dealing with value feelings would mislead rather than explain anything. For instance, the most important social phenomenon of today, economic booms and slumps, are emotionally caused and could be predicted from observations of the value attitudes of people. But paradoxical logic would have to be applied in understanding them. The loss of confidence that causes a slump is born out of the overconfidence that causes a boom. The learned psychologist would be the last person to connect causally such two opposed emotions, though life shows that the slump does follow when the boom and confidence have reached their highest accumulation.

There are many such important social phenomena. But without understanding their seemingly paradoxical causation, the psychologist does not even suspect that he can explain or predict anything about them. The most important social and political phenomena are determined by opposite causation. Overindulgence in positive emotions by people leads to emotional negativism and all kinds of social "neuroses." We shall discuss later the wars, persecutions, witch hunts or disastrous policies that a people may pursue without really wanting them, due to the paradox of opposite causation. At the moment we may mention election and popularity polls, as the surveys that could least possibly raise any problems.

Election polls are purely factual, since they state in figures how many voters are ready to vote for what party or candidate. But even they have led to big surprises and contradictions. The reason is that the survey does not account for the emotional factor which follows its paradoxical logic. A party may lose an election against all expectations, because it overreached in emotional appeal at one moment and the voting day fell at the moment of emotional reversal. In popularity polls a President may be rated higher than any reasons warrant because there was an equally unwarranted undervaluation of him before; or he may become less popular for no apparent reason because he enjoyed an equally unwarranted overvaluation.

BEHAVIORISM

More than any other school behaviorism has tried to make psychology scientific in the sense of the physical sciences. In those sciences the same factor always has the same value or effect. Correspondingly, the behaviorists tried to build their system on stable causal relationship between stimuli and responses. Nothing can be more misleading in psychology. As we saw, psychologically there are no definite values for stimuli. A response to the same stimulus can be anything, from completely positive to completely negative, depending upon previous background. We may recall here the phantom nature of really important emotional problems, and the opposite causation, which is contrary to everything the

74

scientist learns in the physical sciences. In the physical world, when you add heat to a heap of sand, it "reacts" by losing water. But if you apply heat to a living piece of matter, then *as far as the living reaction is concerned* it will consist of absorbing or seeking to absorb water.

Experimentalism was the main goal of the behaviorists. They wanted to make psychology a "purely experimental branch of the natural sciences," in the words of its founder, Watson. The behaviorists did not recognize that their experimentalism would lead to nothing but confusion if applied to truly psychological reactions. Due to relativity of effects, opposite causation, reversals and dependence of effect upon opposite value or previous opposite background, any conclusion from the same experiment is possible depending upon factors completely outside the experiment. The behaviorists saved themselves from incongruities only by limiting their experiments to the never-changing behavior of animals and to purely physiological reflexes.

The attitude of the behaviorists rests on one of the deepest fallacies of the natural scientists. The endeavor of the behaviorists amounts to trying to reconstruct behavior from its elements. It is like trying to rebuild an animal from its physical components. Scientists often do not realize that nature in its multiplicity is ungraspable by the mind and therefore must remain a virtual miracle if looked at in this way. Time and again scientists have rediscovered the fact that, for instance, the human body acts in ways inconceivably more miraculous than was thought of. There is no need to resort to mystery. Nature does not work in ways superior to the human mind. The two simply do not match. That is why the only possible mechanistic explanation of nature is one that deals with principles, or, in the case of psychology, with unified wholes or values. The naïvest kind of scientism is the one which assumes that nature can be grasped or dealt with in the terms of the few processes that man has finally happened to master. Three centuries ago London students proclaimed that the existence of God was disproved by the discovery of the circulation of blood by Harvey. Behaviorism is an example of this attitude, always persisting in the sciences.

75

By the way, even if a behaviorist succeeded in his endeavor, he would arrive only at the last over-all integrated response, grasped as a unified concept. In other words, he would be dealing with purposes and values in the end. It all amounts to trying to reconstruct life when it is there already in all its streamlined perfection.

The ideal goal of the behaviorists was to establish what stimuli evoke what responses and then to predict behavior by finding out the stimuli which apply in the given case. Watson said that the response of even a nation could be predicted by finding all the stimuli it is exposed to. Logically, this seems to be correct and in the physical sciences such a procedure would give the right results. But none of this works in psychology. A people exposed to one stimulus more intensively or for a longer duration respond so much the less to it. If continued without relief, any condition or stimulus is accepted as "normal" and ceases to evoke any specific response. Watson's assumptions are correct only for experiments with animal or purely physiological human responses.

The popular appeal of behaviorism lies in its implied promise of transforming human psychology by scientific means. Watson's book was hailed as "marking an epoch in the intellectual history of man," in the words of the *New York Times*. Watson said that he could train a child to become a successful man in any chosen field — or to be a beggar or thief — by conditioning his instinctive reflexes, which, according to Watson, were fear, rage and love. Watson proved experimentally that a child can be conditioned to fear furry objects by being frightened with noise every time he touches such objects. This experiment was considered epoch-making by other psychologists.

One can be sure, however, that if only such a reflex of fear is conditioned, the child will either get gradually used to it, and will return to touching furry objects, or will develop a phobia toward a specific kind of objects like furry animals, but will continue dealing with the rest of the world as usual. Actually, a greater capacity to counteract the noise or any further similar condition would be evolved by the growing child, striving for the satisfaction of multiple new and different value goals. He would become more callous to such interference with his emerging deeper *purposes* and *values*. In brief, just the reverse of the expected result would be achieved as far as such conditioning is concerned.

Not the external reflexes but deeper general needs determine behavior. Reflexes are products of the needs, not the other way around. Upon repeated satisfactions certain patterns are evolved. In the strongly established automatic behavior of animals, or in physiological reactions, the reflex coincides with the satisfaction of the need. But as soon as nonautomatic psychological behavior is involved, reflexes are changed if they do not conform with general and conditioned needs. This is too evident to be discussed, but the behaviorists had to stick with the reflexes because only these remained consistent under experimental methods. Thus the behaviorists reached the absurd position of assuming as force what is only its outlet. The value or pleasure is the force that has to be channeled in conditioning. A mother simply wanting to see her child happy, but also wanting him to renounce his natural egotistic pleasures, produces the right conditioning. In comparison with this, Watson's conditioning is a parody. It is like driving a faucet in the wall and expecting water to flow, or like trying to reorganize a factory by changing handles or outlets on machines.

Incidentally, Watson included love in his reflexes. We can only agree that by conditioning love everything can be achieved. But then by love has to be understood the whole system of values and purposes by which the child lives. The same applies to rage, if one understands by it displeasure in general. Here we can see that when it comes to practice the behaviorists have enough common sense to think in terms of values and purposes.

True to their intention of viewing everything in terms of machine-like reflexes, the behaviorists tried to reduce all experiences to the senso-motor reflexes of muscles, or to the reactions of glands and viscera. Thought was construed as implicit speech concentrated in the larynx, emotions as visceral or muscular movements, and so on. Here the endeavor to explain living processes mechanistically borders upon a naïve anthropomorphic conception of mechanisms. Theoretically, it is possible to speak of all behavior as consisting of reflexes, the same as it is possible to speak of life as a chemical process. But why limit the reflexes to muscles and viscera? Why not extend them to the infinitesimal processes in the brain? The brain is a more likely seat of thought than the larynx, as lesions in these organs show. Behaviorists, however, could not extend the reflexes to such innumerable invisible mechanisms which can be grasped only through the value reactions they produce. These are meaningless under the experimental approach. Behaviorists have persistently denied the existence of value feelings as well as of images of thought, though other psy·chologists have pointed out that such images undeniably exist.

On the important question of learning the behaviorists tried to explain it by a simple frequency or recency of reflex activity, without regard to pleasure or satisfactions. As the law of effect established by Pavlov and Thorndike shows, learning depends on satisfaction. Every animal trainer knows that satisfaction in the form of food or safety from punishment, is the source that is to be utilized in training. If learning were due to repetition, like engraving a plate with traces of behavior, the animal would unlearn more than it learns. For there is much more random activity than coinciding activity in every behavior, especially before the fundamental pivotal patterns are learned.

This may be sufficient to show how the endeavor of the behaviorists to make psychology scientific in the sense of the experimental sciences precludes it rather from becoming a science. Everything that is real in psychology — values, purposes, thoughts or images — is nonexistent for the behaviorists. If these realities, which clearly do exist, are not explained mechanistically, then mentalistic concepts, which were the main target of the behaviorists, remain the only explanation. The use of the concepts of love or rage, in the sense we explained above, by the behaviorists themselves may show what happens in practice.

We saw how the psychological realities can be explained by the concept of pleasure or need-satisfaction, as mechanistically as by biochemistry or by stimuli and responses. By concentrating on the purely external aspects of stimuli-responses the behaviorists have chosen what is not only humanly ungraspable in its whole causal significance, but also leads to answers exactly opposite to what is true. As far as truly psychological experiences are concerned every stimulus becomes part of the background and a cause of a *reversal* of its own effects. The introduction of the concept of intervening variables by later behaviorists, Tolman and Hull, is a step toward recognizing background causation. But in general behaviorists never even suspected the reversed logic of psychological causation.

Like all believers in experimental logic, according to which the adding of good means more good, the behaviorists are supporters, directly or indirectly, of methods aiming at an increase in releases. Behaviorism and its experimental discoveries can give comfort to psychologists advocating satisfactions; to educators favoring freer education; to writers selling their happiness formulas; or to doctors getting spectacular cures with miracle drugs. They all can refer to experimental proof. When the inevitable opposite effects or "side effects" appear, experiment again can prove that unexpected new negative factors are producing them.

GESTALT PSYCHOLOGY

The next most important school in modern psychology is Gestalt psychology. It seems to be gaining ground. Reasons are not far to seek. The belief of psychologists, especially the behaviorists, that the elements they deal with have consistent or logical effects, the same as in the physical sciences, collapses under closer scrutiny. The Gestaltists have proved this amply.

The most important part of Gestalt psychology are the perceptual illusions and inconsistencies that we are going to discuss first. The whole theory started with the practical observation of these illusions. The theoretical part was constructed to explain them. In fact, these illusions are excellent examples of relative causation in the field of perception. The Gestaltists did not realize that much more important are similar illusions or phantoms in the fields of emotion and motivation. Perceptual illusions are often mentioned by other psychologists, but have remained unexplained. If such conspicuous psychological phenomena cannot be explained by psychology, there must be something wrong with it. No wonder, the Gestalt theory is preferred, in spite of its mysteries.

79

One series of illusions arises from simple relativity or contrast. A line placed along a long line seems shorter than the same line placed along a short one. A circle amidst big circles seems smaller than the same circle amidst small ones. A space between broad parallelograms seems narrower than between narrow ones. The same applies to any value. White close to black is whiter. This explains the often shown illusion in which grayish spots seem to appear in the middles of the crossings of white stripes drawn through a black background. We saw before how color derives its value from its relative difference in regard to another color. Gray in spacial or temporal proximity with red appears green. A sound amidst strong sounds seems weaker than in silence. The saying about hearing a pin drop exemplifies the fact.

In this connection we may mention a phenomenon for which the Gestaltists postulated a special Gestalt. Two equal tones are sounded one after the other. When the interval between them is less than three seconds, the first seems stronger; when the interval is more than three seconds, the second seems stronger. The explanation does not require the existence of any Gestalt. In the first case the first tone is louder because it follows silence. In the second case the longer interval makes the second tone distant enough from the first so that it can appear stronger because of the general rule that the last impression is always stronger.

A second series of illusions is due to relation or contrast with background. The most interesting one is the Zoellner illusion. A line drawn through a stretch of lines slanted in one direction seems to be a little tilted in the opposite direction. If two parallel lines are drawn through two such stretches slanted in opposite directions, they do not look parallel. A straight line drawn through a uniformly distorted background seems to be slightly distorted or bent in opposite ways. This explains Herring's illusion, in which two parallel lines, drawn one above and one below a center from which ray-like lines fan out, seem to be slightly curved toward each other.

The reason for these illusions is the relative value or contrast. The onlooker adopts the curved background as normalcy, therefore expects everything to curve the same way. But since the straight line does not do so, it is judged as having the opposite curvature. The best practical example is the sides of skyscraper which seem to broaden at top. Because we see them against the dome of the sky, we expect them to narrow, the same as the segments of the sky do when they go toward the center of the dome. But since the sides of a skyscraper do not narrow, we evaluate them as having an opposite character. Of course, the evaluation is automatically felt rather than reasoned.

A third series of illusions is due to the way we relate objects. The moon looks larger when closer to the horizon because we relate it to real objects there and conclude that it must be pretty big to bear that relation to them. In fact, all celestial objects appear bigger when closer to the horizon for the same reason. The dome of the sky itself looks flattened out due to a similar relation, as its sides extending toward the horizon are seen longer.

The same reasons lie behind the fact that objects at a distance appear much bigger than they should on the basis of their picture on the retina. The object at a distance is related with other objects there and retains its normal value. If we did not have to relate it to objects closer to us, it would seem of normal size. As it is, we make a compromise. For the same reasons a pencil held at arm's length is seen longer than it should on the basis of its physical picture on the retina; and a dime seems smaller than the moon though on the basis of the retinal picture it is bigger.

The manner of relating explains other illusions. If two equal triangles are placed one on top of the other, the upper one appears bigger. The reason is that we make the comparison or relation between the broad or *large* lower part of the tringle above and the narrow or *small* upper part of the triangle below. The same illusion can be obtained by placing other equal figures, like trapezoids or ring segments, so that the broader part of one is related to the narrower part of the other. This illusion is so natural that even chickens have been found to have it.

The relative value of the illumination of objects explains another series of illusions, demonstrated in various experiments. A black sheet of paper placed in a strong light actually gives off as much light as a white sheet in normal light, but still is seen as black, not white. Apparently the comparison is made with the immediate environment. If the environment is artfully concealed, the black sheet does appear white; but as soon as a white slip of paper is placed near it, the black sheet is seen as black again. Of course, the same applies to colors, or to any other sensation. If all objects in a room are of graded red colors, the sensation of red disappears and only differences are seen. Similar experiments can be made with all kinds of sensations or their combinations. The interesting experiment of touching curved objects for a time and then finding normal flat objects curved in the opposite direction belongs here.

As we can see, all these illusions are due to the relativity in evaluations. In simple words, it means that things are neither big nor small, bright nor dark, good nor bad, except in relation to other things that are different. Any value in itself is nonsensical. It can exist only through its opposite or disvalue. Our recognition of things derives from what they are not. Only relations matter, and the same thing may seem different, or different things may seem the same, depending upon what we relate them to. Here we may mention the transposition of tunes into different keys, which gave the first idea of Gestalt to Ehrenfels. The transposed melody consists of completely different notes but the tune is recognized as the same — because the relationships are the same. The Gestaltists did not have to postulate any special Gestalt here, nor in any other case of illusions. The general laws of psychology, that is, the laws of relative causation, are sufficient to explain them.

Before we proceed with the rest of Gestaltist discoveries we wish to recall that relative causation ultimately rests on the correspondence of satisfaction to need. Satisfaction or value can exist only to the extent, and in the form, that need exists. In other words, we see the world not as it is but as our needs and values tell us it to be. For instance, a chick assumed to have only one need in the world, picking grain, would see only the grain in the world. The rest would be emptiness or nothingness for it. Our impression that we see everything there is in the world arises from our inability to imagine things that we cannot know or imagine; and from the vast potential of our consciousness to have innumerable needs. Consciousness arises as a result of restriction of satisfactions with regard to most reactions. Consequently, the search for release extends to every possible combination of reactions and sensations; their number can be astronomical, according to the mathematics of combinations.

Now we may turn to one of the main discoveries of Gestalt theory. Wertheimer and others after him demonstrated by the use of dispersed dots and shapes that man tries to organize them in certain definite and preferred patterns instead of viewing them as the separate dots or shapes that they are. For instance, dots happening to group themselves somewhat crosswise are immediately seen as a cross. Gestaltists formulated special laws in explanation of such tendencies: the law of pregnancy, the law of good form, the law of closed form. If we view our mental processes in terms of values, the postulation of special laws here is not necessary.

We simply see things in accordance with our value preferences or, in other words, in accordance with what makes more sense. At the same time an automatic exclusion of other values makes the chosen form appear more regular, clearer and simpler than it is in fact — just as the Wertheimer's law requires. The chick, when it gets a visual impression, sees either a grain, complete and simple, or nothing. In the above example, the figure of the cross has important value preference because it represents verticality and horizontality, which are very important in orientation, in their most distinct relation: contrast. Therefore we see the dots as a cross even if they do not form a regular cross.

All the principles of organization postulated by the Gestaltists can be explained by such natural value preferences. For instance, proximity, one such principle, rests on value preference because we deal more easily with objects closer by than with those far away. Similarity means the saving of effort and the increase of reliability in evaluation. Continuity, as well as symmetry, renders relating easier. There can be as many such principles as there are preferred ways of relating things or dealing with the environment. Of such ways the underlying biological ones are common to all living beings, while the learned ways may produce what Gestaltists formulate as factors of familiarity and of set or attitude.

Now we may look at the rest of the illusions. A vertical line seems longer than an equal horizontal line. Apparently we evaluate lines according to the sweep or movement by which they are covered during visual evaluation. A movement vertically means more in effort because of our visual organization; and more in value because of gravitation. By thinking in terms of movement we can also explain the Mueller-Lyer illusion. A line with a pair of prongs at each end seems longer when these prongs extend out from the ends in the direction of the prolongation of the line, but seems shorter when the prongs are bent backward toward the middle of the line. Apparently the movement or sweep of the line is enhanced by the prongs in the first case and restricted in the second. Also, the configuration is seen as a whole, and in the first case it is longer. For similar reasons, when a triangle is divided at the middle of its height, the bigger lower part looks taller than the smaller upper part. A similar value prejudice explains Sander's illusion. A line bracing a smaller slanted quadrangle (between narrower, more distant corners) appears shorter than an equal line bracing a larger one (between the nearer corners). Apparently the sweep of the first line is more restricted; and the line has less general value because of the smaller figure as a whole.

Value preference means preference for what "makes sense." At bottom, "sense" or understanding is value or satisfaction. When in a completely dark room an illuminated large point is moved toward a small one, the observer has the illusion that the small point is moving toward the large point and that the latter is standing still. Apparently the person attributes greater agility to the smaller point and greater stability to the larger one, or assumes the larger point as the base to which the smaller one is then subordinately related.

Innumerable illusions are accepted as truths in everyday life because of the same preference for what makes sense. The extension of blue sky that we "see" is an illusion. In fact, our eye gets only samples of blue patches. The disappearance of a small gray spot on a red surface is explained on the same grounds. The hundreds of rustling leaves that we "see" on a tree are an illusion, for we see only a few. Most of our ordinary patchy sensations are consolidated by such illusions, especially in perception of movement. In the classical experiments of Wertheimer two lines that were made to appear one after another produced the illusion of one moving line. This illusion makes motion pictures and moving neon signs possible. Here the preference for sense-making interpretation combines with the slowness of vision.

More generally, the same tendency to see preferred values rather than truths is the cause of our unconscious falsehoods, emotional convictions and rationalizations. Many of these lie at the bottom of our great systems of supernatural and moral beliefs as well as our prejudices. Some theories of psychology, like the intentionalism of Brentano, could derive strong arguments from this dependence of experience on intention rather than on objective fact.

Another phenomenon dealt with by the Gestaltists, often together with illusions, is the oscillation or reversal of a figure. If a drawing is made so that it can be seen as a rabbit's head facing one way, or as a duck's head facing the other way, then the drawing oscillates between the two in our perception. Many kinds of such drawings have been made — transparent cubes which appear to have at one moment one side in front, at the next the opposite side, and similar figures. Gestaltists like to use drawings where the oscillation involves figure and ground. This enables them to refer to their law of figure and ground. A white goblin in the middle of a black square can be drawn so that the black backgrounds at the sides of the goblin look like profiles of human faces. Oscillation between seeing either the goblin or the profiles then results.

The explanation of the oscillation suggests itself if one thinks of opposite causation or aftereffects. Seeing only one value in a thing that has two equal values amounts to a one-sidedness or exaggeration, which automatically leads to its opposite and recognition of the opposite value. We cannot help the one-sidedness in these cases because we can see only one thing at a time — either the rabbit's head or the duck's head — and not both together. Whether the evaluation is automatic or accompanied by conscious meaning makes no difference, since it is always a value process subject to the same law.

The causal similarities between figure oscillations and aftereffects are so close that the Gestaltists could not miss noticing them. But the Gestaltists were bound by their multiple laws of Gestalt and never recognized the simple underlying common principle. Typical in this respect are the comments of Koehler, the leading Gestaltist, on the Gibson experiment in which subjects looked at curved lines for periods of time and then saw straight lines as being curved in the opposite direction. Koehler advanced two hypotheses in explanation. One refers to the Gestalt principles of figure and ground. The other is termed by Koehler as a specific figure process viewed in terms of physical field effects. Koehler stated that this process "tends to block its own way if the figure remains for some time in the same location." This is close to the concept of satiation, which, as we saw, constitutes one phase in the most evident instances of opposite causation. The second leading Gestaltist, Koffka, came close to the same explanation. In his *Principles of Gestalt Psychology* he explains afterimages as being due to "reversible chemical processes, material having been decomposed, and the products of the decomposition now recombining themselves to form the original substance by reverse process."

In spite of such close guesses the Gestaltists did not see the simple general principle on which not only reversals of figures and aftereffects but all the other illusions and contradictions discovered by them rest. Here we have to make a general observation on Gestalt psychology. We find in it an extensive observation of relative effects, even close guesses as to their cause; but also a lack of simple unified explanation. Instead, we find a multiplicity of laws. Boring says in his *History of Experimental Psychology* that 114 such laws have been listed by one encyclopedist. If the Gestaltists had been aware of the illusions and contradictions in other fields than perception, they would have had to postulate hundreds more laws. Actually, all the laws of the Gestaltists are reducible to the simple principle of relativity. We have seen already how this principle explains all the phenomena from which the Gestaltists derived their laws, and we hardly need to repeat the explanations for each law separately.

The contribution of the Gestaltists is undeniable. They showed that experience is determined not by the logical or absolute values of elements perceived but by the configuration or Gestalt in which they are presented, which means by their relation. "Gestalt" translated means configuration, figure or pattern. Why did not the Gestaltists make the last logical step and recognize the general rule of the relativity of experiences? Apart from the seemingly paradoxical ultimate conclusions that relativity implies, it would have required a complete change in the notions of scientism in psychology. Dealing with relativity means dealing with values, but values as concepts have no place in the scientism to which the Gestaltists aspired, namely, scientism in terms of the physical sciences. Accordingly, the Gestaltists resorted to concepts from the physical sciences, mainly, those of field and isomorphism.

The Gestaltists used the physical concept of field quite literally. The distribution of electric current in a system or field of electric conductors, or of water in a pipe system, were taken as concrete examples. For instance, Koehler explained aftereffects like those observed in the above Gibson experiment as effects of equalizing and polarizing electric currents in the brain. By the way, when this explanation was checked in an experiment on the brains of monkeys by Lashley, Chow and Summers, none of the predictions was confirmed.

Equally physical and literal is the concept of isomorphism. The Gestaltists assumed that to the physiological constructs in the brain correspond similar physical constructs of objects perceived. Since the constructs from both sources have to coincide before perception results, man sees everything only in certain forms or *Gestalten*. As Woodworth explains in his *Contemporary Schools of Psychology*, the assumption meant that to the external world of objects, like a country, there corresponds a system of structures in the brain, like a map.

We cannot go into more detailed explanation of these concepts, nor do we need to. The real point lies somewhere else. Whatever physical processes or forms are assumed, *it remains unexplained what makes them so miraculously purposeful in the animal and sensemaking in the human mind.* This purposefulness and sense or value would require intervention by a supernatural creator having human-like intelligence in the creation of all the *Gestalten*. There is only one way of explaining this purposefulness and sense mechanistically and that is in terms of selective adaptation working at every infinitesimal instant through millions of years of adaptation. But such adaptation, with purposeful behavior as its product, can be dealt with only in terms of purposes and values. These, however, have no place in the scientism of the Gestaltists. Consequently, adaptation cannot and does not have any relation to Gestaltist isomorphism, fields or any of the *Gestalten*. They are all physical concepts, and as such do not derive their causal value from any development in the past. In physics, the law of gravity does not act differently on a stone with a different past; and the same applies to the laws of field, isomorphism or *Gestalten*. *Gestalt psychology has remained deliberately ahistoric.*

Some interpreters have tried to point out the correspondence between tension in the Gestaltist field and in actual emotion. Even this isolated endeavor to bring value notions into the Gestalt theory fails. For a higher physical tension or energy level in an organism may mean precisely a lower emotional tension.

Insofar as Gestalt psychology offers explanations of the ultimate nature or origin of *Gestalten*, it is philosophical. Apparently, serious scientists prefer to hold to orthodox classical methods, even if that means adding further mystification. Koffka, the chief interpreter of the Gestalt school, says in his major work, *Principles of Gestalt Psychology*, that there must be a Gestalt for each ego, each world outlook, like intellectualism, and each personality, like Michelangelo, Raphael or Leonardo da Vinci. Abandoning philosophical loftiness, one could say that there also must be a Gestalt for each apple, or everything that is organized as an entity in our perception. This agrees with the definition of Gestalt by Koffka and Koehler, as a "concrete individual and characteristic entity, existing as something detached and having a shape or form as one of its attributes." In truth, Gestalt psychology requires an underlying metaphysical causation. Koffka says that Gestalt "cannot be explained by mere chaos, the mere blind combination of essentially unconnected causes," and that "its essence is the reason of its existence." Though Koffka protests against any metaphysical interpretation of his ideas, they cannot be interpreted otherwise if they are to have any meaning. In the conclusion of the above book Koffka says that the Gestalt theory rejects the positivistic attitude according to which all natural events are irrational.

What we have said may be sufficient to show that Gestalt psychology precluded rather than helped a mechanistic understanding of psychology. It did this by trying to make psychology scientific in the sense of the physical sciences. A system that has scores of laws and innumerable constructs, like the *Gestalten*, which cannot be reduced to simple natural principles, but rather require philosophical explanations, cannot be scientific. The concept of Gestalt is, however, very comfortable to psychologists. Whatever the phenomenon to be explained, the psychologist can say it is due to the existence of a special Gestalt. And a Gestalt cannot and does not need to be explained: it is an "individual entity," as Koffka has said. Nor can a Gestalt be analyzed as to its simpler elements: the wholeness is the very essence of Gestalt. The same can be said about the increasingly popular concept of field, which is often interchangeable with the concept of Gestalt.

The practical implications of the Gestaltist approach are neither too important nor convincing. The new concept of *insight* that Gestaltists claim to have discovered appears to be the same trial-and-error process. Gestaltists have repeatedly used as an illustration the observation by Koehler that an ape happening to join two sticks into one suddenly uses it to rake in a banana. Does not this confirm rather than supplant the trial-and-error theory? The learning by insight or from whole to parts, postulated by the Gestaltists, contradicts the common practical knowledge that things learned are not revealed to us suddenly, after meditation, but have to be painfully built up bit by bit. The Gestaltists suffer here from a general lack of understanding of background causation. They do not notice the accumulation of background, which makes the sudden insight possible, because this background as the opposite of the things learned never seems to have anything to do with them.

Gestalt Therapy. This is another sample of modern alchemy. Gestalt therapists prescribe ritualistic techniques, the acquisition of specific skills, the direction of one's thoughts and many other formulas. They advise orientation of the self, the direction of awareness, manipulation of the self, retroflection, introjection, projection, and so on. As important special techniques of therapy they consider: muscular concentration; tightening of the chest in respiration; taking small bites of food to "wreak vengeance" or to increase the feeling of oneself as an active agent; practicing chewing, swallowing and vomiting of bites of food, and others. Of course, such ritualism would never attract either sensible writers or readers if it were not for the underlying idea of *release* that the Gestalt theory consciously or unconsciously embraces. Such things as *"growth and excitement"* are the real substance of the therapy, as the subtitle of the *Gestalt Therapy* by Perls and others shows.

FIELD THEORY

The field theory of Kurt Lewin represents a prominent example of the modern approaches in psychology, seeking explanations in physical concepts. Lewin was explicit in describing his theory as ahistorical, the way physical sciences are. His theory is also typical of an endeavor to deal with psychological concepts in terms of mathematics, so useful in the physical sciences. Lewin used topology to map the life space, and vector analysis in explaining motives. As other psychologists have pointed out, the use of diagrams and technical mathematical terms amounted to adding complexity in description rather than producing explanations. Let us see how helpful such ahistorical theory is in practice.

In the classical experiment by Lewin, Barker and Dembo, children who had learned to play constructively with toys — "writing a letter" with a pencil, or "calling" through a toy telephone — were offered other very attractive toys. Then after a while they were shut off from these toys by a wire partition and were left with their previous toys. Now the pencil was not used for "writing a letter" but for sheer scribbling and the telephone became a mere rattler. Lewin interpreted the experiment in complex concepts of dedifferentiation describing the process in topographically represented sensory regions, and arrived at the discovery of Freudian regression.

The simple fact is that the more pleasant toys enjoyed in the immediate past made the present toys uninteresting. As the interest was lost the toys could serve only as general excitants of grosser releases which the children now badly needed in their ensuing state of emotional negativism. As to the regression to more primitive behavior, the children simply started behaving in ways characterized by grosser releases and the loss of more refined releases. This resembles the characteristics of earlier versus the later ages of children, because maturing and conditioning consists of restricting the grosser releases and channeling them into more refined interests. In any event, the past background was the deciding factor and an ahistorical approach was the least suitable one in providing the true though simple explanation.

Another experiment, by Zeigarnik, established the now classical observation that subjects seek to return to uncompleted tasks. Here the past accumulation of needs, as a kind of emotional investment, is clearly the cause. A background of *needs* is built up in approaching a task. As completion or solution takes place, the corresponding *satisfactions* follow. Naturally, these are sought after. The importance of the past background is clear here. Still Lewin thought that his ahistorical approach was confirmed by these experiments.

Experiments by Hoppe, Frank and Gould showed that persons assessed their future success high, but not too high. Here again an analysis in terms of aspiration level and ego level according to Lewin's field theory was used. In fact, everybody likes to enjoy the greatest possible success in reality or in anticipation. But everybody also has learned early that displeasure follows if enjoyment is greater than warranted by the success when it comes. To avoid disappointment one does not aspire too high. An ahistorical approach that disregards the relative dependence of an experience upon its counterpart in the past can lead here to confusion rather than explanation.

We cannot discuss an experiment in which Lewin showed that students worked better under a "democratic" work arrangement than under a "dictatorial" one. Here the negative background causation was missed: every restriction or discipline produces at first a seeming stalemate. Also missed was the background of social conditioning, which makes democracy as well as dictatorship succeed or fail — and was responsible even for the prejudices that permeated this experiment.

HORMIC THEORIES

The hormists recognized purposes or instincts as the fundamental sources of behavior. Hormic theories represent a revolt against the formalistic and barren scientism of other schools, especially behaviorism. McDougall, the founder of the hormic school, said he wanted to see psychologists deal with human experiences, not with the reflexes of mice. But the hormists could not liberate themselves from the deeply rooted tenets of scientism as they are known from the physical sciences. The simple concepts of purposes and values should have been the cornerstones of the hormic, i.e., purposive, psychology. However, such concepts were not considered scientific enough by the hormists. McDougall recognized that sentiments modify instincts, therefore are the fundamental reality behind instincts. But the concept of sentiment had no place in a "scientific" system. Instead, the purposes or instincts were construed as mechanisms corresponding to human notions about man-made devices used in the physical sciences and mechanics.

For instance, McDougall considered such machine-like mechanisms as sneezing and coughing to be typical instincts. He listed them on the same footing as his other twelve instincts, which ranged from hunger and sex to gregariousness and acquisitiveness. This is typical of all hormists. They wanted to explain the widest social and cultural phenomena, like property interests, as products of machine-like mechanisms. Such endeavor could lead only to incongruities. This shows in the fact that the hormists could not agree on the number and nature of instincts, though these, as the basic simple principles of nature, evident everywhere, should have been clear the moment the hormic theory was conceived. No two hormists had the same set of instincts. Some hormists listed over a hundred of them, and some discovered only two or three.

In fact, instincts as mechanisms are a million. Think of the innumerable instincts that must operate in order to make a bird seek for a mate, respond to the mating song and ritual, find a nesting place, build a nest and feed the offspring. Each such instinct has innumerable subordinate "instincts" of the same nature — actually as many as there are living reactions. Classification of instincts around a few anthropomorphic notions, like gregariousness, acquisitiveness or constructiveness, can explain the cultural background of the psychologist who makes the classification, not the way nature works. Nature does not know such humanly meaningful, complex principles. The principles of nature are elementarily simple and few, though its mechanisms are innumerable. The hormic theory, on the contrary, arrived at the scientifically absurd position that there may be in nature scores of complex intelligent principles, but that the number of mechanisms of nature could be exhausted by a certain limited number.

If hormists had dealt with instincts as true psychological purposes, they would have found, as McDougall did, that emotions, with pleasure as the ultimate principle, are the determining psychological realities (we have shown why exactly these concepts permit the only possible mechanistic explanation). Of course, any endeavor to deal with values, emotions and pleasure requires the causal understanding of these psychological realities, and of the paradoxical logic that governs all psychological causation. Because this logic is repugnant to a learned psychologist — even more than to a common man — neither the hormic, nor hedonistic, nor any related theories could add anything more than confusion.

OTHER SCHOOLS

The older schools — one thinks here of associationism, introspectionism, intentionalism, functionalism and structuralism — rightly saw that emotions, and states of consciousness, as well as purposive behavior, are the proper subject matter of psychology. This is evident from the works of such prominent pioneers in psychology as Wundt, William James or Dewey. However, the older psychologists had as little understanding as anybody else of the paradoxical effects of psychological causation. Consequently, they produced more confusion than explanation; and their mistakes were conspicuous because they attempted solutions of the very basic primary problems, as is to be expected in a new science. Dewey's theories on progressive education are a good example.

The most frequent source of fallacies was the lack of understanding of *background causation*. As we saw, a psychological cause is so different from — actually opposed to — its effect that the causal connection between them is never suspected. Moreover, what is *omnipresent* and therefore causally all-important does not appear as having any psychological meaning at all.

For instance, the older schools could never prove their contentions about the association of mental states. On the contrary, the epoch-making experiments of Kuelpe and Marbe proved that there was no association of any *kindred* mental states or images during judgments. The explanation is that an association or thought, like any experience, is a need-satisfaction process, but the needs that are accumulated and make the satisfactions or judgments possible are so different from them that no connection is suspected or felt. Actually, the causal connections are exactly opposite to what is logically assumed. This explains why all the logical attempts to demonstrate causal connections between mental states or experiences of any kind only added more confusion. This finally led to rejection, not only of all methods dealing with mental states and introspection, but also of the images, ideas and mental states themselves.

What was perhaps even more important was that in plain practical terms the theories missed the *omnipresent* and therefore causally most important factors of psychological life: conditioning, fundamental needs and the role of pleasure as the universal source of motivation. This, together with the confusion arising on every line of attack due to the paradox of psychological causation, discredited the older schools. Thus the only sensible approach of dealing with psychological realities directly and in their own terms was abandoned. The schools that followed got rid of the contradictions by getting rid of the realities of psychology as such. These were replaced by various secondary phenomena that could be dealt with in the scientific ways of the physical sciences.

The result has been, as we saw, a useless vast formalism, barren elaborations and more confusion: in a word, an imitation of scientism leading away from true science.

Behaviorism, Gestalt psychology or operationalism have superseded the older functionalism, structuralism and associationism, if not as schools then at least as approaches. According to a quotation in Woodworth's *Contemporary Schools of Psychology,* behaviorism and psychoanalysis are now dividing the whole field of psychology between them. We have seen the misunderstood scientism of behaviorism and we shall discuss the typically alchemistic nature of psychoanalysis in another chapter. As to operationalism, it is a good example of the same imitation of the physical sciences. Operationalism is ordinarily connected with the philosophical school of logical positivists represented by Carnap, Schlick and Feigl. According to the philosophy of operationalism, physical entities have no meaning except in operations by which they can be observed. We can fully agree with such philosophy. But the question is which are the relevant psychological operations observed: the fractional secondary data, about which we do not even know their causal connections, or the value experiences evolved to perfection precisely for operational use. The same operationalism that is right for the physical sciences, where only external operations can serve the understanding, has a completely different meaning for psychology, where the causally understood operations are the inner experiences. But psychologists accepted only the implications of operationalism for the physical sciences.

There has been some revolt against this imitation of the physical sciences with their positivism and atomism, which were the keys to their success. Concepts derived from mentalistic notions or from values and principles of organic wholes have no place in the physical sciences. But in psychology precisely such concepts are the ones that are causally meaningful. We find the best objections to misplaced positivism and atomism, especially that of the behaviorists, in the holistic or organismic theories of Meyer, Coghill and Goldstein; in personalistic psychology, or the psychology of the self, of Calkins and Stern; in the "understanding" psychology of Dilthey and Spranger, who opposed the explanatory psychology imitating the natural sciences; and in various "dynamic" psychologies.

These schools, however, seem to have little influence on the general trend. The reasons are not far to seek. Theories on the self or the organism as a whole become only a more conspicuous source of contradictions if the theorists completely misunderstand the causal logic according to which the organism operates; and do not even notice the most important causal realities of the self: basic needs, their conditioning, the universality of pleasure, and the causal role of negative backgrounds. The personalistic psychologist is bound to pick up what is exceptional, or what is most *salient*, as Stern stated, and therefore causally least fundamental. For instance, the most salient feature of a person with a background of insecurity is a callous lack of a sense of insecurity, whereas the salient characteristic of a person with a background of the fullest security is a mystifying anxiety.

The same applies to "dynamic" psychologies. Their tendency to deal with the fluidity of living adjustment is realistic, but if the paradoxes of the psychological dynamics are not understood, the approach leads to endless controversies or outright fallacies. For instance, on the main problem of psychological dynamics, motivation, it seems clear that release is its source, whereas in fact it is the previous restriction — the exact opposite of release. Opposite conclusions can be reached depending on what phase of motivation the psychologist looks at or what aspect he prefers to emphasize. Goldstein could emphasize tension, where the hedonists or Freud saw only release as the dynamic source.

Probably more important practically, but also more misleading, are the hundreds of "theories" presented by popular writers offering their various miracle remedies. One thing that, predictably, is common to all of them is the advocacy of release in all its diversified forms — pleasurable interests, "positive thinking," relaxation, the joys of life, play, excitement, emotional enrichment, pursuit of natural interest and avoidance of repressions. Such writers can always "scientifically" prove their theories, by referring to experiments or case observations.

In the end, the confusion that has resulted in modern psychological theory is complete. Every psychologist postulates different forces, principles, mechanisms or instincts, often dozens of them. You can imagine what would happen if in physics somebody advanced a theory that there are not only mechanical energy, gravitation and electromagnetism, but a dozen more forces; or that energy can be derived not only from other equal sources of energy, but also from coincidence of shapes of objects, and so on. In psychology numerous, even more radically diverging theories exist within the same school or area of study. For instance, in the area of personality, there are: the personalistic theory with its elaborate process of growth, functional anatomy, traits, self and ego functions; the organismic theory with the Gestalt concept of organism, self-actualization and the biospheric holistic entity; the field theory with the principle of the regnancy of the brain, 13 viscerogenic and 28 psychogenic needs, need integrate, different functions of the regnant process, and ego strength; the biosocial theory with the person as a nodal region within a larger field, with an infinite number of motives, the process of canalization; and so on. In other areas, like motivation, learning or social psychology, there is a similar variety of theories, each postulating scores of new principles or laws. We have already mentioned the scores of instincts postulated by the hormists and the even more numerous principles or laws discovered by the Gestaltists.

With such confusion, nobody can be expected to rely on theory when real problems have to be solved. Psychologists themselves have no trust in the theories, unless a particular psychologist is defending his own. As Woodworth says in the previously quoted book, practical psychologists are reluctant to call themselves followers of any school. In psychology, as in all fields dealing with man, we still have only an art, not a science. There are many psychologists who can claim to be doing straight scientific work. They are experimenters and compilers. The wide branch of experimental psychology has stayed above controversies. But to the same extent it has avoided any theory, which in the present state of things amounts to avoiding the search for causal understanding of psychology. This reflects the prevailing tendency: to proceed in a "scientific" way in the hope that some progress will result.

In truth, such efforts lead to a deepening of the fallacy. There is a difference between progress here and in the other sciences. In engineering, for instance, the basic law, gravitation, is so well understood that the engineer does not even have to mention it. Other truths are equally well understood. Who, for instance, would believe that the color of a material adds to its strength? But in psychology just this kind of nonsense is possible. Moreover, the deepest convictions that man holds, as well as the very logic of the sciences, are exactly contrary to the actual causal logic of psychology. Imagine what would happen if irrigation engineers were averse to the truth that water flows downward. They would produce innumerable theories — about the influence of colors, shapes, or any possible coincidental event on the flow of water — all equally defensible; but the simple truth would be buried deeper under such "learning."

In modern psychology progress in traditional scientism is producing enormous amount of learning and theorization on every possible aspect. Such programs as an international conference on galvanic skin response are the order of the day. And the amount of theorization, all conflicting and complex, even mystical, is possibly greater than that of all the other sciences taken together. All this enormous effort aims at getting closer to causal understanding in psychology — to an insight into its causal laws. At the same time these laws, like all natural laws, can be only elementarily simple.

All this means that only a complete change of direction can lead psychology out of its impasse. But no psychologist would have the power or even the courage to oppose the present "progress" of psychology, advancing with colossal inertial weight. How can a highly learned psychologist state or even consider the idea of something that would make him appear a freak and a simpleton in the eyes of everybody and in the light of everything he has learned? Contemporary ideas about what is "scientific" and what is ridiculous have always been part of the cultural atmosphere that dominates the minds of men, even the best minds of scientists; and our times are no exception.

IV

THE PARADOX OF NEUROSES AND PSYCHOSES

The key to understanding the mysterious grip that a neurotic complex has on a person is the paradox of *worsening through improvement*. When a person overenjoys, opposite feelings become inevitable and have to be lived through. But a neurotic person, instead of living through such feelings, tries to avoid them by still further overenjoyment. Thus, as more is overenjoyed, the feeling worsens, and as the feeling worsens, more is overenjoyed. A *vicious circle* results that can drive emotional negativism to any degree. Neurosis means such emotional negativism, which increases as the neurotic strives for positive emotions in an exaggerated way. This explains the main characteristics of all neuroses: the *contradiction* between aspiring to the highest emotion or value feeling and reaching the lowest one; *fixation* on an exhausted source of release to the farthest, seemingly ridiculous detail; desperate *defense* against a menacing, deep, emotional negativism; and a mysterious effect of *repression* as the pressure toward normalcy increases.

Naturally, this can happen only when the person derives more release at each step, when he not only gets even while compensating for the arising negative feelings but overdraws a little bit every time. In other words, it requires a neurotic personality, or a constant tendency toward overenjoyment. The neurotic may have an inborn incapacity to operate with finer releases and may need stronger, grosser releases. Or his conditioning may be insufficient: responses along more restricted and more refined releases have not been learned. Such a person will exhaust his releases when he is in a position requiring more motivation. But he will also exhaust them when conditions permit greater liberty or license.

99

Stresses and difficulties in themselves are never causes of neuroses. They actually serve as challenges and sources of strength for the normal person. Even psychologists have observed that a real trouble cures neurosis; special theories have been invented to explain this. Of course, the emotional negativism that constitutes the neurosis does not appear while overenjoyment goes on. It appears when further overenjoyment becomes impossible — when some final difficulty stops it. This difficulty is then blamed, while the previous overenjoyment is seen rather as the period of best adjustment. Actually, what appears as the neurosis or disease is only the pressure toward a return to normalcy. If the neurotic could live through it squarely, he would be cured.

The modern psychiatrist, however, tries mostly to help his patient avoid further unpleasant feelings, which constitute the "disease." He may help to increase releases by use of any of the varied means of stimulation and energization. Or he may use the means of tranquilization and relaxation, which overcome the normal, culturally or biologically conditioned restrictions on release. The psychiatrist can also do this by purely psychological means — by helping the neurotic to lower his conditioned aspirations. This naturally has to be continuously increased, thus deepening further his emotional negativism and narrowing the margin of availability of releases. Finally, the neurotic may be reduced to compulsive hand-washing or nail-biting as the only alternative to complete immobility.

As we explained before, developing ambitions and interests means previous restrictive conditioning. Since this is unpleasant, the neurotic evolves little conditioned interests. He tends rather to abandon restrictions, and therefore the source of interests. If he is permitted by life conditions to have his way completely, the neurotic uses only those releases that need no conditioned investment and are close at hand. Further, due to the vicious-circle effect, he narrows the margin of available releases constantly. Thus he may end with the most primitive releases and their narrowest margins. For instance, the release offered by the natural cleansing functions is always available without any investment. Since the neurotic has no interests left, he may save himself from complete emotional immobility by resorting to this release. Then as he overenjoys the cleanliness of hands, for instance, the opposite reactions start pressing: he starts feeling more uncleanliness of the hands, and washes them even more. Such obsessive fixation may attach, in the same way, to various body functions which are close at hand and offer a release, however slight, without investment of needs or restrictions. Here belong various improvements in the state of the body or its parts — neck-stretching, nail-biting, face-climbing, pimple-pricking, nose-cleaning and many other obsessive "rituals." They may evolve side by side with normal adjustment, as a kind of separate domain where the person is permitted to go to the bottom of his releases.

The clearest and most general instance of worsening through improvement is the unprecedented increase of nervous disorders under the unprecedented improvement in the living conditions of modern man. The age of greatest improvements has become the Age of Anxiety. Of course, psychologists still try to blame the stresses and difficulties of life as the cause. Many, however, are ready to recognize that our stresses and difficulties are a mere child's play in comparison with those of our ancestors who lived in constant struggle for a naked existence. Here we have to mention the psychologists with a social orientation. Supported by famous anthropologists, such as Margaret Mead or Ruth Benedict, they have sought explanations rather in the complexity and lack of integration of our society. However, all such difficulties are a matter of learning, organization, intellectual insight and under-standing. None of these have anything to do with the plain and simple emotional negativism that constitutes neuroses. Other learned sociologists and humanists talk about upheavals in ideologies, deep schisms in value concepts or other abstract conflicts. What does the neurotic care about ideologies or abstract concepts? All he needs and searches for is plain simple pleasure — and that is the cause of all his troubles.

Some sociological theories — that of Burrow may be the most representative — emphasize the lack of biological outlets in civilized society. Repressions imposed by cultural conditioning, especially in sex matters, are blamed by many psychologists, especially psychoanalysts. If this were true, moral license would be the best way to mental normalcy, and neuroses would be suffered most in monasteries or prisons. The exact reverse is true. The Cattell-Sheier scale shows that priests suffer from neurotic disturbances less than any other group; and for convicts the rate is far below average.

Karen Horney, another representative of the sociological orientation, gives appealing descriptions of the difficulties created by modern society. They may seem convincing to the modern reader to whom they are close. But in comparison with the difficulties people are suffering under less civilized conditions they are the whims of pampered children. Incidentally, Horney notices that discomfort or pain can be the source of relief or pleasure. She describes the self-torturing rituals of the Plains Indians, of the Flagellantes of the Middle Ages, and of the Penitentes of New Mexico. These rituals served to induce feelings of the highest well-being. The practices of yogi, shamans and others can be added.

Psychologists elaborate so effusively the whimsical difficulties of modern man because they desperately need some logical explanation. Actually, they would be closer to the truth if they accepted the traditional wisdom that degeneration follows profuse living — the plentiful and unrestricted living which psychologists see as ideal. It is common knowledge that neuroses afflict the lucky, rich, successful and leisurely people who can really afford to enjoy life. When the William Alanson White Institute offered low-cost treatment so as to attract all socio-economic groups equally, only 7 percent of the patients were laborers during an eight-year period. A study by Dr. Lawrence Hinkle shows that neurosis affects most those in the rapidly advancing middle classes, enjoying the greatest new opportunities and the most marked improvements in life conditions. Because of relativity, a person from a higher or wealthier class, accustomed to a better life, does not find any special enjoyment in it. On the other hand, a low group, like the American Negro, even some rapidly advancing groups in Africa, finds its relatively rapid improvements a source of unusual enjoyments — and suffers more from neuroses. No wonder psychologists are puzzled.

People behave normally only so long as there are needs to

provide for the endless play of needs and satisfactions of which normal human adjustment consists. When man is lucky enough to attain a state of full satisfaction without needs, normalcy ends, unless he evolves other cultural needs. If he is even luckier and manages to become the boss of his own releases, he drives himself into the emotional negativism of mental disorder.

In this connection some types of neuroses could be mentioned. Sunday neuroses and vacation neuroses were noticed first by Ferenczi and Abraham, who explained them in psychoanalytic manner, as inherited atavistic reactions originating in the bacchanalia and saturnalia of the Greeks and Romans or in the Purim of the Jews. "Christmas Blues" have been noted, and explained in a similar psychoanalytic fashion by Dr. L. Bryce Boyer. Retirement neuroses have been described by several psychologists. Pathogenic discontents suffered by farmers during winter — the time when they can really take it easy — have been described by Hamilton.

The relativity of emotions, or the dependence of joys upon difficulties and vice versa, is common intuitive knowledge. Everybody knows that kings do not live in continuous happiness, or Hollywood stars in an endless bliss of perfect love. Also, it is easily understood that the person having a permanent defect does not suffer from it. Naturally, man cannot survive with convictions consistent with the truth of relativity. But the scientist should be able to look beyond human delusions and see the down-to-earth truth of psychological causation. If the scientist needs experimental proof, he has it in every one of the innumerable instances he can observe, which show that aftermath, aftereffect or "habit" formation inevitably follows every overenjoyment, intoxication or use of drugs. The rule is confirmed here with such strictness that no amount of human ingenuity can do anything to change it.

By the way, case reports by psychologists themselves show the opposite backgrounds in the past experiences of neurotics: sexual indulgences, overenjoyments, addiction to intoxication — through alcohol, drugs or some special psychological or physiological means — as well as intensified living induced by various causes. Naturally such backgrounds are misinterpreted or incomplete, since psy-

103

chologists remain unaware of their causal significance. The psychiatrist, the same as his patient, considers the period of overadjustment one of the highest normalcy — since it *is* emotionally opposite to the negativism of the neurosis.

Now we may turn to separate neuroses and complexes.

ANXIETY

Anxiety is typical of all neuroses and accompanies most of them — because the opposite feeling of security governs and accompanies all overenjoyments of positive feelings; only to the extent that man feels secure can other things be enjoyed. Of course, the sense of security is highly conditioned culturally as well as biologically. Varied feelings therefore attach to it. For a civilized man security means primarily love by others, social success, even his own moral worth. When the opposite aftereffects follow upon overenjoyment, then hostility from others, fear of failure and a sense of guilt are inevitably the primary feelings. In general, anxiety exhibits just as complex emotions — only in reverse — as the enjoyment of security does. The reverse may not seem to correspond exactly to the previous overenjoyment because the ideational contents, supported by the emotions, may combine differently during the aftermath due to accidental associations. Moreover, emotional reversals are never recognized as such, because opposite emotions are so different in every respect that man usually sees no connection between them.

The means by which overenjoyment of security is attained are equally varied: intoxication, love, success, the comforts and beauties of life, entertainments or any of the innumerable things that make life exciting.

It must be made clear that the particular thing or reason about which the person becomes anxious may have nothing to do with the anxiety. When the underlying emotional negativism is there, any thought or reason can attach to it by purely accidental associations. This is true of all emotions. Everybody knows or can easily observe how people who are angry, irritated or morbidly tense find plenty of reasons for their anger, irritation or morbidity, though such reasons have nothing to do with it. But the modern psychologist has nothing more to work with than logical interpretations of the ideas he discovers in the psyche of the person. No wonder that the mystery of the subconscious and the deliberately entangled methods of analysis are resorted to by modern psychologists.

One can picture the overenjoyment that subsequently causes anxiety as an accelerated living or growth. The aftereffect, then, means a slowing down in the living process, as the body tends to regain normalcy in its dynamics. Such slowing down must emotionally resemble death itself. Imagine what one would feel if his heart or breathing suffered constriction. In anxiety the restrictions are deeper and more general. The deepening of the negativism here is explainable by the same vicious-circle effect that turns every neurosis into a self-tightening knot. The over-adjustment in the case of an anxiety neurosis is reached mostly in regard to conditioned feelings. Because of the high conditioning we live under, there are always plenty of restrictions that can be loosened, by overvaluations or by any kind of psychological intoxication. Likewise the restrictions of biological conditioning can be loosened, by a more physiological stimulation or tranquilization. In either case normalcy has to be re-established under psychological or physiological pressure; and that means an opposite restrictive process, with opposite emotions which resemble slow dying.

The right way of dealing with anxiety is the difficult way of suffering it through. Only this can lead back to normalcy. May we recall here that the highest adjustment means a play between a vast system of releases and restrictions. The constant restrictions are not felt because they are always there — as a counterpart of an equal potential of releases. In other words, man as the highest animal lives with the highest amount of "anxieties" in his system of higher psychic differentiation. These "anxieties" become the cause of stress only after they have been relieved and then are being reimposed during the re-establishment of normalcy. Trying to relieve an anxiety neurosis by further relief from such restrictions or "anxieties" — by further increase in releases — only offers new ways for the vicious-circle effects to tighten. Every time the means of relief is used the neurotic indulges in it a little more than is necessary for the mere equalization of his suffering, and thus deepens the overadjustment.

OBSESSIVE-COMPULSIVE REACTIONS

These reactions can be best understood by thinking in terms of emotional perfectionism. The perfectionist housewife would see all her pride, which she has built up for years, collapse if she left dust in a corner. The object of enjoyment here is the conditioned value of cleanliness and self-virtue. These have to be constantly increased to be still felt. At every step the feeling seems to vanish, as opposite reactions set in, and the cleanliness has to be increased just to keep the feeling alive.

Here, as in all neuroses, this vicious-circle effect can drive the compulsion to any degree. Finally, the housewife may reach the most perfect, elaborate and thorough performance, like a ritual. But at the same time she will increasingly feel the imminence of negative feelings, as the overdriven organic mechanisms that support the positive feeling increasingly tend to start on the opposite process back to normalcy. This explains the neurotic's clinging to nonsensical, minute details, on one side, and his seemingly senseless fear of an abyss of emotional negativism, on the other. These are the main characteristics of all neuroses.

We all may go to unnecessary lengths, resembling a "ritual," in putting things in order, or check the locked door twice even when we know that it is locked. The difference is that we have other occupations, interests and troubles, so that we cannot dwell on such things endlessly. Also, we restrict our tendency to enjoy more and more the sense of perfection or safety. If we did not, we would check the door three times on the next occasion, to be really safe — since checking twice has become just the usual thing providing no positive feeling of safety. By such additions, which alone can yield a definite positive feeling, the obsessive "ritual" grows. In practice, the obsessions may become more involved, because feelings are interchangeable and compensable to some

106

extent. Negativity arising in regard to one thing may be compensated by an exaggeration in regard to another. Further, avoidance of something negative can be as important a source of overenjoyment as the attainment of positive feelings.

There are other complex aspects. For instance, the perfectionist housewife may decide one day to stop the dust-chasing. She may actually abstain from it for a few days. But, having a neurotic personality, she cannot renounce the enjoyment for good, or replace it by other interests, which she does not have. Therefore, she may be only accumulating "exaggerated" restrictions in terms of her "normalcy." The opposite reaction may then break out with such power that she may find herself dusting the pavement. In many cases the neurotic may go to great lengths in trying to abdicate his perfectionism, to evolve new interests, be tolerant, abandon pettiness or adopt nobler goals. But however he maneuvers, he ends with the same neurotic behavior, perhaps in a different form. He does everything except the one and only thing that can help him — endure the suffering that has to be lived through during the re-establishment of normal restrictions.

In connection with compulsive reactions we may mention the much discussed Oedipus complex and other horrible wishes imputed to neurotics by psychoanalysts. The feeling of purity of thought toward parents and love for children are raised to exaggerated heights by conditioning. That one could have sexual desires in regard to one's parent, or wish death for one's own child, are the most revolting ideas. A normal person told of such hidden wishes will not dwell too long on either their possibility or impossibility. But a neurotic person wants to banish for ever and ever the possibility of the recurrence of such horrible thoughts. He exaggerates — overdrives — the specific mechanisms, whatever they may be, that serve to keep such thoughts out of mind. The reverse effect or relapse becomes inevitable. As the neurotic increases his effort at every step, the possibility of the recurrence of such thoughts deepens. He ends with the conviction that he really has the horrible drives.

In reality, such dark subconscious drives are only the inventions of psychoanalysts confused by the ghost phenomena of opposite

107

causation. A person standing at the edge of a cliff and becoming obsessed with the idea that he may wish to jump is further away from doing so than ever. The very exclusion of such a wish by an *exaggerated* emphasis creates the opposite idea, which can reach an obsessive degree due to the vicious-circle effect.

PHOBIC REACTIONS

Perfectionism in avoidance of fear or aversion is the source of phobias. A phobia starts growing when the neurotic tries to derive an extra bit of the feeling of safety or reassurance by avoiding the feared object a little more every time. This starts the vicious circle running, and the abyss of fear deepening to any imaginable limit. This explains why objects that are *repeatedly* encountered become objects of phobias — cats, mice, germs, unlucky numbers, street traffic, bridges, trains and so on. A ferocious animal seen in a zoo or a terrible disease read about in a book are, rationally, more frightening, but they do not become objects of phobias. On the other hand, any common object that can be *repeatedly* avoided is likely to become an object of phobia. A medical dictionary lists some two hundred phobias, all of them centering around the most common objects.

A phobia may play an interesting role as counterpart of positive feelings that a person may be cultivating. As we saw, any positive feeling without its opposite is impossible. The little girl is taught to be clean. The necessary counterpart, the feeling of aversion, then needs an embodiment. The simplest way is to attribute it to objects like mice or insects, around which a deep phobia then grows through repeated avoidances.

In a similar way a phobia may help a person to reach a certain equilibrium in an otherwise confusing world. An overprotected adolescent, when he is let out into the world, finds it full of dangers. He lives under confusing oscillations between threats and reassurances. Then a definite thing like a bridge that he has to cross every morning may appear somewhat more dangerous than other things. After that his life acquires a kind of order in which he feels comparatively secure in regard to other things. As in all complexes, the phobia starts here with a striving for positive feeling — with the endeavor of the person to derive some reassurance, by way of emotional relief, as if by saying: "This is nothing in comparison with the bridge." Actually, the process is an automatic evaluation rather than thinking; and the emotions are more complex. Anyway, the fear of the bridge automatically increases through repeated emotional contrasting. But the person never suspects that the positive feeling he thus derives can have anything to do with the phobia.

Psychiatrists suspect it even less. They seek for hidden horrible drives or symbolic connections to explain the irrational fear that grows as if out of nowhere. The fear of a woman to "walk" out on the "street" has been explained as the repression of a wish to become a "streetwalker." In fact, agoraphobia is only the counterpart of the enjoyment of the securities and comforts of home. It is driven to an extreme by the constant accumulation of positive feelings, which would have no meaning without the opposite feelings, that constitute the phobia.

In some cases the phobia seems to originate from an innate difficulty, like claustrophobia from respiratory difficulty; or from an accident, like fear of animals from having once been frightened by a dog. But here, as in all neuroses, the same thing can serve as a challenge for the normal person, and as a source of neurotic fixation for the neurotic. Psychologists know that anything is sufficient to start a phobia with a neurotic. And if he is cured of one phobia, he becomes the victim of another. His striving for additional positive feelings is the real cause.

Naturally, the only cure for a phobia would be taking a big plunge into the fear or aversion. But this is exactly what the neurotic is least able to do. Only accumulation of some other more important need, like that of survival or conservation of mental normalcy, could produce sufficient potential of satisfaction to operate the motivation. In a really great trouble the neurotic gets over his phobia. But nobody could be so cruel as to inflict such distress on a person deliberately. Moreover, if the neurotic is forced against his will, he may resignedly comply, but at the same time may emotionally live through it as a kind of "restriction" of his "normalcy." Then the opposite reaction and return to the old avoidances may break out with increased strength. Only a genuine readiness to live through the hated and feared experiences can help. Naturally, the process can be only gradual — following an opposite path to the gradual growth of the phobia. Freeman and Kendrick have described in the *British Medical Journal* how a patient suffering from cat phobia was gradually accustomed first to velvet, then to furs, then to rabbit skin, then to small kittens, and finally to cats, whereas the phobia had extended in a reverse order to more and more remote objects.

NEUROTIC DEPRESSIVE REACTIONS

These reactions are as varied and common as enjoyments derived from excitements. They are the opposite reactions to the exaggerations in such enjoyments. The exaggeration may be purely physiological, as when a person uses drugs, intoxicants or other stimulants offered by enjoyable living. Or it may be induced by manipulation of conditioned releases, as when a person overindulges in his own goodness and ends with a complex of guilt.

The most common forms of depressive reactions are overwhelming feelings of anxiety, nausea, irritation or lack of motivation — just the opposites of what excitement and pleasure bring with them. The neurotic nature of such reactions lies in their strangling compulsiveness, that can reach any degree under the vicious-circle increase. Of course, the neurotic, as well as the psychiatrist, seeks explanations not in the overadjustment, which is seen as a blessing, but in all kinds of negative events which stand closer to the depressive reactions.

Man never lacks rational explanations. A person performing an absurd act under posthypnotic suggestion finds logical reasons for it in the closest thing he sees. For instance, a lecturer climbing on a desk under posthypnotic suggestion explained that there seemed to be something wrong with the ceiling light and he wanted to inspect it.

COMPLEX OF GUILT

The complex of guilt is frequent because overenjoyment of one's own goodness is frequent. Cultural conditioning aims at making us experience pleasure upon doing the right thing. Of course, the complex of guilt is phantom emotion, or an aftereffect of previous exaggerations of opposite feelings. Factual circumstances may play a causal role only so far as after the exaggeration of actual evaluations corrections in the opposite direction become pressing. We all tend to exaggerate in order to derive higher feeling of virtuousness and of our own value. What turns the exaggeration and its opposite into a strangling neurosis is a constant worsening through incessant striving for improvement. It can be easily observed that here, as in all neuroses, the neurotic aspires to the highest positive emotion or value belief but ends with the lowest one.

Since the overenjoyment here is derived from culturally conditioned feelings, the guilt complex mostly afflicts individuals who are highly conditioned culturally. But it is not conditioning in itself that leads to the complex. A neurotic individual may need more self-praise, and indulgence in his own goodness, during conditioning. Consequently, exaggerations may result and guilt complexes may follow. But a normal individual can go through conditioning without such exaggerations. Naturally, when the feeling of guilt is there, the person or psychologist finds all kinds of reasons that seem logically related to such feelings, though in truth the causal logic is exactly the reverse.

COMPULSIVE SHYNESS

Compulsive shyness and compulsive blushing are good examples of the paradoxical nature of complexes. Though everybody knows that social inadequacy is the cause of shame, often there seems to be no logical correlation between them. A person with very adequate social qualities may suffer from shyness more than others. Actually, there is a strict causal correlation, but it obeys relative logic. A person who overevaluates himself in an exaggerated way suffers the opposite effects of a feeling of inadequacy every time he faces the very different real truth. As always, the evaluations here are emotionally lived through rather than consciously argued. Naturally, such a person avoids reality and is shy or introverted. Moreover, at every unpleasant brush with reality he may seek for emotional compensation through further exaggeration of the feeling of adequacy, and further withdrawal into his inner world.

The person does not feel the abnormal, higher level of his inner world because it is always with him. Rather he finds, emotionally, the real world abnormal or disturbing. Usually the shy person is an intellectually minded one. The maintenance of an inner world of one's own requires an intensive intellectual life. Also, a highly conditioned person may be shy, as an exaggerated appeal to a person's own goodness and virtue may become part of his conditioning.

The paradox of making the complex worse by trying to improve it is easily observed in such symptoms as blushing and stuttering. The young girl who forcibly and optimistically tries not to blush, and places great value on this, blushes most. A stutterer gets worse when he optimistically attempts to stutter less. Even when a person stutters in a situation in which he seems to feel only helpless distress, he still may be optimistically exaggerating his aspirations. The *relative* value of the reaction is what matters. When the person feels *great* distress only where there is *very great* actual cause for distress requiring a corresponding mobilization of the emotions, he still is living in an optimistic exaggeration. In fact, exactly in such situations is the tendency toward optimistic exaggerations strongest.

The stutterer or blusher gets rid of his plight when his aspirations reach the lowest level—when he gives up. This may require a series of disappointments, and long suffering. That is why such complexes disappear as a person loses his illusions with the advance of years. Incidentally, even if stuttering be due to purely physiological disruptions of innervation, the same paradoxical logic would apply (such disruptions can be thought of as repeated instantaneous aftereffects following repeated bursts of inner overstimulation). Disruption here could be remedied, and steadier release obtained, by restricting the releases. The stutterer should be taught new, more difficult or restrictive, rather than easier techniques of speaking. In fact, the famous Speech Clinic at the University of Iowa has been evolving such techniques. Because of the same vicious-circle effect, stuttering becomes worse when more attention is paid to it, since paying attention usually amounts to an attempt at improving the reaction. Some psychologists have shown that a parent who stuttered when young often unwillingly induces his children to stutter, by his attitude. This may be true. Such a parent, naturally, tries hard in numerous intuitive ways to make it easier for his children — and makes it worse due to the paradox of improvements. Of course, the psychologists try to view the connection in an exactly opposite, more logical way.

As a general rule, the people who are better equipped to deal with their emotions, like highly intellectual people capable of directing their conditioned releases, are also more often victims of complexes, especially those involving feelings of inferiority, guilt, shyness or depression. They know how to manipulate their releases and therefore attain more extensive exaggerations. Equally, those matters which permit more freedom and offer greater opportunities of release become the more frequent sources of complexes. For instance, an adolescent discovering the new field of amorous attraction and adventure may overenjoy them in his aspirations and may develop a complex of inferiority or shyness in these matters. On the other hand, in serious matters where unrealistic aspirations are dangerous, as in matters of a job, no complexes are developed, though in themselves they are laden with more conflict and stress.

The experience of ordinary shame may help to understand what happens in all complexes. A boy falls while dancing, and experiences shame. He may argue that there is no reason to be ashamed, or that falling is natural. But no amount of reasoning will help him. We all try to reason or laugh away incidents that make us feel ashamed, but the shame returns with even greater force. Is there something irrational about it? No, the strictest reason lies behind it, and one can understand it by thinking in terms of opposite background causation, or equivalence of feelings. If the boy had not derived pleasure in the form of pride in the showmanship of his dancing, he would not experience displeasure in the form of shame upon the fall. The same boy may fall dancing and experience no shame if he had no previous enjoyment of showmanship in this matter, as when he is forced to dance, just learns to dance, or is ready to show his lack of grace while clowning. Shame is a phantom experience that derives its meaning, not from anything that is there, but from an opposite emotion that was lived through in the past.

COMPLEX OF INFERIORITY

The complex of inferiority is one of the most frequent complexes because the overenjoyment of superiority is so frequent in our society. For a highly social and culturally conditioned individual his superiority is the main source of pleasure. Moreover, the social success of a person often depends on his appearing and being held as superior. But everybody knows the trick and is on guard against it. Nobody is easily deceived, and any faked superiority is mercilessly despised. Therefore only a capacity to evoke a *genuine* feeling of superiority at the needed moment can help. We all become exaggerators in our feelings of superiority. Especially does a man in public life, a social star, a high executive or any person who deals with people have to exaggerate constantly his feeling of superiority. This explains why precisely these people suffer most from neuroses connected with the inferiority complex, though logically they are the ones who have the least reason to feel inferior and the best capacities for counteracting the feeling.

In connection with the inferiority complex we may mention the concepts of "social image," "idealized self" or "idealized image" which the psychologists of sociological orientation, like Burrow and Horney, have used to explain most complexes. It is assumed that the difficulties of the neurotic arise from his endeavor to live up to a social ideal. The idealization may seem to help explain why the neurotic is tormented with feelings that have no basis in the existing state of things. Actually, the neurotic is the last person to care about images or ideals. He would be more than willing to

114

throw them overboard. And he would be fully able to do so — if the theories of social images were true. Then it would be only a matter of abstract decision. In fact, it is not images or intentions that torment the neurotic, but the plain and simple emotional negativism growing out of an exaggerated striving for positive emotions, especially the sense of superiority.

PROJECTION

Many complexes bearing on feelings toward other persons involve the mechanism which psychoanalysts call projection. In these cases the neurotic imputes to others his own character traits, such as insincerity; or his own attitudes, such as hostility. He may hate, and wish ill to, his boss or friend, but may end up living in fear that the boss or friend has hostile designs against him. The concept of projection is one of the mystifications of modern psychology in which formalistic sophistry is resorted to in order to provide at least some explanation. Anything can be explained by saying that the neurotic projected this or that feeling or idea onto this or that person or object.

Here we may make a general observation about such psychoanalytic concepts as projection, displacement, substitution, identification or introjection. It is true that a man can do curious things, *even unconsciously*, in his striving *for pleasure*. We all know how people can rationalize away anything that is unpleasant and prove anything that is pleasant. There really can be all kinds of projections, substitutions, identifications and so on. But they all are resorted to in order to obtain pleasure. The above psychoanalytic concepts, however, are supposed to be mechanisms adopted by the person with the consequence of bringing him the *sufferings and torments* of neuroses and mental disorders. This is an absurdity worthy of alchemy and witchcraft. The desperate need of psychologists to explain why and how the neurotic brings on himself all the negative feelings is the reason why such absurdities are ever considered. None of them would be necessary if it were understood that the neurotic drives himself into emotional negativism by an exaggerated striving for *positive* feelings. As it is, the above concepts are extensively used by all psychologists.

Now let us explain what really happens in the case of "projection." All the other above mechanisms can be explained similarly.

When a great liar projects his lying onto somebody else, he simply derives pleasure in doing so. He wants to hurt the other person, and chooses the weapon that he knows to be painful because it has been used on him. Further, the vices that a person chooses to impute to another must be emotionally meaningful. Naturally, they are the ones that the person knows from his own experience. But when a neurotic "projects" his own hostile designs onto his boss or friend and develops an *unpleasant* persecution complex, the causal story is completely different. Here we have to understand that most relations between people are built on the "pecking order" — on being "above" or "under." Everybody likes to be "above" with respect to any of the hundreds of ambitions and virtues we live by. A neurotic overenjoys the feeling of being "above." Due to the vicious-circle effect he drives this overenjoyment to extremes and may end by aspiring to exert great power over others, even do great harm to them. Then when the opposite reaction becomes inevitable, the neurotic cannot escape the feeling that he is "under" and the other person "above" him, in regard to the same feelings and designs. A phantom of an unwanted negative emotion arises, as the wanted, positive emotion is overenjoyed, here as in all cases.

CONVERSION HYSTERIAS

These reactions can be confusing if one tries to interpret them from their symptoms, in a logical way, as is done at present. Paralysis of the legs has been explained as a subconscious reluctance "to stomp on mother earth" (Freud), or as refusal to "go on in marital life" (Brun). The twisting of the neck in torticollis has been explained as the subconscious wish to look at libidinal objects under the prohibition to do so (Jones). In fact, the physiological symptoms here are *accidental*.

Let us take the most frequent reaction — paralysis of the extremi-

116

ties. In one case the arm of a girl became paralyzed after she tried to stab her father, in a scene that was unbearable to her. The paralysis disappeared when the girl was induced to relive the scene, emotionally, in all its unpleasantness. In simple terms, the girl wanted to bury all feelings connected with the scene. This meant that every association with it had to be precluded. Since the strong innervation of the arm that lifted the knife must have been the main association, any later innervation of the arm had to be precluded. In many cases of paralysis suffered by soldiers under horrifying circumstances, the cure was brought about by inducing them, under hypnosis, to relive the event with all its horrors. In brief, the real cause of the paralysis is refusal to live through a horror or displeasure, whereas coincidence of associations determines which function or capacity is affected. Any combination between unpleasant past or present experiences and incapacities can result from such unconscious blocking of associations that happen to coincide with the experiences.

How the person achieves such unconscious preclusion of the experience and of the association, he may himself understand as little as he understands how he evokes a feeling, remembers a thing or exerts his will. That some previous practice here is necessary is evident from the fact that mostly persons with previous neurotic history suffer from conversion reactions. Psychiatrists have suspected right from the beginning — we can refer here to the Nancy school, and the famous Charcot — that some kind of self-hypnosis or autosuggestion is involved in conversion hysterias. The similarity of these reactions with hypnosis is striking. Self-hypnosis is ordinarily a difficult thing to achieve, though in fact, it must be more difficult to keep associations correctly related than to mix them up, like wires in a Univac, which is what happens under hypnosis. But such mixing up means disrupting the normal functioning of the mind, which is needed even to carry out autosuggestion. Moreover, disruptions of mental order are feared by man instinctively like death itself. This can be observed in cases where a person suffers from recurring lapses into mental disorder.

But if a person sinks to a low motivational level, and is on the verge of the deepest emotional negativism, he may be indifferent to slipping into a state of mental disorganization, and may readily gravitate toward dissociation by self-hypnosis, which, as we said, may be easier to attain than normalcy. His wish to escape reality may be stronger than the instinctive fear of abnormalcy. Neurotics may often reach such disposition of mind.

By the way, conversion hysterias are frequent in military life under war conditions. The situation often becomes unbearable for the person and his motivational indifference too general. Characteristically enough, when soldiers are placed in a position where they have to exert motivation and evaluate reality precisely, under great need, as when they are sent into actual combat, conversion reactions do not occur. Here as everywhere else complexes and neuroses do not arise when men are exposed to uncompromising difficulties, which then create motives or satisfaction potential. Modern soldiers in war suffer so many neuroses because emotional worsening through improvement is perpetuated on a grandiose scale, from entertainment programs to psychoanalysis made available by corps of psychologists.

The absence of any motivation, leading to an uneasy immobility, explains why the person may resort to the first reaction he observes that may offer some, however slight, restriction-release or need-satisfaction play. Then such a reaction, as the only one present, may become fixational and dominant. This explains, for instance, why some hysteric reactions, like torticollis, become epidemic at a hospital, where one person gets it from watching another. Babinski observed, and others have confirmed, that the neurotic often gets an indirect suggestion for his symptoms from the way a doctor examines him. O'Kelly and Muckler have explained this in their *Introduction to Psychopathology.*

AMNESIA AND FUGUE

Here the neurotic escapes mentally or, in the case of fugue, even physically an unbearable situation by way of the same unconscious autosuggestion. In fact, amnesia and fugue are the ideal, and almost the only, ways of continuing to enjoy, without suffering immediate reversals, positive releases on the basis of

118

optimistic overvaluations of reality. Unless there is complete forgetting and running away, the person cannot escape returning to his psychological normalcy based on reality, or strict correlation between external factors and inner values. And such returning is inevitably accompanied by feelings opposite to those of previous overvaluation or overenjoyment. If we really were to succeed in living according to the suggestions of those advocating emotional enrichment or more "positive" feelings and thoughts, we would have to live under constant amnesia, and be on a constant flight or fugue.

MULTIPLE PERSONALITY

A general reversal in emotional values, combined with amnesia, is sufficient to explain multiple personality. A multiple personality actually never amounts to anything more than an appearance of emotionally opposite characteristics. In a classical example described by Lipton, Sara was sedate, self-controlled, refined, mature, conscientious, and had high sense of guilt; but her double, Maud, was promiscuous, expansive, immature, and had no sense of guilt. Of course, the opposite reactions may combine variously in regard to various traits during various periods. This explains the appearance of more than two personalities, as in the famous case of Miss Beauchamp, described by Morton Prince.

We have to remember that conditioning is the core of every personality. Conditioning is built on the deeper physiological mechanisms. A general exaggeration or excess in the releases of these mechanisms is sufficient to change the emotional tone of all the conditioned traits and produce an expansive, carefree personality, like that of Maud. Then during the inevitable opposite reaction the traits are reversed and exaggerated in the opposite direction, producing a highly restrictive and tense personality, like that of Sara.

The reason for periodicity in such oscillations may lie in the physiological periodicity of organic functions, which has been often observed by physiologists. Moreover, all oscillations — whether of a chord or psychological states — tend automatically to make themselves complete and regular, as each state continues until it reaches its fullest limits, and then reverses. The stronger the neurotic tendency of exaggeration in the releases, the more complete are the cycles. All that is needed to make the double personality then appear is the isolation of the two opposite states, by an unconscious amnesia. The neurotic readily resorts to it in order to avoid all kinds of emotional conflicts. For, as the opposite states continue recurring, each of them becomes more integrated in itself and more conflicting with the other. The process may be imperceptibly gradual. Psychiatrists mostly find ready-made double personalities because patients seek a doctor only after the disorder has reached its full, highly disturbing state, in which the person does not know what he has done or will do.

PSYCHOSES

The cause of psychoses is the same as of neuroses. It is the *emotional negativism produced by excessive releases.* Many psychiatrists recognize that the difference between neuroses and psychoses is only a difference in degree. Actually, in neuroses the excess in releases is attained by manipulation of the more refined mental releases — the sense of security, superiority, one's own goodness and so on. In psychoses the excess in releases is obtained directly, and therefore more strongly, at the physiological level. But, practically, the difference amounts only to a difference in degree, because the finer mental releases are merely elaborations of the deeper physiological releases and depend on them.

We may recall here that the normalcy of a higher animal means an endless play between restrictions and releases, providing all the richness of his adjustment. The natural or pleasurable tendency is always towards releases, but the biological and cultural conditioning, operating mainly through the nervous system, upholds the restrictions. If man had full freedom to act as he pleased he would accept no restrictions and therefore would have no reserves, in static or dynamic terms, for further releases. When man approaches such a state, emotional immobility results. Since he cannot stand this, he tries to remove conditioned restrictions —

thus deepening the disorder and emotional negativism. At first there may be removal of the higher conditioning. Thus the person may sink closer to the animal level — but without the natural controls, such as sexual controls, which have been lost in man. Such a state is fairly typical of psychoses. Then even the removal of biological conditioning may be attempted, with graver organic disturbances.

However it may be, it is important to realize that there is a *single* causal principle underlying all the various psychoses, and neuroses. As a natural principle it can be only simple, and if it cannot be explained in a simple way, it cannot be explained at all. The reason why it has not been understood is the paradoxical logic that it follows. The causation here by a single principle is generally recognized. Any one of the existing theories on mental disturbances is built on assumptions of some one causal principle. Only, the modern psychologist turns any such principle into a mysterious agency, like the personified subconscious, or into some erroneously assumed factor, like the disintegration of the self due to stress, or self-alienation due to an imagined ideal.

The very nature of psychosis shows that its cause is a simple emotional negativism rather than the various mental deficiencies or disruptions that seem to characterize it. A moron has an inferior brain but is not necessarily psychotic, whereas a schizophrenic does not necessarily lose his capacities, as has been often demonstrated, in particular, by Cameron, Wittman, Kendig and Richmond. Further, most forms of psychoses and neuroses may be "cured" by the same simple drug, such as reserpine, chlorpromazine or meprobamate. The way the drugs act, as far as can be followed, is also simple. For instance, Ostow and Kline have shown that the drugs affect the most primitive structures, the globus pallidus in the basal ganglia of the brain. Also, it has been found that a single organic compound, like taraxein, may be responsible for a limitless variety of cases and symptoms in a psychosis like schizophrenia. The taraxein from the blood of schizophrenics injected into a monkey induces in it a temporary state of utter, stupor-like negativism. Apparently, the taraxein is the counteracting agent which here, as in all overadjustment, produces the "disease" by stopping further expenditure in releases, which is its real cause.

Further, there is a striking uniformity in the traits that accompany psychoses. If the causes were varied, there would be the appearance of sudden, unusual capacities and interests, or new ways of thinking and adjustment. None of this happens. On the contrary, there is only one single trouble that affects every psychotic: he fights desperately against emotions that are exactly opposite to those he wants and that increase with his every endeavor. The deepening abyss of emotional negativism and the decreasing margin of positive releases is the main characteristic in psychoses, as it is in neuroses. There is always the same self-generating fear, hate, depression or morbidity, which often becomes so strong that it turns into rage, aggression, stupor or hypochondria. In general, there is an increasing lack of pleasure, that ends with motivational immobility. On the other hand, there is the never-ending persistence to derive more pleasure from the same overworked mechanism. The acts of the psychotic become curiously repetitive and fixational. Hence the ritualism as well as the excessive striving for positive states — for example, the growing delusions of grandeur. In brief, the essence of psychoses is emotional negativism caused by overdrawal on positive releases — a worsening that grows with every "improvement."

Any exaggerated release is bound to lead to its equally exaggerated opposite in the form of emotional negativism. *Opposite emotional exaggerations* are observable in most psychoses. *Cyclic, opposite states* are characteristic of the main psychoses: catatonic, paranoiac and acute schizophrenic reactions, paranoia, manic-depressive reactions, and involutional melancholia of the acute type. The opposite states are less pronounced but can be found in the previous life background, especially as determined by the whole life cycles of aging, in the lighter psychoses: schizophrenic reactions of latent or simple type, paranoid states, psychotic depressive reactions, and common involutional melancholia. This explains why these disorders increase with the approach of a certain age.

The difficulty in establishing clearly such opposite states is that neither patient nor modern psychiatrist pays attention to the exaggerated positive states. These states are so pleasant and rich in motivation that they are considered very normal indeed. And since they may last for longer periods uninterruptedly, they may not be noticed just because of that. Even when the psychiatrist observes an inevitable sequence between the opposite states, in the cyclic psychoses, he hesitates to accept a direct causal connection between them, because of the impossible logic that it implies, and the complete difference in symptoms. Characteristically, in their previously mentioned excellent book O'Kelly and Muckler conjecture that depression and mania "must have something in common," even though they find that the "gross difference in symptomatology" speaks against it. The striking universality of opposites experienced by patients during manic-depressive reactions has been described by one patient himself, in the book *Wisdom, Madness, and Folly* by Custance.

But the opposite exaggerations do not need always to take the form of cycles. In fact, the very nature of psychosis as an excessive striving for releases does not permit accumulation of "reserves" sufficient to produce a lasting positive period. In psychoses the hand-to-mouth pleasure economy reaches its ultimate limit. The slightest release that becomes available is immediately used up and only a stupor of negativism remains.

The deeper trouble of the psychotic is his incapacity to respond to finer releases and his need for grosser releases. Hence the similarity with the less refined, not yet conditioned responses of a child. This similarity has induced psychoanalysts to speak about *regression* to a more primitive mental state. The possibility of such traveling from one ready-made state to another is scientifically absurd, especially since it implies that the person does so even though it entails tormenting himself with psychotic reactions. Primitive states, characterized by grosser releases, result in all cases of removal of restrictions, as can be easily observed in cases of intoxication.

The *ritualistic mannerism* as one of the most characteristic symptoms of psychoses illustrates the worsening through improvement as the underlying cause of all psychoses. As the psychotic tries to improve one release, usually the one that happens to be closest at hand or has been used before, it becomes exhausted and further improvement becomes necessary. What function becomes the object of such fixation is purely accidental. Analysts are wasting their time by trying to discover a causal meaning in such rituals. Usually the psychotic fixations start with tiny occupations like avoidance of unlucky numbers or slight improvement in some body function. Occupations that are important to a normal person, because of cultural conditioning, are not available to the psychotic. He is incapable of accepting the restrictions that conditioning and the evolving of interests require. And since the main natural release sources are already exhausted, the elaboration shifts to insignificant marginal releases. Hence the impression that the psychotic acts out his compulsions merely for the sake of a ritual, especially since no real pleasure is derived, and only the deepening of the seemingly mysterious negativism of feeling results.

Hypochondriacal delusions, which are frequent with psychotics, may illustrate the same point. Any person can discover some small pain or discomfort at any moment somewhere in his body. If he happens to have no other preoccupations, he may concentrate all his attention on it, and thus start a fixational obsession. Anybody reading about a disease usually finds that he has exactly that disease. It has been observed that an article about a disease may fill the waiting rooms of doctors with people complaining of symptoms of that disease. All that is needed to turn similar accidental suspicion into real hypochondria is the psychotic general tendency to overdraw the positive feeling of relief or reassurance at every turn. This then accumulates the opposite feeling, which finally deepens into an abyss of negativism. Since anything can do as a starting point, the psychotic may start with the first often-heard expression, like "to be all gone inside," and may end with a real obsession, the feeling that his insides are gone. Such use of the most often heard ideas is so frequent that special theories have been advanced holding that psychotic reactions are prototypes of beliefs held by society.

Delusions of grandeur are typical both of this concentration on the commonest ideas and of the vicious-circle effects. Delusions of being Napoleon or the Messiah are most frequent because the corresponding ideas are most common. The worsening through improvement shows in the fact that concurrently with increasing grandeur the feeling of helplessness or fear increases. The psychotic may end by believing that he possesses supreme skills and powers, but also by fearing his ridiculous enemies more than ever. Naturally, the psychotic cannot abandon his delusion or even change it. Each bit of it represents a building block in the accumulation of his sense of superiority, security or well-being. Abandoning it would mean coming down all the way in terms of these values. The psychotic therefore advances further and further with the accumulation in his attempt to lessen emotional negativism, though by doing so he increases it at every turn. It is useless to ask how the psychotic can uphold his conviction of grandeur, or of fear, in the face of clear reasons against them. Never in the world have there been reasons clear enough to change anybody's convictions arising from strong *emotional* need or feeling.

An interesting illustration of opposite causation is offered by the *obsession of persecution.* Psychologists have observed that the most likely "persecutor" of the psychotic is his best friend. The reason for this is that, given the psychotic personality, there is a constant overenjoyment of the various, mostly egotistic feelings of friendship. Consequently, the potential of opposite feelings increases at every turn. Such exaggerated enjoyment is, understandably, strongest among two homosexual friends. Freud invented a special theory to explain why so frequently a homosexual suffers from the paranoiac obsession that he is persecuted by his former friend.

The opposite emotional states are not, however, always clearly discernible in psychoses, because, as we said, the increasing emotional negativism is so strong that no positive emotion seems ever to be present. For instance, a psychotic kills his wife in jealousy, as sometimes happens. We know that jealousy can exist only where there was great enjoyment of love. The psychotic overenjoys this love more than anybody else. Hence his great jealousy. But his overenjoyment is spasmodic, short-lived and increasingly interwoven with deepening negativism. It never yields rich experience, because the psychotic needs more release than other people to achieve the same experience. In brief, it may seem that there was never any enjoyment but only a senseless suspicion and faulty reasoning. Actually, the reasoning of the psychotic is absurd only because his emotions are phantasmal and excessive.

The endeavor of the psychotic to increase releases leads to removal of the restrictions of biological and cultural conditioning. This means sinking to more primitive level, culturally as well as biologically, with all possible disruptions and deteriorations. We cannot go into them, but we may mention, as an illustration, the *sexual perversions*. The sexual satisfactions of man are conditioned so that only in the case of a highly suitable partner of the opposite sex is release forthcoming. The intense sexual satisfaction would not be there if there were not this previous restriction. Man yearns in his romantic love to be "reunited" with the "second half." Apparently he has been deprived of it during the period of sexual differentiation. The simplest principle of sexual differentiation is the halving of chromosomes during mitosis. However it may be, the removal of conditional restrictions is bound to leave the psychotic with only gross releases, and without the finer restrictive differentiations that make release contingent upon meeting a proper partner of the opposite sex.

The main general characteristics common to all psychoses reveal clearly emotional negativism as well as the exaggerated striving for more release. First, there is the general *flatness or negativism of emotional tone*, as well as *lack of motivation, interests, energy or persistence*. Apparently these are due to emotional impoverishment. Concurrent *emotional instability, eccentricity, perversity in conduct, undue conceit, lack of self-control* are expressions of the exaggerated striving for extra releases. Finally, such characteristics as *disordered way of life*, which can turn into a mess anything the psychotic deals with; the *lack of common sense, of truthfulness or of social feelings*; and the self-deepening of *all possible negative emotions*, like hate, suspicion, guilt or sense of deterioration — are all results of the vicious-circle effect by which the negativism of emotion and of motivation increase at every turn. The widening depth between such negative emotions and reality explains the crazy order of things, or the madness, the psychotic lives in. We all reason according to our emotional realities and needs. The psychotic lives with the strongest negative emotions — extreme fear, hate, anxiety, threat of deterioration and apprehension of every possible evil — as well as the exaggerated striving for more release. He is unreasonable for the same reason that we all are when under emotional stress.

Naturally, when the removal of conditioning reaches the deeper physiological levels and affects the brain itself as the center of all restrictions, normal reasoning may become disrupted. Also, because of this role of the brain as a restrictive system, all kinds of psychoses may develop as a result of injuries and illnesses of the brain. When a person finally gets the chance to control his own releases, in disregard of all restrictions, he inevitably drives himself to the deepest psychotic negativism. Such capacity to live in an unreal world of his own making is typical of all psychotics.

The question arises, how to explain the extreme agitation in some psychoses if the impoverishment of releases and of motivation is their cause. The answer is that a pleasure release as intensified living at the deepest levels is often very different from an external release of physical energy. As we saw, energization as well as tranquilization can be sources of overenjoyment. Actually, states of sedation are more frequent sources of enjoyment than states of energization. The feeling of ecstasy is mostly accompanied by immobility. Such states may be induced by the organism itself, and their enjoyment may accumulate. Then when the opposite reactions set in, agitation, together with feelings of anxiety or fear and dissatisfaction or rage, is bound to take over. The dual nature of agitation has led to confusions. Psychiatrists recognize as manic and may treat similarly both the excitement in the affective manic reactions and the oppressive agitation of schizophrenia or hyper-mania. In fact, the two kinds of agitations are on opposite sides causally. The first is an overadjustment, that later causes the psychotic reactions. That is why it is pleasant. The second represents the reverse endeavor to re-establish normalcy after overadjustment. It is an aftermath. That is why it is unpleasant.

TREATMENT OF NEUROSES AND PSYCHOSES

From what we have said it is apparent that the application of the usual medical logic of seeking immediate improvements may lead only to deepening the disorders. The basic misunderstanding about the causes of mental disorders is the reason why they are increasing in numbers and gravity with the advance of the "scientific" attitude toward psychological problems. With good reason our age is called the Age of Anxiety. Supposedly one in every twelve Americans now needs institutional care, some time during his life, because of nervous disorders. Incidentally, the statistics showing increasing number of discharges from hospitals are misleading. So many people have been turned into hospital patients that the number of discharges has to increase, especially as such patients finally evolve counteradaptation even to the strongest "improvements," and as doctors are beginning to realize that institutions are the worst places for mental patients to be in.

If there are some treatments, like the shock treatment, that do work, they are contrary to what the present theory or general understanding is based on. In no other field has science such an opportunity to overcome difficulties by use of nothing more than the mind itself. But in no other field has science failed more conspicuously to provide a causal understanding for doing so.

Drug Treatment. Drugs are very crude and simple compounds in comparison with organic matter. A drug can never rebuild anything in a living cell, consisting of millions of molecules arranged in incomprehensibly intricate ways. Even more complex must be the interaction between the billions of cells of the body. This interaction reaches the height of its complexity in the mental reactions. Any intrusion by a nonliving matter into a living one can mean only destruction or disorganization. That is what drugs are doing. They remove the restrictions by paralyzing in a gross general way the mechanisms in the nervous system, which is primarily a system of restrictions. Naturally, this cannot cure anything, though the immediate relief may be miraculously effective as more release is obtained. A drug addict also is "cured" by the administration of the same or a stronger drug.

The relief brought by drugs is absolutely convincing under experimentally scientific logic. Any kind of experiment, observation, measurement, statistics, factual conclusion or logical analysis shows the beneficial effect of the drug. For decades now continuous breakthroughs have been announced, each capable of wiping out mental disorders — with the result that these have increased. Dozens of compounds in various combinations have been repeatedly hailed as miracle drugs: reserpine, chlorpromazine, prochlorperazine, meprobamate, perphenazine, amphetamine, pentothal, promazine, phenobarbital, paraldehyde, seconal, mephenesin, nembutal, azacyclonol, even iproniazid, glutamic acid and tolbutamide. Some of them have acquired famous names — Miltown, Serpasil, Thorazine, Mellaril, Compazine, Equanil, Luminal, Dial, Marplan, Niamid, Merrill, L-Glutative, Librium, Deaner, Orinasse.

In spite of such clearly demonstrated cures, every sensible doctor knows that there is no drug which really cures mental disorders. But typically enough, doctors blame mostly the "side" effects, as if these were something that could be avoided by improving the drug or its dosage. The "side" effects, however, always appear sooner or later. A subtler, improved drug may delay the effects longer, by driving the disturbance to a deeper level. In fact, the "side" effects are aftereffects of overadjustment deepened by the drug and constitute an effort by the organism to regain its normalcy, thus adding to the neurotic reactions.

Some doctors have realized the self-defeating effects of drugs. The former president of the American Psychiatric Association, Howard D. Fabing, reported that the side reactions of reserpine — the foremost drug on the list of miracle drugs — "often lead one to defeat"; mental depressions that it produces may require electroshock to get over them. A study of 8,200 patients by Herman A. Dickel and Henry H. Dixon has shown that tranquilizers can hurt the emotional health of the patients, cause serious problems, even lead to suicides. Dr. Richard Asher, writing in Lancet, blames the use of drugs for the increase of tensions in patients. Also in Lancet, reports by F. H. Smirk, E. G. McQueen, J. G. MacArthur and B. Isaacs show that disturbing symptoms, mental depression, anxiety and agitation may follow the use of tranquilizers. Even the discoverer of Miltown, Frank M. Berger, has warned that the drug should not be used as "happy pills"; and has pointed out that patients may feel worse after taking tranquilizers than they felt before.

A report by Neville Murray on a more advanced drug is typical in showing how an improved drug may drive the disturbance to deeper levels. This drug allays rage and anxiety in more subtle ways than the previous drugs, but its effects have been mental dissociation and confusion that first shows in accidents. A report by Frank Orland is similar. A man taking reserpine started showing defective judgment, had to be taken off the drug and needed six months to recover. There have been repeated reports, especially by authorities concerned with traffic safety, about similar effects from the miracle drugs. Pilots now are forbidden to fly if they have used tranquilizers.

The *addiction* to drugs, which increases in direct proportion to their "beneficial" effects, also shows that we have to deal here with another form of the vicious-circle effect which deepens overadjustment at every step, just as in ordinary drug addiction.

It is clear that drugs can have decisive causal effect on nervous disorders. But if this effect is to be positive rather than negative the logic of drug medication should be reversed. The only sure way of increasing the potential of positive emotions is by imposing restrictions or negative emotions first. Modern psychiatry is, however, dominated by the endeavor to increase positive emotions without regard to the equivalence of emotions. The similarity with alchemy is strong here. Practically, drugs could be used to limit the positive emotions, or rather the overadjustment as their source, so that there would be no causal possibility for the negative emotions or emotional negativism to arise. When the negative aftereffects of psychosis start, it is too late to do anything about it; the cause lies in the past. It can be prevented only by first preventing positive overadjustment.

This would mean a treatment aiming at antistimulation, antitranquilization and antienergization. If this seems absurd, think of the shock treatment — the only clearly successful treatment so far. Antistimulation would amount to a low-intensity, adaptable "shock" that would derive its effectiveness from continuous duration, which would also make the restriction less felt. Thus the present stab-in-the-dark shock therapy could be replaced by a treatment as adaptable, gradual and many-sided as there are possibilities of drugs, their combinations and ways of application. Of course, such treatment would be difficult, because the psychotic is the last person to accept restrictions readily. And no doctor can build a practice, or even a theory, on a method that makes his patients feel worse. The main difficulty would be the necessity of applying in every aspect and detail a logic that is opposite to the one everybody considers as right.

Actually, even now there are some drugs, among the hundreds that have been tried, which have the antistimulation effect and so far produce real improvement. But it is all accidental, misinterpreted, and often counteracted by the whole treatment, because the causal understanding is missing.

Shock Treatment. Shock treatment reveals fully the paradoxical nature of mental disorders. Influences that usually induce reactions similar to those of psychosis have beneficial effect when lived through by the psychotic. This has been observed in the cases of febrile diseases, treatment of thyroid condition, influenza, injection of foreign proteins or salt solution, as well as the regular shock therapies of insulin, Metrazol and electroshock. These therapies have been evolved without causal understanding. They are contrary to every existing theory in psychiatry and to the very notion of treatment as now understood. They are blind hits that lack any adaptation or continuity, which are the most important requirements in dealing with mental reactions.

Each shock amounts to a separate sudden infliction of negative feelings concentrated to such degree that something similar to the agony of death is experienced. Psychiatrists have pointed out that unless this agony-like experience is there treatment is not successful. In some cases this agony may be more physiological than psychological or conscious. This may be sufficient if the disorder itself is more physiological, as may be the case with the deeper psychoses. But even such a primitive method produces positive results. The shock makes the overhigh emotional level collapse and leave

131

room for a new emotional ascent — for the new play of positive and negative reactions, of which normal adjustment consists.

Of all treatments shock therapy is the most successful. It is generally used to correct disorders originating from other treatments, like drug therapy, play therapy or hypnosis. According to statistics, in more than 50 percent and up to 75 percent of cases the shock treatment produces improvement that is definite. This is impressive considering that other therapies end with the "side" effects or, actually, reversals in such an inevitable pattern that there are only controversies whether they are of any benefit at all. One can imagine how much greater the success of shock therapy would be if it were causally understood and made adaptable to the ills it has to cure. In the Middle Ages the insane were cured by being lowered into snake pits. Now we use electricity or insulin, but the cause of the cure is just as little understood and the treatment just as blind. We have indicated the possibilities of an unlimitedly adaptable "shock" by the use of antistimulating drugs.

Actually, the best means of inducing a perfectly adaptable "shock" are *direct psychological means*. If the neurotic is made to realize that abnormality will follow unless he accepts painful restrictions, which are no loss even emotionally in the end, he may gain a new direction in the avoidance of overadjustment. The incomparable advantage of direct psychological "shock" lies in its built-in purposefulness. Think of the ungraspably purposeful, exactly fitting, innumerable reactions with which the organism responds when a person recognizes a certain danger. Of course, such realization can be best imparted only through life itself — through constant reminders and standards that become cultural tradition and conditioned needs. Purely abstract realizations have little weight, and any endeavor to enforce a conviction or "shock" on somebody directly would lead only to an opposite reaction.

Psychiatrists should at least not try to isolate the psychotic person from the already existing cultural restrictions and traditional stresses of life. At present just the reverse is the aim of treatment. In all possible ways the psychotic is isolated from stresses or pressing needs; and the loosening of restrictions or the increase of releases is the direct goal of every therapy. It is not even suspected that

132

the "disease" here — the pressures and negative reactions — is the cure. Hence the increase in mental disorders, specially as the same attitude permeates the whole of modern life. Only recently have doctors started to realize that patients do better if let out of hospitals, in which isolation is greatest, and are placed back into life. But there is no causal understanding of this beneficial effect, and the rest of the treatment counteracts it.

Analysis. The most popular therapy in modern psychiatry is analysis. It is also the least useful, though under experimental logic it appears very satisfactory. It certainly gives the best satisfaction to the patient. Neurotics love to talk about their problems and to have so much attention paid them. Talking is indulged by emotionally less stable people because it serves as a means of autosuggestive reassurance — permitting further overadjustment. The atmosphere of absolute permissiveness, together with a mysterious theory spiced with sexual ideas, offered by psychoanalysis suits the neurotic just fine. Schilder says in his *Psychotherapy* that even an appeal to will power should be avoided because it increases the feeling of guilt. As can be expected, the final results of such seemingly satisfactory treatment are negative rather than positive. Statistics show that the rate of recovery among patients treated by psychoanalysis is the same as among patients not treated at all. And some studies show that it is even lower. We shall return to this in the next chapter. Of course, a very different picture appears from studies on the subjective feelings of immediate "improvements" gained from analyses. Probably the most important such study is that of A. T. Jersild. Such approaches perpetuate the fallacy for good — by virtue of its own errors.

It cannot be overemphasized that analyzing, discussing, reasoning or explaining are the last things a neurotic needs. He has enough insights to make him the strongest-willed and best-adjusted of men — if only he could follow his insights. As O. Hobart Mowrer has explained, it is not insights that the neurotic lacks. All the needed insights can be formulated in one sentence: have more positive feelings. And everybody knows what positive feelings are — satisfaction, love, joy and so on. The trouble is that any satisfaction is attainable only through the accumulation of needs, which means the restriction of satisfaction. Analysis with its absolute permissiveness is the least suitable method to induce the neurotic to accept restrictions. In fact, analysis hinders the natural pressure toward normalcy or the reimposition of restrictions, which is the function of neurotic reactions. These conflicting reactions exist exactly because the neurotic feels organically and knows intuitively all the "insights" but is unable to live up to them. The analyst then helps the neurotic to continue avoiding the difficulty.

Equally futile is analysis as a means of discovering the causes of the disorder. The more general and therefore causally important a factor is, the less felt or noticed in any form is it by the neurotic. The esoterically involved, indirect methods of analyzing subconscious meanings permit the psychologist to construct suitable explanations while he is facing a completely illogical and incomprehensible picture.

This is the main reason why analysis persists as theory and therapy. It enables the psychologist to continue doing at least something while real understanding is missing. Moreover, in practice any analysis becomes something more than just analyzing and providing insights. Psychology is an art, and the sheer intelligence of the analyst prevails over his theory. He understands and learns intuitively the right procedure, namely, the *enforcement* on the neurotic of the unpleasant realities and needs. Every analyst feels that he must work hard and make the neurotic recognize, accept, or decide to do, things that are hardest for him — that he is avoiding. The very atmosphere created by the presence of another person with higher intelligence makes all this inevitable, whatever the theory. In brief, each analysis produces, in practice, a certain amount of the psychological "shock" that we mentioned above. The greater the amount of such enforcement, the more successful the analysis. This explains why the recently emerging religious therapy is becoming one of the most successful methods though it is least scientific. Of course, in any enforcement the motivations of the patient himself must be utilized; otherwise only opposite reactions may be evoked.

The Freudian analysis is least beneficial because in it the

permissiveness and emphasis on pure analyzing are greatest. But even here the practice has become very different from theory. Some psychoanalysts have used methods that amount to pure psychological "shock." The "character analysis" used by Reich, and to great extent by Horney, is typical. Under this method the neurotic is forced to realize his own unpleasant character traits. Reich's analysis produced emotional outbursts by patients so violent that he thought the method would be dangerous in hands of less experienced analysts, though he found it very successful. Actually, the whole psychoanalytic theory and practice is moving toward the recognition that emotional *enforcement* rather than analyzing should be the aim of the treatment, as we shall see in the next chapter. It does not matter under what theory and for what reasons something unpleasant is forced on the neurotic. As long as he lives through unpleasant, restrictive experiences he acquires a background for experiencing the opposite, positive emotions. That is what every "shock" does.

Incidentally, psychoanalysis was born out of a treatment of the enforcement of unwanted reactions. The girl treated by Breuer and Freud was cured by the method of abreaction or *catharsis*, as Breuer called it. The girl had to be forced, by use of hypnosis, to relive her harassing past experiences. Freud started his theory from this case, used hypnosis in the beginning, but soon ran into insurmountable difficulties and ended with a system of mystifications permitting every possible explanation. Freud's theory dominates modern psychology because of this easiness of explanation as well as the broad growing interest in it by the general public, always ready for a mystery, especially on such themes as sex, dreams and the depth of the soul.

The sad truth is that those psychologists who do not subscribe to Freudian mysteries have to limit themselves to explanations that are clearly inane. All they find as causes of neuroses can be summed up under faulty learning and the formation of wrong habits. As we saw, the learning or insights can never be a problem. The real problem is the lack of one elementary thing: pleasure. All the troubles of the neurotic disappear the moment he can enjoy more release, induced by drug, other intoxication or any exciting experience. As to the formation of habits, nobody in the world forms habits that are unpleasant; and the reactions in neuroses or psychoses are highly unpleasant.

A good example of what the most reasonable men in modern psychology are offering is a pamphlet that has been widely advertised and distributed by the National Association for Mental Health, entitled *How to Deal with Your Tensions.* It lists eleven things that patients should do — talking it out, escaping for a while, giving in occasionally, doing something for others, shunning the Superman urge, giving the other fellow a break, and so on. It concludes that the main thing is to have Faith. It all amounts to advising that the person strive for more positive emotions, and exert more positive motivation. In truth, the very trouble of the neurotic is that he strives too much already for positive emotions or satisfactions, and that he does not have any motivation just because of that, since only the accumulation of needs can provide it. Without available motivation all the nice things suggested become a travesty, as the neurotic subsequently seeks for more indulgence elsewhere in compensation for whatever effort he exerted. The pamphlet simply elaborates the logical emphasis on positive emotions and experiences, though exactly the opposite kind of emotions and experiences are what the neurotic has to live through first. It is not by accident that the neurosis itself forces such reactions on the neurotic. These reactions are natural processes, and the function of all natural processes is to maintain or re-establish normalcy.

This is only an example. There are hundreds of books and pamphlets that elaborate the same logical emphasis on more positive emotions, under the assumption that negativism in behavior comes from lack of insights, faulty reasoning, wrong learning or unfortunate habits. The book we referred to before, *Introduction to Psychopathology,* by O'Kelly and Muckler, underlines that therapy should be understood as a process of learning and acquiring new ways of adaptation. A fairly representative book, *Introduction to Psychology,* by Karn and Weitz emphasizes the learning of psychological know-how and correct reasoning which, it finds, is "a rare psychological commodity." Accordingly, it offers certain

136

methods of better reasoning, and various problem-solving techniques. Another fairly representative book, *Dynamics of Personal Adjustment,* by Lehner and Kube, emphasizes problem-solving attitudes, and sees psychotherapy as a learning process. It blames wrong generalizations, and advises the method of careful definitions and correct analyses, used by the scientist in his work.

Specific theories seeking for similar logical explanations have not discovered anything more than the same lack of insights and faulty reasoning. According to the psychobiology of Adolf Meyer, therapy should attempt to explain to the patient the meaning of his behavior established by past experiences, and to give him new insights. The sociological approaches cannot offer anything more than the same teaching of better insights. The semantical approach is the last word in the emphasis on meanings and insights. There is also the existential approach, popularized by Dr. May, which sees the cause of neuroses in an existentialistic preoccupation with problems of being and nonbeing. This constitutes an attempt to explain why modern man, enjoying the greatest security, suffers so much from anxiety. In truth, general or philosophical preoccupations are the last thing the neurotic worries about.

If these endeavors are at least harmless, there is another group of books and theories that can do harm. When the president of the National Commission on Mental Health tells us that unhappiness may be the principal cause of death from coronaries, strokes, ulcers or high blood pressure, and that satisfaction is as important as nutrition in the preservation of health, one may really start on a spree of overadjustments and end in a mental hospital. Or when we hear from such an authority as Karl Menninger that the richest emotions, such as love and hope, are to be enjoyed as sources of better adjustment, the door is opened for even greater emotional overindulgences, which are already the cause of our alarmingly increasing rate of nervous disorders. Schindler, another authority, tells us "how to live 365 days a year" by making every moment an emotional success, by avoiding unpleasant thoughts and by cultivating pleasant emotions.

The emphasis on enjoyment, release and increased stimulation dominates modern psychology. Unfortunately, the experimental approach invariably leads to proofs of the immediate beneficial effects of release as opposed to restrictions on which our cultural tradition and normal adjustment rest. In his book, *Prescription for Rebellion*, Robert Linder tells how he cured neurotics by teaching them to throw off "domestication" and the fetters of "adjustment." There is no reason to doubt that such cures were obtained, especially after the patients had gone already through an extended period of neurosis. The best "cure" for a drug addict is giving him the drug again. The special Release Therapy, in which a child is permitted to break dolls, smear paint or throw clay, is typical of this kind of "cure."

Another source of the fallacies of modern psychiatry is the alchemistic formalism according to which a great harm may result from an insignificant thing if you happen to handle it improperly. *The Interpersonal Theory in Psychiatry*, by Harry Stack Sullivan, another great authority, is a good sample in this respect. A child's adjustment may be warped for life if you happen to let him slip without support, restrain him from fingering his sex organs, or do not handle him properly in feeding, cuddling or stool habits. The adolescent's adjustment may be crippled forever because of unsatisfactory first sexual intercourse. The number of such rules and complications are hundreds. Esoteric complexities always appear where simple causal understanding is missing.

In fact, the simple but inexorable rule of equality of emotions governs all psychological causation. You never get something for nothing here, as in any other field. No serious complex can arise from an accidental experience and no amount of skill, know-how or maneuvering alone can help, whether it be group therapy, play therapy, body-building therapy, hypnotism or music therapy. Only the availability of positive emotions can provide motivation and normal adjustment. But positive emotions or satisfactions are impossible without equal negative emotions or needs. By the way, group therapy has the best possibilities because there the tendency of the neurotic to enjoy his own superiority turns against him. As he observes the neurotic behavior of others he loathes it deeply, and by the same token is later emotionally forced to avoid it in himself.

We cannot discuss these therapies, but we would like to mention lobotomy. The effects of lobotomy confirm the fact that the primary function of the brain is to impose restrictions which make the highest adjustment possible. By isolating the highest part of the brain in lobotomy the highest set of restrictions is removed. Consequently a release of pleasure and temporary improvement in adjustment is experienced. In terms of experimental approach this means improvement; and lobotomy was hailed as an epoch-making breakthrough. But the final effect is a sinking to a lower, almost animal level of adjustment. Even the temporary pleasure gain disappears as the normal play between needs and satisfactions on the lower level of adjustment re-establishes itself. The effects of lobotomy also confirm that neurosis, or psychosis, is a pressure toward normalcy. When the mechanism that sustains the conditioned normalcy is severed, the neurosis disappears.

Cure, or rather prevention, of neuroses and psychoses *is* possible. In usual cases their cause is simple, namely, overadjustment, and their prevention requires nothing more than imposition of sufficient restrictions. The difficulty lies in the lack of means, understanding and general attitudes sufficient to maintain such restrictions. No deliberate or forcible restriction can help, because of opposite causation. For the same reason the shock treatment wears off. Even the continuous "shock" induced by anti-stimulating drugs, that we mentioned above, would require at least a gradual increase of dosage. The perfectly adaptable psychological "shock" is the best means. But it requires that the "shock" or system of restrictions be so general and complete that it is not even felt and, therefore, evokes no opposite reactions. Men can live under any level of such restrictions and find it normal. In other words, it requires that the restrictions permeate life throughout everywhere around us. The present increase in mental ills in direct proportion to the easiness and permissive "scientism" of modern life shows the dependence of these ills on the general social atmosphere. Another difficulty is that restrictions which are sufficient for a normal person may be insufficient for a person with an inborn neurotic propensity.

Psychotherapy should, at least, not try to isolate the psychotic person from the stresses of life, as it does now. In more primitive societies where such a person faces clear dangers to his existence if he fails, he never deteriorates to a state that in our society requires treatment at an institution, which mostly ends with complete insanity. Recently psychiatrists are discovering that out-of-hospital treatment is better. But there is no causal understanding, only conflicting theories, why it is so. The play of needs and stresses which are as necessary to normalcy as valleys are to mountains, and which can be sustained only by the pressures of real life, is least suspected as the favorable cause. If the cause were understood, the approach to treatment would reverse completely: the engagement of those predisposed to mental instability in strict work with hard duties and discipline would be seen as the first goal. In Russia this method has been applied extensively with good results. In our country similar experiments have been successful but have not evoked interest because they are completely incompatible with the basic tenets of our present approach. Even chronic patients can engage in a full day's work, with no absences, as a report by a manager of a Veterans' Hospital, Peter A. Peffer, shows. Of course, it is particularly difficult to impose duties or restrictions on a psychotic person, but all such difficulties would lessen to the extent that the present attitude of emotional "improvements" and increased releases were reversed, and a completely different general atmosphere emerged. For, as we saw, it is such atmosphere and psychological pressures, inner or external, rather than any enforcements, that can really sustain restrictions.

CONCLUSION

It cannot be overemphasized that man can be normal only so long as he lives under difficulties which impose restrictions on him. Difficulties and restrictions are the very basis of biological and cultural evolution. Adjustment without restrictions can mean only a short-lived formless degeneration. Satisfaction is the source of all motivation and normalcy, but it is impossible without needs, or restrictions on basic satisfactions. Now that man is overcoming his greatest difficulties without evolving new needs, he is also losing his normalcy. Modern man has outlived the old-fashioned morals that kept the net of restrictions tight. Now he looks to science. But experimental science shows release, as opposed to restrictions, to be the source of better adjustment and the goal to be strived for. Science could attain its greatest progress in the field of human motivation, adjustment and mental life by continuing in a planned way what evolution has done blindly. Instead, science has become here a source of grave fallacies.

V

THE GHOST WORLD OF FREUDIANS

As we saw, the emotions and experiences of the neurotic are aftereffects of past exaggerations. They are pure phantoms having no reality of their own. They are like the curved world seen by the subject who takes off the glasses that curved everything in the opposite direction. If opposite causation is not understood, this world of phantoms must seem miraculous indeed. It is as rich and varied as was the previous positive exaggeration. The causal connection between the two is never suspected because as opposites they are different in every respect.

Psychoanalysts have discovered this ghost world, and have explained it with an equally ghostlike theory. The negative phantom emotions recur as ingeniously and persistently as the neurotic exaggerates his positive emotions. Therefore only an intervention by *person-like agencies*, such as the Id or Superego, can explain it all. Psychoanalysis agrees perfectly with the experimental approach of recording observations and explaining them by sufficient logical causes. Psychoanalysis offers the only complete explanation that there is, in modern psychology, of the inner world of neurotics. It is unattackable as long as present psychology cannot offer any better explanation.

In truth psychoanalysis has as little basis in reality as had the beliefs in devils and spirits in the age of alchemy and witchcraft. Personification is typical of all prescientific disciplines. Where the simple mechanistic causes are not understood but the desire to find some sufficient cause behind the varied phenomena persists, only an assumption of person-like agencies can do. The psychoanalytic causal agencies are like persons inside the person.

142

The Id. Psychoanalysts have tried to define the Id innocently enough as a totality of instincts. But as soon as psychoanalysts start using the concept of the Id, it becomes an agency that has wishes and performs acts which require observation, reflection and judgment. For instance, the all-important Oedipus drive, consisting of the wish to kill the father and marry the mother, requires cognition and intent. And since the person does not know anything about it, another person inside him must be thinking and planning.

We explained before that unconscious acts are possible, under the avoidance of pain or the striving for pleasure which governs all psychological phenomena, including the appearance of the opposite emotional phantoms. But the person would never resort to the difficultly attainable unconscious adjustment in order to torment himself or perform something senselessly gratuitous. Yet it is exactly acts which are tormenting and senseless for the person that are the supposed work of the Id. Moreover, psychoanalysts ascribe to the Id wishes and drives that the person himself would never even dream of. For instance, why and how should the person suddenly wish to return to his mother's womb (Rank); and how could he come to the idea that the penis is the uniting symbol for such a return (Freud)? Or how could a person want his death under the death instinct (Freud), have a cannibalistic wish (Abraham), be obsessed with castration idea, have penis envy and so on?

The Superego. Similar person-like capacities are attributed to the Superego. It punishes the person, often in very ingenious ways. It can avert the attention of the person at a precise moment so that an accident may occur. It can make a person attract illness (Menninger); or make him commit a crime and deliberately arrange things so that he himself gets caught (Alexander). In melancholia the Superego "abuses, maltreats and humiliates the Ego"; and in some cases it may be "far more irrational" than necessary, so that it may punish a person with blindness because the person wants to look at forbidden objects (Jones).

Psychoanalysts may try to define the Superego somewhat scientifically, for instance, as the residue of parental influences

(Freud). But such definitions are forgotten when it comes to practical application of the concept, as we just saw. It cannot be overemphasized that the personification is the very essence of psychoanalytic concepts. For otherwise they can explain nothing, in view of the above ingenuity and subtle persistence of the neurotic reactions. Even infants appear to have strong Superegos, though one could hardly speak in this case of a residue of parental influences. By the way, psychoanalysts like to place causal events in early childhood. This helps to explain why the person knows nothing about them.

The Censor. According to Freud the Censor acts as a watchdog, especially in the dream work, and cuts out any indecent material that may issue from the libidinal wishes of the Id. Considering that extensive symbolism, with more than dozen devices, is used to beguile the Censor, it must be quite intelligent. Other psychoanalysts have used the concept of the Censor independently of dream work. Alexander sees it as a general moral judge and source of repressions. The concept of the Censor is comfortable for purposes of explanation. The Id and Superego act like two opposed spirits. Because of the value-disvalue structure of all experiences two such spirits should be enough to take care of everything. There are a god and a devil in all unified dogmas. But due to paradoxical causation contradictions arise even under such a dual system. The existence of the Censor then is assumed as the reason why things have been deliberately mixed up, or disguised as symbols by the Id.

The Subconscious. In most cases psychoanalysts do not even care to refer to various agencies but simply use the Subconscious as an all-purpose person hidden inside the person and acting for its own reasons. An appearance of scientism is given to it by terming its acts as mechanisms of fixation, regression, displacement, substitution, inversion, introjection, projection, identification and so on. But under psychoanalytic method these mechanisms become subconscious schemings, plannings and reasonings, which the person himself could never imagine. Under regression the person returns to an infantile stage in order to come closer to the fulfillment of the Oedipal wish. Under displacement the neurotic suffering phobia has displaced his fear of a "castrating father" to fear of animals, in order to escape him. Under introjection, the neurotic shows the syndrome of melancholia because of introjection of another person "toward whom accusations have been made."

Instincts. Personification permeates every concept psychoanalysts deal with. The instincts of Eros and of destruction or death, two opposites, are endowed with intents, perceptions and judgments. How else could the cigar the person smokes be evaluated as a substitute for the mother's breast under the operation of the instinct of erotization? Or how else could the dream be used as a means of reviving a trauma for the purpose of its abreaction under the operation of the death instinct? Infants, even embryos, who naturally have only instincts, are supposed to have ideationally meaningful traumas, subconscious wishes and so on.

Also, the repository of all sexual instincts, the *Libido* is often endowed with capacities of cognition and intent. For instance, it may float out to objects because of their ideational meaning, or may attach to them because of their symbolic value. Psychoanalysts like to use the personified concept of the Libido in ways which give the impression of dealing with something mechanistic that can flow, float, accumulate, attach, become exhausted or misdirected and so on.

What all these personifications imply is scientifically absurd. The reflection or thinking with which the personified agencies are endowed could take place only if there were other separate physical organisms inside the person. Any intellectual activity is a product of the whole organism, absolutely integrated, down to its tiniest cell. There is nothing unintegrated or superfluous that could function for the other "persons" inside the person. In the usual unconscious acts, committed under the *striving for pleasure*, it is the integration of the organism as a whole under the pleasure principle that makes the person gravitate toward such acts. The possibility of multiple personality does not prove anything different, as we saw before. Of course, psychoanalysts are aware of the awkwardness of their anthropomorphic personifications. That is why they are advancing definitions that do not agree with their own practical application of the concepts. But they have no choice, because there is no other logical way to explain the endlessly ingenious persistence of neurotic reactions. Freud said that psychoanalysis should not be judged by general standards and that its explanations rest on the realities discovered in the psyche of the neurotic. This would be justified if there were any such realities. In fact, what Freud discovered as realities are phantoms that derive not from anything really there but from completely different, actually reversed, psychic realities that lie in the past.

Such phantom effects are found everywhere in human experience. Freud discovered some more melodramatic ones in folklore, customs, religions, errors of speech, slang, swearing, even wit and humor. Freud was always looking for sensationally mysterious phenomena. A more sober view and a causal understanding reveals the same phantom effects everywhere; and there is no cause of mystification. But if one seeks for mystery, these phantom effects are a rich field for discovering it.

For instance, why are folklores rich in curiously similar tales about beings having more than one head, spitting fire, being invisible and so on? Peoples living on different continents or having no contact may still have the same tale. The similarity is there because the opposite backgrounds from which the tale derives its emotional meaning are similar. All people have only one head and are visible, therefore the most striking being should have many heads and be invisible. Here the explanation is simple, though psychoanalytic anthropologists find mystery enough in such similarities. But the point is that any human experience, custom, legend or sense of value derives its meaning from the opposite backgrounds behind it, therefore in itself may appear as a curious phantom.

Every possible speculation about the subconscious psyche of peoples or individuals can be supported by observations from the world of such phantoms. The discoveries of Freud can be supplemented by many more curiosities — the strangeness of primitive art, the weirdness of tribal rituals, deliberate perversion in solemn oaths, esoterism in teachings, mystery and splendor in

religious or regal ceremonies, the meaningfulness of our supernatural and aesthetic beliefs, as well as every value notion. They
all may be shown to surge from undiscoverable sources, which
are consequently assumed to be subconscious, as the real causal
source, the opposite background, is never even suspected.

The founders of psychoanalysis, especially Freud, Jung and
Rank, often based their theories on curious customs, beliefs,
folklore and legends. [The idea of the Oedipus complex — the
central concept in psychoanalysis — was picked up by Freud from
the Greek legend.] Apparently, the legend was told, made into
a play and enjoyed because of the horrible, unheard-of things it
tells about. The legend derived its emotional meaning here from
an *opposite* general background which constituted the psychological reality the people lived with. But Freud accepted the
direct meaning of the legend as revealing such reality. Psychoanalysts are at the stage of scientism where the sensational or
extraordinary is seen as important, while the really important
general causal backgrounds are not noticed.

Swearing, slang, wit and humor, errors of speech, and finally
the material discovered in free association derive their main
characteristics equally from an opposite background. In themselves these characteristics are phantoms, having no causal reason
for existence of their own. A person swears to produce or express
sharp emotion, therefore utters something sharply contrasting with
the usual cultural behavior, that is the real causal source from
which the effect derives its meaning. The same applies to dirty
speech and slang. A thing is humorous not in itself but because
of a contrast with which it is tied in. In free association the
neurotic picks up what is emotionally salient, which means contrasting with the general background, or exceptional to it, therefore
causally least important. If there is a tendency by the neurotic
to pick up libidinal ideas during free association, it only shows
that the neurotic with his lesser capacity to bear restrictions feels
them as excessive, or as exaggerations, and therefore lives through
opposite reactions to them.

The emotionally more interesting errors of speech may be
equally due to opposite causation. Let us take a reportedly true

147

story as an illustration. A lady was inviting to her home a famous man who had an extraordinary nose. She warned her little daughter not to question the guest about it. Everything went well, and after the little girl was put safely to bed, the lady asked the guest: "Would you like to have cream or sugar in your nose?" There existed an exaggerated repression against pronouncing the word, and as an opposite reaction it broke out.

In the classical example described by Freud, a speaker wants to say, "Let us drink [in German *"anzustossen"*] to the health of the honored guest," but says instead, "Let us belch" [in German *"aufzustossen"*] on him. Apparently, the speaker had exaggerated his feelings. Therefore, the opposite feeling broke out with all its accompanying reflexes and words. The speaker may still have had high esteem for the honored guest, but might have tried to exaggerate his feelings beyond that. In any event, phenomena of this kind are aftereffects, obeying a simple law of opposite causation, and do not reveal any subconscious agency.

All these phenomena — folklore, customs or peculiarities in daily reactions — were made part of psychoanalytic theory by Freud. In fact, this theory becomes convincing because it can be extended to such a wide variety of psychological phenomena. The absurd personifications are therefore forgiven. Psychoanalysts, especially Freud, discovered many of the emotional phantoms or illusions that are due to aftereffects and negative background causation, just as the Gestaltists discovered most of the illusions of perception. In both cases complex mysterious explanations were offered. The simple opposite causation was too paradoxical to be thought of.

By assuming conflicting agencies with the unlimited capacities of personified spirits, psychoanalysts could explain everything. But there remained the problem of *why* these agencies should act in such absurd and extremely unnatural ways. Why should they torment the neurotic *without any natural reason or cause*, while as natural mechanisms they are there to provide harmony in his adjustment, and should therefore follow the pleasure principle that Freud himself recognized? To explain this incongruity and the irrational absurdities following from the application of the theory, psychoanalysts have postulated psychic drives so horrendous and nerve-racking that the craziest irrationalities can appear possible. The Oedipus complex, castration complex, death instinct, Electra complex, penis envy, playing with feces, traumas connected with sexual intercourse and sexual organs, birth traumas, even a cannibalistic drive have been selected as explanations because of their emotionally horrifying or shocking meaning.

Oedipus Complex. This complex has become the most important concept in psychoanalysis. If one reflects what it implies — desiring to have sexual intercourse with one's mother and to kill one's father — it certainly is sufficient to lead to the maddest conflicts. What is the scientific basis for the Oedipus complex? Apart from the singularly horrifying legend, Freud tells the story that somewhere in the prehistoric past sons killed their father in order to have their mother to themselves but later experienced remorse which led to the complex. Freud tells this as an isolated story, like a legend; and one can only wonder how the memory of such a crime could have survived through millenniums without anybody else knowing about it — not to speak of the continuance of its emotional impact.

Even if it be admitted that the killing of the father was a general custom, only a naïve kind of psychological speculation could lead to the conclusions that Freud reached. If it were a custom to kill the father and marry the mother, the sons would feel shame and remorse if they did *not* do so. Freud refers to the sexual life of apes, in which the older male tries to keep the other males away from the females. This is imaginable for deeply prehistoric groups of men. But here again, if it was the natural rule, the sons would feel badly only if they could not live up to it. Freud also writes about the great fear of incest among primitive peoples. All taboos are emotionally excessive and irrational. Fixation is sufficient to explain this, especially since the fixaton here bears on a matter so continuously present.

Cannibalistic Drive. The idea of cannibalism has fascination for psychoanalysts. It is supposed to have originated together with the Oedipus complex. According to Freud, the infant wants to devour his mother. By inversion he later fears to be eaten by his father, a fear which according to Freud is present in the "typical primal stock of childhood ideas."

In one case, explaining why the little Arpad who was afraid of animals "danced" when chickens were killed, Freud found that it was a re-enactment of "that first great act of sacrifice which had proved to be indestructible despite all attempts to forget it." Supposedly in that act the sons killed the father and devoured him to acquire his strength. We shall show later how Abraham, and others, have explained manic-depressive states as a symbolic re-enactment of the feast of killing and eating the father. Klein, Isaacs and Brierley, the foremost child analysts, have found the cannibalistic drive of infants to be very important.

Castration Complex. This complex is a favored concept in psychoanalysis because of its horrifying and shocking meaning. It is possible that the neurotic, who usually overindulges in sexual enjoyments, often suffers an opposite debilitating feeling. Then if the castration idea is suggested, it may turn into an obsessive reaction, as the feeling deepens under the exaggerated endeavor by the neurotic to avoid it. Freud found that the trauma of castration arises when a boy happens to see a naked female body and notices the difference in genital organs. However, when a girl sees the not less strange differences in the organs of the opposite sex, she is not horrified but develops penis envy. According to Freud, penis envy dominates the whole development of the female child; the girl never forgives her mother and turns to her father because of the wish to have a penis.

Supposedly traumas are also developed from observing the sexual intercourse of parents, or upon being exposed to attempts at seduction in childhood. Freud admitted that most of the stories of such traumas are invented by patients during analysis. Psychoanalyzed patients become quite expert in the theory. But Freud thought that these stories reveal important psychic reality and therefore are to be accepted as relevant even if they are not true.

Sexual Drives. Sex in general is the favored subject of psychoanalysts. Its hidden and shocking character suits well their explanations. To be sure, the sexual drive often is the cause of

150

trouble, because it is an ever-ready source of high enjoyment and therefore of overadjustment. There is also something more: modern man is obsessed by the subject of sex. The taboo on sex is as strong in modern society as it is in any society. No culture could exist without it. There is no trouble as long as the taboo is uniformly accepted; psychological normalcy is completely relative. But modern man has started to rationalize that he should be, and *is*, free in sex matters. This is an exaggeration and the opposite feeling of the mysterious strength of a taboo follows. Thus the taboo becomes a source of compulsive fixation, strengthened at every turn as the person tries to ban it forcibly. Psychologists and people interested in psychology are particularly exposed to this obsession because they rationalize more in these matters. Theories are determined by the emotional convictions of their authors and followers. The modern psychologist, unconsciously struggling with his own irrational obsession in sex matters, furiously exposes sex as the culprit in his theory. We may give here a couple of examples, trying to reproduce the terminology as closely as possible.

Melanie Klein, the great authority in child psychology, says that loss of the nipple by the infant institutes a compensatory search for a penis and a desire to incorporate it. The infant girl attacks her mother to obtain this coveted organ, and the frustration leads to later feminine anxiety. For the infant boy hatred of his mother's body becomes concentrated on the penis, which he wishes to destroy inside her. Later this anxiety becomes fear of castration by the father. The infant's frustrations in regard to the breast lead to the oral and cannibalistic stage. In his mind the infant "attacks the breast with poisonous urine and explosive feces, and therefore expects it to be poisonous and explosive towards him." Klein also holds that the splitting of personality springs from the notions of a bad breast and a good breast; and that persecution anxiety is aroused by the process of birth and loss of the intrauterine situation.

Another authority, Susan Isaacs, holds that the infant wants to drown and burn the mother with his urine. He may be completely intolerant of his parents' intercourse and wishes the father to put bad feces into the mother—dangerous explosive substances which will destroy her inside, or to urinate into her. The later "feeling of emptiness" arises therefrom. To show that this is not merely a theory, Isaacs tells of a man who failed to become an officer because he felt that "it was impossible for both of them, himself and his younger brother—ultimately himself and his father—to be potent." This notion arose in him from "early phantasies of incorporating father's genital." He felt that if he himself "sucked out father's genital from his mother, swallowed it up and possessed it, then the good genital would be destroyed, his younger brother could not have it, would never grow up, never become potent or loving or wise, indeed, never exist."

Psychoanalysts are so obsessed with the mysteries of sex taboos, emphasizing their salient, purely erotic aspects, that they have missed the real, far greater importance of the reproductive drive. This drive permeates all our emotions, especially those of beauty, love, goodness, nobility and the social sense. When conditioned, this drive may serve as source of motivation in any field. All our aesthetics, and a great part of our ethics, religion, education, social institutions and cultural interests derive their essence from the sexual drive. Psychoanalysts, however, see only the salient erotic, or purely genital, functions of this drive, which represent only a short-lived and narrow release phase in the whole process. The psychoanalytic approach is too naïvely sensational to reveal the really important, ever-present influences of sexual drive and the universal, paradoxical effects of its restrictive conditioning.

Because of this superficial narrowness psychoanalysts have arrived at a weird theory about the nature of sex and its conditioning. The most important part of this theory is early pregenital erotism and its "sublimation." The mystery of early childhood serves psychoanalysts well in upholding their assertions.

Oral erotism is made responsible for the smoking and chewing of tobacco, as well as kissing. The cigar or cigarette is assumed to be a symbol of the breast. When this was suggested to Freud himself, he said that his cigar was not always a symbol but sometimes just a cigar. Kissing might have led psychoanalysts to the postulation of oral erotism. Use of the mouth, or biting, may be involved in sexual play, as can be observed in animals. Actually, kissing has become a conventional form of expressing intimate erotic consent, which in any form evokes erotic pleasure. Cultural fixation increases the significance of such forms, whether it be kissing or nose-rubbing. However it may be, it is a fallacy worthy of alchemy to see superficial resemblances as causes, where the deepest cause of all, the search for pleasure release, is clearly evident. Even overeating has been attributed to oral erotism — just because the food passes through the mouth.

The concept of *anal erotism* is one of the most popular among psychoanalysts, who are delighted to discover an "anal character." Coarse language, swearing, assiduity in work, pedantry, the liking of enemas, all kinds of intestinal and rectal symptoms, even catatonic delirium involving smearing with feces, are attributed to anal erotism. Prohibition of this erotism is assumed to be the cause of stammering, apparently on the basis of Freud's discovery that stammering resembles the noises of defecation.

Urethral erotism, observed in children as competition in who can urinate farther, is made responsible for the development of ambition in life, also for bed wetting and various urethral symptoms of adults. Here again Freud discovered the resemblance between the "burning" ambitions in life and urination. *Exhibitionism,* another kind of eroticism, seen in children's enjoyment of being admired, is made responsible for voyeurism and exhibitionism, also for fashions, art and sports. It is also supposed to turn into excessive prudishness, or be punished by weak sight, hysterical restrictions of the field of vision, even blindness.

Sublimation. The all-important process of cultural conditioning is explained by psychoanalysts as a weird sublimation based on superficial symbolic resemblances. For instance, retention of stool in childhood is sublimated as retention of money, therefore as parsimony or avarice in later life. The child's smearing itself with feces is sublimated into meticulous cleanliness and pedantry in later life, by way of a reaction formation. The child's obstinacy in passing stool is later sublimated as perseverance. The propensity to cut or shed blood may be sublimated into the profession of surgery. As Menninger says, this propensity may appear beautifully disguised in the surgeon, less prettily so in the butcher, and unhappily so in the neurotic. Symonds covers almost every cultural occupation by such sublimations, in his *Dynamics of Human Adjustment*. Acquisitiveness or "taking in" of knowledge, "devouring books" and absorbing new fields are sublimations of oral tendencies. Niggardliness, scientific "retention" and classifications are sublimations of anal erotism. "Burning" ambition and the scientific fascination of tubes, conducts, hydraulics and electricity are due to urethral sublimation. There are many more, but this may suffice as illustration.

Resistance, Distortion and Symbolism. Now we may turn to another center of difficulties in the psychoanalytic theory. It is the need to explain why patients — at least those not initiated in the theory — face with bewilderment the discoveries by the analyst of their weird subconscious wishes or fears; and why they refuse to get well after the analyst has discovered and made conscious their complexes. Psychoanalysts have assumed that *resistance* is the reason. Considering the warring agencies inside the person, with their jealousies and disguises, it is easy to find an explanation why the resistance is there.

A related concept is *reaction formation*. Freud and other psychoanalysts recognized the ambivalence or reversal of emotions as a fundamental characteristic of psychological life. Since they could not see how negative emotions could originate from positive ones, they assumed a special mechanism as the explanation: the reaction formation. It was assumed that due to the various conflicts, fears and disguises, between the Id, Ego and Superego, a pleasurable emotion is turned into its opposite.

The most comfortable explanation of inconsistencies in psychoanalytic theory and in practical psychoanalysis is, however, *symbolism*. The ghost phenomena that analysts deal with are endlessly varied and paradoxically related. In spite of all the personifications and opposed spirits, the explanations often do not fit. The easiest way out is to assume that the phenomena are not what they appear to be, but are disguised or symbolic. All that is needed is to make this symbolism flexible enough. And psychoanalysts have achieved this perfectly, as can be seen from their interpretation of dreams.

154

Dream Interpretation. Seeking important hidden meaning in dreams fits well with the occultist nature of psychoanalysis and with the mass demand for easy mystery. Dreams have always fascinated man because they are so real and unreal at the same time. In truth, dream content is purely accidental. Freud himself explains how accidental the dream content is. For instance, he tells how he dreamed that the Pope was dead and later discovered that church bells had been ringing while he slept. He refers to the two-volume work on dreams by J. Mourly Vold, and explains how the dream content depends upon external stimulation of the senses during sleep. Application of a perfume made the subject dream of exotic adventure in Cairo; drops of water on his forehead, of perspiration in hot Italy; a pinch on the neck, of the application of blisters and the doctor who treated him, and so on. However, after all such explanations Freud turns around and asks: but what about the rest of the dream content? Naturally, it is impossible to explain all the innumerable details of a dream, or of any thought, since they depend from millions of associations. Once the causal principle was established, there was no need to ask for explanations of infinitesimal details. Apparently, Freud was looking for mystery.

The purpose of psychoanalytic dream interpretation is to reveal hidden, mostly sexual, meaning of dreams so that the shocking subconscious wishes and complexes can be construed. However, nothing shocking is found in most dreams. Occasionally a person may dream of nightmarish intercourse, even incest. The reason is the same as when he dreams about urinating in impossible places. In the case of an incestuous dream the person may crave for physiological sexual release while still retaining a psychological inhibition against it. But in usual dreams no such shocking material occurs. Therefore psychoanalysts claim that dreams are disguised to look innocent because of the Censor. Psychoanalysts claim that there are some twenty kinds of such disguises and distortions: opposites, reversals, absurdities, transpositions, twistings, modifications, references, symbolizations, fusions, contradictions, substitutions and so on.

The end result is that anything can stand for anything. For

instance, the male genitals can be represented by hundreds of objects. There are not only sticks, poles, trees, firearms, pencils, planes, fishes, hats, cloaks, limbs and so on, but also everything that can be grasped, used as instrument, be injurious, or be hollow, or round, or elongated and so on. Female sex organs have an even richer symbolism, including not only holes, pits, caves, boxes, bottles, pockets, ships, but also landscapes, houses, buildings, rooms and practically anything that can serve as a receptacle, enclose space or contain something. It can be reasonably asked whether there is anything that could not be interpreted as a sexual symbol.

This disguised symbolism is not limited to dreams. Important neurotic reactions are explained by it. We may take as an illustration the case of the nineteen-year-old girl, to which Freud referred several times. She developed a neurotic ceremonial in her arrangement of her bed and room before going to sleep. Apparently, this was a simple case of obsessive perfectionism. But Freud explained the ceremonial as a result of the girl's attributing sexually symbolic meaning to the objects around her. According to Freud, she was so meticulous about placing the vases so that they could not fall because they represented to her the female sex organs. Or she arranged the pillow so that it did not touch the bolster of bed because the pillow meant the female sex organ and the bolster the male sex organ. Every one of her endless compulsive acts was explained in a similar way. Incidentally, Freud tells that at first the girl received his interpretations with "scornful doubt" but that later she helped herself find hidden sexual meanings in her acts.

The method of symbolism, particularly, makes psychoanalysis resemble alchemy. The emotional weight or continuous duration of a background becomes of no importance. Psychoanalysis seeks for accidental, curious and symbolically suggestive events. The very core of the theory, analysis, rests on the assumption that the causal event is hidden or forgotten. This can only mean that it has been of no significance in terms of weight and duration of emotions. Analyses last for years because the event is so completely unsuspected that everything in the neurotic's past has to be turned over. The equivalence of emotions is nonexistent for psychoanalysts.

The gravest disturbance may originate from a mere symbolic connection or abstract whim. A writer may become unable to write because of a symbolic connection of the fluid-emitting pen with the penis (Freud); or because writing on paper is seen as soiling, reminding of "early anal sadistic fantasies" (Alexander). A neurotic may develop a most disturbing tic of the leg just to "show the power in the leg comparable to the strength of the father's penis"; or a tic of the head in order to "see the valuable objects coming from his bowels" (Schilder). We mentioned earlier how a person may suffer paralysis of the legs because he connected the idea of walking with "stomping on mother earth" (Freud). The whole sexual drive is explained "not so much as a natural desire" but as a "motive of proving to oneself that it is safe to commit what another part of mind tells to be forbidden and dangerous act" (Jones). Or a deep emotional complex is created because the person merely reverses or misplaces the sign so that "I hate him" becomes "I hate myself." By similar misplacement love is turned into rejection, joy into grief, or aggressiveness into masochism. This construction has been used by many psychoanalysts, especially, to explain the reversals, or what they call the ambivalence, of emotions that they could not miss observing.

The underlying idea of psychoanalytic theory is that the person somehow wishes or imposes on himself negative emotions. This is the only way to explain why the emotions of the neurotic persist as ingeniously as if he himself were operating them; and why he does not give up his phantom convictions even after it is made clear to him that they are not real. (All opposite phantoms persist in spite of present reality). Freud proposed the theory of omnipotence of thought, according to which emotions can be created by a thought. Anybody having a minimum of insight into psychology knows how absurd such an idea is. But if it is not understood how the neurotic brings on himself negative emotions by his very striving for positive ones, this is the only possible explanation.

157

Self-Punishment. The most popular concept among psycho-analysts who want at least to remain logical and to avoid the Freudian sex lore is self-punishment. Menninger describes in his books, *Man Against Himself* and *The Human Mind*, self-punishment and self-destruction as the main source of mental ills, even of physical diseases, including tuberculosis. Alexander, in his *Fundamentals of Psychoanalysis*, points to self-punishment as the explanation not only for psychotic reactions, like the manic-depressive states, but also for masochism, professional failures, accidents, eccentrism, even alcoholism and crime. According to him, the criminal becomes a recidivist or subconsciously makes deliberate mistakes so that he can be caught, because he wishes the punishment.

Defense. Another concept used to explain how the neurotic imposes endless disturbances on himself is defense. As we saw, there is an extremely strong element of fending off the negative emotions in all neuroses. The exaggerated avoidance of negative emotions is the very cause of neuroses. But the psychoanalytic concept of defense as a means of protection — whatever the supposed threats — is absurd. Why should a person continue using as a defense something that does just the contrary of protecting? Freud recognized defense as the cause of neuroses in his latest theory, but did not see in it any other meaning than this same protection. He argued that the person resorts to the defense in order to take "into own hands the direction of the trauma." Thus the person scares and torments himself to avoid a trauma that he realizes only as an abstract possibility. When Freud came to explaining what this possibility is, he arrived at "object loss" — which can mean any of the undesirable events that can occur by the dozen every day. But Freud apparently wanted to return to some reality in his latest theory and stated that the object loss "alone has utility for man." To justify the need for such strenuous defense against so little, Freud concluded that "an instinctive recognition of dangers threatening from without does not seem to have been among Nature's gifts to man." Something more unscientific could hardly be stated.

We may mention here one fundamental characteristic of the

psychoanalytic approach: the claim of inherently disruptive instincts and drives inside the organism. Psychoanalysts needed this badly in order to support their explanations, even if it meant going against every basic and self-evident principle of the natural sciences. Freud postulated the death instinct to explain the negative reactions of neurotics. If we really had a death instinct, we would not last for an hour. Holding out against death is the incessant imperative of everything living, since even an instantaneous discontinuance of a single function can cause death. Before the death instinct Freud had the destructive or sadistic instinct as opposed to the erotic instinct. Freud used to postulate new drives freely, and mostly as conflicting opposites: love vs. hate, activity vs. passivity, masculinity vs. femininity, pleasure vs. unpleasure, and so on.

Freud saw pleasure as the main principle but could not explain how the pleasure of the neurotic turned into displeasure. He admitted in his book, *Beyond the Pleasure Principle*, that the process was "not yet clearly understood." In the same book Freud postulated a new fundamental drive, "compulsive repetition for the sake of repetition." Later Jones accepted it as a very important drive. Psychoanalysts are always ready to postulate new disruptive instincts, or to see any natural function as disruptive. The birth trauma, postulated by Rank and Ferenczi, is a good example.

Repression. Even though Freud later replaced the concept of repression with that of defense as the source of neuroses, repression has remained the core of the psychoanalytic theory. It is also the concept that has led to the most erroneous, even harmful, approaches. If absence of repression were a source of better adjustment, neurotics would be paragons of adjustment, since the main characteristic of a neurotic personality is evasion of restrictions. As Mowrer has pointed out, neurotics are not persons who lead moral, highly restricted lives. Actually, psychoanalysts are here perpetuating the great general fallacy of the experimental approach. Release always seems to be the source of positive emotions and restriction of negative ones, though causally only restrictions can make release or positive emotions available.

To be sure, the neurotic experiences repression. Neurosis is a pressure toward the establishment of normalcy. This means the reimposition of restrictions, so that there can be room again for the normal play between restrictions and releases. Neurosis means emotional negativism or immobility, which becomes inevitable after satisfactions have been exhausted by the removal of restrictions. In brief, not repression but lack of repressions in the past is the cause of psychotic disorders.

The error here is serious for practice as well as for theory. Some psychoanalysts go so far as to warn against the moral restriction of children. Jones says that it is perhaps less harmful to punish a child in anger than to enforce a moral principle. Our cultural tradition and conditioning mean restrictions more than anything else. The traditions are confusing in themselves because they are not causally understood. Then when psychoanalysts, speaking in the name of medicine and mental sanity, demonstrate the harmful effects of restrictions, people can become really scared. Particularly obnoxious are assertions by psychoanalysts that unless one gives free expression to a natural drive, such as the sex function, there will be complications. In truth, everybody can easily observe that any repression of a natural drive leads only to the most perfect and pleasurable performance by it at the first opportunity of release. And those who are capable of deeper insights can see that the repression of natural drives is the source of subsequent greater motivation and more refined pleasures. Repression, by conditioning, is the source of all cultural motivations.

The Success of Psychoanalysis. The success of psychoanalytic theory and practice is actually the strongest argument in its favor. As we have already showed, under the present experimental approach and state of knowledge psychoanalysis is an unattackable theory. Its real over-all strength, however, derives from the mystery, spiced with sex and sensationalism, that it offers. The human mind does not change in hundreds of years. And mental sciences today permit as much mystification as sciences in general permitted when our forefathers burned witches three hundred years ago. Theories become known and expand depending upon the

160

basic general interest. Sex alone is sufficient to keep alive the interest of the general public in a thing or person; and psychoanalysts have added mystery to it. The psychoanalysts have the advantage of blaring away about sex, which really is important, while the others keep silent about it, for reasons of cultural conditioning.

As the most assured prophets of emotional freedom psychoanalysts stand at the head of the modern movement, which grows out of our unprecedented ease of life and is supported by present-day "scientism" and "enlightenment." Psychoanalysts have showed more dramatically than anybody else how the superstitious, restrictive tradition represses the free and natural flow of psychic energy. Humanity has lived through many rationalistic movements, and has evolved protection against them. But psychoanalysis hides behind the cloak of medicine and scientism. Usually a rationalistic movement discredits itself as it attracts mainly the cultural misfits, who are incapable of enduring cultural conditioning, and are therefore eager to expose cultural superstitions and hypocrisies. But psychoanalysis is protected here as well. Who can blame it for attracting sick people, or students seeking scientific enlightenment?

Psychoanalysis also derives its prestige from the fact that psychoanalysts have been doctors, and doctors can cure. A few centuries ago barbers were surgeons because they could cut. In regard to psychoanalysis as a *psychological* theory, in the field of the human sciences, doctors are only narrow specialists in a different *art* in the different field of physiology. Medicine is still an art, not a science, especially as regards the functional diseases, which represent the closest parallel to mental disorders; there causal understandings are conspicuously missing. As specialists in an art of a different field doctors are less apt to face critically or to analyze relevantly such a theory as psychoanalysis than would be students of the human or even social sciences. Doctors, generally, are uncritical on the wider questions of scientism, as can be easily seen from their uncritical attitude toward supernatural beliefs. This goes well with specialists in a practical, narrowly specific, though intricate art. As such specialists doctors

161

are rather glad to find a complete and easy explanation of mental disturbances — which *is* provided by psychoanalysis — and are ready to disregard the absurdity of the personified agencies. A background very different from medical training is needed to see how absurd the theory is. A critical historico-scientific attitude extending to the very fundamentals of evolution and existence, including the delusiveness of spiritual phenomena, is needed here.

But how to explain the fact that psychoanalysts reach case explanations which the patients find perfectly fitting in every respect? The emotionally distressed neurotic easily accepts everything as fitting him. Even a normal person shows an amazing ability to relate everything to himself. Forer took thirteen statements from an astrology book, and every one of the thirty-nine students in his experiment recognized them as applying to himself. Peterson used a standard description for "reading character" and 90 to 95 percent of the people recognized it as fitting them. Further, most people still believe in fortunetelling, dreams, astrology or "destiny"; and there are more quack doctors of all kinds in the world than real doctors. Psychoanalysts have it a hundred times easier than fortunetellers or quack doctors, who have to deliver hard facts. We have seen the unlimited symbolism and excuses available to psychoanalysts.

As to psychoanalytic predictions of human motivation, an example by Eysenck illustrates what happens. When a household article did not sell well in England, it was blamed on sexual symbolism, while at the same time favorable sales of Life-Savers were attributed to the same symbolism. Eysenck concludes that the explanation could fit equally well one way or another, and that the analysts are wise only after the facts.

As regards cures, psychoanalysts themselves are not so sure. A fact-gathering committee of the American Psychoanalytic Association has stated that "no claims regarding the therapeutic usefulness of analytic treatment are made" by the Association. Eysenck demonstrates that according to statistics the rate of improvement from analytic treatment is exactly the same as from any other treatment, or as when no treatment at all is given: namely, two-thirds. Statistics gathered by Myerson and Strauss, referred to in Salter's book, *The Case Against Psychoanalysis,* show even lower rates of improvement. We have explained the fallacy of studies based on statistics of immediate and subjective improvements. Immediate improvement from analysis, which is what patients are looking for, can mean only a delay in the return to normalcy. This explains why analyses drag on for years. Finally, recovery comes in spite of analysis, since analysis cannot stop for long the pressure toward normalcy that constitutes the "disease." If psychoanalysis does produce a change, it amounts to a lowering of standards of motivation and behavior—leading to later, deeper difficulties.

Psychoanalysts themselves have repeatedly realized how elusive the cure under their treatment is. The older psychoanalysts held that discovering the subconscious conflict and making it consciously realized by the patient was all that was needed to cure him. Freud used for a while the apparently perfect method of hypnotizing patients, so as to overcome resistance, and discovering the subconscious conflict at once. But, when all these things were done, nothing happened. Psychoanalysts then blamed resistance, reaction formation or transference, and had no choice but to drag out analyses in length.

The confusion shows in the fact that almost every psychoanalyst has his own theory. Since analysis rests on the application of a definite theory, and since the treatment here consists of nothing else but such an analysis, this means as many different treatments as there are analysts. Finally, the analysts are starting to question the usefulness of the method of analysis itself. At the recent half-century anniversary of the American Psychoanalytic Association the idea of analysis and understanding by the patient has been de-emphasized and emotional influencing by the doctor emphasized. This is contrary to the very idea of psychoanalysis, according to which an emotional influencing is exactly the source of unforeseeable disturbances.

By the way, the *transference* that we just mentioned has been explained by psychoanalysts on various grounds, from father image to attachment of free-floating libido. The real reason has not been understood. While the patient is allowed to talk, is

163

being analyzed, and paid so much attention to, he overenjoys it all under various emotions — love, friendship or respect between him and the analyst. Opposite feelings are bound to emerge, especially when it all is to end. The patient tries to avoid them and clings neurotically to the continuance of the relationship between him and the analyst — for seemingly mysterious reasons. Actually, the transference is the only concrete result obtained in most analyses. No wonder psychoanalysts are increasingly trying to build their therapies around it, under various alchemistic theories.

Now we may mention a few typical aspects from the work of the masters.

FREUD

All the anthropomorphic agencies and alchemistic symbolism were products of Freud's imagination. Freud was a doctor who wanted to explain the irrational, contradictory and stubborn ghost reactions he observed; and who was not bothered by any scruples of strict theoretics in stretching his theory until it fitted. From an isolated sensational legend and a self-fabricated story he elaborated the horrifying central concept, the Oedipus complex, embellishing it with the cannibalistic drive, castration complex, penis envy and so on. Together with the personified agencies warring inside the person, this offered Freud unlimited possibilities of explanation — from simple inferiority complex to involved fetishism: a person suffers the inferiority complex because he cannot have intercourse with mother; in fetishism the person cherishes the "mother's phallus" which he "as a little boy once believed in and does not wish to forego." Freud never hesitated to stretch his imagination. A phobia about mice was attributed by him to a hidden sexual wish because women sometimes lifted their long skirts when seeing a mouse.

Nor did Freud hesitate to add new disruptive instincts and drives, as we have already seen. With equal ease he changed his basic principles. Apparently, the theory was based not on any fundamental thinking but on expedience. By one stroke Freud could reverse a theoretical view, announce a new principle or postulate a new fundamental mechanism. In one of his last books, *Inhibition, Symptoms and Anxiety,* which constitutes his last reformulation of principles, Freud recognized that repression was not the cause of neuroses though the whole psychoanalytic theory was built on repression as their cause. Now defense was postulated as the cause, and avoidance of mere *"Unlust"* — which means nongratification — was adduced as the ultimate reason for the defense. Thus after thirty years of grandiose theorization all that was found was that neuroses arise because of nongratifying feelings. But Freud had come down, with the years, to some measure of realism, and concluded: "From this standpoint everything falls in place." In the same book Freud announced a new fundamental mechanism, that of "undoing," as a means of explaining the contradictory behavior of the neurotic. Such a fundamental mechanism would have tremendously important consequences — if it existed. But Freud did not even bother to establish a natural basis for it.

Freud lacked the ability — so essential to a psychologist — to see how "abnormal" values or feelings can be completely "normal," and vice versa. He imputed his own normal feelings ot a well-conditioned, civilized man to everybody, even to children. In the all-important explanation of the origins of subconscious conflicts, the child is supposed to live through traumas because of the horrible Oedipal wishes. In fact, if a child had the Oedipal drive he would find it only good and nice. Any scruples could start arising only with *conscious* learning or conditioning — which is of no importance according to Freud. We showed how naïve was the imputation of the trauma to the killers of the father in the Oedipal story; the sons would have felt bad if they did *not* kill the father. If a drive is natural or accepted as normal, it can never create a conflict: it is felt only as right and fine. Nor can its repression create a conflict, since restriction can lead only to its opposite — release and satisfaction. Psychoanalysts completely lack relativistic insight, which explains how a thing or event can

165

acquire any possible emotional meaning, and give more satisfaction precisely because of previous dissatisfaction.

The fundamental principle of psychoanalysis, repression, originated from just such a lack of relative insight. Psychoanalysts did not understand how any repression or abnormalcy becomes normalcy under conditioning, as a matter of the most perfect general rule. If Freud and psychoanalysts had realized under what repressions and "abnormalities" they and other people live without feeling anything abnormal, they would have seen how pointless the concept of repression is.

To show, briefly, how Freud applied his theory we may mention a case to which he himself referred several times. Little Johnny had developed a phobia of horses. Freud discovered through analysis that under the Oedipus complex and reaction formation it was not horses that Johnny feared but castration at the hands of his father. Further, by displacement, Johnny substituted horses for father so that he could avoid them by not going on the street, whereas he could not avoid his father. Of course, all this was going on subconsciously, so that Johnny had not the slightest idea what he himself was fearing and scheming. Freud mentions incidentally that Johnny had seen another boy being hurt by playing horse riding. In an overprotective environment, this would have been sufficient to start a fixation and a phobia in regard to horses that were encountered frequently. But Freud did not even consider how such ordinary things could have anything to do with the strong irrational phobia.

ADLER

The second greatest master of psychoanalysis is, recognizedly, Adler. His main contribution was the establishment of the *inferiority complex* as the source of neuroses. He logically assumed that inequalities of life — the weakness of children, the secondary status of women or sibling rivalry — are the causes of the inferiority feeling. But Adler was a keen observer and saw that the cause-effect relationship was contradictory here. He saw that neurotics suffered from inferiority exactly while they aspired to superiority, and along the same lines on which their aspiration to superiority centered. We know why this has to be so. But Adler had to resort to the subconscious to explain the contradiction. He evolved a special theory of the "style of life."

According to this theory, the person evolves certain high goals for himself, but because he cannot attain them he subconsciously creates excuses for not reaching them, by inflicting all kinds of incapacities and negative reactions on himself. These then constitute the symptoms of neurosis. Adler termed them "distantiations," constant movements "back-and-forth," "cessations," "safety arrangements" and so on. Thus he could explain why every incapacity or disturbance arises exactly where success was aspired to most — actually, enjoyed most. Adler could observe this amply in his case studies.

For instance, the boy whose life seemed to be directed toward social success, and who enjoyed all the social graces to the highest degree, later turned away from society because of feelings of inadequacy and lack of interest. In another case, Adler observed that a woman who tried to consecrate her life to religiousness became obsessed with ideas of sin and her religious inadequacy. In still another case, the son of an industrialist, who threw himself enthusiastically into advancing the well-being of his workers, later developed neurotic attitude of isolation from them. We cannot go into all the interesting cases Adler describes — one in the book, *The Case of Miss R.* — but in each of them we find paradoxical opposite causation at work.

Adler further worked out the thesis of compensation, to explain exactly how the inferior person suffering some handicap develops especially high aspirations as required by the theory of the style of life. The thesis of compensation is the most popular part of Adler's theory. People find it interesting to think of a high, ambitious personage as suffering from feeling of inferiority, especially since this often can be observed to be true. But there is no foundation in Adler's assumption that because a person is in an inferior position he sets out to compensate for it by excessive superiority. Any position or experience that is permanently there is accepted by the person as simply normal and can evoke no specific feeling. Adler might have observed in his extensive work with children that the handicapped child more often has the inferiority complex, with all the exaggerations between superiority and inferiority. But the reason is neither the handicap in itself nor any compensation. Out of compassion parents and educators try to make the handicapped child feel that he is just like other children. Thus there is a constant exaggeration. Then when the child has to face hard reality, he suffers equally exaggerated opposite feelings and the complex of inferiority. Then he may really "compensate" in a world that he finds, emotionally, to be below his standards.

Adler and his followers have viewed the inferiority complex as the source of all neuroses. This is erroneous. There are myriads of feelings, with their exaggerations and complexes. The complex of inferiority is very frequent in our society because exaggerations in the feeling of superiority have become a daily necessity. But theoretically the inferiority complex is only one among many kinds of complexes and their combinations.

JUNG

Undoubtedly Jung is one of the foremost masters of psychoanalysis. His work is typical in that he uses the psychoanalytic theory to its maximum capacity. There is in his theory the conscious, the unconscious, the personal unconscious, the collective unconscious, the shadow, the anima, and the persona which surrounds the Ego. The latter is an islet in the sea of consciousness, which in its turn is an "islet on the boundless sea of the unconscious." The shadow of man is masculine but his anima is feminine. Woman has several animi. Then there are the archetypes which are practically images and ideas supposedly inherited from the subconscious past of mankind. Since inheritance of ideational experiences is plainly untenable, Jung has given a definition of the archetypes as mere predispositions. However, this definition is forgotten when it comes to meaningful application of the concept of archetypes. For instance, Jung invokes repeatedly the archetypes of the form of snake, rebirth, the Great Mother,

168

eternal femininity (probably inspired by the popular expression of Goethe), as well as such ideas as the conservation of matter "harbored in the collective unconscious."

Jung readily personifies any function of the psyche. We can mention here his Eros, Logos, Soul, Libido, Instincts, Spirits and so on. Even such functions as feeling and thinking may become personified. For instance, feeling is feminine, thinking masculine. Libido can be almost anything — will, desire, interest, love, regulator of all functions of the soul — can regress, be split, transformed, detached, withdrawn or tamed. According to Jung, dreams can reveal the future. A person's destiny is inescapable like a law of God. It is hidden in the unconscious. But "only a few persons dare to say 'Yes' to their destiny." The unconscious is an eternal being — infinite, unchangeable and almost immortal.

Jung's theory amounts to a new kind of mythology, and that is what his followers are looking for. There is human need for such mystification, and arguing about it would be as useless as arguing about religion or poetry. The real argument is that a completely legitimate use of the psychoanalytic theory permits the construction of such a system, with limitless personifications, pseudo history and supernatural etiology. It is only natural that other psychoanalysts recognize Jung's methods and discoveries as a great contribution.

We cannot go into a discussion of Jung's practical views on therapy, which are very reasonable and can be beneficial. This further points to his religiously moral world outlook. His well-known theory of extravert and introvert types is equally of little interest for our discussion here of typical psychoanalytic aspects.

RANK

Among the foremost masters should also be counted Rank. In his fundamental work, *Psychology and the Soul*, Rank proclaims four pseudo-historical eras. In the first, Emamism, man does not yet understand the notion of death. The sense of immortality is the same as the social sense. The survival of the group is the main motive. In the second, the presexual era, sex is viewed as something spiritual rather than a means of pleasure or reproduction. In the third, the sexual era, the playful activity of sex becomes taboo because of the belief that man can lose his soul by sexual intercourse. This becomes the root of sexual resistance and accompanying anxieties, which for Rank are spiritual. In this era the will is seen as bad, capable of bringing death. The fourth era involves dealing with the broken will and the collapse of old ideologies.

Rank admits that such eras need not have existed historically, but that they may appear in every person whatever his origin or race. In support of his theories, Rank adduces the myths of the Egyptian Amon cult, the Mycenian Minotaur, the Jovian bull that eloped with Europa, and the dramas of Don Juan, Hamlet and Faust. To the mysteries of the past Rank adds the obscurities of modern quantum physics. He arrives at the conclusion that the present is determined by the future and that his Will principle is the causal principle.

Rank's theory is interesting for its fusion of overt pseudo scientism and mysticism, its naïve attempt to explain drives as products of formalistic reasonings or spiritual judgments, and a deliberate irrationalism as well as epic style in exposition. The important thing is that Rank's theory and discoveries are recognized on an equal standing with other psychoanalytic theories. In fact, Rank has only drawn more richly on the possibilities offered by the psychoanalytic theory; and psychoanalysts or their followers have no reason to object. Some of them find it the highest achievement of modern psychology. Progoff, in his *Death and Rebirth of Psychology*, recognizes Rank as the most advanced of all psychologists, especially because of his combination of the "rational and irrational elements in a world view based on the conception of the supernatural."

JONES

The biographer of Freud, Ernest Jones, is recognized as the most prominent psychoanalyst of the English-speaking world. He subscribes to all the mystifications of the psychoanalytic theory without reservations, and adds his own expansive elaborations. Space does not permit us to discuss them but we may mention here, as an illustration of his approach, one of his case analyses, namely, that of the chess champion Morphy. Apparently, the Morphy case represents one of those cases where a sudden extraordinary success places a person on an exaggeratedly high level of enjoyments, and precipitates overadjustment with all its emotional negativism. Morphy won the world championship of chess, in Paris, and left France "in a blaze of glory." He was presented with a golden crown in Boston, and was the subject of "great Morphy demonstrations" in New York and other cities. After living through the period of high glorification and fame Morphy became paranoiac.

In explaining the case, Jones goes back to the historical origins of chess, discovering that the figure of the king in chess represents the father figure. According to Jones, Morphy was sublimating his wish to kill his father into the chess playing, and because he succeeded in his endeavor the strain became too great. Jones refers to Freud's theory and says that such a wish can be endured in the subconscious imagination, but when it becomes reality it is too much to bear. He says: "To castrate the father in a dream is a very different matter from doing it in reality."

There are too many other famous psychoanalysts to be mentioned here. Characteristically enough, those who try to find some at least less mystic explanations come out least convincing. We mentioned before the explanations by use of the concept of self-punishment, offered by such authorities as Menninger and Alexander. Other explanations have been offered on basis of such concepts as alienation of self, self-hate, self-denial, self-idealization, idealized social image, or refusal to recognize one's own self. Such concepts have been worked into more sophisticated theories by Horney and the psychologists of social orientation whom we mentioned earlier.

But however sophisticated such explanations are made, they remain nonsensical. Why should the neurotic hold to something that he wants to get rid of with all his might and that he could

171

just as well abandon, by simple and pleasant determination—if such theories were really true? We saw what the real cause is and that nothing less than fear of great suffering, which becomes pressing under overenjoyment, is what produces the contradictory neurotic behavior. The person does bring on himself the emotional negativism or the "disease," but for the supreme reason that governs all adjustment: the striving for pleasure. The causal relationship is paradoxical. But if it is not understood, no amount of sophistication or mystery can help.

As the best illustration of the spirit of psychoanalysis we can mention a compilation of articles written by prominent psychoanalysts, edited by S. Lorand under the title, *Psychology Today*. It also shows how uncritical doctors can be in regard to the psychoanalytic mysteries.

In the article on "Juvenile Delinquency," Dr. I. T. Broadwin explains the case of Jerry, nineteen, who killed a man in a holdup. As the description shows, Jerry had made quite a hit with boys and girls, and used to say, "Well, you know how I feel when somebody gets in my way." He was pampered by his mother, who would allow nobody to discipline him. She always took his side. He had also been the favorite of his father, who died when Jerry was four. Mother showed him off to others, dressed him in sissy clothes, spoiled him and allowed him his way too much, as Jerry admitted himself. Jerry had early sexual experiences with girls, and took pride in his violent temper.

Now the analysis by Broadwin gives the following explanation: Jerry was dominated by the death wish. The mother was actually a depriving mother, a castrating mother. His instinctual life was thwarted as he could not achieve identification with his father. Mother shook his feelings of security. The nuclear problem was the Oedipus complex (though father was not there). His sense of guilt was strong and he feared punishment for subconscious sexual relationship with his mother. The dictates of the Superego were severe. All other girls were only substitutes for his mother. Because of interrupted masturbation his penis was denied to him and money became a symbol of masculine power. He got drunk in order to commit symbolic suicide and was subconsciously

172

driven to seek further punishment. By stealing money he took penis with which to function. In actual fact, Jerry held up the man because he needed five dollars for entertainment. Broadwin concludes that the homicide was a substitute for suicide. In fact, Jerry was driven into a corner by the man and shot him to escape.

In discussing "Obsessional Neuroses" in the same book, Dr. B. D. Lewin explains the case of a man who had to count to a hundred, had good and bad numbers, and developed a magic system of numerology. Apparently, the obsession here was due to the simplest kind of perfectionism in avoidances, driven to neurotic heights through the vicious-circle effect. But Lewin explains it all as a subconscious wish by the neurotic that his father die and as the Superego's demands that he undo his crime or else suffer fear of death.

"Manic Depressive Psychoses" are explained by Dr. G. Zilborg as self-punishment. The punitive agency is the "introjected" father, mother or teacher. In the depressive state the neurotic hurls inwardly his sadistic oral impulses against those he introjected, that is, "ate up." They are the ones he loved. As a result he develops his symptoms, including lack of appetite. Zilborg is also ready to accept as an explanation the atavistic feasting on the totem animal, when after the death of the father the yoke of the Superego is thrown off. He refers to Freud, and to the discovery by Abraham that after a period of mourning follows another outbreak of libido, which is ended by yet another symbolic killing and eating of the dead father in repetition of the Oedipus act. Apparently, such elaboration was necessary to explain the repeated oscillations between the opposite, manic and depressive, states.

Writing on "Psychology of Religion" Dr. E. Jones confirms the Freudian theory about religion, which is quite popular among psychoanalysts. According to it, the core of the Christian religion is the Oedipal conflict, and Christian practices represent ceremonial parricidal cannibalism from the ancestral past. The return to the mother's womb — another popular concept among psychoanalysts — is seen as the meaning of burial. The fear of extinction which lies at the basis of religious feeling is assumed to be only

173

the fear of castration. Any erect structures, such as prominently placed stones, are supposedly symbols of the father's phallus, as are such externally resembling presentations as snakes. The idea of sin is explained as an expression of the Oedipal conflict. Repressed sexuality of an infantile and incestuous kind are assumed to be the sources of religious reactions.

In a second article on crime, Dr. P. Schilder also resorts to the theory of self-punishment. He holds that criminals would not commit crimes if there were no punishment to be expected.

Art enjoyment is explained as an interplay between Ego, Id and Superego, in the article, "Approaches to Art," by Dr. E. Kris. He finds that during art enjoyment the Ego opens the way to an interplay with the Id, and later asserts its position by warding off the fear of demands by the Id and of the presence of the Superego.

The article "Psychoanalysis and Anthropology," by G. Roheim shows how the psychoanalytic anthropologists make their discoveries. The article gives a description of a witch play in Bali. The players, at one stage, attack the witch but instead of killing her turn their daggers against their own breasts. Apparently the play uses here the simple device of surprise, emphasizing the power of witchcraft. Roheim, however, interprets this scene as revealing childhood trauma and coitus with the mother. He says that the players "complete symbolically the cycle of childhood trauma — the approach to the mother, the rejection and the turn upon themselves." The pointing of daggers at their breasts by the players is interpreted as symbolic coitus with the mother. Roheim draws the conclusion that specific goals of primitive societies "are by no means conditioned by their environment or practical conditions" but are "a series of solutions offered by various human groups for the pre-Oedipal and Oedipal conflicts inherent in the infancy situation."

We may as well conclude here. As we saw, the psychoanalytic theory not only lacks any scientific basis but is absurd in every respect. It could be therefore dismissed as a pseudo-scientific faith, similar to astrology, alchemy or belief in witchcraft. Sober scientists are doing just that. *But this does not help, so long as modern psychology cannot offer any other explanations of the ghost phenomena that are clearly there and for which psychoanalysis provides a sufficient though equally ghostlike theory.* We hope we have covered enough of this theory to show how unnecessary and absurd it is in the light of *relative causation which provides simple causal explanations instead.*

Before we end, we wish to point out two most objectionable errors perpetuated by psychoanalysis. The first is the scaring of people by the claim that repressions are the source of mental illnesses. Actually, all higher cultural, as well as normal, individual adjustment rests on repression or restriction, which alone can make available more varied and wider satisfactions. But experimental "scientism" shows just the reverse to be true; and psychoanalysts are by far the most articulate expounders of freedom in emotional life. They can scare people because they speak as doctors in the name of medicine. Who would risk his mental health against the advice of a doctor? The fear of restricting children, and the anxiety that a child's personality may be warped because of the slightest incident, have been dominating many of the more advanced homes and schools thanks to the psychoanalytic "enlightenment."

The second error is the perpetuation of the alchemistic reasoning that an emotionally unimportant incident may cause great emotional distress, or that a skillful manipulation may produce emotional gain. As we have showed repeatedly, the law of the equivalence of emotions is as strict in psychology as the law of the equivalence of matter is in chemistry. The practical significance of this truth is important. To the extent people realize that they cannot get something for nothing in their emotional lives, they are more ready to accept the restrictions and cultural conditioning that make more normal motivations available. On the other hand, the alchemistic beliefs can lead to endless and wasteful fixations on cures and emotional improvements, ending with more neurosis. On the theoretical side, such an approach obscures further the simple causal truths on which psychology as a science will be built.

175

VI

THE PARADOX OF ADJUSTMENT

The main paradox of adjustment is that a *person can be normally adjusted only as long as he has disturbances or needs — which he considers as maladjustment.* Satisfaction or pleasure is the source of all motivation, but no satisfaction can exist where there is no need, which means disturbance. To the extent that a person attains a state without disturbances — which to him means ideal adjustment — he finds himself in a state of complete immobility where there can be no motivation, will power, love or anything. The next step is overadjustment and neurosis. The right education consists in imposing as many needs as possible on the growing individual. This is done by restricting or not permitting the natural satisfactions, and by conditioning them into more circuitous, cultural behavior.

Another paradox of adjustment is that *the individual who lives under the tightest system of conditioned restrictions does not feel them.* We do not feel the atmosphere we live in. We feel only the changes or differences in it. A highly civilized man living under constant conditioned restrictions feels only his freedoms, whereas a person with few conditioned restrictions — a juvenile delinquent, for instance — feels strongly the restrictions by others around him, and the stifling of his natural interests.

A further paradox, connected herewith, is that *the really important factors determining adjustment are causal backgrounds so general that they are not noticed.* This is important, because the modern psychologist or human scientist is looking for factors that are felt as salient or remarkable. In fact, such factors are exceptions to the general backgrounds, therefore causally least

176

important. We may recall here what we said about the conditioning of the most general needs of growth, security or competition. Neither the conditioning nor such needs are noticed, though they determine that the person is or does.

We are being conditioned at every moment and in regard to every reaction. The cultural environment determines what we can do and in what way. But we do not notice what is happening because of its universality. We notice only exceptions to what is "normal." We never feel strongly about the fact that we, like all people, want to do the "right" thing, are ashamed of doing what is "wrong" or "indecent," are afraid of losing the love or respect of others, obey some authority, love our parents or children and so on. Only if somebody does *not* have such reaction do we notice it — and find it utterly freakish, though in itself it could be equally "normal." For the same reason we would notice, and find it extraordinary, if somebody did *not* want to be secure, grow or be superior.

EDUCATION

The fact that the conditioning of the fundamental needs remains unnoticed is a source of endless confusion in the theory of education. Everybody knows that education is the hardest task and an art requiring hundreds of years of perfection; hence the decisive importance of tradition. But at the same time education seems to come about by itself, as if completely naturally. An additional source of confusion is the fact that the restrictions of conditioning can be imposed only in the name of pleasure, the same as a stream can be turned, so that it finally may flow in an opposite direction, only by its own flow.

The confusion shows particularly in the theories about the role of natural interests in education. Great theorists have stressed the freedom of self-expression, the fulfillment of the individual nature, and the fostering of the child's own, natural interests. In a controversy about the goals of our present education, Clarence H. Faust, President of the Fund for Advancement of Education, stated that the full flowering of the individual and the discovery of truths by the individual himself is the goal. Dewey held that all we can do is to let the interests of the pupil prevail, and to permit him to engage in activities that he is interested in for their own sake. Huxley considered the "warping of the structure of personality" a grave danger. Bernard Shaw said that the vilest abortionist is he who attempts to mold the mind of the child. Hutchins has stated that human nature is given at birth and is not conditioned. Whitehead emphasized that the student should be exposed to interesting ideas — which can only be natural interests — rather than forced into learning. The movement of progressive or free education, with Bertrand Russell as its great philosopher, is based on the belief in natural interests.

Of course, there are equally strong opponents to such ideas, especially among practical educators. This is exactly the point. There is a lack of theoretical understanding of what makes education work. The great thinker looks inside himself, and sees how he himself can do only what interests him. And any experimental observation shows that only pleasure can provide motivation. Actually, neither these interests nor the pleasure are possible without an opposite background of restrictions or needs, which has to be created by conditioning. But such causal explanation is completely strange, in its every aspect, to any theorist because it implies that feelings of disvalue are the real source of our feelings and notions of value. Theorists therefore see interests as being there by themselves. And since it is not fashionable any more to refer to Providence directly, these interests are assumed to be given by nature — to be natural.

What are our natural interests? First, there are the fundamental biological needs like hunger, sex and physiological growth. Then there are the functions that are conditioned only biologically. From these derive the interests of a child in hitting or breaking things, splashing paint, exploring the environment in primitive ways, playing with water or mud and so on. A higher animal, like a chimpanzee, exhibits such interests strongly. One level higher are such interests as hunting, fishing, shooting, playing ball, showing one's own strength by attacking an adversary or erecting something that has instantaneous, splashy effect. In a word, everything that is "cheap" and crude, or that releases pleasure without effort, constitutes the natural interests. The cheap Western, the crude comic book, the grisly criminal or sex story—they are the real treasures of natural interests. People enjoy them easily, and their producers can make them cheaply because they come naturally. Those who enjoy them are not abnormal. They are more normal and natural than other people. They can rightly call all other interests phony and hypocritical. If our natural interests were not crippled by conditioning, we would also consider the above interests as the only genuine ones.

There are other relative aspects without which conditioning must remain a mystery. One of the most important is obsessional perfectionism, under which a person feels a greater lack of and need for a value as more of it is given to him. For instance, protection or love is given to a child to the highest degree in a highly cultural environment. But the more protected a child becomes, the more he seeks for further, exquisite love and protection. A civilized adolescent is turned into a soft-skinned perfectionist, for whom the need for love becomes as compulsive as obsessive reactions are for the neurotic. This applies to all cultural values —social success, excellence in knowledge or virtue, compliance with moral or religious beliefs, and competition for any value that happens to come to the general attention. This also explains the mysterious self-perpetuation of social uniformity. In a word, cultural refinement and perfectionism become a source of self-increasing, cultural pressures.

Naturally, such cultural fixations require a hothouse atmosphere into which stronger, more natural interests have no chance to intrude. Hence the importance of close family life, and of the general cultural level of the social environment, which explains in its turn the mysterious role of long cultural tradition. The cultural environment or previous background determines the methods of education. A refined method applied to children from a rough environment becomes a parody. The controversies about more progressive versus older methods rest on a misunderstanding. The practice of corporal punishment in earlier education, for

179

instance, was not due to mere ignorance. A nice theory could not have replaced the rod. Teachers have always known how love works. Theories like those of Rousseau, Pestalozzi or Froebel did not appear earlier because they could not have worked earlier, and therefore would have been nonsensical. Such theories were products of cultural advance, not the other way around.

The modern theorist has plenty of opportunity now to observe how excellently these free and refined methods work. But if he accepts freedom or refinement in itself as the source of success, and misses as usually the background causation, he is in for a great misunderstanding. A practical example may illustrate best what happens. Redl tells in his book, *Children Who Hate*, of an experiment in which maladjusted children taken from a rougher cultural environment were put for eighteen months on a special educational program. They were placed in a special home which offered them complete, unconditioned freedom, all refined opportunities, protection from the slightest threat, total self-decision, no enforcement of discipline, and nothing but unconditional love. The result was just the reverse of what was expected. The hardened children "progressed" in their independent status and in their crude, truly natural interests — which always resemble delinquency. The love was completely wasted on them.

Actually, they did not feel any need for love because they knew that whatever they did would be met with the same love and approval. Love is conditioned satisfaction of the need for security, which in value terms is as contrary to love as every need is to satisfaction. If there had been implied threats or discipline, the children would have started to develop some need for cooperation — which gradually could have turned into more refined satisfaction and love. Redl was surprised at the ingeniousness of the children in preserving their "delinquent" ways, and at their "legalistic" skill in finding weak points in the arguments of their educators. In fact, it is not difficult to see the inconsistencies of moral education if one is free from the distortions of conditioning and preserves his natural viewpoint.

Redl concluded that the children were a special kind of Children who Hate — having delinquent Egos, and "beyond the reach of education." He found that there were twenty-two functions of the Ego that had gone wrong, and needed a "large-scale research." In fact, the children seem to have been quite normal. In a close traditional environment, average sensible parents would have turned them into normal persons — without any large-scale research or concern for any twenty-two functions. It would have been difficult to catch up with the lack of conditioning in their past. Something that has gone for years, especially the formative years of early chilhood, cannot be changed in days or months. But sensible parents could have coped even with that — by firmly and gradually imposing a discipline first, then transforming it into a more refined dependence, which is the natural source of love.

The role of negative feelings, largely threat and restriction, is completely misunderstood in modern theory. Of course, it is love, and release in the form of self-realization, freedom and pleasurable interest, that constitute motivation. But these feelings are satisfactions that cannot exist without needs, which emotionally are as different from the nice satisfactions as hell is from heaven. Love is a feeling of security, but without a concurrent threat it has no emotional basis. Naturally, the threat has not to be realized. If it is, it loses its effects. If one starts beating his child, he has to beat him all the time. The threat has to be maintained as an object of obsessional avoidance, which becomes more compulsive as it is perfected. If this neurotic perfectionism in avoidance of threat is not there, as need, there can be no satisfaction in doing right things. Then threat has to be applied in the form of punishment.

The disadvantages of punishment are apparent. Man evades thinking of bad things and forgets about the possibility of punishment until it is too late. That is why it is important to create a background of threat first so that only satisfactions lie ahead and are eagerly sought for. A further disadvantage of punishment is that a forcibly repressed behavior breaks out with double force after the restraint is removed, because while restriction is enforced a person enjoys by anticipation the forbidden behavior. However, punishment is not a complete loss. A twig when bent springs back; but it grows bent if the force is unremitting.

During restraint under punishment the person may suffer a little bit more and lose the hope of return to the old habit a little bit more than the anticipated enjoyment. Such suffering and resignation may amount to a gradual accumulation of background enabling new, more refined interests.

An ironic situation results where a permissive and a restrictive educator bring up a child together. The first gets all the praise, though he lowers the motivational level, and the second all the blame, though he raises it. In a family with a permissive mother and stern father children follow the wishes of the mother and resist those of the father; have all the love and readiness to co-operate with her and only hate and resistance toward him. But if the sternness of the father is taken away, the permissiveness of the mother loses meaning. Then there is nothing to be relieved from. The mother could continue to be more and more permissive, but she would end with complete licentiousness, from which it is only one step to delinquency. The same applies to "free" or "progressive" education. The free educator gets his spectacular results by debasing the background of the pupil, built by others.

As can be expected, the question of love becomes confusing. On one hand, we all know that the child who is loved without restraint becomes a spoilt child. And cultural tradition tells us that the spoilt child grows into a maladjusted person, or a criminal. L. Navratil found, by studying hundreds of alcoholics, that the spoilt child or favorite son is the potential maladjusted individual or alcoholic. On the other hand, everybody knows that the greater the love in which children grow, the greater the cultural success. Why should the great love do harm in one case and good in another? The mother of a juvenile delinquent has the right to ask what could she have done wrong when she had nothing but endless love for her boy.

Psychologists are trying hard to blame restriction even in the case of the spoilt child. When a research team at the Medical Research Council found that the "mama's boy" is the one who gets ulcers, it explained that overloving mothers are dominant and restrict their children. This explanation is probably the most popular one among psychologists, though every sensible man can see that the spoilt or overloved child is the one who gets everything the way he wants it. There are other theories which attempt to explain why excess of love becomes harmful. Deepening of the Oedipal complex, the vengeance of the Superego or splitting of the libido may be blamed by those who tend toward mystifications. But the more rational explanations are equally inane. Adler held that the overprotected child concludes from the attitude of his parents that the world must be dangerous — as if rational conclusions mattered. Anyway, psychologists see restriction, fear or other negative experiences as the source of the negative attitude of the spoilt child. Plain common sense and cultural tradition tell us that the reason is lack of training and discipline, which rest exactly on such negative feelings of restriction and fear.

There are no mysteries, and no sophisticated formulas, to be observed. Love does not work differently because there is too much of it. The difference lies in the completely different approach to love. The right kind of love cultivates obsessive perfectionism in avoidance of implied threats. Because such conditioning is started early, it grows out of nothing more than fear of withdrawal of parental protection or favor and never needs any other threats. Parents achieve such masterful conditioning by simply treating the child as a part of themselves. This is the natural basis for parental love anyway. Sensible parents wish happiness for the child as they wish it for themselves. They suffer when they have to be harsh; the perfectionism of refinement is maintained high. But they also fear that something terrible will happen to the child — as they believe it would happen to them — if he does wrong. They want to avoid this as they would avoid harm to a part of themselves. Thus the love, which means security for the child, is subordinated to, or conditioned on, the avoidance of wrong under threat.

It is true that a child who loses the love of parents or the security of home is the potential delinquent. But the reason is not a feeling of insecurity or inadequacy. Just the reverse is true. A child who has lived through such an all-powerful trauma no longer has the childish feelings of insecurity or dependence that normal children have. The paradox of opposite causation shows here clearly. Homeless children, like the *"bezprizornye"* in Russia after the Revolution, are fearless, self-sufficient, hardened, premature "grownups." They can resist and ignore anybody. Of course, such children deserve compassion, but it is naïve to imagine that they feel insecure or crave love and dependence, however sophisticated such an argument is often made.

In education as everywhere in psychology, the weight and duration of emotions matter, not incidents or skills in manipulating them. For instance, you can have a most liberal occasional discussion with a child on sex matters, and it will make no difference in his feelings about the taboo of sex. Actually, the behavior that is really important is so much taken for granted that nobody speaks or even thinks about it. For the same reason, there is no harm in a child's arguing, or rising in revolt against a suggestion. As long as he remains in the same atmosphere of values, he will deepen his fixations on such values even while arguing that he "knows better" — as children constantly do. He will only gain the impression that he decided for himself. All this explains why keeping child away from outside influences and within the family or selected cultural medium is more important than anything else. The family is the hothouse of cultural growth; and a rich family life is the miracle panacea of education.

The good advice, logical arguments and great truths of educators, which seem so important to everybody, have in themselves little influence. The greatest philosopher or moral teacher has less influence than the insignificant guy one happens to live with continuously. *The real influences come from where our continuous emotions lie.* Even a reasonable person placed amidst criminals evolves criminal standards and ambitions rather than reasonable ones. This dependence of everybody upon others around him, as regards the evolution of his sense of values, explains why the *average* cultural level of a given society determines the cultural standards of everybody.

Those who resist integration, at school or in social intercourse, with culturally lower groups like Negroes are not just brainless bigots. Logically, it may seem that one does not have to follow the lower standards of the group. But practically, even by despising or trying to ignore culturally lower people, *with whom one has to be together constantly*, one lowers his own cultural standards. When one despises somebody, he elevates himself, which means becoming more complacent about himself. A person living among people who do not wash would feel himself excellently clean even by washing only once a month. The psychological life is determined by *emotions*. Therefore the simplest constant factors that evoke emotions are decisive, not any reasons or remarkable and involved influences.

We do not intend to say that the segregation of Negroes is desirable. On the contrary, by recognizing that the general environment is decisive, we recognize that Negroes would be handicapped forever if left in their segregated environment. No "equal" opportunities can help without actual integration. Practice has shown this to be so. Integration is desirable because it brings about an over-all improvement in the end, as the more cultural tendencies finally prevail. At least it produces equalization, which is necessary for effective social cooperation. But while the integration goes on, the higher group suffers debasement in its cultural standards. People resisting integration know this intuitively, from practical experience, and try to protect their children from it.

Though conditioning is the basis of education, its theoretical understanding is not necessary in everyday education. The traditional attitude, based on the plainly naïve beliefs in God, morals and conscience, is the best. As we saw, conditioning implies deceiving. But the educator has to be sincere in his wish to care for the happiness of the pupil, the same as the loving parents are. If he were not, the pupil would feel it and would instinctively resist him. Education is an intuitive art. As long as the educator strives to make the pupil cultivated, the right means of conditioning are found. Even the "free" educator produces restrictive conditioning, by simply trying to make the pupil as cultivated as he is himself. In fact, such an educator would tolerate as little as anybody else natural interests which he *theoretically* tries to promote.

Neither the believers in the soul and Providence nor the progressive educators follow their theories in practice. If there were a Providence and a soul with a ready-made conscience, education would be a clearly sacrilegious interference with God's design. Actually, the believer in the soul works as hard on the *transformation* of the behavior of his children as he combats nature while cultivating his fields; "Providence" is either fought against or ignored as nonexisting. By the way, the conscience — the great gift of Providence — follows the same paradoxical rule that all natural or conditioned feelings do: it effaces itself by its own operation. Logically, the feeling of conscience should increase by accumulation. But everybody knows that it is lost if one keeps accumulating it, namely, by doing wrong, which is the way to arouse this feeling. Apparently, conscience is not part of normalcy or a permanent mechanism: as such it would improve upon exercise. Rather, it is a conditioned value feeling — a result of disturbance in normalcy — and as such grows out of opposite values. The same as love, the noble feeling of conscience derives from a conditioned base threat or need for security, and grows into a compulsion through perfectionistic refinement.

Actually, the generality of the belief in conscience proves the generality of conditioning. The "conscience" is certainly the most important factor in behavior. If this feeling is missing, no amount of reasoning or rational skill can help. There is nothing reasonable or natural in morals. We follow its rules only because we are conditioned so that we cannot obtain the satisfaction of our need for security in any other way. If a person does succeed in obtaining the satisfaction in a *direct* way, he easily throws overboard all morals. This happens in the cases of drug addiction as well as all physiological or psychological intoxications, one of which is sexual love. Conditioning also explains why morals can be so different for different people or for the same people living in different societies. It can be said that *all cultural values are conditioned satisfactions or pleasures.* This explains causally everything else in motivation.

As to the belief of the free educator in natural interests, if they were there, education would be sought irresistibly like the pleasures of eating, drinking or sex. And the more you restrained this striving, the stronger it would break out. The delusion of a "natural thirst" for higher interests arises from the fact that the accumulation of needs, through conditioning, which cause the "thirst," is not noticed. Nobody pays attention to needs as everybody strives only for satisfactions; and as we saw, a causal connection between the two is never suspected.

Another strong reason for the belief in free education is, probably, the observation that any endeavor to force something on the pupil produces rather an opposite reaction. An exaggerated enforcement of religiousness, for instance, may produce an ardent atheist. This cannot be different, in the light of opposite causation. Hence the importance of the method of conditioning, by which new pathways are formed in the name of satisfactions. These are determined by the needs and value goals generally accepted in the society. Anything that goes beyond them is felt as exaggeration and can lead only to opposite reaction.

Actually, in every conditioning a resistance and opposition, or at least a temporary paralyzing moment, are the primary effects. Conditioning means a gradual blocking, like a damming up, of the more natural drives, so that a potential for new satisfactions, like a pressure for breaking new pathways, can accumulate. In other words, the restriction or need in the form of nonsatisfaction is the source of satisfaction here as everywhere else. But the "scientific" approach reveals only the immediate resistance upon restriction; and the rule of the equivalence of emotions is not even suspected. As a result, restrictions are blamed for all difficulties, and an alchemistic formalism is used in explanation. Naturally, this has led to endless contradictions and alchemistic mystery, whereas even the common-sense rule that you never get something, good or bad, for nothing could serve as a better guide.

As the mystery deepens, explanations are increasingly sought in the experiences of early infancy. Apparently, the experiences that a person can remember and analyze for himself do not fit the proffered explanations. It is true that the formation during early infancy is important. But it is so only for the physiological substratum, for the animal stage, on which the personality depends only indirectly. The psychological personality begins with conscious experiences and with its own strict pleasure-displeasure economy on which everything else depends. The theories of modern psychologists about dangers in handling infants, teaching them stool habits or enforcing discipline are products of mystified minds searching frantically for some explanation. Stool training is stool training and ends with the acquisition of that skill. Enforcement of discipline, which means, of restrictions, is the very essence of education. This is the basic truth to which theorists return after they have had to deal with the full scope of long-range practical problems. The oldest authority in the field, Dr. Spock, has gradually reversed his views in regard to parental authority, and recognizes in his latest book, *The Problems of Parents*, that such enforcement follows from the very nature of parent-child relationship.

If what modern psychologists say about the influence of restrictions during early infancy were true, most of the primitive peoples would be wretched neurotics. Most infants in Eastern Europe, Asia, Africa and among American Indians were, and often still are, kept stiffly bound, or restricted in other ways during infancy. It certainly looks as if tradition has taught these people that restriction has value in itself. In any event, such people suffer least from neurotic disturbances. Even as regards temporary physical deformation, the tenacity of the organism takes over and the infants grow into healthy normal individuals. For instance, it was found that Albanian infants, bound stiffly to wooden cradles for a whole year and kept in darkness, with cloth over their heads, soon recovered from a certain amount of muscular uncoordination and later scored in tests as well as Viennese children.

Interesting in this respect are experiments on the influence of cuddling on the growth of children. The experiments showed that lack of cuddling produced slower growth — just as the experimenters expected. But fortunately the children were still there after the experiments were over, so that later effects could show. The final result was that there was no difference between the children who received more cuddling and those who were deprived of it.

At this point we may mention the curious fact that persons who have some physical handicap attain, in general, success, even prominence, more often than normal persons. At the same time it has been proven that physically well-developed individuals have

188

higher intellectual capacities — as can be easily understood. Apparently, a person starting with a definite maladjustment does better even with less capacities. We can only conjecture how much more success physically well-developed persons would gain if our educators knew how to impose on them "maladjustment."

ABSTRACT LEARNING

What we just said about education in general applies to abstract learning as well. Conditioning and learning are the same universal devices of adjustment — the transformation of cruder reactions into more refined ones. In abstract learning as well, the purpose is the evolution of new, more refined and more numerous satisfaction pathways. In practice, the main task is the creation of the specific needs that make such satisfactions arise. Such needs are created by restriction of the more general satisfactions and leaving only certain satisfactions open, as in all conditioning.

What is usually seen as learning or understanding comes by way of satisfactions that follow easily and automatically from previously formed needs. Here we may mention the classical experiments on judgments and reaction time, by Ach, Kuelpe, Marbe and others. These experiments showed that the preparation for a mental act — judging or giving a right response — took time and effort, whereas the actual judging or response was almost automatic. Another interesting phenomenon is the sudden emergence of a solution after one has worried long enough over it. Apparently, after the hard and unwanted part in the process is completed, the part that man sees as the learning proper follows easily by itself, as all satisfactions do. This agrees with the commonplace observation that learning is hard but also pleasant. How we learn or understand a thing we never know. We strive only for the end result, and in spite of ourselves accumulate the unpleasant background of needs — while looking all the time only for the satisfaction, here as everywhere else.

But when the theorist takes over, he ends with a completely erroneous theory. He sees the pleasant satisfactions as the essence of learning and tries to promote them, but rejects the unpleasant part in the process, which is the real source of the learning. No wonder "advancement" in our school education almost ended with the offering of not much more than entertainments, and with the rejection of the "old prejudices" about hard work.

One version of the theory of more pleasant teaching stresses the direct conveyance of what is interesting, to avoid dreary detail. Whitehead argued that interest should be given to students like a "contagious disease"; and that the higher teaching should aim at disclosing the main interests of the subjects learned rather than drilling in dreary details. We can understand, for instance, that an old history professor finds the policy of a certain ruler interesting and the whole story emerging before his eyes. Why not convey this interest to his students? The truth is that there are no ready-made intellectual interests. Anything can be interesting or not, depending upon previous background. To see the interesting point of a story, or to live with it, the student must first have a need to learn about it and an accumulated background relating to it all. That is where the enforced work and dreary details come in. The professor has forgotten that his own interest grew from his need to know, enforced by his own educators and life necessities. Once evolved, the set of the specific need-satisfaction pathways became an exclusive or fixational source of further satisfactions in his life, or a "natural" source of interest. In brief, the well-meaning humanists who reject dreary detail and enforced learning are rejecting the very source from which interest in learning grows.

In another version of the same thesis, theorists urge the teaching of the universal and immutable ideas expressed in the great books, instead of the transitory and changing secondary particulars. The great American educator, Hutchins, has been a prominent representative of this view. Theoretically, it may seem silly indeed to waste our efforts on trying to find out what has already been found out by the greatest minds. Why not start directly with the great truths of the human genius? The fact is that the great truths say nothing to those who do not have the background of sweat and toil lived through while finding them. A satisfaction, knowledge or truth acquires meaning only through previous need, laboriously evolved interests or enlarged background learning.

There are other educational theories and "discoveries" based on the worthy and seemingly logical observation that learning and spiritual interests are pleasant in themselves. Why not show this to others and induce them to share in the spiritual enjoyments? The learned scientist or humanist, the same as the common man, cannot accept the paradox of relative causation: he never sees the negative feeling as the cause of the positive one. He may understand that there can be no enjoyment of resting without the previous hardship of exertion, or of drinking without the suffering of thirst. But he can never accept that the background of unpleasant and negative experiences which he rejected and avoided have anything to do with the completely different pleasures and interests of learning which he now enjoys.

This misunderstanding about the causal source of learning is only a part of a wide general misunderstanding. Man values, strives for and formulates positive experiences, whereas he rejects, ignores and has no formulations for negative ones, which, however, are the real causal source of the former. Man does all right in practice, but theorists, proceeding with the same logic, produce completely wrong theories. *The end result is that in every field of the human sciences the theorists see positive values or reactions as the causal essences or sources to be valued and promoted; but deplore and try to eliminate the accumulation of negative backgrounds, that actually are the real causal sources from which the positive responses follow automatically, even irresistibly, as all satisfactions do. At best, these backgrounds are not noticed, especially where they are so general as to be omnipresent.*

The illusion that learning is caused by satisfaction takes subtle forms in practice. As one example we can mention instruction by use of vivid illustrations, movies or other pictorial presentations. The immediate success may be great, as more direct natural satisfactions are offered. But at the same time the background for learning in more abstract and less exciting ways is debased. A teacher using such methods alone could keep the interest and achievements from sagging only by offering more and more exciting presentations. Finally, he would have to end with cheap Westerns or comic books. The same applies to learning by doing things in naturally interesting ways, as advocated by the "progressive" educators. Receding toward what is naturally interesting means regressing from what is more complex and intellectual. If success were to continue in this way, education would have to continue regressing to entertainments of a primitive kind, and would end with the collapse of intellectual interests.

It is true that man has a natural predisposition to learn, or a natural curiosity, observable even in animals. But this is also a product of needs and restrictions. The chipmunk investigates a new thing in its environment under the restrictive conditioning of the same need for security that makes it run away from danger. A child strives to learn new things, or to contrive a more complex play, because, due to *restrictions* of inherited physiological conditioning, this is the only way he can obtain normal release. Though we do not know exactly how the restrictive mechanisms in the brain work, a simple principle is sufficient to explain it. If the neurons are restricted in such a way that releases can be obtained only upon connecting with numerous other neurons controlling other sensations, then such richer connections will be automatically searched for. The ways in which such a search goes on are then offered by the environment or cultural conditioning. Any more complex explanation is neither necessary nor possible for such clearly inheritable predispositions.

Apparently, we have to deal here with the continuation of general evolution, which, as we saw, proceeds by restrictive conditioning, with the development of the higher nervous system — the most restrictive mechanism — as its main characteristic. Anyway, more direct release or improved satisfaction can only destroy or weaken such predisposition. To be sure, the goal in the exercise of such a predisposition is satisfaction, therefore it may seem always to improve when better release is offered. The general paradox applies here as in any adjustment.

At this point we can mention IQ testing. The capacity to accept restrictions is the source of intellectual attainments. This capacity can be given by nature, and IQ testing measures it correctly so far. But this capacity can be further fostered, or hampered, by the influences of cultural conditioning and temperament. These cannot be accounted for by present IQ tests. This explains why IQ tests often assess the intelligence of some individuals or racial groups higher, or lower, than life shows it to be.

Another peculiarity of the way the mind works has to be mentioned. As we saw, natural or instinctive reactions in animal or man proceed along millions of points at every instant, whereas intellect works by way of generalizations or reduction of everything to "ones." Consequently, whereas somatic responses or the lower natural ways of learning are improved by enrichment of stimuli, the truly intellectual responses or learning are improved by the reduction of stimuli to single barest essentials. The less of natural stimulation there is, the easier and richer is abstract thinking and learning. It is not by accident that the scientist does his best in a windowless room, and with mathematical methods, which pre-eminently reduce everything to the barest "ones."

On the question of learning and effort, one cannot pass without mentioning the experiments by Ebbinghaus, or by other experimenters using his method. We cannot go into detail. But these experiments showed sufficiently that there is no way to learn well easily. The ways that were found more successful were also those that required more effort. The only advantage resulted from the possibility of relating material to be learned with sense-making ideas, which practically means with previous backgrounds of values or needs-satisfactions.

From all that we said, it is clear that restrictions and backgrounds of needs are the sources of abstract learning. In simple terms, the goal of learning is to restrict the releases to such an extent that even those stimuli are found interesting which offer only remote resemblance to true, natural interests or satisfactions. When the pathways of such satisfactions are established, a person has acquired a "natural," self-operating intellectual interest, without which learning is impossible.

But we have to remember that conditioning is to be used in imposing restrictions. This means they have to be imposed by way of offering pleasure, which is the only motivation in attaining any adjustment. That is why teaching is such a great, intuitive

193

skill and requires constant, strenuous effort. In the simplest case the young child is shown that the new way is also pleasant, though the purpose is to make him abdicate the more natural and inherently more pleasant old way. This device becomes extremely complex as education advances. Methods vary depending upon the tightness of supervision and the extensiveness of means used in channeling the interest. A course may be designed which looks like continuous play. In some experiments children permitted to play with specially designed machinery, under step-by-step guidance, have shown spectacular success. The famous Montessori method is based on the same principle, except that the devices used are simpler. There are several such methods using various devices and machines. They are useful if they make the channeling of interests easier by establishing more fitting or more continuously gradual transitions. But if only certain tricks or narrow subjects are learned, the purposes of education are not served. There is always the danger that the easiness and pleasantness of such methods may rather debase the restrictive backgrounds and lessen the interest value of more abstract reactions, as in the case of pictorial learning. The rule that you do not get something for nothing applies, in the end, here as well, since any form of learning or interest is a need-satisfaction process.

Now we may turn to specific problems of adjustment.

JUVENILE DELINQUENCY

The great social problem of our times, especially in the more advanced countries, is juvenile delinquency. It is an indicator of the downward trend in cultural conditioning. Every trend, positive or negative, is difficult to establish because the old inertial fixations perpetuate themselves automatically. But a new, easier trend has more chance of influencing the younger people — before they are steeped with years in the prevailing old tradition. Thus delinquency reflects the modern trend toward freer and more natural behavior. Such directly more satisfactory behavior has been made possible by the unprecedented improvements in modern living conditions. Of course, the feeling of improvement is relative.

A class of people may be still poor but they may feel that they can afford freer attitudes upon reaching an improvement that is high *in relation* to their previous condition.

What are the main characteristics of a juvenile delinquent? Under the logic of experimental observation he seems to suffer from maladjustment, lack of love by his parents or others around him, excessive restrictions and denial of self-expression. That is what is usually discovered in his personality. But as we saw, a really restricted individual would neither feel nor complain about any restrictions; or an individual so strongly conditioned that he has no "self-expression" at all would never know that he is suffering from lack of it. As to love, children who are expected to do their duties before they are loved have no complaints about a lack of love, whereas the pampered child clamors constantly that he is not loved enough.

In this light we can understand the general confusion among psychologists as to the real causes of delinquency. During the previously mentioned Cornell Conference (see *Mental Health: a Critique*) psychologists recognized that the mysteries of personality have not been solved, and that psychologists are unable to explain or predict the development of either a normal or a delinquent personality. If the psychologist wants to obtain a prediction, he has to use the old traditional rather than scientific criteria. In this connection can be mentioned the research project of Sheldon and Eleanor Glueck, which has been operating for decades and has produced a prediction method that has been widely recognized. The common sense criteria of cruelty, neglect, hostility, erratic discipline, lack of love, lax supervision and dissolute family ties have been used in these predictions. Naturally such an approach is as good as an intuition, and cannot offer a really scientific reliability. The Citizens Committee for Children of New York City complained that the predictions were wrong in two out of every three cases. This is understandable if we consider that such common-sense criterion as love, for instance, may represent two completely different things in terms of psychological causation.

The juvenile delinquent ends with the feelings we mentioned, because he starts with the highest freedom from restrictions and from childish fears or dependence. He has attained the best adjustment and the highest self-expression of his truly natural interests. These then mean the exertion of his physical force over the environment, breaking, destroying, assaulting; and unrestricted striving for own pleasure, which further means removing the resistance of others. Stealing, robbing or killing may become useful and necessary means. Justifications are always found, especially since the others around have become detestable obstacles. It is ridiculous to expect reasonable consideration for the feelings of others. Even a highly cultivated person does not hesitate to assert his superiority or power — in permitted ways — though this certainly hurts others. Characteristically enough, the juvenile delinquent often prides himself on being "tough." This expresses his natural self-assertion in its entirety. He intuitively knows that refinement — which is the key characteristic of everything cultural — means emaciation and crippling of the natural self.

Conditioning is sufficient to explain why delinquency may often look like it is inherited in a family. The capacity to be conditioned or restricted is inheritable. And the art of conditioning is inherited in each family from the previous generation as the way of life or moral atmosphere. The inertial self-perpetuation of traditions cannot be overemphasized. Of course, where the social medium is highly cultural a person with a low aptitude for conditioning becomes rather a "beatnik" or some other kind of freedom seeker, or simply a "difficult" person, rather than a criminal.

SEXUAL MALADJUSTMENT

In sexual maladjustment the paradox shows equally clearly. Under the logic of experimental observation the cause of maladjustment in sex matters is clearly restrictions or lack of satisfaction. But it is generally known that people who live under real sexual restrictions, as youth does in a morally high environment, or as monks do, suffer little from sexual maladjustments. On the other hand, those who have better opportunities for sexual satisfactions, like morally undisciplined youth, and persons living in a licentious atmosphere, have real sexual maladjustments. The truth is that even animals can live without ever satisfying the sexual drive at its genital stage. In fact, man or animal lives longer and is healthier under such conditions. Especially in man the sexual drive is highly elastic, since his sexual needs are not dictated by strict seasonal or biological factors.

We have to remember that sex as usually understood means only the genital stage of the reproductive function. This function is too important to be ever suppressed. But the suppression of the last, pleasurable phase of it means only reserving the pleasure for other, related motivations. Enjoyment of art, literature and beauty in general, social attractions and social play are the more direct outlets for such sustained sexual pleasure. Trouble starts when there is full satisfaction and a further tendency to derive still more direct sexual pleasure. This leads to overadjustment with all its physiological and psychological disturbances.

Sexual perversions, such as homosexuality, are due to removal of the restrictions by which sexual differentiation and attraction to the opposite sex evolve. The restrictions may be lost upon strong, continuous sexual overenjoyments. The perversion may be innate — probably as a result of such overenjoyments in previous generation, just as our intuition, common sense and moral tradition tell us. We shall discuss genetics later; it is enough here to think of the simple fact that the biological self does continue, as if uninterruptedly, through generations. Of course, a perversity may originate as a habit. Once a way for release is found, it strengthens itself automatically. Absence of conditioned or sublimated sexual outlets is to blame, more than the strict segregation of sexes. Incidentally, there may be some truth in the story of psychoanalysts that the son of a widow is often a homosexual. Exaggerated lavishment of feminine love on him may induce an opposite reaction. Or he may be emotionally averse to connecting femininity, of which he received so much from his mother, with the very different sexual feelings.

If permitted to be enjoyed unrestrictedly, the sexual function would become the whole fulfillment of life, as it biologically is meant to be, and the only genuine enjoyment. Human culture, as well as biological conditioning among higher animals, has advanced side by side with restrictions on sexual satisfactions. Family life among animals and men is nurtured by continuous, never fully satisfied sexual needs. All cultural norms, religions and morals invariably aim at the restriction of sexual enjoyments. But, as usual, humanistic superstitions are given as the reasons. Therefore, it is easy for a rationalistic "scientist" to demonstrate how we are crippling our nature and opposing the greatest, most beautiful force in ourselves for stupid reasons. The call for more realistic attitudes toward sex is the main characteristic of modern scientism in the field of adjustment. The cultural tradition, which restricts sexual enjoyments, harbors an intuitive compliance with relative causation. The sexual enjoyments are so strong that any lesser interests, especially the more refined, intellectual ones, lose their effect beside them. Complete sexual satisfaction approaches the fulfillment of all goals, but higher adjustment requires that there be continuous search for new, varied forms of attaining satisfaction that is never complete.

Sexual compatibility in marriage has been made a great issue in modern life. Whereas in other times cultural tradition has been against sexual criteria in marriage, modern man can afford to be free in this matter as well. The belief in the pleasure release as the means of better adjustment supports such an attitude. It is true that in marriages which break up the most frequent cause is sexual dissatisfaction. But this is so because those marriages which break up are mostly those which have been founded primarily on sex. In such marriages dissatisfaction or "incompatibility" becomes inevitable. Here we may recall what we said about a person finding one fault or another with food as he becomes satiated with it.

Marriages last in proportion as other interests than sex are their goal. The great simple truth about marriage is that it has to be much more than a sexual relationship if it is to meet the demands of reality squarely. A spouse who is loved during the night more than he, or she, deserves will be so much hated during the day for his inadequacies, of which there will be plenty,

198

as a person interested mainly in sex cannot be too successful in other things. Marriages founded on sex are turmoils of strong love and strong hate. Improvements in sexual enjoyments, such as instruction in better love techniques, is the worst thing that can happen to a marriage. That is why cultural tradition abhors them. But psychologists, proceeding in the logical experimental way come to different conclusions. Such an authority as Karl Menninger praises in his book, *Love Against Hate*, the doctors who give instruction in techniques of love-making.

The selection of a sexual partner on the basis of attraction is an important matter. It has remained the only form of natural selection for the improvement of the human race. Nothing can compete with the miraculously purposeful natural mechanisms in combining couples so that the best reproduction is insured. The goals of nature coincide here with cultural goals insofar as healthier offspring are also more intelligent. But nature has also the goal of rapid and vigorous reproduction for the sake of reproduction. Correspondingly, mere sex appeal often attracts more than do other qualities. The solution lies in the cultural refinements of romantic love, which bring in intellectual and spiritual factors. This gradually changes tastes in the selection of partners. That is why cultural tradition favors many forms of sexual romance though it generally imposes taboos on the subject of sex.

OVERWEIGHT

A typical maladjustment of modern man is overweight. The reason is overenjoyment of food. Any food is tasteful to the extent that it offers release in the rate of growth and metabolism. Exaggerated acceleration of this rate must lead to its slow-down or to organic sluggishness. Since modern man disposes of a wide variety of means of stimulation, including every possible refinement of foods, he meets any such slow-down with even further overadjustment. Thus organic sluggishness deepens and the person has to eat more of the tasty foods just to derive some release. Overexpenditure in the rate of metabolism, followed by overweight, goes together with an exciting, more stimulating life, as everybody can easily observe. Sometimes a person cannot help overexpending, because he may need more stimulation or motivation to carry out the tasks which engage him.

Since striving for more release of pleasure is the cause of overweight, it can tie in with other psychological problems. Loss of one stimulation, as when smoking is discontinued, may be compensated by overeating. Psychologists speak of substitution of the "mouth satisfactions of infancy." Leo H. Bernstein, in his study on connections between oversmoking, overeating and overdrinking, has used this explanation. In fact, the person simply seeks for more release, and if one means is discontinued, he turns to another. The person may be unable to operate with lesser releases due to previous overstimulation, even in the previous generation.

As in all cases of overadjustment, the relation between cause and effect here is seemingly paradoxical. The same food that reduces leads to overweight in the end; the increase in rate of metabolism leads to increased exhaustion and slow-down. Inversely, food that gives less stimulation, and therefore is usually fattening, can help reducing in the long run. This has led to unsolvable controversies. Dr. Taller wrote a best-seller, showing that a person can eat fats and still lose weight. Naturally, those who hold such views, like their opponents, seek for logical explanations of the paradox, and produce only more confusion.

The best evidence of the paradox is probably the Rockefeller Diet. Subjects were permitted to eat as much as they wanted of foodstuffs, like fats and starches, which ordinarily are fattening. But they were permitted only a certain amount of proteins. Reducing in weight resulted, but subjects complained that the foods tasted hopeless. The paradoxical logic that this experiment implies is, naturally, unacceptable to scientists. Dr. Harris, who directed the experiment, sought explanations in the corruption of natural tastes by modern techniques of food promotion. Roy de Groot, who wrote a book on the Diet, held similar views.

Under the same paradoxical logic, all the means that reduce weight spectacularly, through increased metabolism, lead to increased overweight in the end. Here can be mentioned smoking, drinking, drugs, sensational reducing techniques, as well as psychological overstimulation. The stimulating overbusy modern living that is clearly weight-reducing in its direct effects leads to overweight in the long run, as everybody can easily observe.

SMOKING AND DRINKING

The purpose of smoking and drinking is to remove the restrictions of biological and cultural conditioning so that more release, in the form of increased metabolism, becomes available. We do not need to repeat here the seemingly paradoxical effects that follow every overadjustment. But we would like to say a few words about the breaking of the habit. The first rule is that it brings exactly as much negative emotion as there were positive or pleasurable emotions derived from the habit; and that the process is equal but opposite in all other respects.

Usually there is a strong paralysis of the restrictive mechanisms, such as the supposed Nissl's granules, during the initial stage of addiction, with corresponding strong pleasure release. Later the restrictive mechanisms intensify, in order to re-establish normalcy in spite of the narcotic; and the person only keeps at bay the excessive onrush of restrictions which would follow if the narcotic were discontinued. During later stages, therefore, there is no additional enjoyment. Reversely, during the initial period of breaking the addiction there is a strong opposite feeling of displeasure, as the mechanisms, used to operate under suppression by the narcotic, take over excessively. Soon, however, the mechanisms readjust to normal functioning and there is no more suffering. Of course, the person may have compensated for the initial suffering by some anticipated future enjoyment or some other emotional compensation, and therefore may continue having emotional difficulties much longer.

In any event, plain, readily accepted suffering, rather than any skills, formulas or sudden decisions, is necessary to break the habit. One should prepare long and thoroughly, drawing together all one's motivation, if the breaking of addiction is to be successful. The main motivation can be derived from the evaluation of alternatives between slavery to the habit and a free productive life — neither of which can give more, or less, in the total enjoyment or happiness anyway. This coming to grips with hard reality explains why an alcoholic is helped better by Alcoholics Anonymous, where he faces reality and sees the real-life alternatives, than by the existing psychological analyses and therapies. These rest mostly on sophistry. Psychologists find all kinds of causes for smoking except the simple real cause — pleasure. Dr. Maurice J. Barry, for instance, explains that smoking is caused by a desire to defy authority, share mutual companionship or obtain oral gratification. Dr. Lester suggests psychoanalysis on the assumption that a smoker smoking twenty-five cigarettes a day is giving himself twenty-five breast feeds. But those who eschew ghost stories cannot give any better explanation, and may see cigarettes as an aid to social poise or keeping the hands busy. The simple real cause, the pleasure release, the same as the rule of the equivalence of emotions, is not recognized at the present alchemistic stage of modern psychology.

USE OF DRUGS

Increased use of all kinds of drugs and pills is a prominent characteristic of modern life. The expenditure on drugs in this country is to be counted not in millions but in billions of dollars yearly. Sleeping pills alone are consumed at the rate of twenty million a day. More pills and drugs are used for other purposes — stimulation, relief from all kinds of pains and headaches, or the removal of any unpleasant reaction — without asking what is the cause of the ill or what function the reaction performs.

The typical fact is that the same simple pill, such as aspirin, gives relief from all kinds of pains or reactions, somatic as well as psychological. Apparently, the function of the drug is simply to paralyze the mechanisms of control and alarm. The drug is too ridiculously simple to rebuild anything in the organic tissue — but completely sufficient to disrupt its normalcy. It all amounts to shutting off a warning system when disaster is on. Naturally, the real ill accumulates. It may be driven deeper by use of an increased dosage or another subtler pill. The result may be real abnormalcy or malignancy.

As more ingenious means for the control of releases become accessible to man, he destroys more successfully the limitations of his normalcy, in a misunderstood and ultimately self-defeating effort to derive more pleasurable feelings.

HEADACHES

Use of drugs against headaches is a typical example of the attempts of man to overcome his unpleasant organic reactions. A headache is an alarm signal serving to initiate organic readjustments against various abnormalities in the blood, internal organs or intestines, in which the pain may not be felt directly. At present people have incomparably better means for improving and enjoying all those functions that can cause headaches. But the end result is that 60 percent of the people in this country are suffering from headaches, according to a study on 5,000 persons, reported by Dr. Henry Ogden. The main sufferers are people to whom the means of improvement are most available: medical students topping the list, professionals, executives and the more educated people. Farmers, to whom such means are less available, suffer least.

In simpler cases the paradox of opposite causation in regard to headaches is directly evident. A drink or cigarette relieves the reactions of stress and tension which are generally recognized as the causes of headaches. But everybody knows that smoking and drinking is the surest way of landing into headache trouble. In most cases, however, the opposite causation is not so clearly evident. It is always difficult to see a correspondence between opposite emotions. The pleasant emotions that we enjoy upon release are felt as being rich and varied, because we follow them closely and attach so much ideational content to them. The headache may consist of equally rich and varied opposite emotions, but who cares to elaborate them? They are all felt as one big misery.

Study of headaches without regard to overadjustment is more confusing than revealing. This is the reason why existing explanations of the causes of headaches have remained superficial. Such things are blamed as the straining of neck muscles, glare of light, bending over work, postures producing contraction of blood vessels or tensing of muscles. Dr. Arnold P. Friedman, the foremost researcher on headaches, has pointed out such postures and tensions as being typical of headache sufferers. If physiological stresses and muscle tensions were the causes, farmers or physical workers would suffer headaches most, and medicine students or executives least.

Any attempt to explain the headache by logically connecting it with some definite body function or reaction is futile. The same body function or reaction may have a completely different meaning depending upon its relative purpose. There can be as great increase in circulation during the clogging up and exhaustion of tissues as there can be during their cleaning up and restoration. Dr. Harold G. Wolff, another prominent researcher on headaches, discovered experimentally that dilation of blood vessels can be the cause of headaches. But the dilation of blood vessels under stimulation by alcohol or drugs has exactly the opposite immediate effect. If the headache comes with the dilation of blood vessels, it may be an opposite aftereffect of a relaxant, like nicotine, which at first relieved headache by letting the vessels remain restricted.

SLEEPLESSNESS

The overadjustment nature of sleeplessness is best evident in connection with the use of sleeping pills. Doctors know that the more the pills are used, the deeper the problem of sleeplessness becomes. Of course, doctors see such "side" effects as an unfortunate incidence rather than causal inevitability.

Curiously enough, modern science does not know what sleep is. Study of separate body functions offers no explanation. The reason is the relativistic nature of sleep. Viewed as an opposite aftereffect of overactivity sleep is a causally simple phenomenon.

Apparently, animals having exaggerated awareness during the day, though suffering the opposite effects during the night, have advantage over other animals. It is self-evident that the nature of sleep is opposite to that of activity. But the opposite causation that this implies is not understood. Doctors have invariably advocated relaxation in various forms as a means of falling asleep more easily. This conforms with the traditional logic that like comes from like. In organic adjustment, however, just the reverse is true. Need for rest comes not from relaxation but from exertion. The best way to fall asleep is to try to exert an *exaggerated* effort. This happens when one tries to read an uninteresting book or follow some other unexciting task. The exaggeration has to be understood in its *relative* causal terms. For instance, a person exerting great effort in an exciting task may still not be exerting an exaggerated effort, because the energy release or excitation offered by the task may be even greater than the effort. Techniques of trying to relax may work because the person is exerting so much uninteresting effort in following the technique that sleep is induced.

Opposite causation in sleep is interesting in understanding or controlling its other effects. An elderly person suffers from sleeplessness not because there is too much of alertness or wakefulness, but because there is too little of it. Since there is a lack of activity, sleep as the opposite of activity is also lacking. On the same grounds, if one wants to stay awake for a long stretch, as a pilot sometimes may, he should use sleeping pills, plenty of them, during the days before the period of wakefulness is to begin.

Another error of straightforward logic is the assumption by a person who worries about certain matters during sleepless hours that these matters are the cause of his sleeplessness. Actually, they are only the accompanying effects; in the same way, the sleepless person may blame noises which he would not have noticed if he were normally sleepy. It is true that a thought may become obsessive during sleepless hours. This is due to overenjoyment of the pleasant aspects of the thought. Such overenjoyment is fostered by the general attitude of the person to get even with the harassments of the day at the end of it, and to enjoy the relaxation. As the thought is overenjoyed, opposite unpleasant feelings become inevitable. Since the person tries to overcome these by further overenjoyment, the complex deepens and becomes obsessive.

The only sensible way to deal with sleeplessness is to get up and do something useful; or to keep strict hours, sleeping rather a little less than is needed, in the first place. This is hard, but the pleasure of rest comes just from the hardship. There is no reason to fear that by getting out of bed you will get further away from sleep. Logically this may seem to be so. But organic adjustment proceeds by way of opposites. This may be clearer in the reverse case of too great need for sleep. The sleepiness there can be overcome not by trying to stay wide-awake but by dozing it off.

WORK

One of the most important factors in human adjustment is work. Whenever man wants to transform his environment or himself for the better, he knows he has to work. *Work is continuation of the hard, adverse method by which evolution has produced the highest forms of adjustment*. Nothing useful comes without work, and work is unpleasant, which means it goes against nature, as all progress does. Work makes us advance in the direction of less exciting, more complex, slower and longer life — in the general direction of evolution.

Though work means spending energy, therefore may seem to mean more release and faster living, the unpleasantness of work shows that this is not so. Apparently, the energy expenditure is only peripheral, with minimized central releases. The restriction-release economy of achieving most with the least attains here its highest realization. Increased *peripheral elaboration* is the characteristic of all higher adjustment reached by the bigger and longer-living, more evolved animals. The restrictive nature of work also explains why it is good as therapy in all cases of over-adjustment, such as mental disorders, functional diseases, even heart troubles. Doctors are beginning to realize here the paradoxical truth that what seems like increasing the stress, weakening a function or burdening the heart has an exactly opposite final effect.

As can be expected, scientists seek for more logical explanations. Psychologists have found one in the popularly plausible theory that work gives outlet to aggressive drives. In fact, work requires self-discipline and care, which are the exact opposites of aggressiveness and destruction. The formalism of modern psychology borders here upon absurdity. Just because a person swings his arms or exerts force, the act does not become aggression. Other psychologists — Woodworth has used here his concept of behavior primacy — think that work is beneficial because it keeps the neurotic occupied, gives him something to do. Actually, work is good therapy to the extent that it imposes restrictions and needs, thus making possible a wider need-satisfaction play, which constitutes every normal higher adjustment. The restrictions or needs are imposed more easily through work because our whole cultural tradition and way of life are built around work. If the neurotic has any conditioning left, it is more easily brought to life through work.

The frequent retirement neuroses have been attributed to loss of outlets for aggressiveness. In fact, the explanation is simple. There is a long-accumulated overenjoyment, as a person anticipates the pleasures of retirement while working for it through the years. Then when it comes, the previous anticipated overenjoyment makes it appear less exciting. As extra enjoyments are sought in compensation, overadjustment and neurosis inevitably follow. Every anticipated enjoyment decreases the pleasure. The child who joyfully lives in expectation of a gift is easily disappointed. In whatever way man derives his pleasures, he cannot eat his cake and have it.

Some interesting aspects of work arise from the fact that it requires motivation, or plainly pleasure, to be carried out. This motivation can be derived from anticipated enjoyment of success, or any other enjoyment. A person often derives it from the sense of his own superiority and his own achievement during the work. This is the reason why some people work better when there are "assistants" around; and why people need recognition of their work. Naturally, all such forms of enjoyment involve exaggerations, or disregard of reality. The opposite emotions of dissatisfaction, rage or irritation then follow, as the opposite reactions to previous exaggerations emerge in all possible combinations. Also, the stubbornness of people in clinging to their "accomplishments" or ways of doing things is due to such emotional investments.

Many problems arise in industrial psychology. Big companies have their own psychologists to deal with workers. The present psychological theory offers only controversies in this field. For instance, on the main question whether the disturbed worker should be protected against hard reality, or be forced to face it, as Dr. Gordon of Du Pont's program holds, there are two opposing views. Psychologists can be useful in evaluating the permanent capacities of workers and accordingly finding the best work arrangements. But when it comes to psychology as such, the paradox of immediate effect and later reversal inevitably applies. Experiments may show how increased efficiency results from shortened hours, improved cooperation from more freedom and so on. But those who have to live with such improvements know how disappointing they become.

There has been much talk about replacing the monotonous tasks of assembly-line specialization with more interesting ones. It is true that a more complex task offers pleasure in its completion. But here again the background through which this pleasure is made possible is not seen. Completion of an involved task is interesting because there was previous investment of needs that were experienced as anxiety, fear of mistakes and so on. These are unpleasant, which is the reason why everybody tries to avoid complex tasks. The persons who become unskilled assembly-line workers would be the last ones to like them. The same can be said about giving workers more responsibility. To be any good, responsibility must rest on even more difficult background effort.

A more subtle aspect of the paradox of opposite causation is illustrated by such instances as increased motivation in work after enjoyment of a vacation. This may seem like a proof that easing the work increases performance. The truth is that the vacation represents an unusual or "exaggerated" ease after a year's work and therefore evokes an opposite reaction of a feeling for duty which accumulates and gets its outlet in increased performance during the first days after the vacation. But at the same time the vacation serves as a new background against which work now appears an "exaggeration." In the total there is some lowering of the sense of duty. We all know that it is constant work, not ease, that makes men duty-conscious.

In this connection we should mention a curious, very general effect of opposite causation. One can often observe that relaxation of discipline in regard to himself or others brings about a greater motivation or better results. The truth is that every one of us has evolved a certain "normalcy" in our state of restrictions and conditioning. Then, when the level of this "normalcy" or conscience is lowered, there is the opposite reaction, as in all cases of change in one's normalcy. But it should be clear that this "normalcy" can be only destroyed by such repeated debasements. For it is not a deep natural normalcy, but one growing out of cultural conditioning. Living in wrongdoing destroys the feeling of conscience, though logical analysis of every individual case shows that wrongdoing augments the feeling of conscience.

THE SHELVING OF WORRIES

Forgetting or postponing worries is seen as a logical means of better adjustment by all theorists. Why not shorten the clearly disadvantageous emotions by worrying only when needed? The truth is that worrying is the natural anticipated accumulation of the background of needs so that there will be motivation or satisfaction available when the task has to be carried out. The worry is not just a useless incident. The organism knows what it is doing. The worry often means the replacement of optimism, inertial complacency or self-assuring comfort with a realization of the real needs and dangers — and getting ready for them. The best thing that can happen to a person is to experience as much worry and fright as possible before the crucial event, exam or public appearance begins. A realistic person who worries hard is calm when the critical event comes. Moreover, a worry disappears as one lives through it. The avoidance of it is what creates neurotic worrying. Unfortunately, we try to delay worrying as much as possible — even without the psychologist's advice. Such advice can only precipitate any neurotic tendency that there may be in the person.

PLAY

Psychologists see play as one of the best means of straightening out maladjustment. The reason is that play is an excellent source of release. Play means reconstructed life in which the needs and satisfactions, struggles and successes are similar to those of real life, therefore offer real pleasure. But in play one can dismiss his failures, which in real life would mean feelings of anxiety and needs. That is the whole meaning of play. In play man tries to beat the general rule of the equivalence of positive and negative emotions. In their play men have discovered the perfect form of adjustment that psychologists, "positive" thinkers and sellers of happiness are advocating — life without its negative side.

Unfortunately, life cannot continue in playfulness. If it did, there would be no motivation and no emotional resourcefulness. There can be no satisfaction or motivation potential without the accumulation of needs. Only children and primitive savages who have not yet learned, by intuition or tradition, this truth cling to playfulness as long as possible. In simplest terms, eternal playfulness makes real life uninteresting. The successes of real life fade in interest value in comparison with the great success enjoyed in play. And the failures of real life become less bearable after one has got used to avoiding them in play. Of course, play of one hour matters as little as a drop in a bucket, but the principle is clear.

Plays and games may be used in education and conditioning as gradual stepping stones from easier, more natural tasks toward real-life tasks. The gradualness is important because of the way conditioning is imposed. *This is the only use that play and games can have. They are to be outlived by children, not perpetuated by adults.*

We are victims of fixations in our enjoyment of plays and games — baseball, football, fights, races and sports in general. Something that is done better by an animal with quick reflexes than by an intelligent being cannot serve as an example for man. It all amounts to glorification of physical superiority. The next step is glorification of the fight, attack and the justice of the fist. Add the emphasis on natural drives and you have juvenile delinquency. Of course, it is easy for clumsy youth organizers to obtain cooperation in this way. But it is a crime to inveigle normal youth, capable of intellectual interests, into fixations limited to the interests of man as an animal. Such interests are strong in man and sufficient to keep a fixation going. The fixation becomes sacrosanct with tradition. Everybody can judge that there is no value in such occupations, but the great traditions have become so sacred that one who opposes them appears abnormal. We agree that tradition is mostly wise. But it can be wrong also. Roman circus games and Hottentot war dances were also sacred tradition.

Of course, in practice, an intelligent educator finds compromises, which may even be necessary in cases of youth with unusually low intelligence, or of low cultural background. But it must be understood that the same general fixation on primitive interests is largely responsible for the low cultural background. The example of grownups and their value notions is what determines the interests of children. Naturally, in the absence of outlets for intellectual interests — competitions, shows, places of interest or other activities — parents or teachers have to subscribe to sports just to keep children out of the street.

PHYSICAL CARE

Physical adjustment is equally governed by the paradox of reactions. What is pleasant and seems like best adjustment may be worse than what is unpleasant and seems like maladjustment. Boring and toilsome work, which is unpleasant because it requires performance at more sparing release rates and in more complicated ways, leads to the best adjustment. Restriction and complexity are sources of all higher adjustment. Life in general shows that boring and difficult work is salutary in the long run. But when it comes to complex scientific analyses, the logic of immediate positive reactions is followed without the slightest hesitation. Only recently is medicine discovering, in the most evident cases, that a seemingly undesirable reaction, like the apparent burden on the heart, is beneficial in the end. The common man has long known that enjoyments ruin health. But it is not realized that there is no essential difference, for instance, between enjoyment of exciting food and enjoyment even of the exciting "outdoors," which is accepted as unquestionably beneficial. In its natural forms the outdoors is good because it means hard physical exercise, but as an enjoyment it may end with a headache at best. Also a one-sided, grandly stylized "physical culture" that is enjoyed with great gusto leads rather to excesses and abnormalities. Any excess, whether in ease or hardship, is bound to exhaust a body function sooner, as it means stronger opposite oscillations in either case. Improving one's own body in the Theodore Roosevelt style is good if it involves acceptance of hard, unexciting work. But in most cases the person is only deceiving himself that he is exercising his will power whereas actually he is seeking for increased physical release.

The best physical adjustment is attained by leaving the body alone. If a person is genetically constituted to grow big and strong, he can be kept in chains and be fed only bread and water, he will still reach his full size and strength. Everybody who brings up animals knows this, and man is physically only an animal. Dietary deficiencies are often too easily proved in the laboratory, where limitations are imposed with mechanical strictness and long-range adaptations are excluded. The frequent physical weakness of modern youth is due to all the "improvements" and ease in nutrition and living conditions, rather than any lack in food or exercise.

Excessive care of the body leads to overadjustment in one form or another. The negative reactions then inevitably follow. If mother overfeeds a child, even while using a fully balanced diet, there is excessive acceleration of growth. Then in conservation of its dynamic normalcy the body has to stop growing for a while. Since some functions may not be able to proceed at all unless the growth goes on, complications may result.

DAYDREAMING

Dreaming about success and a grandiose future performs an important function. Man mostly advances by erecting a glorious future for himself and investing his aspirations in it to such extent that he cannot abdicate it later without a grave emotional loss. Therefore he prefers fighting hard for it than giving it up. Man thus lures himself into straits from which he can hope to get out only by advancing. In other words, man drives himself forward by his spiritual powers, which are always higher than his other capacities.

Naturally, feelings of inadequacy and maladjustment appear here in unmistakable form. Modern psychologists therefore have been recognizing daydreaming as an important source of maladjustment. They have been trying to help the person lower his aspirations when such maladjustment appears. Actually, the "maladjustment" here is the real gain. It means the accumulation of needs so that satisfactions as motives for future performance become available. Real maladjustment and neurosis start when a person, incapable of standing restrictions, tries to avoid such accumulation of needs. With the normal person, this "maladjustment" is more fruitful than the mediocrity attained by the lowering of aspirations. As regards playing with future ideas, the progress of humanity depends on the capacity of men to imagine how things can be different.

SOCIAL ADJUSTMENT

In social adjustment we meet with the inherent adversity of the interests of people. If one wants to gain cooperation from others, he has to serve their interests. But if anybody really did so, he would have to disregard to the same extent his own interests

— and would sink into misery, where nobody would want to have anything to do with him. Consequently, the forms of social intercourse have become an extremely elaborate and refined system of hypocrisies and pretensions. Nice words, smiles, pretended benevolence or implied condescension constitute the social atmosphere we live in. Naturally, everybody has become equally skillful in discerning the pretensions and guarding himself against the deceit. Everybody also fears to be discovered in his pretensions and be despised for it. The contradiction explains why a person who does not care to make a good impression and does not try to be interesting, becomes really interesting. Also, the person who has abandoned seriousness, the cause of which is always self-concern, is the one whom others find amusing. But not often can a person afford to be disinterested; and an intended disinterestedness is a hard thing to attain.

Making friends and influencing people by design is a tricky business. Everybody loves to "influence" others and hates to be "influenced" by others. No amount of superficial refinement can help, since everybody knows the game too well. Only real reciprocal usefulness can do. *To win friends really, one had better do useful work so that he be able to offer something real and important in exchange.* Even good listening — which is highly appreciated — requires that the listener be important as person; that he fully appreciate how interesting the things said are; and that he be able to make stimulating comments so that the other person can further show how interesting he can be. All this means real capacities and interests. Mere exclamations — "How interesting!" or "Oh, really?" — by a nobody will make him only more despised.

Even the professional seller of social success has to admit that unless a person has genuine interests for others, he will not win friends. But the thing is that an endeavor to create a feeling artificially leads to an opposite feeling. The person who has read a book or taken a course on social success is in for great disappointment. This does not mean that the effort has been wasted. If the person tries time and again, he ends with greater indifference as regards his personal emotional involvement. Such an attitude, accompanied by real expertness in social intercourse, which the person may have acquired through the effort, is exactly what can make person interesting.

Here we have to mention a very general secondary effect of opposite causation: *adjustment on the basis of a previous opposite reaction.* To take a simple example, a person brought up in over-protection will find social realities full of insecurity. Consequently, he will develop special capacities and attitudes for overcoming that insecurity. He may succeed so well that an attitude characterized by self-assurance and a sense of security may finally result. Superficially, it then may seem that the original overprotection contributed to the later overassurance, whereas in fact there were two consecutive reversals.

In social life, more than anywhere else, the backgrounds that seem like maladjustment — feelings of threat, restriction and dependence — are the sources of better adjustment. When such negative backgrounds become so general that they are not felt anymore and only the positive satisfactions which they make possible are primarily felt, then social cooperation reaches a smooth, "natural" course. Then the humanist can start pointing out how love, harmony and freedom between people are providentially there as the causal essences of social cooperation. Under the same humanistic delusion, every author on social problems condemns negative or restrictive social phenomena — insecurity, inequality, competition, status seeking, clinging to reputation, social gossiping, class feeling or repetitious boredom in social intercourse. In fact, these are the real causal sources of our positive social feelings and motivations that lead to better social adjustment. They are there not by accident, but by virtue of selective social evolution. On the other hand, all kinds of negative reactions, including the mystifying solitude experienced amidst the most intense social life, appear where people have really attained the social enjoyments they considered as the essence of happy adjustment.

OLD AGE

Maladjustments of old age are becoming an increasing problem. The wider reason is the same general attitude toward the enjoyments

215

of life. The unprecedented prosperity permits poeple to live in the expectation that after a certain age they will not have to continue the struggles of life. That is where the trouble starts. Man without disturbances or needs is like a clock with its spring not wound up. Work has never hurt anybody. Naturally, the older person has to work at a slower rate, but this is automatically regulated by the organism itself, provided no special stimulation, psychological or physiological, is applied. The economic arguments are not valid. The economy can adjust itself equally well to fifty million or one hundred million workers, and to a retirement age of 45 or 85. The older, experienced, people should be easier to absorb than the young newcomers.

The most complex old age problems would find solutions if older people did not consider their tasks and struggles completed at sixty-five. This, however, is not a matter of decision, opportunities or programming. If a person has lived for years under the emotional expectation that he will take it easy after sixty-five, he cannot change his attitude suddenly, however convincing the reasons.

SUICIDE

The ultimate form of maladjustment is suicide. There have been many endeavors to explain the causes of suicide. Durkheim's study is a prominent example. He attributed the cause of suicide to something like the individual's loss of identification with his society. Modern psychology has no explanations, apart from the psycho-analytic ghost stories about self-destructive drives or the symbolic loss of sexual potency through material loss. Psychologists are bound by the logic of experimental scientism, according to which a person reaches the state of highest despair upon the maximum accumulation of nonsatisfactions. In reality, just the reverse is true. The wretched poor, the handicapped and the rejects, whose every hour of life would seem a torture to us, go on cheerfully with their own hopes and delights. On the other side, the rich, the meteoric stars, the persons reaching the highest successes in love, wealth or adventure — those commit suicide more often. No wonder the practical sociologists admit that the cause of suicide is not known.

In fact, there is no contradiction, nor need for mystery. What does a person care about identification with society or symbolic loss of sexual potency? Or why should his destructive instinct let him first ride high and then strike him down like a Mephisto? Actually, suicide is as logical as taking a bus out of a town where one has accumulated only debts and has no credit left. When a person has accumulated such a high background of enjoyments that anything he can think of for the future means lowering himself emotionally, his best course is to leave. If there is only suffering left, why continue?

Of course, enjoyments are never seen as the cause of subsequent displeasure, for reasons we have explained repeatedly. Any added source of enjoyment actually keeps the person from thinking of suicide. But with each new enjoyment the causal background for experiencing opposite feelings increases. Then any stop in the addition of further enjoyments or any unfortunate event may start the backward movement. In practice, an event of a more lasting negative effect is necessary to precipitate the suicide. If the negative effects are short-lasting, they become part of the background and the source of positive feelings even before the person decides on the fatal step. As in all cases of background causation, the enjoyment may not be felt as anything special, because of its uninterrupted continuance. A person born in wealth may not feel that he has had an unusually good time, but when he loses his wealth suddenly, his past life still can serve as a background against which the future appears hopelessly dark.

By the way, suicide is always a hasty miscalculation. If the person waited a little longer, the negative feelings would start effacing themselves through reversion; time cures all ills. Value feelings are expressions of deeper physiological mechanism, and as long as these remain unimpaired the value potential is still there. The person committing suicide realizes his error only at the very last moment, of the horrors of death, as only then do these deeper mechanisms start disintegrating and the loss of the remaining potential is excruciatingly lived through.

Statistics on suicides confirm the fact that overenjoyment is their cause. Suicides are committed most frequently in May and

June, which are the months of the first and strongest cycle of enjoyments and their aftermaths; also on Mondays and Tuesdays, which are clearly the days of aftermaths. This has been confirmed by a study on more than sixteen thousand cases, conducted by Howard A. Rusk; and by a study at the Harvard School of Public Health. Lawyers, artists and businessmen head the list, whereas clergymen and miners are at the bottom of it. Another study, by Dr. Richard A. Kern — which confirmed the observation about the months and weekdays — showed that worries, even illnesses, help to prevent suicides, and that suicides are more frequent among the rich than the poor. Statistics on suicides classified by nations and years are equally revealing but have remained uninterpreted. Apparently, they say nothing to modern scientists not seeing the paradoxical law that they illustrate.

Before we conclude we would like to show by concrete examples what help modern man usually gets from the theorists on adjustment. We may look at a couple of the most popular and most representative books. They all reflect sufficiently and comply fully with the certainties the "science" has in this field. This is easily done, because all the certainties here are presently only expressions of the general certainty of experimental logic, according to which positive feelings are increased by addition to satisfactions.

The Power of Positive Thinking by Norman Vincent Peale has enjoyed great popularity. It urges people to strive for every possible positive feeling: maintain a happy state of mind, stop worrying, expect the best, have faith, develop the habit of happiness, etc., etc. Numerous examples are given to prove how people succeeded because of their positive attitude of mind. We do not doubt that a person having positive feelings can achieve anything. But the problem is that by trying deliberately to enjoy such feelings one drives himself into an emotional negativism. If a person would follow perfectly the advice given by the book, he would end with a neurosis. Reliance on God, which is the second theme of the book, may indeed have positive effect. A religious person has been conditioned all his life to fear and believe in the power of God. Then, if a guardian of religious power tells him that God is on his side, the person may get additional release from that.

But it should be understood that if the background of fear and respect for God is used in this way it effaces itself, or becomes degraded, and is so much the less effective next time.

The Mind Alive, by Harry and Bonaro Overstreet, equally extols positive feelings, but also deals with another characteristic matter: the blessings of love, tolerance and tenderness, especially toward children. There can be no doubt that love can do miracles, even transform our social and economic life into a utopian paradise. But the problem is that love cannot be had by wishing or deciding to have it. Everybody would like to have much love — for everybody and for the whole world. Love is the most precious motivational capital. But people lack it the most and suffer from the opposite feelings of hate. The reason is that the love — that nice heavenly satisfaction — comes from the hard accumulation of ugly, disturbing needs by way of restriction and conditioning of satisfaction. Without these, any love for others, i.e., limitation of the self, is an "exaggeration" and inevitably breaks out into opposite feelings. Hence the increase of the negative feeling of hate as people strive to derive more social motivation in easy ways — by the enjoyment of love that the book advises. The hate is accompanied by obsessions of mistrust because everybody equally overenjoys the egotistic confidence that he is lovable to everybody and needs to fear nobody.

In education, heavenly love is nonsensical without the ugly threat to, or need for, security. Giving a child fullest satisfaction of this need, the fullest love, which the book advises, means taking away or exhausting the very basis of love. In practical terms, a true tolerance can lead only to moral license, deterioration of discipline, and finally hate of everybody. We have explained the paradoxical role of refinement in love, which gives the illusion that permissiveness is the source of love. A theorist should be able to see beyond such delusions. Otherwise his theory becomes a nuisance.

How Never To Be Tired, by Marie Beynon Ray, is illustrative of another characteristic topic: interests and the motivational energy that follows from them. The book gives numerous examples from experiments and case studies, to show that a person can have endless energy as long as he has interest. Consequently the book advises avoiding boredom, worry, fear and indecision, learning to summon vitalizing emotions, acquire courage, get one's mind interested and so on. No doubt, such positive feelings and interests can work wonders — and are pleasant. Why not have them? The truth is that they are satisfactions that can be created only through accumulation of needs, which means restrictions, hardships and boring, monotonous effort. These are exact opposites of the excitements that the book advocates, and that are the surest means of landing into emotional negativism with collapse of all interests.

Naturally, the most frequently suggested way to a better adjustment is the use of reason. The simplest and most frequent approach here may be illustrated by the one we find in the book, *Freedom from Fear*, by Lester L. Coleman. The book urges abandonment of distortions, confusions, fear of pain, ignorance, inferiority, guilt, frightening oneself into illness or being afraid to live. It sees solutions in taking decisions without fear, looking at fear in the daylight, discovering and destroying the sources of fear and working hard for freedom from fear. It all amounts to showing that there are no logical reasons to live in fear, and every reason as well as advantage for not fearing. All this is absolutely correct under the logic and methods of experimental sciences, but nonsensical in psychology. If pleasant emotions could be created by adding or increasing them directly, without first living through their unpleasant opposites, there would not be one negative feeling in the world. Actually, the exaggerated striving for positive feelings that the book advises can lead only to more anxiety, emotional negativism and neurosis.

Other authors offer more sophisticated solutions to be attained through the use of reason. In the book, *Problems of Human Adjustment*, by Lynde C. Steckle, we find emphasis on correct reasoning, analyzing the facts of life, taking account of reality, understanding the aspects of living and escaping the restrictions of self. Similarly, the book, *Psychological Foundations of Personality*, by Louis P. Thorpe, suggests getting a rational view of one's own qualifications, learning to react normally, eschewing fixed ideas, learning to adjust to the requirements of environment, facing life as it appears in terms of causation. Many such elaborate suggestions on the use of reason can be found throughout psychological theory. The elaborations, however, can only gloss over, not remove, the fallacy of "scientific" logic. As far as reasoning is concerned, the formula of the most perfect adjustment is known to everybody. We all know which are the positive attitudes and emotions. They can be expressed in one sentence: have more satisfaction. But satisfaction cannot be created by reason. It can be created only in the seemingly illogical and difficult way of living through its opposite: need.

CONCLUSION

Man, by nature, is never to understand the seemingly paradoxical laws of his adjustment; and modern science has deepened the misunderstanding. But practical life has never depended on causal understanding. Men have always strived for more freedom or release — and imposed on themselves more restrictions. Modern theorization has been equally counteracted by practice. In fact, the more disturbing modern attitudes become, the subtler the countermeasures which are emerging. The important thing is that even the theorist who advocates more release works to see the culture, which means more restrictions, prevail in practice. The only thing to fear is that in our age of scientism "scientific" theory may end by exerting an over-all influence on the general cultural trend. The increase in juvenile delinquency and in psychological as well as physiological diseases, exhibiting the vicious-circle effects of overadjustment, are the indicators of this change in trend. A true causal understanding of adjustment could help to stop, or even reverse, this change in trend, thus strengthening the restrictive attitudes embodied in cultural tradition.

Furthermore, it can always be hoped that a causal understanding of adjustment can lead to a science, like engineering, in the field of human adjustment. In our age of scientism, a replacement of mere blind tradition by science could be achieved in few generations, with results we can hardly imagine. A beaver builds a good dam by instinct, but the Tennessee Valley Authority is a very different thing.

VII

EVERYDAY VALUE DELUSIONS

Values determine what we feel, believe or do. But value depends upon equal and opposite disvalue. Our feeling of freedom, for instance, depends upon the amount of restrictions we live under. If there is absolute freedom, there can be no feeling of freedom. Even the highest satisfaction gives no feeling of value if there has been no previous need. One who always has plenty of water never knows the satisfaction of drinking, or one who rests all the time never knows the pleasure of resting. Only deprivation or need can give satisfaction or value. The same applies to all values — happiness, love, beauty, harmony, reason, purpose or sense of humor.

Man never realizes what this dependence of satisfaction upon need, or of value upon disvalue, really means. It means that his striving after happiness, beauty or freedom is a self-defeating task comparable to chasing his own shadow. The very act of obtaining a value means losing it. The only way to obtain a value is by searching for its opposite — going away from it.

Naturally, man cannot live with such understanding. If he did, he would lose every motivation, and would perish. He has to continue chasing his delusions like the squirrel turning its wheel in the cage. Belief in positive values or pleasure is the very essence of life. The striving for release, on one side, and the restrictions imposed by evolution and the adverse world, on the other, constitute our whole living existence, in its simplest forms as well as its ultimate philosophical contradiction. Opposition is the very essence, and normalcy, of everything living — which does not make delusions about human values any less general.

222

Before we go further we wish to make it clear that we are not motivated here by any indignation over the lack of recognition of rational truths, or by a righteous zeal to turn people away from their delusions. We have shown repeatedly that cultural superstitions harbor wisdoms which are intuitively followed by those who have higher intelligence; and that it is precisely the rationalist with his arsenal of truths who is incapable of following or grasping the cultural tradition. Our purpose is a general causal understanding of the value experience. The values we are going to discuss serve us only as material for analysis. We are eager to expose the general delusion about values only because this explains the simple facts of relative causation, especially the question why the truths of psychological causation have never been recognized. We are perfectly aware that explaining away as delusions the deepest beliefs that all men hold is not a graceful or respectable way of writing. But a relativistic approach can never look respectable or graceful; so we may as well forget about it.

Anyway, our purpose is to explain values causally without bothering about conventional beliefs, practical consequences, or the seeming ridiculousness of the conclusions we come to. Man as an intelligent being deserves to understand what makes him tick, wherever that understanding leads him. Such understanding is also the precondition of ever making human adjustment scientific. The disillusionment that a relative outlook could bring about belongs with the higher maturity gradually approached by the race of intellectual beings. Cultural attitudes based on the emotional espousal of values are comparable to the turbulent excitements of children or primitive men. To primitive men a civilized person seems an emotionless and helpless invalid — until they learn to know his real strength. We explained before how diversification through restrictions rather than the deepening of emotions produces richer motivation.

HAPPINESS

The ultimate measure of all values is happiness. It is the goal of all human strivings, recognized as such even by our Constitution. There is no other thing that man strives for or thinks about more. But there is also no other thing about the attainment of which man knows less. All of us know intuitively that our striving for happiness is delusory, though we cannot help doing nothing else but strive for it. A person with good common sense knows that anybody who tries to sell a happiness formula is a crank.

The virtuous humanists have extolled spiritual or cultural interests as the safest road to happiness. One may think here of the lofty pronouncements of the Greek philosophers from whom our humanists derive their tradition. Bertrand Russell, in his *Conquest of Happiness*, sees renouncement of personal ambitions and development of intellectual interests as the surest way to a happy life. Interests are undoubtedly pleasant. They are satisfactions. But as such they require an equal previous accumulation of need, or restrictions of satisfactions, through long learning and conditioning. This means an equal previous displeasure.

Another method suggested by promoters of happiness is the plain resignation of personal ambitions, and of emotional involvements that bring unhappiness. Resignation of ambitions certainly makes things easier, for a while, as any lowering of needs does. Russell's book emphasizes resignation and disengagement from material interests. Resignation is a high price to pay for something a person does not get anyway. Disturbing ambitions, emotional involvements and "maladjustive" imagination are the necessary counterparts in any motivation or higher interest. Of course, nonpersonal and nonmaterialistic ambitions are more productive in the end. But then it is a question of the best ways of channeling ambitions, not resigning them; and of choosing the most effective, indirect, means in the attainment of materialistic progress, which is the only possible progress in the end.

A state of happiness reached by resignation has been an element in many philosophical and religious systems. Oriental teachings and religions — one may think here of Buddhism — as well as Western Cynicism, Stoicism, even Christianity, can serve as examples. They bear witness to man's realization that satisfactions even when fulfilled bring only unhappiness in the end. Actually, a blessedness gained by the evasion of aspirations does not produce more happiness, but means sinking toward the level of vegetation. Walter B. Pitkin, describing the "blessed" in his *Psychology of Happiness*, finds, among many prominent cases, that a Pennsylvania farmer, Timothy Tubb, came closest to undisturbed blessedness. Timothy Tubb had no worries, nothing disturbed him, and all he did was enjov the good meals his mother prepared. It may seem that he had no unhappiness in life but only satisfactions. In truth, even the already given natural enjoyments require an opposite experience before they can appear. Appetite requires hunger. The same applies in reaching less natural states of blessedness. The ecstasy reached by yogis, ascetics or shamans requires previous mortifications. Even a meditator, according to the teachings of Buddhism, has to concentrate first on the delusory, transitory and pain-causing aspects of this world.

The most frequently suggested way for reaching happiness is by increasing our capacities to see, and respond to, the pleasures of the world around us. The fame of Thoreau, the author of *Walden*, rests on the popularity of this idea. John Cowper Powys wrote a book, *In Defense of Sensuality*, in which he exaltingly described the thrills that are waiting for us in nature around and in ourselves. Such thrills are certainly there; and it can be demonstrated, by facts of experimental observation, that they are always available to everybody. Unfortunately, anybody who gets himself into a state of overenjoying them finds opposite aftermaths in the end. Every narcotic addict knows how inevitably the ecstasy changes into its opposite aftermath. Thomas De Quincey has described vividly in his *Confessions of an English Opium Eater* such opposites in the emotional experiences connected with narcotic intoxication. The results are the same whether the extra release is obtained from more direct physiological overstimulation by narcotics or from less direct psychological overstimulation by various means ranging from auto-suggestion to an exciting way of life.

Martin Gumpert tells in his *Anatomy of Happiness* of many elaborate ways, from wearing new clothes to believing in miracles, to derive more happiness in life. Naturally, the aftermaths become too varied and inconspicuous here to be noticed. However, the same causal rule applies whether the overadjustment is tiny or great. Still, there have always been theorists who have thought that their more reasonable insights could help. The theory here has not changed much. In 1621 Burton wrote a book on the *Anatomy of Melancholy*, in which he advised that the melancholic person turn away from too much fasting and meditation, and turn toward recreation and all kinds of good thoughts so that the "Muses can sing and Graces dance all life long." Our theorists also think that the reluctance of the common man to espouse pleasurable emotions is due to ignorance. Russell has said that man forgot how to smile during his dark historical past, and that his salvation lies in opening his heart to joy. The modern postulation of dark subconscious forces inside man is another way of blaming wrong insights.

Recently psychologists are beginning to admit that unhappiness or negative feelings are part of normal life. But this is still a far cry from realizing the seemingly reversed logic of psychological causation. Hardly any book or article on adjustment fails to urge the cultivation of brighter positive experiences, richness of emotions, greater vitality, a fuller life or the readiness to enjoy things.

It is interesting to note that the experts on happiness do not understand the causes of their own emotions, and fail to see the causal meaning of the backgrounds that they themselves describe. Pitkin in his book tells about a moment of bliss that he experienced during a rest after a long painful ride. The unpleasant background is vividly described, but the causal connection is missed. Gumpert in his book tells about his own "severe attack of unhappiness," but does not notice its connection with the previous period of intensified living that he himself describes in the book. Vinning tells in her book, *The World in Tune*, about a moment of ecstasy that she experienced by observing locust blossoms falling. She gives it as an example of the "minor ecstasies" that she thinks are available to all of us. But the circumstance that this moment of bliss occurred after "long months of sorrow had clamped tight her heart" is mentioned only incidentally. Whitman, writing on the art of cultivating the joys of life, tells of a moment of blissful joy that he experienced during a tiresome trip, after struggling with discomforts, weariness and gloomy thoughts. He also tells how a pilot, after flying desperately through turbulent, dangerous weather, suddenly experienced the "beauty and perfection of the world as if he were one with it." In another story he tells of a moment of ecstatic vision experienced by a man who had just lived through the worst experiences of the Depression. But Whitman does not notice the causal connection between the opposite backgrounds he describes. Elisabeth Byrd, in urging us to develop our sensitivity to the delights of life, tells how after weeks of near-fatal illness she experienced a blissful moment by looking at an otherwise ordinary scene; and how from that experience she learned that the wonders of delight are always available to us.

Trying to live a life filled with happy events is like trying to write a book with nothing but happy endings. We do enjoy the happy ending and read a book avidly to reach it. But if the happy ending is not preceded by worries and anxieties, it is pointless. In life as well there can be no happiness without a previous experience of need or unhappiness.

Restoration of normalcy is not possible where there was no previous disturbance of it. A person who had his every wish fulfilled — wealth without limit, the highest satisfaction in love or godlike power — would be the most miserable man in the world. There would not be anything more for him to wish or feel. He would not even have the feeling of being alive. Nor are spiritual enjoyments inexhaustible in terms of emotions. There the negative aftereffects do not follow because the restriction in satisfactions precedes instead of following the enjoyment. But the equivalence of opposite emotions is there, however it manifests itself. The great scientist, moral giant or genius suffers more from a lack

227

of knowledge or imperfection of achievement than other men. Whether the values enjoyed are physically concrete or purely mental, the rule of equivalence applies equally; it is the only causal principle under which any organic release can work. Only children and mentally unstable people try to live in a rosy imagined world for purposes of enjoyment.

In brief, the rule of satisfaction and need applies at all levels and to all aspects of experiences, physical or mental. Attaining happiness means losing it. The process is like being given a million dollars in one series of operations, and then being deprived of it in another. What is often seen as a richer, happier life is just having been involved more frequently in such operations, or having avoided unusually great losses at any one time. Also, many people hate to admit failure in their ambition to have a happier life and in their "expertness" at attaining it.

BEAUTY

The feling of beauty is a natural satisfaction. The underlying needs are mostly sexual or reproductive needs. That is why seasonal influences, which mark natural rhythms in reproduction, evoke in us strong moods of beauty. Our needs of growth and biological well-being are also involved. We find light in all its variations an inexhaustible source of beauty. Light as the fundamental source of all biochemistry serves as the triggering factor. Beauty of color is a further facet of the beauty of light.

The same applies to all natural factors which have biological value. When you look at the play of shadows, calm waters, green fields, luxuriant growth or blue hills in the distance, you are automatically evaluating the presence of life energy, the undisturbed persistence of elements, the richness of natural resources, the mildness of air and the freedom of space — all of which are values of our biological well-being. The correspondence between the love call and musical enjoyments is not more difficult to trace. Even the love call of birds evokes in us feelings of beauty. We all know how every release overflows when the love or reproductive function is being satisfied. More mysteries of heavens

228

have been poured into poetry on account of sexual love than anything else. All such heavenly spirituality disappears when the simple sexual drive is absent or fully satisfied.

Mystery shrouds our feelings of beauty because they have evolved through millions of years and myriads of processes of which man has no idea, but the effects of which involve his whole being. The functions that underlie our feelings of beauty are innumerable and intricately interwoven, as all natural functions are. We can discern only some general principles. For instance, the beauty of cleanliness or aversion to uncleanliness means avoidance of biochemical harm; symmetry, regularity, continuity or smoothness of forms and relationships means advantages in dealing with the environment. These and other principles of beauty combined with the above elements of light, space, energy, richness of nature or suitability of objects can explain all aspects of beauty.

Like all organic satisfactions, the experience of beauty depends on an equal previous experience of needs or opposite emotions, and therefore complies with all the laws of relative causation. Even a child knows that the warm, bright spring is found beautiful because of the preceding cold, dark winter. Where there is continuous "spring," there is no experience of spring. Similarly, the beauties of nature are not felt by those who live amidst them. Peoples of nature, or peasants, never exalt the beauties of nature around them. European peoples started to discern their feelings of beauty toward nature when they became urbanized. The fashion of writing or talking about the beauties of nature was then introduced, mainly by Rousseau.

The degree and contents of our feeling of beauty derive from previous deprivation or need. When in the depth of the woods you feel a calmness which reveals eternal harmony, it is an opposite to the noisiness and disturbances of the city, which were intruding on every minute of your life with disturbing harassments. A person living in the woods all the time would not feel anything particular about that calmness. The richness of your feeling of eternal harmony is supplied here by the "richness" of opposite negative feelings in the past.

We must say more about the mystery of the spiritual richness of our experiences of beauty. When you listen to a piece of music, or look at beautiful scenery, you may have the most complex feelings, of unity of being, harmony, eternal continuity, revelation of an enigma, soothing redemption and so on. Viewed in themselves such feelings are a mystery necessitating a source as complex and intelligently meaningful as the feelings themselves. But if we see them as opposites of equally varied and rich negative experiences which we have all the time, then their mystery disappears. Naturally, the human value approach never permits one to see a causal connection between the feeling of a deep sense of harmony and the feeling of senselessness of harassment. But as in narcotic intoxication the most incongruous negativity arises from the most harmonious sensation, here *the very meaninglessness of the past gives the feeling of deepest sense* to the subsequent experience of beauty.

It has to be understood that the deep sense revealed through an experience of beauty is only felt as such but is not there as a fact. Every enjoyer of beauty must have had the experiences described by Somerset Maugham in one of his novels. The opium smoker there feels that he comes so close to the revelation of the existence of God that he almost sees all the mysteries of Being revealed to him. To be sure, the opium smoker is no closer to any true revelation. But during the intoxication he feels deep satisfaction in regard to everything, including his previous preoccupation with the problem of God. The negative answers thus are turned into positive ones, *emotionally*. The revelations felt by a person under the enjoyment of drug, music or any aesthetic stimulation have the same truth value as the conviction of an intoxicated man that he knows all solutions. You can observe this for yourself. While listening to music you may feel that you suddenly have a deep insight into something. But later when you recall what exactly the insight consisted of, you can find that nothing very meaningful was there.

Relative causation implies unacceptable truths in aesthetics as it does everywhere else. For instance, the humanist extolling the sublimity of beauty should actually thank the harassing experiences in his past from which that beauty derives its meaning. In every aspect or detail of aesthetics, value derives from disvalue as satisfaction derives from need. We saw how the requirement of opposite effect, or contrast, explains the intricacies of aesthetic laws. We shall see later how all artistic effects, as well as styles, even the seeming absurdities of modern art, derive from the same relative causation because of the dependence of value upon disvalue. At present, we may mention a simpler, curious observation. Polar explorers suffering from cold and privation sometimes have vivid dreams of warmth and plenty when they manage to relax during sleep. Equally, men suffering from thirst in the desert have reported vivid dreams about cool refreshments and green meadows. These cases show how relative causation works. When the highest limit in a need is reached, a phantom satisfaction appears. When the swing away from normalcy has reached its limit, it starts back at the slightest opportunity.

Another related paradoxical consequence of relative causation is the enrichment of the experience of beauty by restriction. A hermit living with his dreams or books may have richer experiences of beauty than the world traveler feasting on the wonders of the world. Not only is any emotion matched with equal opposite emotions, but its total potential is also predetermined for every person. This cannot be otherwise, because any emotion has its basis in physiological functions which are organically predetermined. Therefore one's feelings of beauty can only be varied within a given total. They can be intensively spent on a few experiences, or they may be extended to more numerous and varied, less intense experiences. Naturally, the world traveler concentrates on the deeply enjoyable, more nearly unique, great experiences, like brightness of color or grandeur of form in the enjoyment of scenery. He may even fixate, and thus narrow himself completely, on a few, natural or artistic enjoyments. The hermit, on the other hand, may spend the amount of emotional reactions that he has to live through anyway on all possible inner experiences, and combinations of elements in his mind or imagination. Since the mind is not limited in its products and possibilities of combinations as nature is, the emotions of the hermit may be spread over incomparably more varied and extensive *ideational* constructs — which alone are of importance to man as an intelligent being. A world traveler can never see a mountain of gold, or a dragon, but our mind can produce them in an instant.

Experiments on persons isolated from outside stimulations show that their own thoughts and imagery can become as sharp as realities and that the images they have may be more exotic than anything they have seen. It can also be easily observed that a person with rich experiences in the past does not find much beauty in simpler, less perfect and more varied day-to-day experiences. Only specific and strong stimulations can arouse his interest. Of course, his specific interests may be "worthy" ones, like the enjoyment of art. But apart from the notion of worthiness they represent only deepened and narrowed fixations.

Here we come to the cultural value of aesthetic experiences. Culture and art go together. But art is a consequence, not a source, of culture. Because more direct natural pleasures are denied by cultural tradition, men turn to more indirect enjoyments and find them in the objects of human art that accumulate with civilization. Especially has the enlightened and modern attitude of favoring enjoyments strengthened the fixation on aesthetics as a source of pleasure. Fixation, then, has turned aesthetics into an unquestionable sacrosanct cult; fixation can turn any occupation into a cult. The religious nature of this value fixation shows in the superstitious attitude of modern man toward art. He professes unquestioningly to recognize the value of art and to like it, though he does not know on what its value really rests, and may even not genuinely enjoy it. In the Middle Ages everybody professed religious zeal for fear of being considered uncivilized. All cults derive their unquestioned authority from the higher status of their priests and followers, so that any doubts of common sense are overridden. The priests and followers of art come from the more civilized and learned milieus for reasons we have just mentioned.

Actually, aesthetics or the enjoyment of beauty does not help culture. Conditioning is the source of culture, but enjoyment of beauty never serves conditioning. First, the aim of such enjoyment is satisfaction, whereas the basis of conditioning is restriction of satisfactions. Second, any feeling of beauty is a strictly specific reaction that accompanies or measures a definite physiological function. *Such reactions cannot be changed and are not intended to be changed by aesthetics.* For instance, aesthetics does not aim to change our appreciation of a beautiful human body or of beautiful things, but rather to enhance it. Therefore aesthetics can lead to deepening rather than restricting and conditioning our natural feelings and reactions. In terms of simple common sense, enjoyments of beauty are useless pleasures; and pleasures stem from what is closer to the animal than to man. Historically, peoples aspiring to higher culture and spirituality have, rather, opposed useless artistic enjoyments. Only during periods of greater ease, as opposed to those of intense spirituality, have such enjoyments multiplied. Naturally, since greater ease follows greater breakthroughs, the impression remains that civilization and art go together. Finally, in our age, that of the greatest ease of all, art has become a cult in itself, and history has been reconstructed in the light of this cult.

It can be argued that the culturally restricted man should be permitted at least this innocent form of enjoyment. But in the light of relativity there is no loss even in terms of enjoyment if man channels all his natural interests, including those serving the sense of beauty, into culturally useful work.

HARMONY

Belief in the harmony and purpose of the world is one of the most delusory human beliefs. The very reason why harmony, purpose and lawfulness in nature are so prominently noticed as values by man is that nature is governed by an all-pervading disharmony and chaos. Because man has constantly to struggle against this chaos in nature, constantly to seek for some regularity and law in it, he values and notices these above everything else. He finally sees everything in the world under the aspect of harmony and purpose. Here we have a typical instance of the general fallacy of the human *value approach*. Positive values are

233

prominently noticed whereas the general negative backgrounds which are their real causal source are not even suspected.

This fallacy has been brought to its heights by humanistic theorists and philosophers. Under their value approach, the striking discoveries and salient truths are the ones in which the value emerges with the greatest strength, that is, where the true causal background of disvalue is strongest. This explains why thousands of years of humanistic philosophizing had the effect only of keeping man away from discovering the simplest general truths about nature and himself.

For instance, so far the greatest discovery in the natural sciences is the theory of natural selection. It is so simple that even the intelligence of a child is sufficient to understand it. At the same time it is so revealing that the greatest miracles of nature become clear in its light. But this truth remained unnoticed so long because it went against the value outlook. The recognition of natural selection represents the first instance of reversal in the value outlook: selection shows adversity or opposition as the real source of progress and "harmony" in nature. The breakthrough here is, however, rather accidental and isolated, since the general causal principles have been perceived here only in regard to one specific field. All fields of the natural sciences could attain equal breakthroughs by recognizing negative universal causation or negative causal backgrounds. We saw what can be done in the field of psychology by such a change of approach, and what revolutionary changes it could bring in every area of theory, even in that of the physical sciences.

The one-sidedness of the value outlook, however, still keeps its grip on man's thoughts and shows him as true what is least true causally. For instance, on the major problem of man's place in the universe and on the source of progress, the humanistic value outlook is, scientifically, the worst possible help. Under this outlook harmony and purposefulness in nature are seen as its inherent essences. In simple words, this means a belief in Providential creation through a human-like intelligence, and an intention to comply with such Providence, whereas exactly the opposition to what is "provided" for is the real source of all progress. It is true

234

that the harmony and purpose which man recognizes in nature are of the same kind as the purposefulness or reasoning of the human mind. But we have to remember that human intelligence itself is a product of endless adversities embodied in man's adjustment during his evolution. That is what makes man different from an alga. The alga shows a far more harmonious adjustment. It has been left in water, provided with everything it requires to exist without the need to move, protect itself or know how to hunt and fight. But man sees little harmony in such an adjustment. In other words, man sees the greatest harmony where there is causally the greatest disharmony.

But could it not be that an animal evolves by discovering the advantages that are Providentially there? It is true that a better adjustment results from evolutionary change, as additional means of meeting difficulties evolve. But *to imply that an animal can strive for a better adjustment means endowing it with prescience.* The only "good" or "better" adjustment that an animal can strive for, by itself, automatically, is that which serves to maintain its *existing state.* That state is its only criterion of satisfaction. A change in it can be produced only by forcible pressures from outside, which always are felt as unfavorable and are resisted. If an animal were offered more of what it feels as pleasant and as improvements, it would degenerate, become sluggish, and would reach its goals of maturing or reproduction faster, which would mean a shorter, less complex or more primitive life, and less worthy progeny.

Any improvement in the animal can be produced only through forcible intervention from outside. This intervention, however, can be only negative or adverse in this world. There are always millions of possible processes that can harm an organism for every one that could fit it harmoniously. The living process is the most unsuited process in our universe, governed by the dispersion of energy and the destruction of organization. But due to the persistence, especially by way of reproduction, of living beings and their inner processes, *every adversity has the unexpected effect of improving them.* A difficulty may block or destroy most of the given processes or organisms, but amidst the surging myriads there may be some that find a way around the difficulty. They thus become more complex and more capable of dealing with the difficulty. By reproduction the new capacity is consolidated and serves as the basis for a cumulatively increasing, further selective progress. Of course, there are innumerable organisms and processes which are irrevocably extinguished under these difficulties. Our world is not the best of all worlds, but only such as happens to result from the interaction of adverse processes.

By the way, Being itself, as the basic concept of everything, means adversity. If something existed without opposition, i.e., differentiation from anything, even the perceiving mind, then it would have no form and could not be perceived. It would be equal to nothingness.

The above process of improvement through adversity is much more general than natural selection in its usual sense. Adversity or chaos exerts its selectively improving influence in all instances where there is some self-persisting or self-reproducing phenomenon sufficient to sustain the play of opposition. We saw how adversity working on the inner organic mechanisms that intensively persist under the pleasure principle produces what we called inner selection (without which the selection, as usually understood, would lead to extinction rather than improvement of the species). All conditioning and learning, on an evolutionary as well as individual level, result from encountering adversities and selecting new ways, under the same persistent search for satisfaction or pleasure. The intellect itself serves as an infinitesimal miniaturized experiment for encountering difficulties and persisting under them. The mind realizes innumerable dangers and difficulties through foresight and selects the way out of them. Thus incomparably richer selection can take place without the individual having to be physically involved in the adversities. If he had to, he could rarely survive. Further, societies, and culture with them, evolve because of selection under the greatest of all difficulties for man — hostility and threats from other men.

In the physical world, the few aspects that exhibit harmony, law or order are equally due to adversity. Atoms, planets and suns show in their fundamental aspects such incredibly uniform, wonderously orderly effects and forms that a universal lawgiver may seem to be at work. Actually, the real creator of the fundamental laws is the fundamental opposition between forces — we shall explain them later — an opposition that is universal, inexorable and blind. This explains why these laws are so uniform everywhere, so endlessly repetitive and so inhumanly simple. Fundamental opposition further explains the miracle of universal order. The order is so great because the absence of freedom is so all-inclusive. Due to opposition, only that which fits permanently and thoroughly or "harmoniously" with the rest can persist. Everything else is eliminated forever. Here we meet with the widest realization of selection: everything exists by reason of its capacity to persist under adversity — by virtue and for the sake of existence. Here we also meet with the self-realization of such selection at its very basis. For all evolution starts with, and is ultimately determined by the fundamental physical processes.

Actually, our very notions of "fundamental laws" are due to the fact that this same *opposition* is the *identical* principle by which both universe and man exist. This identity is what makes these laws appear so *simple* or *orderly* to man — what makes them into "fundamental laws."

Apart from the miraculously orderly and "alive" fundamental effects of atoms and suns, the rest of the physical world is endlessly chaotic, dead, and shows little harmonious adjustment. The reason is that in the rest of the physical world there is little persisting opposition. But where such opposition does exist, "harmonious" formations appear. Rushing waters form wondrous rivers, waves battering against the land build sea walls, and winds streamline the surface of the earth.

Naturally, the greatest opposition is reached where the opposing forces are closely matched. If one side is too strong, it overcomes the other, making opposition nonexistent, and loses itself in a formless diffusion. To that extent there can be no notion of any form or even of Being. This is the reason why the most harmonious forms in nature — from atom to human intellect — are found where there is more of such "balance" between the opposing forces. And the richest harmonies are found where the closely equaling or balanced opposing forces meet on numerous fronts or in numerous aspects, as is the case with human adjustment.

The value outlook, which reveals only harmony and order, implies looking at things in their last, as if ready given state. Under this outlook understanding a phenomenon means seeing it in its existing specific value or essence. Going into the past history or evolution of the phenomenon is therefore pointless, since that can only disturb or unnecessarily complicate the view. If there is historical inquiry, it extends only to a search for a causal source of a *similar* essence or value. In view of the universal *opposite* background causation, the result is that the value outlook, by way of avoiding contradictions, inevitably gravitates toward explanations which exclude anything truly causal or evolutionary. This is the reason why philosophy as the most characteristic discipline of the humanistic approach deals only with the given value essences and their idealistic sources, never with the truly causal or materialistic origins of phenomena.

We wish to illustrate the fallacy of the value outlook by a simple example. Let us look at some simple "harmonious" creation—for instance, a river. Viewed in its essence, or already evolved stage, the river would clearly appear to be built and directed in a most ingenious way. It flows through innumerable valleys connected so wisely that over hundreds of miles it finds its way to the ocean in the straightest possible and most economical way. The terrain is ideally hewn out for the river to flow smoothly and quickly. The banks are streamlined and exactly sufficient to hold the water in the most efficient stream, and wise provision has been made for more water during peak periods. The route is streamlined so that the flow encounters the least resistance. The river bed is cut in a most rational way. Where harder rocks are encountered, the channel is detoured through softer ground, but if that would mean too great a detour, the rock is attacked— in its softest parts first. There seems to be an ingenious calculation between what effort would be wasted and what advantage gained by breaking a new channel or enlarging an old one. Where there are too deep depressions, they are filled in to provide a more efficient flow. In case a tributary flows in, the river bed is enlarged so as to take care of the additional water. Further, provision has been made even for the users of the river. Where deepwater fish live, the river is deeper. Where delicate water plants grow, water is not permitted to rush in torrents. Where animals come to drink, the river bank is made more accessible. And where people have to construct a bridge to connect two meeting roads, the banks are made more suitable for it. Also where cities depending on navigation are situated, the river is made deep and large enough for ships.

The naïveté in this example is exaggerated to bring out the point. Incidentally, an English geographer a century ago pointed out that fortunately the great English cities have been provided with good natural harbors. The point is that any final stage, or state of balance, self-establishing in nature, when looked at with "harmony" in mind and in its final, already evolved stage seems to be intelligently planned. The adjustment in living nature is not different from the formation of a river, except that incomparably more forces are involved and that due to reproduction the "harmonies" are cumulatively amplified through millions of years.

What we said may be sufficient to show that due to his value outlook man sees in an exactly reversed way, causally, the universe he lives in, and his own evolution. He sees the greatest harmony or Providence where there is the greatest adversity and lack of Providence. The deeper reason for this delusion is that man cannot accept disvalue as the source of value. And it is *exactly the most important aspects of man's world that are affected by this fallacy, because in these aspects his value feelings are strongest.* The result is a complete causal misunderstanding in regard to the most important problems of man's adjustment and progress. As we have said, a complete submission to "Providence" is seen as the goal, whereas only opposition to what is really "provided" can lead to progress. Of course, in practice the wise, though blind and dismally slow cultural tradition makes man act against all "Providence." To explain the resulting contradictions, men have resorted to unbelievably complex, endless, anthropo-

morphic mystifications in religion, philosophy and every humanistic theory. This humanistic delusionism is deepening with the
ascendancy of theorization, but a *planned* progress would depend
on the exact reversal of every tenet and discovery of such humanistic theorization.

REASON AND TRUTH

Equally delusory is man's belief in his own reasons and truths.
Everybody believes that he is living according to pure reason
and is pursuing only the truth. From the Papuan seeking to kill
a tribesman pointed out by the witch doctor to the philosopher
writing volumes in defense of his theory, everybody acts according to reason. Thousands of conflicting beliefs held by men through
millenniums have been accepted as expressions of incontestable
truths. Sensible people, in their practical business of living, look
with derision on those who are seeking for truths. But the humanist
philosopher or educator considers it his life goal to find truths and
show them to others. What he usually finds are rationalizations
of whatever moral views are held in his society.

We do not intend to say that there is any better way at present
to teach, or to defend morals and culture. Everybody knows that
reason is the most precise instrument man has for finding out
what is right. That is why everybody devises reasons for what
he emotionally wants to do. The moral theorist does the same.
As long as he succeeds in convincing himself and others, he is
the best teacher or spiritual leader. At the present state of knowledge, the cultural tradition, however delusory, is still better than
any of the half-understood truths of our "scientists" and rationalists.

In any case, innumerable volumes are written by our spiritual
leaders about the right way to reason, discover rational proofs
and have or not have reasons for doing this or that — as if the
reasons could really determine our motivations. Any reason can
be turned the way a person feels — the way he is conditioned to
feel. For instance, all great scriptures are similar as far as truths
or reasons are concerned. But they have been used to justify

conditioned dissensions so great that people have seen the exter-
mination of each other as the only way out. Communism is the
most perfect system as far as reasons are concerned. But since
it does not provide corresponding motivation, it becomes a nightmare in practice. Rationalists have always been the pest of
humanity — so much so that people have developed an instinctive
aversion and immunity to them. But it is exactly the rationalist
who attains most nearly what every humanist proclaims as the
goal to be attained, namely, rational truths.

People are unreasonable not because they lack reasons but
because their emotional negativism turns them into irrational
neurotics. But as we saw, the causes of such emotional negativism
are paradoxical. Striving for positive emotions the direct and
easy way, as advocated by the reasoning theorist, the experimental
scientist or logical rationalist, leads exactly to such negativism.
No wonder "reasonable" people and rationalists are more often
unreasonable than emotionally well-conditioned people.

Though our humanistic education sees the revelation of reasons and truths as its goal, its real contribution is the creation
of an atmosphere of superior authority, necessary for conditioning.
Reason is used because it gives an aura of intellectual superiority
to that atmosphere. But as to the reasons acquired, they could as
well be anything else, as they are in different cultures. The
maxim that knowledge makes one free is a gem of humanistic
delusionism. If the student were made free through knowledge,
he would become a rationalist, just like any other rationalist —
something to be avoided like a plague. Humanistic education
supplies convictions and arguments, labeled as truths, to be used
against rationalistic tendencies — which represent the closest approach to free reasoning.

The feeling of a person about his own reasonableness is paradoxical, as all feelings are. The less reasonable, a person is, the
more he feels that he is reasonable. This can be easily observed
from everyday life. Reason has emotional appeal while it is
emerging, while the satisfaction is going on. When reason becomes
established, and is really worth something, the satisfaction has
worn itself out. This explains the fervor of youthful convictions,

and the resignation of wise men. Also, emotional investment determines the degree of conviction. A person having cultivated certain views for life cannot abandon them overnight. Emotional investment also explains why people who live by emotions rather than reason find their reasons more strongly convincing than people who really live by reason.

The existence of higher reason in the world is one of the main humanistic tenets. The problem, approached philosophically, is puzzling indeed. Why is everything in the world around us meaningful in terms of reason, and everything we think of comprehensible? How can natural phenomena coincide with the forms of the human intellect? Actually, there is no mystery if one abandons the philosophical approach and thinks how our intellectual notions evolve historically. There is an infinite number of ways in which man could think or adjust so that it all would *not* make sense. For obvious reasons he does not choose them. His life is a constant effort to find the few ways which happen to make sense. Through generations, these few *selective* ways become embodied in all human traditions, habits, speech, notions of thought, cultural environment and everything man deals with. All the things that make sense are like a thin thread through an ocean of nonsense. But this thread is the only thing we follow or know.

In a word, man first arranges the world to suit his reason. then overlooks the endless arrangements he has made and wonders at how miraculously everything is there to fit his reason. We do not mean to say that man is fooled this easily. The common man understands intuitively and the scientist scientifically what is happening, and they never proclaim any mysteries here. Only when the philosophical method of viewing things in their essence or final stage is applied, does mystery result and give rise to abstruse philosophical theories.

PURPOSE OF LIFE

Belief in the purpose of life is related to belief in higher reason in the world. Naturally, the less purpose there is in man's life, the more he feels a need for it, the more he values it and the stronger is his belief in it as the essence of life. When men lived primitively amidst real dangers and dire needs, their lives were full of immediate purposes, as well as fears of death. But men evolved no formulations then about the purpose of life or the problem of death. These emerged when civilization eliminated man's pressing purposes and fears. Then the inherent purposelessness of existence gave rise to a strong need for some abstract purpose and to a deep belief in it. Likewise, the inherent fear of death accumulated into and abstract immensity, under the absence of everyday fears, and gave rise to the belief in immortality. This is reflected in all higher religions and philosophies.

The same development can be observed in individual lives. As long as a person follows real purposes in life, he never thinks about life's purpose. Only after he reaches an emotional state of purposelessness, does he start evolving deep beliefs about the purposefulness of human existence.

LOVE

From the behaviorist theory of conditioning to the deepest religious belief in God love has been invoked as an explanation. This can be done because love actually means the general availability of motivation. Common speech reflects this: one can "love" alcohol as well as his fellow man. Scientifically, there is only one kind of motivation or love: satisfaction growing out of the innumerable egotistic needs. But the paradoxical logic of the enrichment of satisfaction through its opposite — need or non-satisfaction — applies here as well. The more there is of such non-satisfaction or restriction, the greater becomes the potential of available motivation or love.

The richest potential of love or motivation is reached when the egotistic satisfactions are restricted so highly by conditioning that they have gradually been turned against themselves and become selfless love. This is the hardest endeavor for man, but to the extent that such conditioning is reached everything else becomes attainable by him. If men had more selfless love, every utopia, social as well as economic, would become a reality. The plain

243

availability of such motivation or enriched satisfaction is the measure of all success in adjustment. If a person has rich motivation, he can do anything, and performs automatically the noblest deeds of love. That is why everybody wants to have love — love for all the world.

Of course, the humanist outlook reveals only the satisfaction stage — the pleasant, rich, all-powerful feeling of love — never the hard opposite process by which such satisfaction is made possible. We have explained repeatedly how a heavenly love, as an enriched potential of satisfactions, grows out of the accumulation of needs and restrictions because of ever-present implied threats and insecurity that rather resemble hell. The delusion about love as a natural altruistic feeling is deepened by the fact that man tends to attach his notions of love primarily to the love between parent and child or between lovers. There the one partner needs the other, and is therefore fearful of seeing any harm done to him. Also, the cooperation is so reciprocal that more is received as more is given. The more pleasant a lover becomes, the more love he gets. Through long evolution, the very act or capacity of being pleasant or attractive becomes a pleasure in itself.

But it should be clear that the natural forms of love have not much to do with the truly self-denying love that makes higher adjustment possible. The loving parent can be so much more intolerant toward others because of his love for his child; the same applies to romantic love. Parental love is love of self. The offspring is felt, treated and protected by the parent as if it were part of himself. This is clearly evident in the case of animals; and the basis of natural human parental love is the same. Human parents as well have no regard for the well-being that a child might have while being separated from them. A mother often kills her children before she commits suicide. If she had the slightest feeling for her children's own happiness, she would see this as the most horrible act under any circumstances. Also, the mother who sees the love of a child taken away from her throws to the winds all considerations about the well-being of the child. Likewise, the child does not hesitate to inflict pain on the parents if

244

he is jealous; or to oppose them if he feels safe enough on his own, and is free of conditioning.

Love for one's child or one's own family member grows also out of a fixational attachment that increases as it continues. Animals adopt as their own strange offspring put in the litter. In case of man, the attachments are more-sided. A person who has cared for years for his child or brother cannot abandon him suddenly without great emotional loss. For the same reason an adopted child becomes as loved as a child of one's own blood. The belief in ties of blood is just a rationalization. But it may nurture other wider rationalizations, such as objection to artificial insemination. The surest way of transforming the world is by transforming man himself. His own genetic improvement is the first and most important task that man as a planning, intelligent being should undertake. It is the lever by which he can achieve what nature could never achieve. Unfortunately, human value fixations prevent man here, as in many other cases, from stretching out his hand and taking what is right before his eyes.

Romantic love is even more obviously motivated by egotistic needs. More cruelty is inflicted because of love than for any other reason. As soon as one partner seeks his own happiness, without the participation of the other, the latter is ready for any cruelty. Jealousy serves as the surest measurement of love, but there is hardly any feeling that is more markedly egotistic than jealousy. By the way, in romantic love the paradox of opposite causation is particularly evident. Logically, it would seem that a person who has received much love should have only a rich treasure of happiness left when it ends. In fact, the more he has received, the greater his suffering when the relationship ends.

The richness and depth of romantic love reveal how the psychological self is built. Plainly, primitive sexual or reproductive need is the source of such love. If that simple need is not there or is satisfied fully, there is none of the heavenly idealistic romance full of the varied value emotions and the noblest thoughts. Apparently, values and cultural ideas are conditioned on the deeper releases, and when these are stirred, everything else moves with them. Every need seems to reach its glorious satisfaction for the lover.

This amounts to intoxication and the aftermath is inevitable. It is, however, mitigated by the continued love relationship. Only when this breaks down is the aftermath felt in full. Then every enjoyment lived through has to be paid for by an equal suffering. Suicide then may seem to be a logical escape. Goethe's *Werthers Leiden*, the prototype story of tragic love, is so convincing because Goethe describes in it every opposite aftermath of every enjoyment previously lived through. But even in a lucky, continuing relationship the aftermath manifests itself and becomes a source of puzzling reactions. Sullivan, in his previously quoted book, looks for subconscious causes to explain the contradiction that couples often are not satisfied with each other but are even less satisfied without each other.

Falling in love is interesting. Though "love on first sight" is not taken too seriously, people still believe that unhappy falling in love can bring unearned suffering. In fact, there can never be suffering without previous enjoyment. A person may discover the most suitable partner, but if he is realistic about it and avoids previous enjoyment, the effect is the same as seeing a beauty in a movie. In most cases, however, a person falling in love enjoys in imagination or reality whatever goes with such intoxication. Then the suffering becomes inevitable. Such emotional investment, together with fixation, can increase the love for one person to a degree not warranted by any reasons. Hence the belief that there is something fateful about falling in love, or that one can love only one person. The truth is far less romantic. Though we would all consider ourselves "born for" a beautiful movie star if we had the opportunity, we take what we can get, but by fixation elevate it into sacredness. The misunderstanding here — coupled with the unwillingness to face suffering even temporarily — is responsible for the modern attitude according to which nothing can be done once adolescents have fallen in love.

The intoxicating nature of love is revealed best in literature and art. There the love theme is so persistent and repetitive that a Martian unacquainted with the feeling would see it all as an incredible bore. He would not see any essential difference between it and the endless croaking of frogs on a spring night. The purpose and nature of both are the same. But because of his intoxication the lover feels that he is attaining something sublime and having an experience so unique that nothing else can compare with it. The realization that every man, even a moron, has experienced an equally deep feeling means nothing to the lover.

The intoxicating nature of love shows in its influence on motivation as well. There is a great release of positive emotions — all of which have to be paid for later — but it is all squandered. The perennial lover produces little. On the other side, the suffering of the unlucky lover leads to great achievements; it serves as the background for increased motivation.

We have mentioned before how a naïve romanticism in love performs the important role of refining the tastes so that the more spiritual qualities become preferred in reproductive selection.

When it comes to real, selfless love, satisfaction has to come from its opposite, nonsatisfaction or the imposition of needs through restrictive conditioning. There full opposition between the sublimity or pleasantness of love and the baseness or unpleasantness of its true causal source is the law. We shall not repeat the explanation of why it is important, at least in theory, to see beyond the humanistic delusion. But perhaps an illustration may help to bring out the point in practical terms.

Let us look at the behavior of a well-trained animal. We would find in it eagerness to please the master, to follow his every wish, to bear sacrifice for him genuinely and without reserve. We would also see satisfaction after a good performance, which we would interpret as noble pride; and interest in the master, as the animal tries to discover his every wish; as well as refinement in the mutual relationship. In a word, it all adds up to a big, genuine love. Yet the trainer knows that nothing but beating, threat or exploitation of the animal's hunger and need for security can produce this behavior. If the trainer let the animal do what it really loves — to be satisfied and free — it would revert to a vicious beast. Typically enough, when training is complete, the animal as well as the master really do love each other. When satisfaction is there, the need that created it is forgotten. We have explained before why in the training of man refinement rather than enforcement augments the efficiency of the threat.

The highest expression of love, love of God, shows the same need-satisfaction structure. The most typical fact about all beliefs is that gods are not invented in those situations where there are no needs, threats, dangers or deficiencies. If men lived in a true paradise, immortally, with every need satisfied, there would be no belief in gods. The same applies in individual lives. As long as a person fares well, he does not care about God. But a calamity, or the threat of the ultimate calamity, death, brings forth religious zeal and love of God. It is certainly true that man, like the dog, has the greatest love for his Master when beaten by Him. One can easily observe that the more wretched a person gets, the more love he has for the Great Master on whom his fate depends. And the love here is genuine. There is so much genuine satisfaction because there is so much need.

In this connection we may mention the curious self-accusations of prisoners under despotic regimes, like the confessions of accused counterrevolutionaries in Russia. We do not need to go into detail. We have just seen how a genuine love and sincere submission emerge from a threat or need which is their opposite. All that is required is that the despotic power be absolute, like that of a god; that the person have no hope of saving himself by resistance; and that he have no recourse for reassurance to any other authority or god. Then the need to comply with the will of the despot becomes the only need. And the satisfaction of it becomes genuine: the person invents his own accusations and sincerely believes in them. We always invent reasons and beliefs when the corresponding need is there.

HOPE AND FAITH

As with love, hope or faith means only a degree in one or another specific emotion, satisfaction or need, which in this case are derived by anticipation. Opposite causation applies here as in all emotions. If one tries to increase hope artificially, by intoxication or exaggerated optimism, he ends with an equally exag-

248

gerated depression. That is why more foresighted people never engage in unfounded hopes, though everybody knows how pleasant hope is and how much positive motivation it brings.

This does not mean that feelings of hope or faith should be shunned. Man's progress is only as great as his imagination. But this imagination should serve the accumulation of needs, not the enjoyment of satisfactions. Psychologists see only the satisfaction factor in hope as beneficial. Enjoying such satisfaction means losing it, and ending with its reverse — anxiety. Imagination should paint the future as glorious and real, but the person should suffer rather the pain of not having it, and should develop a burning need to attain it. Faith can do more than move mountains. Socially, if everyone believed that upon the abdication of his egotistic interests everybody else would do the same and that all would benefit far beyond what they abdicated, then in fact all the aspired benefits would be attained. Also, confidence could sustain a never-ending economic boom at any level, which would lead to virtual utopia.

Utopias are unrealistic not because they could not work, but because there is not enough reciprocal faith and realistic hope. If we could emotionally believe as fully in the future of a thousand years from now as we can construct it in our minds, we would soon make that utopian future come true. Some kind of Science of the Future, still better a Religion of the Future, is the most needed and appropriate discipline that could be taught men as planning, intelligent beings. We do not have it because the inertia of the past rather than imagination has shaped our methods of education.

FREEDOM

Enjoyment of freedom dominates the minds of modern men. Everybody, from teen-agers resenting parental interference to new nations expecting miracles from independence, extols the value of freedom. The general attitude is that freedom in itself can provide all the benefits of better adjustment or social progress. This is a fallacy perpetuated by the same one-sided humanistic value outlook. Freedom in itself is nonsensical. A lone savage having all the freedom he wishes has no feeling of freedom. The meaning as well as the motivational force of freedom derive only from its opposite, restriction. Freedom has increased as a value in the highest societies exactly because restrictions have increased with the advance of culture. No wonder the ideals of freedom have dominated all the social movements of the most civilized peoples in the recent times. Then the humanistic theorist, looking at the cultural history, constitutions, declarations, slogans and theories, sees freedom as the essence and source of culture.

Actually, in social movements as well as in individual lives men advance because of the lure of freedom or release, but learn in the end to accept greater restrictions. This is evident from all revolutions, the history of political parties, or "corruption" of religious teachings, as well as in everyday education. It cannot be otherwise. Advance in adjustment always means restriction, but restriction can be imposed only through the operation of release.

The misunderstandings that result from the value delusion here may have practical consequences no less serious than bloodshed. We teach the young African leader that his people should fight for freedom, whereas they need subordination and restriction more than anything else. Perhaps the end result is not too different either way. People who gain their freedom soon drive themselves into greater subordination than before. But, as always, such learning through misunderstanding is costly in suffering, even lives, full of passionate conflicts, and often brutish in practice in spite of noble pronouncements.

The delusion about freedom is deepened by the fact that people living under the tightest system of restrictions, like an atmospheric pressure, feel only lessenings of it and therefore extol only their freedoms. Further, the means of restriction have become extremely refined. In a highly civilized society everybody tries to live and bring up his children in such a way that the more severe restrictions never have to be applied to them. This increases the sensitivity and further refinement of restrictions to the point of obsessional perfectionism. Also, the amount of restrictive pressure is increased by seemingly giving more freedom to everybody under democratic systems: everybody becomes exposed to pressure by everybody else at every moment and in every matter.

SENSE OF HUMOR

The nature of the comic is intriguing. Many theorists have written about it. Bergson wrote a whole book on it, *Le Rire,* which is regarded as one of the main treatises in his system. Most theorists have seen contrast as the basis of the comic. But contrast explains nothing, since everything is experienced by differentiation or contrast. The real essence of the comic is a release from the restrictions of the tense seriousness of normal life. In other words, the comic means a rich and strong experience of unseriousness or lack of seriousness, just as common sense shows it to be. The question is, how can the lack of something be presented richly and strongly? That is where contrast as the method comes in. *The comic results from presentation of the lack of seriousness in rich and sharp contrast with seriousness.*

Actually, such a presentation has to be surreptitious so that the person is induced to accept it against his intention. Otherwise he would reject it. For the main task of normal life is to uphold restrictions, which constitute seriousness, so that normal releases or "serious" motivations are kept available. This explains why men lapse very easily into mirth when normal tensions or restrictions are removed, as in the case of intoxication or when there is implied permission to ease restrictions, as when other persons around, especially higher-standing ones, are laughing.

The requirement of contrast and surreptitiousness explains why a joke must start with seriousness and follow an inevitable logical sequence. The listener has to be led into accepting the situation seriously, and only at the very end should discover the unseriousness involved; the joke ends with that because that is its very essence. The more subtle and sudden the discovery, the greater the contrast and feeling of the comic. Further, the joke has to provide this in an ingenious way, never imagined before, since

251

any easily imagined humor has already been tried by everybody and has become no longer enjoyable under the general need for seriousness in life. Because that which is comic is difficult to imagine, jokes are difficult to recall. Above all, the whole situation must exclude any real seriousness, for it is the unseriousness that is enjoyed.

That laughing means release is evident even from the way it goes off — like a pricked balloon. Naturally, there can be no release if there is no previous restriction. This explains why *only man as the most tense or most restricted of all animals is capable of laughter*. It also explains why the more cultured, which means the more restricted, person has a higher sense of humor. The low-grade, primitive person who is ready to laugh at every moment never has a real sense of humor. Everybody knows, intuitively, that the sense of humor reveals a richer personality, and everybody wants to show it off. But to really have it one must pay in previous restrictions and suffering. The person who has a true genius for the comic is actually the rare person who has a background of deep seriousness but also the readiness to abandon it. This may come as a result of disappointments and resignations in life.

DISVALUES

Any disvalue derives its meaning and existence from a previous value which is its opposite. There can be only as much disvalue as there was previous accumulation of value — as much disturbance as there was normalcy. In physiological terms this means that there can be only as much pain as there was previous accumulation of growth. Something that has not grown cannot deteriorate or die and, therefore, cause pain. A person who has never grown a certain part of his body, or has been born with a restricted system, feels nothing in particular about it, though a normal person would feel excruciating pain if he were reduced to such a state. Equally, a person who has already lost a part of his body, or fully lived through certain restrictions of his system, as happens with old age, experiences no further pain.

In brief, the relativity rule applies to disvalue or pain just as it applies to any value. This means the strict equivalence of opposite emotions, and the paradoxical logic of increase through decrease, or vice versa, in regard to any kind of experience.

An important aspect of disvalue or pain is that while it is felt it is accompanied by a striving to restore the previous state. That is the function of all negative reactions as the need side of the universal pleasure mechanism, which ultimately serves the maintenance of organic normalcy. We explained before that higher living adjustment is a complex interplay between two opposed principles: the natural tendency toward pleasure, which leads to accumulation of growth; and conditional restrictions, imposed by circumstances during evolution and individual life, which make growth more complex, longer-lasting or, actually, retarded, and skillfully refined. To the extent that either side is left unsustained normal adjustment collapses. Therefore the negative reactions which serve the conservation of the already attained state of accumulated pleasure or growth are absolutely essential. *Artificially* eliminating negative reactions means abandoning the body's effort to protect or restore growth. At the same time, elimination of pain *naturally*, by the successful restoration of normalcy, mostly through strenuous trial-and error efforts and painful readjustments, is the very purpose of organic life.

But man does not make a distinction between artificial and natural ways in the removal of negative reactions. In other words, man is ready to shut off alarms and skip safety procedures when these impose hard, strenuous adjustments. Here we have one of the greatest dangers to man as a conscious, planning being. Only his incapacity to produce means subtle enough to eliminate all negative feelings especially the "side" effects, has kept man from destroying his normalcy. But with the advance of science this incapacity is gradually overcome and the danger progressively increased.

PAIN

A prototype of all negative feelings is physical pain. As can be expected, there has been little study of pain, and there is even less understanding of its nature. One thing, however, is clear: the rule of relativity, or of diminishing effect, applies to pain. This rule is confirmed by the generally recognized Weber-Fechner law, which represents a mathematical approximation of the relativity rule. In terms of this law, if a certain pain is caused by an injury of, let us say, ten units, then an injury of a million units would increase that pain only six times. Practical observation shows this to be true. A person feels acutely a prick in the finger, but may be able to endure, with only a few times greater pain, an amputation of the whole arm.

Experiments with pain thresholds have confirmed the Weber-Fechner law and the relativity of pain in general. Dr. Hardy's study of pain thresholds showed that once the excruciating pain maximum is reached, as when skin has been exposed to the temperature of 152 degrees, the pain remains constant upon further increase of injury. The experiments showed that an intractable high-intensity pain is a physiological impossibility. Medieval torturers wasted their time in adding greater efficiency features to their machines. Pain, like any emotion, consumes itself. The famous surgeon Le Riche has explained that pain persists only so long as a person tries to avoid it. Under the relativity rule pain returns if it is avoided. Drugs or anesthetics only delay pain. During an operation under anesthetics organic normalcy may be disturbed but also restored. So far there is no cause for later pain. But insofar as such restoration has not been made, e.g., when a limb has been amputated, the pain is suffered afterward, as the anesthetic wears off. Hence postoperational pain.

Other experimental observations have confirmed the relativity of negative experiences. Yacorzynski gives in his *Medical Psychology* a summary of experimental findings on depression, which is sufficiently typical of all negative emotions. According to this summary, the emotion of depression involves the same mechanisms as the emotion of excitement. Secondly, the emotion of depression is produced only by conditions which first produced an emotion of excitement.

More painful than physical pain is the psychological pain that we know as anxiety, fear, depression or threat of death. Man is ready to accept the greatest physical pain or inconvenience to avoid such feelings. Though the two kinds of pain may not always appear to be clearly related, nature has organically integrated them in an incredibly precise, commensurable order. The whole miracle of adjustment rests on our capacity to assess precisely in terms of mental emotions any physical pain or difficulty awaiting us. Anxiety builds up in exact proportion to the threatening pain or difficulty; and to avoid that anxiety anything less painful or difficult is undertaken. The organism knows how to relate these so precisely because it has been evolved in its every part and detail through the operation of the same universal principle of pleasure.

It cannot be overemphasized that pain should not be treated by scientists as just an accidental feeling accompanying other reactions, as psychologists now hold. Even without going into theorizing whether the feeling *is* the reaction, as the James-Lange theory implies, we can say that pain guides the organism away from harm. This is so evident that it hardly needs explanation. We would perish in a day if we did not feel as painful, and therefore did not avoid, injuries, cold, fatigue, thirst or any other damaging influence. The processes here are so incredibly complex, but also so miraculously purposeful, that only the integrated value feelings of pain and pleasure can serve as guides. To try to replace this guidance by any intervention based on other data or on analytic interpretation in other terms amounts to madness. Only the imitation of "scientism" and the complete misunderstanding of the causal logic of value reactions has prevented psychologists and human scientists from recognizing here the simple but all-important significance of pain in dealing scientifically with human reactions. A true science of living adjustment can be built only on such value phenomena and their causal laws.

In connection with pain as value feeling we have to mention the erroneous imputation of the feeling of pain to animals. An animal does not know that it exists. Still less can it consciously feel anything. The animal reacts the same as man; but in any value terms such reaction is as meaningless as the "reaction" of a cloud to the wind. Conscious life emerges only with the specific restrictions that make a new additional system of "reserves" and reactions possible. All these would be automatically excluded as superfluous hindrances in the animal's more direct adjustment, even if they had arisen in the first place.

The imputation of feelings to animals, just as our love for them, is an animistic fallacy due to lack of insight beyond superficial resemblances. That is why primitive people, or children, have real "friends" among animals. Generally, those who love their dogs only extend the domain of their own egotism, whereas they should restrict it so that the real love of other men would become possible. But what about infants, who are equally without consciousness? There we are too close to a future conscious being in every respect to withold the fullest compassion. But, as a matter of fact, the infant equally feels no pain, just as he does not know that he exists. What would it have mattered to me, for instance, if even the greatest pain had been inflicted on me before I started to acquire the first inklings of consciousness, which reach importance only with the beginnings of speech?

DEATH

Death means the ultimate degree of pain, because it takes away the last bit of our previous well-being or growth. Man starts from zero and returns to zero in his physiological life and, with it, in his psychological reactions, which depend upon it. The "ups" and "downs" in between are finally equalized. If there is much of the accumulated growth left before the end, the descent is so much the steeper.

But cannot a person die suddenly without experiencing anything? Death means the disintegration of every physiological construct. Since our psychological expriences are all locked in such physiological constructs, every experience finds its final conclusion, the return to zero, upon death. Here we have to remember that time, psychologically, is nothing more than an amount of experiences.

256

Consequently, the psychological duration of even a split-second death can be as long as years. Reports by persons who have lived through threats of sudden death confirm this, though such people must have been only preparing for the real final closure of accounts. Such reports show that the whole life can be relived in a few seconds. Several psychologists have described reports or their own observations showing that a surprising number of experiences can be crowded into the shortest instant.

When faced with its full realization, every man knows intuitively this meaning of death. If offered a choice between a split-second death and long suffering leading to equally certain death, a person may prefer the latter. Only after the suffering has lasted long enough is the person ready to die. By instinct a person knows that the only way to ease the final closure of accounts is by paying off, by abandoning, as much as possible of the remaining growth or well-being. It never works the logical way of getting more well-being and then departing in satisfaction about it. The young person at the peak of his life is most afraid to die, though logically that would be the perfect moment for quitting, since everything good is behind and everything bad ahead. Logically, a person who knows that he is to die should rush into fuller, more joyful living so as to get more of the good things of life while it lasts. In reality, he does just the reverse: he starts declining by his own will so as to leave less to be paid for at the end.

But what about those people who look forward to death as a deliverance? The young and robust person is the first to say that he has no fear of death — because he is actually furthest away from it. As to a person committing suicide, he proceeds under the wrong assumption that a quick payment will be easier. Those who cultivate beliefs in a life hereafter are only accumulating the anguish for the very last moment. Actually, even the most convinced believer knows instinctively what is involved, and fears death, or is ready to live through any misery before dying, the same as everybody else. In practice, the religious person shows deeper insight here than others: he starts paying off early by way of disengagement from the pleasures of life. In fact, any

257

belief as such has little influence. Beliefs as well as feelings only follow physiological changes. That is why the staunchest believer in heaven may see hell open before him or the most assured unbeliever may lose his assurance when his condition becomes critical.

CONCLUSIONS

We could not help being cynical, but our purpose was to look beyond the delusions that the value outlook implies. As we saw, man values most what is lacking in his world. Consequently, the value outlook means seeing as the causal essence of our world what is causally least essential in it. It matters little in practice whether man causally understands his own adjustment or not, so long as he lives by cultural tradition. But tradition is being replaced by "science" and rationalism. The humanist theorist himself helps this change by his insistence on rationalizations based on reason. Thus the value delusions become a source of fallacies. It is pleasant as well as clearly beneficial to have positive emotions, like happiness, love, the feeling of beauty, freedom, hope or faith. But if one tries to promote these emotions in the pleasant direct way, he ends with exactly opposite emotions or emotional negativism as a result. Even the common-sense intuition that you cannot get pleasant emotions without equal effort is lost in "scientific" and humanistic theory. That is why theorists in the human sciences are producing more confusion, mystery and conflicting theories than certainty, especially in regard to the problem of restrictions, on which our "reactionary" cultural tradition rests.

Our cynicism has one excuse: we do not expect to convince anybody. Theorization cannot change man's striving for values. Insofar as any influence could result from the realization of the relativity of values, it would only mean furthering the advance toward the more resigned as well as more productive maturity of civilized people. The persisting delusory value approach means emotional excitement and good intentions but a lack of causal understanding. As in all such cases, the result is passionate conflicts, bigotry and backwardness, in spite of lofty pronouncements.

VIII

CULTURAL VALUE DELUSIONS

Cultural behavior is determined by value feelings. Consequently, the value outlook with all its delusions and fallacies dominates the understanding of cultural phenomena. For instance, the humanist sees the prominence of moral or social values, and attributes them to the moral or social nature of man. In fact, the absence of such a nature is what makes moral norms necessary and highly valued, as well as requires their enactment in the complex normative forms that they have. Or, in the field of religion and philosophy, values like order or harmony, and security or love, are seen as the essence of the world and of a higher order from which they are believed to emanate. Actually, the absence of order or security in the world makes them the highest values for man with all his intense beliefs about their supernatural source. Similarly, in aesthetics, the sublime, deeply meaningful feelings of beauty actually derive from the base, senseless harassments of previous experiences, just as all satisfactions or values derive from needs and disvalues. But all these simple causal truths are the last thing that the humanistic theorist or aesthetician would accept.

As to culture itself, the most important truth here is that *culture evolves in spite of man's intentions.* As we saw, all higher adjustment means more hindered and forced, and with it more complex, resourceful and indirect, adjustment, evolved *through encountering difficulties.* This is the universal rule in all learning or conditioning as the general method of higher evolution, including cultural progress. Man tries to avoid learning as he tries to avoid all difficulties. He wants to remain the way he is, as every animal does.

People live for thousands of years in the same way if they are left undisturbed by pressures (competition may become one form of disturbance or pressure).

All learning is found unpleasant, as every child knows. Of course, human foresight, as the indirect source of pressures, can force man to learn. Further, by long tradition the need for learning becomes a built-in pressure or a value in itself. But even with thousands of years of experience man still has not overcome his resistance to cultural progress. We can easily see by looking backward how dismally slow and blind human progress has been. A few hundred years from now people will wonder how we could have clung so stupidly to our narrow-minded values. We may know, abstractly, even now what the road toward future progress is, but we will not embark on it unless forced; and we will not progress much on it until the majority of men have assimilated more culture in the same painfully enforced way.

Man resists his own cultural inclinations, imposed by way of inertial tradition and conditioning. He finds his feelings of shame, and his inhibitions, even his "conscience," unpleasant, often calamitous hindrances that he constantly tries to get rid of or lessen. He fears his taboos and religious spirits, and seeks to overcome that fear. Every moral rule is felt as a pressure and is obeyed only because of conditioned fears that cannot be overcome. Our acceptance of gods or any authority may seem voluntary enough, but it is so only because we want to get friendly with those who have the authority so that we may escape its severity. Only when we cannot overcome our fears and pressures, conditioned in us, do we comply.

But we seize every opportunity to escape that fear. We like intoxication of every kind because it helps us in this effort. We like mass movements of liberation, because by feeling others around us rebelling against the yoke of restrictions we feel safer in doing the same. And we like all kinds of "enlightenment" and rationalism because they help us oppose cultural restrictions in the name of reason. Human history is characterized by such revolts and movements — which defeat themselves as the people start realizing their consequences and learn the necessity of the same old restrictions. Here belong the perennial conflicts between generations, between fathers and sons.

Moral rules always mean unpleasant restrictions. There have been no morals yet which were pleasant to follow, especially for those not conditioned to them. Religious dogmas and practices are even more onerous. All cultural education means hard work applied to every individual during long formative years; and cultural tradition takes thousands of years to build. Even those things that would be to the greatest advantage of all are resisted desperately. Utopian advantages would flow from closer social integration, but man clings to his individuality, tries to remain as he is, with a sacred fervor. Nothing comes easily or by itself in civilization, as it would if culture were in accordance with human nature. The very feeling that cultural attitudes are valuable and deserve great merit is due to the essential natural absence of such inclinations in man, and a desperate need for them. In a word, man is forced to evolve civilization in spite of his nature and against his will.

The force that presses man into civilization is hostility between men. After man evolved intelligence he became the king of nature. Difficulties of nature could not longer force radical changes on him. That is why man, with all his intelligence, stagnated in an incredible primitivism for hundreds of thousands of years. The advantages that social cooperation and learning could have brought men were right before their eyes. But that is not how men have advanced. They had to be faced with the choice of survival or death before they accepted changes in their adjustment. Only other men with an equally high skill at hunting and killing could force men to such choices. This explains why only in the last few hundred years, as the world became overpopulated, did civilization start advancing. It has advanced exactly in the same exponential rate that populations increase.

The main form of advance has been the evolution of social cooperation. We do not need to explain how any human effort can be increased a hundredfold by cooperation, leading to specialization and exchange, or how the most important tasks, which are not possible for any single man or family, become possible for a larger group. But these advantages were not realized

261

directly and were not the primary goal of social cooperation. Societies emerged for the simple reason that in encounters between men survival depended upon getting together into larger groups. Even a few men forming a group can defeat thousands of men if the latter do not form equal groups.

Humanists hold the view that man is a social animal. This has been considered one of the great certainties since the time of Aristotle. Such a view goes well with philosophies of the Aristotelian kind, which lack a deeper insight into how selective adaptation created by adversity rather than Providential creation is the source of harmonious adjustment. The sociability of men is certainly a most valuable thing. But it is so highly valued, and is discovered so saliently by the humanist thinkers, just because it is so wanting and rare. On the other hand, the egotism of man is so universal that there is nothing to discover about it; and it is too commonplace to be dealt with by any higher mind seeking for striking, noble and "meaningful" ideas.

Actually, man is the least social of animals. He has no social sense at all. A soldier ant feels the injury inflicted upon another ant, and a worker ant feels the hunger experienced by another ant. Man has none of such senses that the social insects and animals have. He simply has no organs or reflexes for them. The only sense he has for another human being is his sexual love for his mate and, subsequently, for his family. This is his only "social" sense, and by conditioning it has been stretched to its limits. But not much can be done with it, because of its specific nature. Man is not adapted to living in any group beyond the family. Even such mechanisms as the establishment of a strict pecking order, which is the minimum requirement for group existence, do not operate with man. Like the manlike apes and highest hunting animals, man lives in isolation and is ready to attack on sight any other man intruding upon his living space. A state of independence and isolation is what man craves to regain at the first opportunity. That is why *freedom and individuality have remained the highest values of man*, even in the book of the humanists themselves.

Observation of peoples of nature shows the true social nature of men. Tribes evolve as an extended family which continues due to inertial fixations and the advantages for survival offered by the group. But outside their tribe, when men meet they know only how to kill and enslave — or eat each other, which other animals do not do. Cannibalism may continue even in spite of the obvious dangers that it harbors for individuals inside the tribe itself. Though the advantage of cooperation between tribes is obvious, they remain on terms of killing on sight, modified by fear of reprisals, even while living for ages side by side. The only thing that can unite these tribes is the appearance of some stronger society of men. Then by instinct as well as long trial and error they unite. As soon as such a union becomes strong enough, it tries to subjugate other, isolated tribes, and induces them to unite in their turn.

Obviously, a snowballing effect results: larger and larger societies emerge as soon as contacts between increasing populations in a certain region become closer. The exponential rate of population growth is thus reflected in the rate of increase in size and the degree of integration of societies and, with it, in civilization itself. Peoples in more sparsely populated areas have always remained less civilized, in spite of the natural advantages that such a state insures.

The need for self-protection shows itself as the force that has created empires even in the era of recorded history. The prototype of all empires, the Roman Empire, is said to have been built by the Romans in sheer self-protection. The Romans lacked imagination, as most historians hold, and never had imperialistic dreams. H. G. Wells has pathetic things to say in his *Outline of History* about the lack of imagination of the Romans, and the blindness of Rome and Carthage in not realizing that they could both prosper side by side. But this blind hostility and obsessive mistrust toward other peoples were exactly what had made the two nations great in the first place.

The prototype of all states — the national state of modern Europe — further illustrates the process. The national states of Europe emerged suddenly all at the same time. The cause was the rivalry and hostility between them. As soon as one of them advanced in its strength or social cohesion, others had to follow. The emerging similarity in structure and degree of integration of the European national states was so striking that political historians have looked for the causes of the process in the evolution of new ideas, such as sovereignty, realization of natural rights, or a mysterious historical predetermination. In fact, abstract ideas or realizations had as little influence here as in any adjustment.

Not rational decisions or altruistic feelings, but conflicts or threats of oppression have produced the unification of peoples. Wars and disasters created by men have brought about unprecedented social integration, with all the advances in economic and social progress that follow from it. The nearest examples, the two world wars, confirm this spectacularly. The present tendency toward unification of the European states has been induced by the threatening presence of the Russian giant. But Russia in its turn emerged as a counterbalance to the Central Asian population outbursts, which have been the most violent that humanity has known. The Hun onslaught almost succeeded in unifying the whole of Europe. Similar onslaughts created on the other side of the world the unique giant China, with its wall as a monument to them.

Hostility between men, especially in its chain-reaction effect of reciprocal tightening of threat, is what produces the closer social integration which is the primary source of all civilization and progress. Political historians often wonder why it is that no nation has ever been without its enemy. A nation cannot exist without enemies, and if it lacks them, it creates one as a means of emotional justification of its own integration efforts. This world will become unified only when Martians start attacking it. At present *the only hope of progress without wars lies in providing other forms of hostility that do not require physical killing.* Unconsciously, as always, we are moving in that direction. Competition in economic and scientific excellence, in foreign aid, in the conquest of space or for world opinion as well as the cold war in general, which we are so desperately trying to end, may be the beginnings of unsuspected solutions that humanity is approaching.

MORALS

The nature of morals shows best in the fact that morals do not appear before there is society. If morals were something natural to man, they would always be with him; and would not depend, as they do, upon the peculiarities of the society in which a person happens to live. Actually, the existence as well as the forms of morals are the product of social selection. Those societies prevail and take over in which the greatest cooperation is offered to neighbors inside and hostile aloofness or aggressiveness toward people outside. By fixation the rules become sacrosanct. As such they form part of religions. All religions have the same great laws: not to kill, wrong, deceive or steal from anybody in one's own society; and to obey the highest unified authority, which often becomes the authority of one unifying God, vested in His priests or kings. Recognition of a foreign authority or strange gods — in its modern version this means lack of patriotism — becomes the first of sins, and expansion of one's own religion or society the highest of virtues.

Naturally, under the value outlook morals appear, in their final, as if providentially given stage, to be eternal dictates rooted in human nature. Two brothers, separated and brought up under opposing religions or patriotisms, would be ready to kill each other in the name of "universal moral dictates" or man's "innate moral nature." Morals or patriotism *are* worthy, but not because they are part of a sacred human nature; nor because there exists a higher Providential moral authority. On the contrary, morals and culture are products of conditioning which *transforms* human nature because of needs imposed by the *hostility* between men and *adversity* of the world.

The history of morals and religions shows them to be products of selective social integration. The highest moral law, the love of all men, has emerged as a rule only in the last two thousand years, which is a short moment in the history of man. It emerged as the core of all universal religions — Brahmanism, Buddhism, Confucianism, Taoism, Christianity and Mohammedanism. But these religions were products of a closer and more extensive social

265

integration evolving together with the emergence of empires. People adopt those teachings, and teachers adopt those rules, which correspond to existing social realities. Every one of the universal religions has had an empire as its basis. This fact is so striking that Toynbee, the greatest historian of our times, has built on it his main thesis. According to it each empire fulfills its mission by leaving the chrysalis of a universal religion behind it. By the way, the rule of an eye for an eye or of just vengeance corresponded to a tribal world in which peace was maintained by the threat of reprisals. This rule was already an advance over the truly natural, boundlessly egotistic rule under which man lived for hundreds of thousands of years.

The formulation of the rule of love is interesting. In all the above religions the Golden Rule tells man not to do to others what he does not like being done to *himself*; or to do to others what he likes being done to *himself* (see *World's Great Scriptures* by Lewis Browne). Thus it is the appeal to oneself, to one's own feelings, that has been found the real basis on which to build human cooperation. If man had a real natural mechanism for cooperation or for brotherly love, such as there is in sexual cooperation, then the rule would tell one to do to others what others like to do to him, or to let others do what they like best. You can imagine what kind of social cooperation we would get with such a rule for a start.

The Golden Rule is wise. All social cooperation derives its reality from the inexhaustible, egotistic sensitivity of every man to wrongs done to him by others. In an integrated society, where vengeance is prohibited, the only thing that a person can do against one who injures him is to loathe him. This means placing him, emotionally, in the worst possible, despicable position. Naturally, the person would hate to find himself later in a similar position. Consequently, he avoids injury to others. Though all this happens only mentally, it is more real psychologically than actual happenings or reasons because it means strong emotional experience. Thus there evolves, under prohibition of physical vengeance, a self-perpetuating "altruistic" mechanism by which everybody avoids wrongdoing in proportion to his own boundless sensitivity to the wrongdoings of others.

As egotistic trespasses become loathed and virtues praised, competition between men does the rest to deepen moral feelings. Everybody wants to be more virtuous than others and gladly denounces the immorality of others. Since competition and jealousy are constantly there as emotional realities, the deepening of moral feelings becomes a self-sustaining fixation, approaching obsessional perfectionism. Martyrdom becomes highly desired, especially by those seeking immediate satisfactions, because it proves the other person morally wrong and oneself morally superior. Most of our everyday moral acts have the sweet savor or martyrdom.

We cannot go into a discussion of various moral rationalizations, but we may take as a paramount example Kant's main rule of moral conduct. Kant extols duty for duty's sake and not for the sake of one's own good or happiness. Actually, this rule is scientifically absurd. A person simply cannot act in any other way than by following his own drives, which mean his own pleasures. As to any supernatural basis for such a rule, the law of striving for his own pleasure is implanted in man as in every living being, down to the cell, by whoever or whatever created it all. If there is any universal law, this is it, though evolution and culture have to proceed against it.

Nor is Kant's logical formulation of the rule tenable. Kant argues that simply as a matter of logic a person cannot want an immoral rule to become universal law, for if it does, it will hurt the person himself. Here we have a typical instance of the fallacy of the philosophical method. If social cooperation and culture are assumed as the ready given beginnings of everything, then Kant's argument is right. But actually the beginning of everything for man is his unlimited egotism, the logic of which does not admit any universal laws applicable to him in the same way as to others. Kant's further argument that a person should treat other persons as goals in themselves is not only inconsistent with the logic of egotistic human existence, but also impossible practically. Man simply cannot act for any other goals than his own, just as he cannot get outside his own body. Practically, if we tried to mind each other's well-being, an indescribable mess would result, since nobody can feel what is right for the other person. Man's intellect involves the capacity to use outside factors, including other men, as tools. This capacity is what made him rise above the animal level.

In whatever way the problem is turned, the asocial egotism of man remains the only basis of human conduct. This is what every man deeply knows, and no philosophical sophistication can add anything new to it. The noble theories of philosophers and moralists become a theoretical nuisance. The source of morals is not any higher reasons or qualities of human nature, but the inherent adversities of the world of men, and the transformation, through a contradictory process, of truly egotistic human nature, because of such adversities. No wonder the humanistic theorists remained blind in regard to conditioning, by which all cultural progress evolves. They have remained blind also to the next most important factor of progress — closer social integration. Humanists fanatically oppose, in the name of the sacred nature of man, any ideology advocating subordination of the individual to society.

Closer social integration offers benefits that man at present cannot dream of. If we finally reached the stage of a social beehive or a social organism, there would be, first, the never-ending economic boom that we mentioned before, as any reciprocal fears or loss of confidence would become inoperative. This alone would make utopian attainments possible. Also, the branches of competitive distribution or controlled supervision, which now constitute half of our occupations, would disappear, so that all efforts could go into pure production. Moreover, centralization and specialization would become complete, which means that every effort by man would become hundreds of times more powerful and precise. We shall see later how the concentration by men of overwhelming resources in their struggle with nature would alone enable them to pry open the forces of nature with a chain-reaction advantage. Anyway, such a beehive state is being approached gradually, though blindly, by men as they are being pushed into greater integration and find it beneficial. But every humanist, moralist, educator, philosopher, publicist or political scientist furiously attacks the very idea of "anthill" integration. Of course, social integration can be conditioned only on private interests, here as everywhere else.

268

The present humanistic approaches are based on belief in the sacredness of human nature. Actually, this nature makes men behave like irrational lunatics resisting even the clearest social advantages. Every possible benefit lies before us at the stretch of a hand; all we have to do is to keep our egotism in check so that closer social cooperation can start showing its incomparable benefits at each step. But men do their utmost not to permit any chance for this to happen. The reason is the same deep egotism, that everybody is aware of. Nobody dares to take the first step, because everybody knows that any act of altruism will be exploited rather than reciprocated by others.

Thus we are paralyzed by the universality of egotism. Only threats of survival, originating in hostility or competition with other societies, can make men advance. Then looking backward the ancient ways of life look stupid and miserable indeed. But the humanist outlook, which accepts the existing forms of our culture or existing human nature as sacred, prevents us from realizing how equally miserable and stupid our own way of life or moral ideals are in the light of the completely different possibilities that humanity is inevitably approaching.

The ultimately egotistic nature of our "altruism" in social relations is so apparent that nobody is really deceived. When we perform acts of love, give gifts, exhibit charity or offer compassion, we are only concerned with our own virtuousness and moral superiority, or at least the avoidance of the loathsome negative emotions that attach to egotism. We are not really concerned with the other person. Nobody slips ten-dollar bills surreptitiously into other people's mailboxes. Actually, everybody knows what this all means, and nobody likes to be on the receiving end of favors. At best, the favor is appreciated by the receiver for its material worth or is interpreted as a recognition of his importance. Still, he would be happier if he could have the gift without the giver, or have his importance recognized in another form than a favor.

If we really cared for the pleasure of others, we would, as the first thing, show ourselves at a disadvantage — appear in rags in society or do some other crazy thing. Above all, we would avoid being superior to the other person, or more successful than he, for that really hurts. However, we compete mercilessly, even in the virtuousness of being altruistic. In those cases where we really are glad about the success of a family member, relative or a person we have supported, we are actually enjoying our own success or superiority.

The very feeling of virtuousness about morals shows that man is immoral by nature. If moral conduct were natural to men, they would be as little proud of it as they are about their ability to cooperate sexually or to perform any natural function. In fact, if altruism were innate, *the hard and most necessary thing* would be to teach men to attend to their own interests and abstain from the enjoyments of altruism, just as men are taught now to abstain from their sexual enjoyments. Further, if morals were natural, like breathing, there would be none of the strict, complex and regulative prescriptions for their observation that we have now in codes of justice, moral conduct, social intercourse, education and so on.

Perhaps the universality of inherently asocial human egotism is too obvious to be discussed. But the point is that under the present humanistic approach it is exactly altruism which appears to be the causal source of human behavior and the deeper essence of his nature, revealing the existence of a loving Creator. In other words, *we have here the most important instance of the delusionism of the value outlook.* We can say that *one would be closer to understanding the meaning and purpose of morals and human progress if he reversed every truth and discovery of the humanistic theories.* We do not doubt the noble intentions of the humanistic moralist. But lofty intentions based on ignorance lead only to bigotry and misery. Stupidity is still the first sin. As long as tradition remains strong, the humanist defending it is better than any rationalist or present "scientist." But we are entering the era of science and reason — humanists themselves extol reason — and in the light of reason or "science" cultural traditions appear like webs of limitations based on superstitious ignorance.

What deserves admiration is the intuitive wisdom of practical man. Higher intelligence goes together with morals because both rest on the capacity of man to accept restrictions. The common man does not fail to see the connection. In practical terms, he follows and imitates the ways of morally higher people as the ways that are more intelligent and bring the greatest long-range success. He is wise enough to disregard immediate effects, which may show restrictions to be hindrances to direct success.

RELIGION

All people have in one form or another what we call religion. But any endeavor to define religion by some one characteristic has failed. Religion is as undefinable as life. It represents the missing part in man's emotional life, like a missing half in a huge jigsaw puzzle. Considering how delusory and ghostlike his own psychological life must appear to man, this missing part has to be extensive indeed. We do not need to repeat here how mysterious, delusory and phantom-like every feeling and value appears to man. Further, the conditioning under which man lives is like a mechanism set up inside him, of which he has no idea how and why it is there. Naturally, he rationalizes that it is a conscience, soul or higher authority that he is obeying. Since all these phantoms and mysteries are as rich and complex as man's own adjustment, only a person-like agency is sufficient to explain them. Hence the belief in a personal God.

Religion offers a good illustration of the delusions arising from the value outlook. Because man needs love and protection more than anything else due to their absence from the world, he believes in a Loving and Providential God. The same applies to every value and belief. Where there is real harmony, and an apparent Providence, man holds no beliefs. Gravitation, the availability of matter, its cohesion, plentifulness of air and light and so on are there as if really providentially given for our benefit. But we have neither gods for them nor any value notions about them; we do not even notice them as real. On the other hand, the insecurity of life, the insufficiency of food, the adversities of nature, the dangers and ills afflicting man, recurring disasters, scarcity of rain or lack of fertility are rich sources of beliefs in gods and Providence. It can be said that *the godlessness in the world is the real source of man's belief in God.*

271

We cannot go into a discussion of the evolution of religions or their forms. We can only mention that the delusions have become richer as religions have advanced. Primitive man believed in many gods like the many factors that act in nature. He also avoided attributing to these gods exactly human-like qualities. But as man's endlessly complex psychological needs, especially those centering around the craving for love and around the lack of explanations of the universe, became stronger, God had to be made into such a complex and man-like agency that only one abstract, omnipotent and intelligent Being could be expected to take care of them all.

The belief in life after death is the strongest and most convincing belief, because the need is paramount. Nobody can live without such a belief, though nobody is so naïve either as to believe that it is actually true. An atheist may say that he does not believe in anything, but emotionally he invests in the idea of some continuity after his death. If he did not, he would treat his life as a meaningless episode. On the other hand, even the staunchest believer clings to every misery of this life rather than be ready to pass into the next.

Here we may say a few words about atheism. Belief is nurtured not by reasoning but by emotional necessity, therefore is subject to relativity and its paradoxical logic. The deeper and more general the belief of a person is, the less able he is to formulate it as something specific and the more apt he is to discover disbelief in some particular value or see absence of higher sense in something. An ardent atheist may be a person who believed in a personalized God and now discovers that he does not believe in it anymore, though he may admit that he believes in "something." Most atheists are rationalistic reformers. They may believe very generally and deeply in many things: the redemption of their efforts by the intelligence of men, the continuation of their goals by humanity, and so on. A civilized atheist believes more deeply than an uncivilized believer. Most of the present controversies over atheism are not much different from the old controversies between believers who invoked the name of Jehovah and unbelievers who did not. Emotional replacement of

God by Humanity, Civilization, State, Party, Progress, Art or any Higher Duty goes on in all of us. But these also are only names. Real belief is as wide and undefinable as life is. Reasoned-out convictions do not matter. A person may be convinced that he does not believe in ghosts, but when placed in darkness he may fear them as much as one who believes in them.

The possibility of any kind of life after death is absolutely nil, though man believes in it more than anything else. A Martian not concerned with the problem would regard such a belief as a fantastic fabrication conceivable only by madmen. Any kind of experience we can have is so closely dependent on our physiological normalcy that the slightest disturbance in it changes or interrupts that experience. How can there be any experience after that physiological basis is completely gone? We do not intend to say that there are no unknown, or rather unknowable, possibilities. As likely as not there "are" myriads of other worlds crossing through the room you are sitting in. But the point is that you cannot even say that they "are." Anything that does not exist in the specific terms in which we exist, feel and think can never "be" and has less relevance to us than our turning into dust, which at least "is" something.

Let us be clear about one thing. Man often feels and argues that life cannot be just nonsense, that there must be some reason or purpose behind it all. Actually, man is not concerned here with reasons. All he is concerned with is the avoidance of the negativity of emotions that he instinctively knows death brings. Continuation after death is accepted as a solution. As far as reasons are concerned it is as reasonable for Mr. Jones to become nothingness as for him to continue on and on. If death were not painful in any way, the whole problem would not even arise. The argument that man wants simply to continue, to be there, see or think, even apart from any emotion, is not true. Millions of lives, with worlds of their own, have been lived and are lived, by other men, or even other beings on faraway planets. But we have no pre-occupations with our incapacity to participate in these lives.

Man can have concern only with what is *emotionally* tied inside him. Even the seemingly abstract desire of man to continue merely to exist is a strong emotion. Because it is tied in with the accumulated well-being or growth that constitutes living, death means an equal emotional loss or repayment, which we want to avoid. If the loss or repayment were already made — if there were not even the faintest interest left — the individual would be unconcerned whether it all ended today, a thousand years from now or never. A person committing suicide, under the feeling that death is not to be feared, never resorts to belief in another life, though logically he should be concerned about it more than anybody else. In brief, belief in immortality is an attempt to avoid the equalizing strong negative emotions that death brings. But *this is something that even God cannot give man, just as even He cannot create mountains without valleys.*

Even if man has a soul, it does not change anything. If the soul participates in the emotional life of man, the same inexorable equivalence of emotions applies. If it does not, it is irrelevant: such a soul or its continuation has less relevancy for man than his continuation as atoms or in the results of his work, by which man continues anyway. Actually, a true soul can be thought of only as being in full harmony with the Creator. It therefore could not be part of the disturbances and, consequently, of the need-satisfaction interplay which is the only source of human experiences. A true soul, therefore, could never have anything to do with the feelings, thoughts or any other of man's experiences. Whether man has one or hundreds of such souls, and whether they turn into angels, other men or animals, can make no difference to anybody.

The only thing man can do is to make death and the fear accompanying it more gradual. Man can plan his joys and fears, if he understands their causal interdependence and the inevitability of the equivalence between positive and negative emotions. Belief in life after death can only accumulate horrors for the last moment, as the believer holds on stubbornly to what he has to lose in the end anyway. We mentioned that in practice, however, the religious believer meets the problem, by way of restrictive living, more wisely than anybody else.

In this connection we may mention the strongest attraction that religiousness has: the kind of people who practice it. The moral and religious attitude goes along with a greater capacity to bear restrictions, which also means higher intelligence. The great moral and religious systems are expressions of higher culture. Historical conversions to such religions have come with higher civilizations. People accept a religion because they are impressed by those who practice it.

The way of life matters more in religion than dogmas or scriptures, but due to cultural fixation the scriptures become rigid and excessively sacrosanct. Actually, the ideals and liberties expressed in scriptures serve only as promises or lures, necessary here as in any motivation and conditioning. The final practical result is, however, a denial of these ideals. That is why the less prejudiced humanistic thinkers have always found that the Church has corrupted religious ideals. The Church as the practical preserver of the cultural way of life cannot do differently. If we lived like birds in the sky or lilies in the valley, in the spirit of the New Testament, we would end with moral license and spiritual as well as material impoverishment. Many sects ended that way by following these ideals literally. In practice, even seemingly senseless rituals, prayers and superstitions are more important than ideals. The more pain and attention a person invests in his religion, the more authority it has over him. Ideals or reasons do not count but emotional investments do.

The sanctity of dogmas has been excessive to the point of ridicule. Psychologically this is revealing. Peoples have waged wars and killed millions for the sake of one word. Even a syllable, like the last syllable in *"filiusque,"* or a letter, like the first "i" in *"homoiousian,"* has been sufficient cause of bloodshed for centuries. When the heretic Servetus was burned, his executioners said he would have been spared if he had exclaimed, "Jesus, eternal son of God," instead of "Jesus, son of eternal God." Words become sacred in religion because they are objects of fixation and symbols of conditioning. An animal conditioned to a certain symbol may run to its death by following the senseless sign. The conditioning that lies behind the words may be important for the preservation of culture or society, worthy of wars and sacrifice of life, but as

275

to the words or scriptures — the signs of conditioning — they could as well have been anything else. If the right words or teachings rather than conditioning really mattered, we could build a paradise on earth on the basis of a two-page leaflet.

The same excess in holiness is observable in regard to the Masters. A religion grows out of the whole civilization, as a river grows out of a whole region. But only one name is given to the religion, or to the river. Accident more than anything else determines that name. The river may have its upstream beginning at a tiny source, but the whole river may be called by its name and considered its product. A civilization, tending toward a unifying system, may gradually select one of the existing religious movements, called after its leader. Then, as the symbols of the civilization become sanctified due to conditioning and fixation, the name by which it all is designated becomes holiness itself.

The same process can be observed even today in the formation and naming of social and religious movements. In older times attachment to myth and personification was stronger because of the less scientific approach and absence of historical records. Moreover, religion was then the basis of all cultural and social, even political, organization. That religions grow out of the existing civilization is shown in the similarity of religions of the same period. Historians know, for instance, that Christianity was so similar to other Roman religions that Christians blamed it on the perverse ingenuity of Satan.

Moral and religious beliefs imply the existence of free will. Scientifically, free will is an impossibility. Everything in a person's character and behavior can always be traced back causally to his innate capacities and environment — which are independent of him. However, man sees no sense in a world without purposes, and his belief in free will is one of his deepest convictions. Even scientists are glad to get a chance at speculating about the possibility of free will. When quantum physics revealed effects that scientists could not explain, arguments about the possibility of free will were eagerly resumed. The famous physicists, Planck, Eddington and Jeans, have argued that since final causes cannot be established in quantum phenomena, causal indeterminacy may

276

apply to processes in the brain as well. Scientists know that freedom of the will can exist only where natural causation ends. In simple words this means the requirement of supernatural intervention or miracle.

Here we come to an important point. *Only miracle and mystery can support religious beliefs.* This applies at any level of knowledge — the most ordinary commonplace knowledge as well as the highest science or philosophy. Under the normal causal order one never discovers any evidence pointing to anything beyond the material world. The common believer knows this truth intuitively. That is why there has been no religion which has not claimed miracles as its proofs. Equally, the scientist bases his religious beliefs on the remaining mysteries of the universe.

But miracles and mysteries are disappearing fast, like shadows from dark corners, in the light of advancing knowledge. Even quantum phenomena can be explained causally. What remains are the mysteries of the mind, the ultimate limits of cognition, values, the soul and the mental life in general. These mysteries are still there because scientific or causal understanding has not yet reached the fields of psychology, mind and values. All these mysteries have found their most complete expression in philosophy.

PHILOSOPHY

We have to say more about philosophy. The philosophical method means striving for direct and pure knowledge of things in their essence, as differentiated from scientific or practical knowledge, derived from the enlargement of factual and historical backgrounds. In other words, philosophy represents the highest expression of the humanistic *value outlook* which we mentioned before. Every humanistic mystery arising from the lack of understanding of negative background causation, as well as every value delusion, is perpetuated to perfection in philosophy. The scientific though simple causal understanding of cognition and values can therefore meet here and dispel all humanistic mystifications in their highest, most systematic elaboration, with supernatural reality as the central mystery.

277

We may start by looking at the nature of philosophical endeavor. Philosophy tries to reach its insights not by widening factual knowledge, but by going into the depths of human cognition itself. Ultimately, it amounts to trying to extend the very limits of cognition. The question is whether this can be done.

Here it may be important to point out a very general phenomenon that demonstrates the limits of all thinking, whether it be that of the philosopher or the most common of men. There are more than three thousand languages, evolved in many cases by peoples who never met or knew of each other. However, all languages obey inexorably the same fundamental law of grammar, namely, the division of words into the same parts of speech: nouns, verbs, adjectives, adverbs and so on. Thousands of peoples and uncountable millions of men, through all times, and under the most varied circumstances, have obeyed this law, without failing even once, and without knowing that they are obeying it. If there is a miracle, this is one, though it is too ordinary for lofty philosophies. Naturally, we cannot expect that the above rule be too complex — that the uniformity apply to every modality in the use of the parts of speech. We have to deal here with fundamental natural principles, and these can only be few.

First, let us explain how we can be sure that the parts of speech are the same in all languages. Knowledge of a dozen European languages shows this to be so. Even this uniformity is a miracle, considering that otherwise these languages have varied endlessly through thousands of years of independent development. But the universal proof lies in the fact that if there were a language consisting of words which were neither nouns, verbs, adjectives nor other parts of speech, no human being would ever be able to understand it. *Not only would such words be untranslatable, but their meaning would be inherently inconceivable. For no man, not all the philosophers of the world working together, can invent, or understand, a single word that does not belong to the known parts of speech, and still has any meaning.*

So far all languages can be understood and translated into others, though their modalities — still within the limits of parts of speech — may seem puzzling. There are books telling of sensational differences between languages, but when the differences are shown, one can see clearly that they do not go beyond the parts of speech. A primitive people may say "that which makes things change" instead of "development." Other people may not change the word while using it as noun, verb or adjective. We say the "work," to "work," or "work" horse. There may be innumerable such peculiarities. But the very fact that meaning can be elicited from any language shows that the miracle of new parts of speech does not exist.

What does this limitation of languages mean? Apparently it means the limits of human thought. Though speech is not so quick or rich as thought, it fundamentally represents thought. With greater care thought can be expressed quite closely. Through thousands of years people have had endless opportunities to find better ways for expressing their thoughts, and myriads of such improvements have been made. But not a single one has gone beyond the rule of parts of speech. The meaning of these limits of thought is that man cannot think otherwise than by relating matter in time and space. Nouns are relationships of matter in space; verbs, of matter in time; adjectives, of matter to matter; adverbs, of matter to matter in time; participles, of matter in time to matter and so on. There are as many parts and subparts of speech as there are possibilities of combining the space and time principles in regard to matter. We can disregard prepositions and conjunctions, which only reveal that thought means relating. Thus we are left with matter, space and time as the ultimate limits of all thought.

We can understand that all relationships have to be in terms of matter, for we exist as matter and can get in touch with the outside world only in terms of matter. But why the categories of space and time? Apparently their origin is due to the very nature of living existence and therefore of mind as a form of it. To exist as a living being means to persist as a permanent organization of matter. To think, which means merely to exist in a more complex form, therefore means establishing relationships with the outside world in terms of its stable or constant aspects.

In other words, man grasps the world, primarily, in terms of the static relationships between things. And space is never anything more than such relationships. As to the category of time, it is a necessary complement to the category of space. It enables us to cope with total reality in its endless flux and change while we still cling primarily to the static relationships of space. Time is never anything more than relationships of changes.

The exact explanation does not matter for our purposes. What matters is that *every man, whether he be the most sophisticated philosopher or most primitive savage, can speak, think, feel or have any experience only within the same simplest limits of our own existence — the limits of matter, space and time.* Any pretension or self-delusion of a deeper or wider knowledge, beyond these simple terms of our existence, is due to mere confusion. We shall see this as we go along, but first we may look at other categories postulated by philosophers.

Aristotle had ten, sometimes eight, categories, corresponding to predicates answering the questions: "what?," "how?," "where?," "how large?," "what posture?" and so on. Kant had categories of quantity, quality, relationship and modality, apart from the general categories of time and space. Peirce had the categories of quality, fact and law. Alexander had categories of identity, diversity, relation, causality and so on. The explanation for such category-building is not far to seek. Thought means value differentiation. Any notion is arrived at by differentiation or relation with other notions. The whole system of man's thoughts is like an endless net in which each mesh is connected with other ones, these being connected with still other ones, and so on. You can start with every one as the center and trace everything else to it.

What notion or notions are considered as central depends upon the choice by the philosopher, which is determined mostly by his value outlook. That is why there are as many philosophical systems or sets of categories as there are philosophers. As a rule, philosophers start with the notions that they consider most worthy, serious or important. If a philosopher could afford to be unserious, he could start with the notion of a doorknob and build his whole philosophical system around such a notion. By the way, any logical system can be built in the same way. The non-Euclidean geometrists, Saccheri, Lobachevsky and Bolyai, built their geometries on central assumptions that were otherwise nonsensical.

If one wants to, he can treat the categories of matter, space and time also as mere starting points. But apparently these starting points are so fundamental to human thought, or rather man's whole existence, that, as we saw, nobody can have a different choice. All our thoughts and experiences derive from our existence, which is the last term for all of them — but as such cannot be understood.

The impression that man can think beyond the terms of his existence — matter, time and space — is mainly due to an incorrect combination of notions. In practical life it serves well to use such combinations. We may speak of an "absent," "nonexisting" or "unthinkable" thing, knowing that we are using an improper combination to which no reality corresponds. However, when the philosopher uses the terms "supernatural," "transcendental" or "ideal," he forgets that he is using an improper term to which no reality can ever correspond. Other combinations of notions, for practical purposes, lead to similar confusions. We use thousands of notions like "thought," "life," "to exist," "to feel," "spiritual," "pleasant" only as shorthand signs for lumping together multiple combinations. We intuitively know what we are doing, and never expect that there is such a separate thing as "life" or "thought." But every philosophical system is built on precisely such constructs derived from essences such as "Being," "Idea," "Mind," "Reason," "Soul," "Spirit" or "Will." If the philosopher used such notions in the way they are evolved and applied for practical use — in the way the common man and the scientist uses them — there would be no philosophy.

As a typical example we can mention the ontological proof of the existence of God. It is based on the argument that since a perfect being can be thought of it must exist, for perfection includes existence. This proof, as elaborated by Anselm and reformulated by St. Thomas or Descartes, still appeals to formalistic minds. Kant pointed out that existence does not follow from an arbitrary idea. This is also what common sense tells us. Russell proved *by the use of logic* that an idea of a golden mountain, or a nonexistent King of France, do not imply their existence. But using logic amounts to nothing more than using a different language —as Latin was used in the Middle Ages—to express what we know in the usual terms of common sense.

The real argument is that we do not have any idea of such a perfect being in the way we have ideas of real things. If we did, the ontological proof could be valid. By thinking of a "perfect" being we still think in terms of our past ideas about the same imperfect, limited, material world of ours in which no such being does or can exist. In the same way, while thinking about a golden mountain we use only our past notions of gold and mountain, each derived from something real in itself, but not in combination. When you read a book you may think that you are introduced to new places, but analyzing them you will find that they represent only recombinations of places you already knew.

Now we may turn to the sources of the mysteries and beliefs of philosophy. For our purposes, we may classify these sources under four headings. The first, most important, source is values: the lofty value beliefs, and mysteries about their cause and nature, as well as the presence of the highest values or harmony in nature. The second main source is the rationality of the world as evidenced by the affinity between mind and world. The third source is the virtual miracle of the working of the human mind, incomprehensible to itself and appearing like a transcendental emanation from a soul. And the fourth source is the infinity of the world and its causes, or rather our incapacity to understand them.

I. Value attitudes dominate the earliest as well as the most modern philosophies, even if the older, lofty and nicely reasoned-out value beliefs have been replaced by irrational existentialistic despair and negativism. The ancient Greek philosophers, with Plato and Aristotle as its giants, exalted the rational certitude of moral values and the virtuous life. The world of the Greek philosophers was a rationally ordered world existing for the sake of higher values and virtues. Philosophers demonstrated that the most natural and happiest life for man was the life of virtues, to be discovered by reason. Socrates must have been an absolute believer in a life of reason. No wonder the Athenians had to condemn him to death for corruption of the youth. The Athenians seem to have been very tolerant people. But a fanatic rationalist can become a real pest and wear out the patience of any people.

Plato, who wrote down the Socratic philosophy, maintained the same attitude. For him, the ideas of wisdom, goodness and justice are in man's eternal soul. His most typical argument is the one that uses the illustration of men in a cave: because some men live restricted to the darkness of the cave and become conditioned to its world of shadows, they become incapable of recognizing truth in the bright daylight — the light of reason. The Athenians seem to have been wise enough to keep their youth well under their conditioning and away from the light of reason. Plato's world of ideas or forms is a world of all the highest values. Naturally, he was fascinated by the idea of the Good. Though he believed in the god Demiurge, the world soul, planetary souls and many of the gods of Greek mythology, the Good was for him the dominating idea or form.

Aristotle retained the ideas or forms in all their noble and virtuous perfection. He merely tried to bring them down from their separate heaven in which Plato had placed them. Aristotle also tried to explain the variety and change in reality, which the noble formalism of ideas did not permit. Consequently, he postulated potentialities inherent in men and things. These potentialities, however, were no less rational, noble or virtuously purposeful than the Platonic ideas. Aristotle was the most positivistic of the classical philosophers, and his system can serve as a measure of how far the serious philosophers were from ever questioning the virtuous rationality and purposefulness of the world as ultimate truths. Sophists and cynics who were not sufficiently respectful of such truths became the rejects of philosophy forever.

The naïveté of the value outlook in classical philosophy is best illustrated by the well-known Aristotelian doctrine of the golden mean. It amounts to seeing any adjustment — which is finally reached and accepted as normal — as having been perfectly and purposefully given. One could as well wonder how providentially man has been created — not too big nor too small — for the things that are there for him to use. If heads were different, how could we use hats?

Belief in the perfection and goodness of creation and its Author dominates medieval philosophy. The same certitude about the order and purposefulness of the world of mind and creation underlies the systems of the early modern philosophers. Descartes, or Spinoza, did not question intelligent creation in nature or the reflection of the highest intelligence in mind. For Descartes, mind was a reflection of the qualities of God himself. The pantheistic world of Spinoza represents the highest recognition of perfection in nature. Early British positivists, like Bacon, or empiricists, like Locke and Berkeley, held the same contemporary views about the evidence of intelligence and purposefulness in the world. Even the great skeptic, Hume, did not contest the existence of purposefulness in nature, though he maintained his skeptical attitude and rejected the usual teleological proofs of God. The German rationalists, Leibniz and Wolff, were inspired in their philosophies by the wonderous perfection of nature. Most interesting of all, even Kant saw evidence of transcendental reality in *practical* reason, which means in the moral or value experiences of man.

The philosophies that followed the epoch-making criticism of reason by Kant relied even more on value insights. In Fichte's ethical idealism freedom and moral order are seen as the ultimate realities. In Schelling's identity philosophy nature in its beauty and creative energy was accepted as the expression of a pantheistic Absolute. Overt value attitudes are found in the direct emotionalism that has become more prevalent as philosophy has advanced. We encounter it in the philosophies of Schopenhauer and Nietzsche, where it dominates their main themes. Schopenhauer's Will is an emotional experience rather than logical reality. So is Nietzsche's Will to Power. Bergson's *élan vital* is a value concept. Without its qualitative, emotionally intuited spirit the *élan vital* has no meaning. British utilitarianism is another, somewhat different example of the increasing emphasis on emotional value. The teleological idealism of Lotze, the ethical parallelism of Wundt, and the Neo-Kantian systems of Windelband, Rickert or Eucken are pure

284

value philosophies. Later romanticism and aestheticism — one may think here of modern Italian philosophy, with Croce as its main representative — are characteristic of the shifting emphasis from reason to value experiences. The same shift is observable throughout modern philosophy. Intuition (Bergson), immediacy of feeling (Bradley), loyalty (Royce), even animal faith (Santayana) are the modern equivalents of belief, grace, faith or practical reason.

Existentialism is the most typical example of modern philosophy. It may suffice here to mention a couple from the dozen main themes of existentialism. The helplessness of reason and the impenetrable darkness or silence that surround man in his faith were brought out by Kierkegaard and Jaspers. The realization of death, and an eternal anxiety, formulated as being-in-advance-of-oneself, were introduced by Heidegger. Alienation, strangeness and oppression in the existence of man, his being *de trop* or superfluous, with all his existence as a useless passion, have been the preferred themes of Sartre. Solitude, the feeling of nothingness, of personal guilt and a host of other negative emotions constitute the rest of the themes.

This may be sufficient to show how the sense of values and emotional attitudes have determined philosophies. The fact that philosophers have always conformed with the spirit and attitudes of their times shows this better than anything else. A positivist is as unthinkable in the Middle Ages as an existentialist in the period of the enlightenment. Except for sophists, cynics and rare or unnoticed decadents, few philosophers have dared to think differently than their contemporaries in regard to prevailing beliefs and values. Hobbes was, probably, the only one who dared to oppose contemporary beliefs — before deliberate nonconformity became fashionable in recent times. He received his punishment, which he certainly deserved.

In evaluating philosophical truths based on values, we may draw conclusions in two directions.

First, there is the acceptance of reason and harmony in creation, as well as the mystery of the ultimate source of our values and of the spirituality of our nobler, especially our aesthetic, experiences. Actually, if philosophers understood the true evolutionary causes of harmony in creation, *they would have to extol lawlessness and adversity rather than any order or reason as the real creators of that harmony.* Further, if they understood the true causation of value feelings, *they would have to praise the general lack of values as the source of our notions about higher values; or the harassments and disturbing wants of human existence as the real source of our lofty aesthetic experiences or ecstatic revelations.*

Secondly, there are the subjective emotional attitudes of philosophers themselves. Emotional attitudes always influence the general direction of thought in individual systems. But in some philosophies they have become the direct sources of the central ideas. The philosophies of Schopenhauer, Nietzsche, Bergson, all the existentialists and their predecessors back to Pascal are the more complete examples. *The truth value of such philosophies, as far as they depend on their central ideas, is nil.* The emotional postulates of such philosophies can serve as material for the analysis of the emotional backgrounds of the philosophers themselves, rather than as criteria of truth. An emotional value is always relative and derives its meaning from an exactly opposite emotional background. Therefore, *if there are any truths to be deduced from a philosophy with this approach, they are just the reverse of what the philosopher postulates.* The despair and anxiety of the existentialists reveal the modern background of emotional pampering and overprotection. The same applies to truths from such emotional sources as intuition, sentiment or "immediate" experience, which are becoming prevalent in modern philosophies disappointed with the capacities of reason.

II. The next main source of philosophical mystery is the seeming prevalence of reason in the world, as evidenced by the affinity between mind and world. The plainest argument here is that without such an affinity the mind could not grasp the world. Actually, this argument became interesting and was properly stated only in the more critical post-Kantian era. Early philosophers did not see anything worth wondering about in the fact that the mind can comprehend the world. When at the beginning of the modern era dualism became fashionable — as some concessions to science and materialism had to be made — the question arose how inferior matter could be grasped by the completely different mind. Then the assistance of God was invoked, under the cumbersome anthropomorphic doctrine of parallelism.

An affinity between the mind and the world is an implied requirement of all rationalism and idealism, which have dominated philosophy. But the early rationalists did not perceive the problem, and in idealism of the Platonic or Hegelian type the argument of such an affinity did not arise because everything was postulated beforehand as being of the nature of mind or ideas. The argument became interesting only with the revival of idealism in the more positivistic modern atmosphere. Thomas Hill Green, the pioneer of the new idealism, found that there can be no knowledge of nature without a unifying spiritual principle. Bradley demonstrated that mere phenomena are contradictory, and that a unifying transcendental principle is necessary as the ultimate source of all cognition. Royce postulated the necessity of an all-inclusive consciousness, which he called the Logos. He found that the only thing absolutely certain about this world is that it is intelligent, rational, orderly and in essence comprehensible.

The apparent rationality of man's world is really miraculous — but only under the philosophical method of looking at phenomena as ready given. As we saw, *man first orders everything according to his mind, in a selective way, through the ages, and then wonders at how everything is so miraculously ordered.* A chick which sees only grain in the world and nothing else, due to a similar selective adaptation, could also wonder at how the world is so miraculously ordered that there is never anything else but grain in it. Under the philosophical method any adjustment looks miraculous; we can recall here the example of the river. The mind and its operations seem most miraculous because they represent the greatest embodiment of adversities, through which selection works.

III. With this we come to the third main source of metaphysical mystery: the miraculous operation and capacities of the human mind. Everything in the conscious world of man comes from his mind, as his highest capacity. Since there is nothing higher, mind appears to be *perfection itself.* Only a mind of a different, higher kind could see the limitations of our mind as we can see those of the animal's. Further, consciousness or mind has to remain *inherently incomprehensible* to itself, because understanding means relating to something else or differentiating between one thing and something else. The hand cannot grasp itself nor the eye see itself.

Because of this apparent ultimateness of the mind in its perfection and incomprehensibility, it must remain for man *intrinsically transcendental* — as long as man looks at it philosophically, that is, without going back to its evolution, its integrated mechanisms or its practical use. Even the most modern philosopher could infer a mysterious soul with supernatural origins from the workings of the mind. He does not do so only because, due to scientific advance, he sees how limited and antiquated a strict adherence to the philosophical method would be. But the older philosophers, and even some modern ones (Lotze, Fechner, Wundt), derived complete convictions of the existence of soul from the mysterious working of the mind.

The miraculous performance of the mind, together with its endless and perfect selective arrangement of our world, is too much for any thinker, proceeding under the philosophical method, to escape the conviction of some mystery. Consequently, almost every philosophical system postulates some transcendental or a priori capacities, categories, forms or essences. We find them even in modern empiricism (Mill) or rationalism (Hamilton). Spencer's approach is relativistic but he still saw the need for a transcendental Unknowable or Absolute. Even the modern realistic or naturalistic systems cannot get over the general fact that the products of the mind, when isolated from their past development, appear miraculous and transcendental. Alexander admitted the nonempirical or metaphysical character of his categories. Whitehead's *prehension*, the universal form of cognition, has been compared to the mirroring by monads of Leibniz. Santayana's "essences" have been recognized to have the "texture and ontological status of Platonic ideas."

Idealism has remained strong in philosophy for the same reason. Ideas, as the final, ready-made products of the mind, are for the philosopher the primary realities, wonderful in every respect;

and dealing with nothing but ideas removes all the discrepancies between philosophy and reality. Of course, here again the expansion of scientific knowledge has made philosophers hesitate to limit themselves to the deliberately narrowed view of Platonic forms or the Hegelian Idea. Consequently, more subtle, or at least more ambiguous, sources of the world of ideas are being postulated, such as intuition or the immediacy of feeling. More significant, probably, is the search for the revelation of ultimate reality in emotional, especially aesthetic ideas. Here belong idealistic romanticism (Fichte, Schelling) and aestheticism (Croce), as well as the direct emotionalism and existentialism that we mentioned before.

But whether the mysteries of mind are rational or emotional, they can imply the existence of a higher transcendental reality only under the deliberately limited philosophical method. In scientific or simple causal terms, *the intellect, its capacities and its adaptive arrangements are products of selection by virtue of blind adversity, difficulties and lawlessness rather than any trascendental spirituality.* Mind is more complex and miraculous only because it represents an adjustment that is more adverse or incompatible. Further, *in the light of the causal understanding of emotional experiences the emotional forms of cognition are the most delusory of all.* They depend on the more direct value notions and these derive meaning from their opposite disvalues. The result is that such cognition brings out as important or true the exact reverse of what is causally true.

IV. The fourth source of philosophical mystery is the human incapacity to understand the infinite beginnings and causes of the universe. Man's world seems like an island surrounded by impenetrable immensity. This human condition has been the source of most sophisticated as well as primitive philosophizing. The main theme of modern philosophy is the limitations and despair of the human condition. This is typically illustrated by existentialism. On the less emotional side this theme is repeated in the modern philosophies of positivism, phenomenalism conventionalism and pragmatism. The main arguments of these schools center around the puzzling incapacity of the mind to know ultimate truths. Actually these arguments are what give such schools a reason to exist as philosophies. For the very argument that the mind is incapable of penetrating such truths implies their existence. Likewise, our capacity to ask questions about the wider beyond implies our inherent ability to think in its terms.

Actually, our capacity, or rather necessity, to ask unanswerable questions has a different explanation in the light of the relativity of knowledge as a form of contradictory existence realizing itself through opposition. Due to this relativity nonknowledge or non-satisfaction, which makes the questions arise endlessly, constitutes an inherent part of knowledge itself. But as long as such an explanation is missing, the mystery about the endless beyond, and our delusory endeavor to know it, will persist.

In the naïvest form, the endlessness of the universe and its causes is used as proof of a supernatural cause or God. The argument of the First Mover, worked out in a humanistically perfect fashion by Aristotle, is probably the best-known philo-sophical proof of the existence of God. As Kant has said, there are only three such possible proofs: the ontological, the teleological and the cosmological. These three proofs or arguments, applied also to the origin of the other values, including the spiritual nature of man, constituted the essence of medieval philosophy, as can be seen from the main theory of its most illustrious representative, St. Thomas. Even the early modernists (Descartes, Spinoza) used the same proofs in various combinations. We have already discussed the ontological proof; and we showed how delusory is the harmony or purposefulness of nature, on which the teleological proof rests. Now we may look at the cosmo-logical proof.

The naïveté of the cosmological argument appears as soon as the humanistic value outlook is eschewed. It is humanly *satisfactory* to stop at one point in the endless causal regression, to call that one cause God and to forbid further questioning. But this amounts to simply shutting off the voice of reason, which the philosopher himself invokes as the highest means of proof. Reason still poses the questions, what was before God, and what was His cause? Endless causal regression is an inherent part of reasoning, and we cannot avoid it as we cannot avoid nonsatis-

290

faction in getting satisfaction. If we want to comply with the full extent of reason, we cannot help recognizing that the material world is endless and can originate only from previous material causes. Attributing human qualities to one cause in the endless chain means merely replacing reasoning with anthropomorphism. The deeper reason for this is the value outlook. A critical philosopher has to admit this himself, as Kant, the greatest of all philosophers, did.

According to Kant's famous antinomies, it can be equally well proved that the world has a beginning and that it is endless; that the divisibility of matter has an end, and that it has not; that there is a necessary Being as the cause, and that there is not. Kant states that the positive answers are contingent upon man's practical reason, or his belief in values and morals. Since such beliefs are delusory anyway, the negative answers are the only possible ones. An unrestricted, scientific or even common-sense view shows clearly that the world is endless and determined by its own material causes, therefore requires no ultimate Being, still less an anthropomorphic one.

Of course, such an explanation is not *satisfactory*, and that is where the whole mystery arises. Philosophy strives for satisfaction pure and complete, cognitively as well as emotionally. But such satisfaction is an impossibility. As we saw, cognition is a need-satisfaction process, which means there can be no effect without its opposite. This further means that everything is known only through contrasting or differentiation — through relating with something else, which in its turn can be known only by differentiation from something else further back, and so on. That is why everywhere — in causation, extension, duration, change, movement or substance — we can have only endless chains of relationships, but no final knowledge.

Any one event can be related infinitely in the direction of the endlessly small as well as the endlessly great, or in any other direction. The shortest instant or slightest change can be split into endless phases. Hence the dilemmas, like those raised by Hume, which show the impossibility of causation; or by Zeno, which show the impossibility of movement. Innumerable other, similar dilemmas can be raised. If one thinks of the infinitely small, he has to admit that in every atom there must be further differentiation at some level. Therefore there must be things in it which constitute its universe — with its own smallest units, having universes of their own, and so on. The argument of the endless divisibility of matter which Kant raised remains.

In brief, cognition means as much understanding as nonunderstanding — as much satisfaction as nonsatisfaction. In practical life we have long adjusted to this; and we pay no attention to the nonsatisfaction side, or the negative causal backgrounds, anyway. But when we start philosophizing, it all emerges as a mystery. For instance, we understand practically what infinity is. But when we try to understand it completely or philosophically, we find it incomprehensible, for it then means going on and on endlessly.

The typical thing is that man never worries about the myriad of real or potential instances of such nonunderstanding, but finds deep mystery in regard to the few issues where his aspirations to greatness, continuation, fulfillment and so on are involved. In such matters, of his own immortal continuation or beginning and the goals of his existence, man cries that it all cannot be just meaningless, that there must be some reason behind it all. The reasons here are as perfect, or imperfect, as everywhere else. They are the only kind of reasons that man can have. They are rooted in the contradictions of existence itself as the only mystery; and nonsatisfaction is an inherent part of them. Actually, *man here is not after "reasons," but after a satisfaction that would for once be free of nonsatisfaction. This, however, is as impossible as it would be to have mountains without valleys.*

If man were seeking for reasons as such, he would find all the innumerable instances of nonunderstanding — including the endless universes inside every atom — to be as important as the beginnings and goals of his own world. Why should man's values, standards and purposes be of any particular importance to the universe? These values and purposes are delusory and impossible in the first place. Why should there be any sense in creation? Sense is only another word for these same impossible human values. It is ridiculous to try to impose our incongruous human value goals on

292

the universe. A truly reasonable universe should instead *not* have any human "sense" or "reason," and *not* be governed by any anthropomorphic ultimate Being. A universe governed by senselessness, nothingness and complete disorder is rather more consistently reasonable — as being more remote from the contradictory terms of human existence and values. Even in his own terms man should have learned by now that his world is an insignificant speck in the universe, and he himself rather an accidental aberration, meaning nothing in the eons of time.

In brief, the universe, the same as any other thing, can never be comprehensible, satisfactory or fully understood in itself. For there can never be value in itself, without its opposite, disvalue. Even God could not make it different; even He cannot make shadows appear without their opposite, light. Ultimately, the contradictions here derive from the contradiction of all existence realizing itself through *opposition*. We shall explain the universality of the principle of opposition later. Here it may be sufficient to reflect that Hegel could construct on it the most comprehensive system ever conceived, including everything man can think of. This realization through opposition means that any endeavor is meaningless without its own denial, but nonetheless must persist if there is to be opposition and existence in the first place.

In terms of human existence, any reaction, feeling or thought acquires its value only through disvalue, but the striving for value must be the beginning of everything. Man cannot have answers or satisfactions without opposite backgrounds of premises or needs, but he must strive for the answers or satisfactions alone. This explains why man, like a child, can ask endless nonsensical questions and meet every answer with a further "Why?" or "What is beyond that?" When philosophers postulate the higher worlds of ideas or things-in-themselves, they do not realize that they are only postponing the question one step further.

It must be understood that existence, realizing itself through opposition, is the last term of everything else — as such it has to remain a mystery, the only mystery — and that cognition is only a form of it. As we saw, all the philosophers together could not invent one word or have one tiny thought that would really go beyond the terms of existence: matter, space and time. When Kant explained that mind can never go beyond the phenomenal world, he should have stopped there. To say that there is a noumenal world of things-in-themselves amounts to an incongruous statement. For saying "is," or "things," or "world," or anything means still talking and thinking only in terms of the same phenomenal world. For the same reason, all questions about transcendental reality are incongruous. However one tries, he can ask the questions only in terms of the same material reality.

The more critical and more modern philosophers have realized the self-limitations of cognition, thus recognizing its inherent relativity. But as philosophers they could not stop at that. The result has been mystifications about a different, higher reality behind the one we simple mortals know — actually, the only one anybody can know or think about.

For instance, idealism has always meant postulating a different, higher reality. Since the time of Kant rationalism implies that the *phenomenal* world as distinguished from the *noumenal* one does not represent reality. Fichte, Schopenhauer, Bradley and Royce have used the term *appearance*. All critical or skeptical philosophies imply, by their very criticism of our capacity to know reality, that such a different reality, somehow known to the philosopher, exists. Even philosophical empiricism leads to similar implications. For instance, the early British empiricists (Locke, Berkeley, Hume) came to the conclusion that we can know only our own ideas. Berkeley derived from this his famous thesis: *Esse est percipi,* which implies that the world does not even exist, except in perception, ultimately determined by divine guidance. The later British empiricist, Mill, agreed with the Kantian thesis that we know only phenomena, not things-in-themselves. Even the modern realists have argued that we do not perceive reality but only *sense data* (Moore), *sensations* (Russell) or *essences* (Santayana). In a word, philosophers have found the terms of cognition unsatisfactory and have tried to postulate, directly or implicitly, something more satisfactory behind them.

Actually, all such philosophizing is delusory. It is like trying to answer the same endless question: "What is beyond that?" If the philosopher went one step further, he would have to postulate a further reality behind the transcendental reality, and then one behind that too, and so on; or he could argue that we know only ideas about our ideas about our ideas. Actually, no philosopher can speak or think about a different reality any better than the simplest of men. The world we all know and the way we know it are the only ones that we can ever have. It is silly to assert that this world is only the appearance of something else if there "is" nothing else in the only sense it could "be." Our world or the way we know it is complete because it is the *only* and the *whole* world we can ever know. Beyond that we can neither think nor speak nor feel without becoming incongruous. No endeavor by philosophers, however desperate, can change this. One could even agree to a pure solipsism and say that there is nothing at all except the states of mind of different people. Still, that would change nothing. All these states of mind still work in the same way as before — the way we know reality to be. Causality still remains inexorably strict, no miracles happen, and nothing beyond the terms of existence can ever be conceived.

We may as well conclude. Philosophy, either as a learned discipline or merely as a way of looking at things, has remained the only rational source of mystery, necessary for the support of our moral, religious and aesthetic beliefs if these are to be defended in the humanistic fashion. Other mysteries and miracles have been dispelled in the light of science. In philosophy miracles can persist because a causal understanding of psychology, values and the phenomena of mind is still missing. Relative causation offers such an understanding in its simplest form; and it is sufficient to dispel philosophical miracles. The complexity of philosophy does not matter here. The simplest fundamental scientific discoveries have always been able to dispel the most complex sophistications, without going into their details. By the way, if there were any true mysteries or miracles, common sense would have discovered them long before philosophy. Common sense is so simple because it has been fitted and adjusted for ages so precisely that it can hit the point at once. Complexity always accompanies lack of understanding. There are always thousands of ways to make a mistake as against one simple way that is right. Great truths are as simple as philosophy is complex.

AESTHETICS

Our almost religious regard for aesthetics stems from a mis-understanding about the source of the unearthly feelings we derive from aesthetic experiences. If it were realized that the true source of such feelings are the earthly negative feelings of need, harassment and deprivation, aesthetics as a spiritual mystery would have no followers. Aesthetic release is no different from any other release; we explained before the biological nature of the feelings of beauty. The opium smoker or user of drugs also gains unearthly satisfactions. He may even experience spiritual revelation if he has been previously preoccupied with spiritual problems. But nobody would claim that a divine formula is contained in the poppy gum or drug.

The difference between aesthetic release and ordinary pleasures is that the aesthetic enjoyments are less intense biologically, therefore more compatible with culture. As such they are readily permitted, and enjoyed with an accompanying feeling of worthiness. Second, the aesthetic medium is used by the artist to appeal to so many and general releases that the way for mystery is opened. The artist, aided by the aesthetician, intuitively directs the interpretation of this mystery along spiritual lines, indicated or implied.

But if aesthetics rests on simple biological release, what about the intricacies of the laws of aesthetics? We showed before how relative causation, especially the law of contrast, is sufficient to explain them. We may give here another illustration. Musical enjoyment means the enjoyment of the human love song, which is not unlike the song of birds or the love call of cats. The human love song consists mainly of raising the pitch from a natural low to a natural high (which usually accompanies inhaling and ex-haling). The excitement value lies in the high pitch. But because of relativity and the need for contrast a high pitch in itself means nothing. There must be a low one from which the high can rise.

296

This low may acquire meaning of its own, as relaxation, resignation or preparation for release.

But a repeated contrast between a simple low and a simple high becomes monotonous. In other words, it needs further contrast. Then the whole may need still further differentiation or contrast. Also, the new contrasts that are added have to be as original and spontaneous as jokes must be to have surprise value, which every contrast requires. All this goes on intuitively, as all human evaluations do, but the end product seems miraculous. It offers almost mathematical order amidst unexplainable but meaningful diversity — harmony amidst complexity. According to Birkhoff's formula, the value of aesthetic experience is proportional to the amount of harmony as well as complexity in the aesthetic presentation. Aesthetic theory cannot explain why should there be complexity or disorder, if the enjoyment is, clearly, derived only from the harmony or order, which in its perfection means the highest simplicity.

Another law of relative causation, fixation, explains the process by which aesthetics becomes a sacrosanct cult. Art enjoyment is suitable for fixation. Though its pleasure releases are slight, they are always present. The value of these releases increases automatically, according to the law of fixation, through repeated encounter with objects of art. Such encounter is made possible by the accumulation of human workmanship through the centuries. Due to fixation the vicious-circle effect establishes itself: art is valued more the more often it is encountered, and more of it is produced as it becomes more valued. Here the compatibility of aesthetic enjoyments with cultural demands becomes important. Art enjoyments may even help sublimate more direct biological enjoyments, which, due to their strength, may make other, more refined, cultural motivations fade in importance.

Art becomes the main pleasure outlet for civilized people living under restrictions of natural enjoyments and amidst the accumulated riches of human workmanship and skill. Gradually art becomes associated with culture itself, and fixation helps to turn this belief into a religious cult. Modern man professes a love of art without having any rational reasons why this enjoyment should be more worthy than others. He is simply afraid to be regarded as uncivilized or to miss real culture if he does not. The inertial force of superstition is already there.

But as we explained before, art is of little value for cultural conditioning. It means enjoyment, and enhances rather than restricts natural releases, whereas conditioning means restriction. Art is a fixational cult of the enlightened man who favors releases rather than restrictions. As such it is closer to pleasure-releasing cults, like dance rituals, than to other cultural occupations. The enjoyment of beauty could be conditioned. But this would require the restriction of the natural experience of beauty, so that even such vaguely "beautiful" occupations as education, social cooperation, industry or science could become additionally enjoyable for the sake of their beauty. Something of this happened during the Middle Ages—the period of the highest aspirations of spirituality and culture by which we still live. Then art was not valued for its own sake; but the enjoyment of beauty was often attached to useful occupations or directly cultural institutions, like religion.

Of course, in practice we often have to choose between lesser evils and to use natural enjoyments as attractions to entice people to a more cultural medium. Probably, that is why our cultural tradition does not oppose art, even tolerates its occasional licentiousness. But viewed in the wider perspective of cultural history art has to be placed among the many other purely fixational superstitious cults. This is not the first time that people have elevated into religious sanctity something they have been associating for ages with higher culture without understanding the reason. It is true that culture cannot exist in a vacuum, that it has to be attached to something concrete. But then we should prefer moral cults, with prayer, ritual and all. Though these are equally superstitious, they tie in better with cultural conditioning.

Actually, art is destroying itself due to the need for contrast. As more and more surprise or originality is needed, art reaches its natural final contrast—denial of everything that it originally stood for. Ugliness is the final contrast to beauty, and we find it throughout modern art, from Mauriac's twilight characters to Albright's portraits resembling corpses in putrescent skins. Any one aspect of art — beauty, harmony, loftiness, refinement — has found its ultimate contrast in modern art. It is not true that this is no longer art. It is as much art as any previous art was. Experienced artists, critics or art enjoyers recognize this by intuitive emotional insight. What may appear only a disorderly smear on a canvas may meet previous styles in a contrast at so many significant points that it can give to a cultured art enjoyer a meaningful experience. That is why not every smear means a work of art, though artists or spectators often may not know the difference.

In general, modern art shows its pretentious immaturity in seeking for abstract, which means unnatural and, ultimately, "loud," expressions. Real art consists of finding the extraordinary in the ordinary. The greatest effect of contrast can be produced by using, not avoiding, the background of similarity. Stone or mud would seem to offer the highest contrast to the liveliness or purity of the human body. But only a very similar other human body can serve to bring out the stoniness or impurity of the body. Contrast is greater where more points of reference or comparison are available — where the basic similarity is greater. That is why only the primitive storyteller or poor comedian uses loud exaggerations.

The laws of contrast and fixation can help explain other aspects of art and art history. For instance, primitive art may resemble modern art, because both show contrast to natural beauty. But the resemblance is purely accidental. In fact, primitive art is not art at all: it does not have any reference to beauty either directly or by contrast. Men of nature find nothing particular in the natural or ordinarily beautiful. Their "art" objects are simply objects that serve various practical or ritual purposes, but are provided with extraordinary, unnatural features in order to impress, or to make them appear more efficient. Weird ritual masks and totems, shiny, rare and unnatural objects or materials for ornamentation and witchcraft, contorted designs and so on serve this purpose.

Fixation explains why such objects become stylized. They have to be the same as objects previously enjoyed or admired. If they are not, they will have none of the sacrosanct value which has grown out of fixation on similar objects. On the other hand, differentiation or contrast can make an object appear much more impressive. The two tendencies converge and stylization results: sameness is conserved while subordinate variations are enriched. This applies to all styles and fashions. The modern art historian who searches for artistic meaning in the objects and styles of primitive "art" is imputing his own views or feelings to primitive man.

The story of our own Western art is illustrative. The early artists wanted only to present religious truths and images in the proper way, that is, in the way they had been presented before. Copying from previous presentations led to a fixational deepening of styles. The artists, or rather the craftsmen, like the spectators, did not expect the representation to show the elements of beauty of nature. Those were too commonplace for the early Western peoples of nature. They expected the objects rather to show something weird or extraordinary; and early Christian artists gladly obliged wherever the sanctity of presentation permitted such diversions. For similar reasons of contrast these peoples of nature turned toward classicism, romanticism and everything artificial which came from the higher Roman civilization, including Christianity itself. Only to the extent that life became less natural did the appreciation of nature and its beauties become fashionable.

Aestheticians and art historians trying to discover in logical ways the revelation of the soul of a given people in their monuments of art have produced only endless, conflicting sophistications. Viewed with the usual logic, art shows what is exceptional, therefore least essential, in the psychological makeup of a given people. The paradox of contrast applies to every aspect and detail of artistic experience. Other styles and aesthetic movements of Western peoples have followed the same rule. Realism and rationalism derived from romanticism and the medieval reliance on faith, in varied combinations, in different fields, but were in their turn reversed by more modern irrationalistic tendencies.

Perhaps the best example of the evolution of styles is offered by modern French painting, which can serve as a prototype in art history. It started with the classicism of David, Gericault and

300

Delacroix, and ended with the irrationalism of the Fauvists and Cubists — eminently represented by Matisse, Derain and Braque — as well as the Futurists, Surrealists, extreme Abstractionists and even Primitivists. This reversal followed a pattern typical of all styles and fashions. At each step the established fixational values conflicted with fresh contrasts — offensive and enriching at the same time. This explains why every new style was met with outrage at the same time as it haunted the imagination with fresh richness — to become sanctified in the end and serve as background for the next style. Since opposed forces were at work at each step, and since the new could emerge only against the background of the old, the change had to be gradual. Rouault or Picasso is unthinkable in the time of Delacroix or Rousseau.

The story of the most famous of all styles, Impressionism, may serve as illustration. Even the most masterly Impressionists, Manet, Degas, Renoir and Monet, were at first branded as freaks or savage extremists. But at the same time Impressionism gained its salient haunting brilliance from contrast with the previous style. The momentariness of expression, the divisionism of pure colors or casualness of form were direct contrasts to the studied search for the enduring mood, imperceptible transition of natural color shades or minute exactness of form achieved by such masters as Rousseau, Corot, Millet or Descamps. Actually, the naturalism of these painters had in its time emerged as a contrast to the background of the prevailing classicism and romanticism, and was considered just as crudely inartistic at first.

Thus each style served as the background against which the next one acquired its contrasting brilliance or salient emotional conviction. Impressionism served as a background for the temperamental intensity, even mysticism, in the paintings of Gaugin or Van Gogh, for the hued color planes and monumentalness of form in the paintings of Cézanne, and for the emphatic design or reinforced contours of Gaugin, Van Gogh and Cézanne. The ultimate in contrast was found in deliberate ugliness, probably first introduced intentionally by Toulouse-Lautrec; and in the primitivism made famous by the other Rousseau.

Of course, the explanations given by artists themselves, especially after a style has become famous, are only rationalizations of the emotions evoked by increased effect. All kinds of rational and idealistic reasons, even mystical causes, are discovered, as in all cases when man tries to explain deep or worthy emotions. Cults have always had their abstruse dogmas and esoteric priests, though the emotions that support the cult obey the simplest natural laws.

Contrast used to its best effect and in all possible aspects enables the artist to make an art object more impressive than anything nature can produce. The happy-end marriage of the hero and heroine of a story may make the reader choke with joy, though if presented without the threats and calamities of the story it would mean nothing. A yellowish patch of color on canvas means nothing, but surrounded by darkness in a painting by Rembrandt it becomes a source of everlasting light. In all arts brilliance of feeling is evoked by contrast in as many of a person's natural releases and previous experiences as possible. His previous art experiences also can become important. That is where aesthetic fixation and the play of styles comes in. A person who has enjoyed a certain style or form of art for years has every release operating in him upon the discovery of something new in it. In short, the richness of aesthetic experiences can be heightened to any degree by nothing more than a play of amassed sharp contrasts in which every value is intensified through its opposite. Fixation helps, by deepening the release pathways, and consequently decreasing other, natural releases, due to the predeterminacy of the total of releases. Thus an art object may become emotionally more meaningful than any single natural experience, though at bottom it derives its values from natural reactions.

Art has other advantages over nature. A musical instrument can produce a tune a hundred times more amplified or perfected than the best human voice; think of the human vocal chords and those of a piano. That is the reason why music can arouse such profound emotions. It is like stimulating a nerve with a current a hundred times stronger than natural stimulation. In painting, the main element, light, cannot be heightened directly. But it can be heightened by contrast; and its components of color can be purified or combined more effectively than nature can ever do. As to natural forms and other natural values in painting, they can be amplified unlimitedly. In the crudest instance, the human body can be painted in much more perfect or exuberant forms than nature ever produces. Or a landscape can combine warmth, calm, luxuriance or other moods to a degree that nature can never offer.

Actually, a more refined artist eschews such vulgar effects. He knows that a cultivated spectator wants to discover for himself and retain the value experience rather than have it forced on him in such a strong way that he ends with a feeling of cheap overfeeding. Underemphasis is as important in creating a work of art as it is in telling a joke or trying to convince people. To an emotionally farsighted person underemphasis or underenjoyment becomes a deeply seated wisdom. Avoidance of cheap over-enjoyments is the main characteristic of cultural refinements. For instance, red is the color that means beauty in natural reactions — in the Slavic languages "red" has the same root as "beautiful" — but it is vulgar to use red richly. Used in profusion it loses its effect. Rather, a hue of red, or a fine red pattern on a contrasting nuanced background, is more effective.

Due to relativity, underemphasis may serve to enrich value experiences in other ways. A still life representing a herring on a piece of newspaper can imply more light than a grandiose landscape. The standards here are lower and the effect exceeds expectations. The spectator deduces intuitively that the world must be wondrously rich in light or the mood of reassurance if even such a prosaic object is full of it. By a further step, a deliberate somberness of presentation in itself becomes the inspiration of deep reassurance — which also is felt as enduring because of the avoidance of overenjoyment.

Understanding the art experience can become very confusing if the simple laws of value causation are left out of sight, and attention paid to separate values. To be sure, everybody looks for values in a work of art; and the aesthetician expects to discover, through logical relation, the higher spiritual sources behind the values. Actually, the logic here is reversed, and the real sources of the aesthetic value experiences are their exact opposites — things that are furthest away from spirituality. Also, the values intuitively selected by the artist or art enjoyer are myriad. If one tries to follow them up, he is lost.

Art critics aspiring to explain more by trying to go deeply into all the possible moods or ideas they can discover can confuse more than explain. We may look here at the work of the foremost art critic, Malraux. It is full of profound and esoteric insights as well as culturally exquisite analyses. If we wanted to learn how great and refined an art enjoyer Malraux is, we could not find a better work. But it explains nothing about art causally. The causal laws of aesthetic experience, as of any experience, can only be simple. The humanistic sophistications throughout our culture originate from the lack of understanding the simple psychological causes and a consequent flight into mystery. If Malraux had understood the underlying aesthetic law of contrast which made him choose the very title of his main work, *Voices of Silence*, he would have realized that his endlessly rich insights causally explain not art in general but only his own backgrounds.

At present, however, art criticism has to remain as abstruse and mysterious as art itself, in order to be enjoyed in the religious mood that modern man has acquired for aesthetics.

LITERATURE

We may say a few words about literature. Here art enjoyment sometimes overlaps learning. A person can live manifold lives and learn about inaccessible things by reading. But as regards literary fiction, even the best writers create what resembles a world of freaks rather than reality, because of a lack of understanding of psychological causation. The inner life of people, which constitutes the main subject of fiction, is completely distorted. As we saw, psychological experiences are governed by laws that work in ways exactly opposite to those believed in by every man or writer, as by every psychologist or humanistic theorist. In real life this does not matter much, because the equally contradictory practical adjustment takes care of the delusory beliefs. But in literature it is different. There the writer creates life fully in accordance with his delusory understanding of psychological causation. He creates people with impossible motivations and behavior which would be closer to the truth if they were reversed.

Practically, literary errors matter little. The underlying moral tone and especially the universal rule that the good side should win matter more — whether the moral is brought out directly or by way of contrast through the anguished cry of negativism. Reading means living, though in a less vivid way. Emotional support for simple good intentions is more important than the most elaborate reasonings, moral rationalizations or deep sophistications.

Modern literature has turned toward emotionalism and Freudian mystery. But writing about paramount emotions with a complete misunderstanding of their causal logic is like writing about strange islands with monstrous animals, as was fashionable a few centuries ago. In the light of emotional causation, every bit of the fashionable modern novel or play is as unreal as such monster stories. No wonder the greatest modern literary experts on emotional life — one can think here of Hemingway or Tennessee Williams — are those who are least able to cope with their own emotional difficulties.

As can be expected, the theme of death has led to the richest incongruities, in modern as well as earlier literature. The happy or emotionally redeemed death of the hero upon the attainment of his goal or discovery of love is a virtual travesty of a tragic reality. In truth, the more success or love a person attains, the more horrible to him is death; instinctively the person turns away from it all when he faces death. Further, there is the repetitive yearning for the eternal peacefulness of death by the poet — mainly sentimental in the older literature but more indirect or existentialistic in modern literature. Of course, the poet yearns for deliverance from all his practical troubles, but he does not realize that death is the quintessence of all troubles. No poet or writer would even mention death if he really understood what it means; those who are really threatened by it do not. The recurrence of the theme of death in art has induced philosophers to postulate that there are other sources than life behind aesthetics.

Fixation plays an important role in our appreciation of masterpieces in literature. It may sound like sacrilege to doubt the quality of the *Odyssey* or *Don Quixote*, but a reader untouched by the mystery of tradition would find the *Odyssey* a more exaggerated than imaginative ancient "Western" by an author resorting to impossible miracles, pompousness, mannerism and pretentious virtuousness. And he would find *Don Quixote*, read in the original, a more strained than really witty yarn of practical jokes. But since these works are read as classics from generation to generation, their value increases by fixation, and lofty underlying meanings are ascribed to them. Thus by being literary monuments they have come to be considered perfect works of art.

Critics should try to reread these works as if they were recently written paperbacks. They should forget about the historical peculiarities of style, which are naturally inimitable, as old things often are. Then they would find that the old masters stand on the same level as our third-rate amateurs seeking for effect through sensationalism, mannerism, pompousness, pretentious virtue and flight into unreality. This does not mean that people of previous centuries had less talent. But then a poet or writer was expected to say extraordinary and worthy things. Literature has progressed from pompousness and mannerism to the talent of simple men, which people always had, and which is what we should admire in the past of humanity. One can observe that the same discovery of the simple but genuinely unique talents of humble men is gradually replacing much of our present artificiality and exaggeration in all forms of art, from grand opera and contorted ballet to tearful dramatization and emphatic comedy. Artificialities and exaggerations persist because they are easier than real talent.

The mistaking of an old, inimitable style for talent cannot be so easily discerned in a literary work, because endless interpretations are possible here. But if one thinks of forgeries of other objects of art, including old paintings, he has to admit that the forger has no difficulty as regards artistic talent. He has difficulties only as regards the older, more contorted method. If one looks in this light at any classic writer, even Shakespeare, he can see that the aura of glory woven around them is due to a mere fixation — though this may be even an advantage from the point of view of cultural tradition.

The same can be said about collection of old books and antiques — furniture, china, jewelry or wallpaper — as well as the other collection fads. Due to the same fixation, collection of things of the past has become a value in itself. The real value of the thing collected becomes secondary and serves only as a criterion for rejecting the mere trash of the past. As more and more fixational value is attributed to the objects collected they become sacrosanct and invested with any possible other value. Scientifically viewed, it all amounts to another superstitious cult.

CULTURAL INERTIA

If in the case of aesthetic fixations there is not much harm done, in other fields fixation becomes a dead weight, obstructing cultural advance. People become victims of value fixations without realizing what is really happening to them. The fixational value feelings prevent such a realization. Value feelings always make us find perfect justifications for whatever we do. Take baseball, football, racing, boxing or any sport. As we explained before, there is no value in them either for intellectual or physical development. They are culturally degrading because men compete here in those capacities in which they excel as animals. Objectively viewed it is all part of the natural tendency of man to slide back to the animal level. But if you, naïvely, tried to explain to a sports fan or college alumnus what it all really means, you would be regarded as a person lacking cultural tradition.

If the *billions* of dollars that are now spent on games and sports were invested in education, in creation of institutions offering cultural interests and competitions, or in the organization of youth, we would not have our perennial youth problems, and society could promote a different cultural environment with universal intellectual ambitions as the formative atmosphere. At

307

present the great hero to be imitated may be a man whose only merit is the possession of the reflexes or muscles of an ape. Newspapers consecrate up to one-third of their space to such heroes and their deeds. These can become of more interest to the masses than all other events. As an article in the *Reader's Digest*, said in enumerating the most important events of the last twenty years, the most important event for 1939 was that "Yogi Bera, 14, decided not to return to Wade Grammar School."

We realize we are not discovering anything new here. Everybody knows these things for himself. But everybody also lives in the atmosphere of fixational value feelings which prevent him from thinking differently. Thus we blindly continue doing an absurd thing with the unshakable conviction that it is "all right" just because it has been done before. If we were started on a different track, we would continue doing differently. This is the absurdity inherent in all cultural tradition, especially if the fixation is strengthened by the continuous yield of some natural release. Blind unshakable inertia is, in general, valuable in sustaining cultural tradition. But during periods of ease, fixations favoring release establish themselves more easily than morals requiring restrictions. Life may advance and offer new forms of enjoyment, but morals for their restriction may not have time to evolve. Thus real sins, more culturally degenerating than some outgrown ones, may establish themselves without anybody recognizing them.

The entertainments, games and sports that we mentioned above are only the more conspicuous examples. There are many others. To mention the most typical and "normal" feature of modern life — the car craze of modern man — it consumes so much capital and effort that if the same amount were invested rationally, it could provide free transportation for everybody and everything in comfort and to an unlimited extent, even rides to the moon or Mars. Here the fixation grows out of the natural enjoyment of "riding" which can be easily observed from the play of children as well as the historical customs of peoples. Of course, everybody for himself, and therefore the people as a whole find full justification for their satisfactions, especially if there is a lack of imagination about how things might be completely different.

The economic arguments about the increase in consumption through the entertainment industries rest on as much blind inertia as culture in general. The sin of waste has not yet been generally recognized because only recently have people had enough to waste on a vast scale; just as it has not yet been recognized that capital accumulation is the basal source of all progress. Sins have always attracted man with their glamour and seeming vigor. The deeper reason for this is man's incapacity to see restrictions or disvalues as sources of value. That is why morals are hard to evolve and have required superstitions as justification.

Practically, the most important force behind all fixational enjoyments is the conviction that life would be meaningless without the pleasures we enjoy and the values we find worthwhile. We are unable to accept that what is considered worthwhile by us is relative. Actually, any other, seemingly impossible set of values could provide the same amount of happiness or sense of worthiness. A nobleman of two centuries ago would not have been able to imagine how life could have any value without many servants, spacious castles, carriages, frilly dresses or the aristocratic way of life. Two centuries from now we will be still closer to the beehive society, toward which humanity is inevitably advancing. And life will still have plenty of values, though to us it would look more like the ironic *Brave New World* of Huxley or the *1984* of Orwell.

We can picture the society of the future as an organism with individuals as its cells. Man will neither have nor need individual freedoms or natural pleasures. The sooner man's physical life with all its aspects of vitality and beauty is reduced to stagnation, slowed down to last for ages, the better. It is clear that man will rule the world by his intellect alone. And it also should be clear that the intellect will create a world of its own, which to us might look oppressive, drab, abstract and lacking everything we consider valuable, but which will be richer than anything we can imagine.

CONCLUSIONS

Our cultural values have become sacrosanct through age-long fixations and humanistic rationalizations. In fact, these values rest on disvalues. Morals derive their value, purpose and forms of realization from the egotistic nature of man. Religious values derive, equally, from needs; as we saw, the real source of belief in God is the godlessness in the world. The sublimity of aesthetic feelings has as its source the harassments and needs of existence. But these causal truths are the exact opposite of what is now held as true. Of course, in practice the cultural tradition is better than any current "scientism" or rationalism. But if we try to imagine the future of man, our cults will be seen as no different from other superstitious cults in the past. Superstition and ignorance breed bigotry, passionate conflicts and backwardness, however noble the intentions or lofty the beliefs. Stupidity is still the worst sin. We showed how present humanistic thought furiously opposes the transformation of human nature by conditioning, or social integration advancing toward the "beehive" society, though exactly these are the primary sources of cultural advance. Genetic or racial engineering and experimentation constitute one form of the transformation of man which harbors revolutionary possibilities. But the very thought of such possibilities evokes horror at present.

We must start understanding that even a few hundred years from now our practical values and immediate beliefs will be found to be as backward as those of other cults in the past. Our present tradition helps cultural advance because it harbors intuitive general wisdoms. But the superstitious tradition will soon have to be replaced by science. Ultimately, progress can only be materialistic. The humanistic endeavor to derive the wisdom and force of progress from the divination or guidance of a higher moral authority arises from the delusions of the value outlook.

By purely materialistic, even blind progress man as a conscious being has evolved. Incomparably greater steps of advance await him in a planned future. What they will be we can judge as little as the animal can judge conscious life. This progress has been and will be achieved exactly because of the absence of Providence or values inherent in creation. Any purpose that we naïvely impute to the origin of man will be exceeded beyond our imagination by what man will achieve in the end. The miracles of the future will be greater, in our terms, than the miracles of the present are in the terms of cave men. Man will become his own creator by virtue of science built on causal understanding. Such understanding, however, means exactly reversing the presently dominating value outlook. Because the delusions of this outlook have not even been suspected up to now, man has not yet even started on his road of planned self-creation, the principles of which are adversity, opposition and seeming contradiction.

IX

THE RELATIVITY OF KNOWLEDGE
(From Philosophy to Physics)

Knowledge, like any human experience, is relative. We shall try to show this by looking at the most complex form of knowledge reached in philosophy, as well as man's simplest knowledge of the physical reality around him. The relativity of knowledge means that there can be no knowledge, which means satisfaction, without or beyond an equal not-knowledge or need in the form of negative backgrounds — enlarged factual premises, questions and interests. We saw how nothing can be known without differentiation from something different or opposite, and how every learning as satisfaction requires an opposite background of needs. Only because we try to avoid the experience of needs, and never connect them with the completely different experience of satisfaction or knowledge, can we live under the delusion that we know things directly or in themselves.

This delusion reaches its height in philosophy or the philosophical method, which represents on the intellectual level of adjustment man's ever-present endeavor to reach satisfactions without the previous accumulation of needs. Man, in general, first tries to know things easily and directly — in the philosophical way. Only when he fails to gain real knowledge in this way does he go back to the ordinary or scientific method, which means the enlargement of premises, questions and factual or historical backgrounds. *The philosophical method means striving for knowledge of things in themselves or in their essences.* Naturally, such an endeavor is as futile as the endeavors of the neurotic to enjoy satisfaction without needs. An enormous amount of elaboration is reached in philosophy, as in neurosis, as every possible way is tried to attain directly what seems to lie just ahead. Every satisfaction seems to be directly attainable. We saw how this delusion underlies all the innumerable futile endeavors in every field of adjustment.

The exclusive striving for satisfaction determines another characteristic of the philosophical method. In his tendency to gain perfect satisfaction the philosopher tries to reduce everything to some one essence. If there is more than one position to be taken, in conscious responses where the organism acts as an integrated whole, complete satisfaction is not reached. This is the reason for all generalizations by the mind; and the philosophical method represents an attempt to reach an all-inclusive generalization. *The central aim of all philosophies is to explain everything in terms of one essence.* We showed before how any one notion can be chosen as the center to which everything else is related in the net of relationships that constitutes a person's knowledge. Usually the philosopher chooses such lofty notions as Idea, God, Mind or Spirit — though he could just as well choose Humdrum or Can-Opener.

As might be expected, *all philosophies try to view their essences, and central notions, as "things."* Notions of "things" are most satisfactory because they represent the stability, unity and finality that we seek to establish in our relations with the outside world. No misunderstandings arise in practical life because we intuitively know the pragmatic nature of "things." We never expect a "thought" or "idea" to exist as a separate thing. Further, we never use "things" or nouns otherwise than with verbs, adjectives, adverbs and so on, which restores flux and variation to reality. In brief, we use notions the way we evolve them — as tools for reaching truths, not as truths in themselves. But the philosopher tries to see his essences or "things" as absolute truths sufficient in themselves. Consequently, he is unable to explain change, motion or individualization of reality. But the greatest fallacy in such use of the concept of "things" arises from the fact that things, as products of differentiation, are actually known by *what they are not.* Consequently, the philosopher, who attributes *direct* universal causal significance to his essences or "things" is bound to attribute causal meanings to everything in ways that are opposite to what is really true; he usually exalts some salient value in his essence whereas this value derives from its exact opposite, disvalue.

Above all, the search for satisfaction makes the *value outlook* the primary approach of the philosophical method. But as we saw, the value outlook implies acceptance of every human delusion, and looking at natural phenomena in their final, as if ready given stage, in which they always appear unexplainably miraculous.

It can be said that every possible human delusion and fallacy is perpetuated by the philosophical method. This is so because *in philosophy the contradictory and impossible human striving for satisfaction alone can go on without being checked by any serious consequences.* If man did the same on the emotional level, he would live in a constant neurosis; or if he did so in his physiological adjustment, he would suffer constant aftermaths and overadjustive derangements. But on the intellectual level any activity, even a "neurotic" one, brings more good than harm; and man has learned to keep away from philosophizing when he has to understand or learn something seriously.

Now we may try to illustrate the application of the philosophical method, by looking at a few representative examples of the Western philosophy.

The first Greek philosophers, the **Milesians,** applied the method without much sophistication. They tried to explain everything in one term by simply postulating one basal stuff of which everything is made. Thales said it is water. Anaximander assumed it to be the Boundless. According to Anaximenes, it is air, vapor or mist. The contradictions arising from such simple philosophizing showed in an equally simple form. If everything is some one and permanent thing, how can the variety and change in nature be explained? The problem of change was taken up by Heraclitus and solved in an equally philosophical way. He declared that everything is in constant flux; he illustrated this by saying that nobody can step twice into the same river. He postulated fire as the stuff of which everything consists, and which can change into water and earth.

But even this kind of change was too much for the pure early philosophical approach. The **Eleatic school** that followed postulated Being as the essence of everything and repudiated the possibility of change. Parmenides, the founder of the school, argued that it is impossible for a thing both to be and not to be, as change requires. If Being has changed or become, it must have come either from nonbeing or from being. If from nonbeing, it has come from nothing, which is impossible; if from being, it has come from itself which means it has never changed. Therefore the changing and varied world as we see it is an illusion. There can be no breaks in Being, because if a break "is," it is the same as Being.

Zeno, the pupil of Parmenides, proved that the assumption of plurality and motion leads to absurdities. If being is plurality, it can be divided into an infinite number of parts. If the parts are infinitely small, they would give only an infinitely small total. If the parts are finite rather than infinitely small, then their infinite number would give an infinitely great total, which is equally impossible. Zeno's arguments are best illustrated by his proof of the impossibility of motion in his famous paradoxes. A thing if it is to move must pass through infinite number of points, which is impossible. In his paradox of the race between Achilles and the tortoise, Zeno argues that Achilles, in order to pass a tortoise, which starts a small distance ahead of him, has to pass the distance that the tortoise has moved in the meantime. But while he does that, the tortoise has moved another distance, and so on, infinitely. In another paradox Zeno argued that an arrow cannot move. At any one of the infinitely small instants the arrow is at rest, it has zero motion; but zero motions, however infinitely many, can only add up to a zero total.

These paradoxes are interesting. They reveal better than anything else the impossibility of understanding with finality anything in itself, as a definite final "thing." Modern logicians and mathematicians have demonstrated that these paradoxes can be solved. H. B. Smith does so in his book *How the Mind Falls in Error*. Of course, the paradoxes can be solved mathematically or logically. Mathematics and logic are only other languages for

315

expressing the general truths we all know; and it is clear to everybody that these paradoxes are not true. But the point is that if one persists in the philosophical method of viewing the world in terms of final things to be known in themselves, rather than in terms of endless relations and a humanly ungraspable flux, the paradoxes cannot be solved.

The philosophy of **Melissus of Samos** is probably the most typical example of pure philosophizing. According to him, Being cannot have originated, for that would mean it came from nothing. Being is therefore eternal, and since everything that exists is Being, everything is eternal and unchanging. There can also be no empty space, since that would mean nonbeing, and according to the Eleatics nonbeing is unthinkable. But if there is no empty space, there can be no motion. Melissus supported the general position of the Eleatics that Being is one and that there can be no separation or combination in it, therefore there can be no change.

Solutions to this clearly untenable position were offered by the **pluralists.** Greek pluralism is naïve enough to show clearly what the gist of pluralism generally is. *Pluralism enables the philosopher to say that reality is something "one," like Atom, Monad or Real, and still to account for the endless variety of reality.* **Anaxagoras,** the main representative of early Greek pluralism, assumed an infinite number of substances or "seeds" of specific qualities as the eternal, never-changing stuff from which everything originated due to a whirling motion. As to the cause of this motion, Anaxagoras attributed it to a special principle which he called *"Nous"* or "mind." He referred to it as an exceedingly fine and rarefied matter. He also attributed to it the qualities of mind, though according to Aristotle he did so only where his mechanistic explanation failed.

Empedocles can be mentioned as another pluralist. He postulated that everything consists of earth, air, fire and water, as the unchanging eternal "roots of things." He then postulated love and hate as the principles that make the four elements unite and divide. Empedocles is often mentioned as the first evolutionist. Actually, he shows not an inkling of insight into the simple but radical idea of selection. His account of the creation of bodies by chance combinations of separate limbs or organs seems to have been intended rather as a mystically sensational, even gruesome, poetry. As the historian Meiners says, nobody can make out what Empedocles meant in his poetry. It is clear, however, that he was as far from scientific or common-sense explanations as all philosophers are who endeavor to "explain" things by postulating mysterious substances, roots, seeds, Nous, love and so on — without bothering to explain these in their turn.

Another school of pluralists was that of the **Atomists,** represented by Leucippus and Democritus. Atomists agreed with their predecessors that the ultimate reality can neither change nor be divided. But the Atomists recognized the necessity of explaining variety and change. Accordingly, they attributed the unity and permanence of ultimate reality to invisibly small parts inside things. Atoms were logical postulates for the Atomists and had nothing to do with scientific or practical insights. According to the Atomists, the atoms are not real in the sense that they can be experienced in any way. The similarity between the atoms of Democritus as logical constructs and the atoms of modern physics is purely accidental, and goes no further than indivisibility and smallness. According to the Atomists, the forms that atoms may have are infinite in number. They may have hooks, grooves, eyes, bumps, depressions of all kinds for holding together and thus giving solidity to things, since otherwise atoms are in constant motion.

We have little to say about the **Pythagoreans** and **Sophists.** The Pythagoreans postulated number as the essence of everything. Their system represents a strain of philosophical rationalism a little more formalistic than the rest. All products of the human mind when viewed in their final, ready-made state are miraculous. For instance, one may find it supernaturally miraculous, as some Greeks did, that language and alphabet have been so created that everything can be spelled with just the number of existing letters. Mathematics viewed in this way can seem even more mysterious. Here man first orders or grasps things in certain relations, according to the simplest universal notions of "one," "more" or "less," and then wonders how everything is so miraculously ordered. As to the Sophists, they were ready to turn into absurdities the contradictions inherent in the philosophical method. They also cynically demonstrated the relativity of values, and fully earned the contempt of earnest men. Consequently, the Sophists discredited themselves forever. Recognition went, rather, to the great virtuous philosophies, eminently expounded by Plato and Aristotle.

The main discovery of **Plato** was the world of ideas or forms as the ultimate reality. At the time of Plato the difficulties inherent in the previous philosophies had become apparent. Plato turned to a new kind of solution: if reality does not fit into mental concepts of finite "things," why not *forget about reality and deal only with these mental concepts or ideas as the ultimate reality? This is the gist of the idealistic approach,* which later reached its culmination in the philosophy of Hegel. According to Plato, the ideas are eternal forms existing in a world of their own, and the things that simple mortals know are only copies of these forms. Naturally, in this world of ideas every concept fits exactly the way the mind requires and every value occupies as important a place as it is felt to have — for it is the mind itself that creates it all. The way for every kind of idealization is thus opened up, and Plato did not hesitate to advocate a republic built on philosophical ideas and administered by philosophers.

But the virtuousness of Plato could not save his system from incongruity. Though Plato postulated no other sources of reality than the eternal forms, he did not, and could not, postulate forms for everything. There could be a form or idea for man or justice, but not for a noodle or mousetrap. And the problem of change remained unsolved. How can unchanging eternal forms account for the infinite number of forms that even the tiniest thing goes through at every moment of change? How can things move or become individualized? Forms are "things," but how could there be a thing of, let us say, "to run," "small" or "slowly"?

Aristotle tried to correct these difficulties. He pointed out the empirical origin of the ideas or forms and their insufficiency in explaining change or the individuality of things. He also pointed out the infinite regress that dealing with ideas or forms entails, as every idea about a form or idea requires a further form or idea. Aristotle, however, retained the ideas or forms as the ultimate reality. To account for the continuous processes of change and development Aristotle postulated purposeful potentialities inherent in each form. The realization of the potentialities was compared to the carving of a statue out of a stone.

However, the solutions offered by Aristotle did not remove the difficulties. These lie in the philosophical method itself as an endeavor to grasp the infinite flux of reality in terms of finite essences conceived as "things" or forms. In practice, one can think of stone being carved into a statue as one act. The infinite stages in the carving are simply overlooked. But the philosopher, postulating absolutely everything as existing by virtue of nothing else but forms and their potentialities, would require a literally infinite number of them to account for each phase in the act. Why should the statue at one stage of carving be considered more real than at another? An equally infinite number of forms and potentialities would be required to account for every, even the most prosaic, event or thing. As long as philosophers deal with great worthy concepts, a system of ideas, forms or universals may seem appropriate enough. But when we turn to endless commonplace reality, the system becomes a virtual monstrosity — not to raise the question of who created the infinitely many and varied forms, and how.

After Plato and Aristotle, up to the early modern systems, pure philosophizing declined. Man knows the uselessness of philosophy, and turns away from it when there are pressing practical or emotional solutions to be found. Of course, pressing emotional problems arise when people have it too good, just as when they have it too bad. During the later centuries of the Roman Empire the civilized world lived in unprecedented peace and prosperity. That period brought its puzzling emotional problems, as our modern times do. On the other hand, during the Middle Ages the Western peoples lived under stresses of cultural aspirations more intense than at any other time in history.

The main schools during the period of Roman peace at its height were Epicureanism and Stoicism, which were concerned with happiness and duty, practical living and ethics. Skepticism and Eclecticism grew out of the same indifference to pure philosophizing or system-building. The pressure of emotional problems found, predictably, religious outlets. The Jewish-Greek philosophy that culminated in the system of Philo served the preoccupation with religious problems. So did Neoplatonism. For Plotinus God was the source of all being. Any difficulties of explanation were deliberately precluded by an appeal to mysticism or the religious duty to believe in God. These non-Christian systems were so close to Christian views that the system of St. Augustine is rightly recognized as a re-formulation of Neoplatonism. This shows once more how all religions and philosophies are determined by the same contemporary atmosphere.

During the Middle Ages philosophy became even more sub-ordinated to religion. Scholasticism, the dominant philosophy, reached its height in the systems of St. Thomas, Albertus Magnus and Duns Scotus. But these same thinkers recognized that reason is insufficient to discover the ultimate truths. The Scholastics tried to use the philosophies of Plato and Aristotle. Theoretically, the most interesting point was the adoption of the Forms or Ideas under the doctrine of Universals. But this doctrine evoked an equally strong revival of Nominalism, which found a convincing leader in William of Occam. In brief, the aspirations and emotional realities were too serious to admit much pure philosophizing.

Such philosophizing returned with the early modern philosophers. The system of **Descartes,** who set out to derive all truths from nothing but rational premises, is a typical example. Under the progress of the approaching modern age the intense needs and unquestionable beliefs nurtured by them were lessening. Justifications for supernatural speculations had to be sought in something more than beliefs. The miracle of mind was the logical choice. We have shown how mind appears inherently transcendental under the philosophical method. Descartes started with thought as the first certainty. If he had used a scientific method, or even the ordinary common-sense method, he would have seen that thought is only one form of adjustment or of existence in general. His famous dictum, *"Cogito ergo sum,"* actually amounts to less than saying, "I exist, therefore I am." Descartes only arrived at the last mystery, existence, which cannot be solved, because it is the last.

The advancing scientism of the new age also required some admittance of mechanistic or materialistic explanations. Consequently, the **dualism** of mind and matter became a fashionable system, beginning with Descartes. However, the duality of essences not only left unsolved the old problems of infinitely fluid reality, but added a new philosophically typical problem. As essences mind and matter exclude each other: no one thing can be something else. But how to explain the clearly evident causal interaction between body and mind? The philosophies that followed aimed at removing the dualistic difficulties. Malbranche proposed the elimination of nature as an independent reality; Hobbes, La Mettrie and the French materialists proposed the elimination of mind; and Spinoza postulated an absolute substance with mind and matter as its attributes.

Insofar as dualism is maintained in any system it requires the recognition of the impossible doctrine of **parallelism.** According to it there is no causal relation between physical events and experiences of the mind. The relation between the two, as evidenced by our perfect reactions to physical events, is supposedly due to the specific intervention of God. The extreme form of parallelism is known as **occasionalism,** which was worked out to perfection by Geulincx. According to it physical events are only occasions for God to produce corresponding ideas in our mind. We do not need to discuss how naïvely anthropomorphic the idea of parallelism is. But all dualists, even the most modern ones, are forced to resort to parallelism or occasionalism. Descartes tried to avoid parallelism, but in so doing he only deepened the contradictions of dualism. If the human mind acted through the intermediary of matter, then God as pure spirit could not impress the idea of Himself on the mind. But the presence of such an idea in the mind was the main argument in Descartes' proof of the existence of God. Nor could God as pure spirit impart motion to matter or interact with it, therefore could have nothing to do with our material world.

Spinoza tried to give substance to the ultimate essence, but in compliance with the views of his time sought to retain the dualism of mind and matter. Accordingly, he postulated Substance, with two attributes, mind and matter. The difficulties of dualism then emerged in regard to the two attributes. Spinoza was strict in applying the philosophical method. He had to admit that interaction between the two attributes was impossible; only like can come from like. Consequently, he had to accept the doctrine of occasionalism.

Above all, the usual difficulty of explaining the change and manifoldness of reality remained. Spinoza built his system logically, like a geometric system. Therefore he could not get over the fact that the one eternal Substance could not become many or different. Spinoza sought the solution in postulating Modes, and by further distinguishing them as eternal, infinite modes and temporal, finite modes. The difficulty, however, remained. Though the temporal modes constitute the whole world as we know it, for Spinoza they remained unconsequential and logically hardly necessary details. In truth they could never be derived from his single eternal Substance. Other difficulties arose from the acceptance of matter and mind as *equal* attributes in Spinoza's pantheistic system. He had to recognize that there can be no teleology or plan in creation, for that would mean the precedence of mind over matter; and if mind is the superior quality, then it alone is the real ultimate essence. For the same reason the pantheistic God, being mind *and* matter, cannot have purpose or free will. Still less can man have it.

A daring effort to overcome these difficulties is to be found in the philosophy of **Leibniz.** In fact, his system shows what enormities become necessary in order to explain the manifoldness of reality by the use of ultimate essences.

The center of the pluralistic system of Leibniz is the doctrine of monads as the ultimate essence of everything. They are metaphysical points of view, infinite in number and responsible for the existence of every individual thing in the world — men, animals, plants, even nonliving things. Each mosquito must have its own eternal monad — like a "garden full of plants or a lake full of fish" — determined from the beginning of time and containing a destiny for all eternity. And each molecule, or cell in the mosquito, like any specific unit of matter, must have its own monad — its own "garden full of plants." Each monad has "perception" and "appetition," similar to human intellectual qualities. Each one "mirrors," i.e., perceives, represents and expresses, the entire universe, with every other monad in it, in all their eternal predetermination, to the end of time. Each one is different from any other. And there can be no interaction between monads, so that there is no possibility of things arising by combination or mixture. Since monads have to account for all reality we cannot see how there can be any one thing — a germ or dust particle — without its own monad. And each monad possesses qualities that are usually attributed only to superhuman gods, higher than the mental qualities of man.

Even with this unimaginably fantastic system, permitting every possible anthropomorphic miracle, explanation was not attained. The monads as "things" cannot explain the endless flux of change, development or movement. If monads are to determine every one of the infinitesimal and infinitely many phases of that flux, they must themselves have been predetermined with equal infinite multiplicity and complexity. It amounts to postulating another just as complex reality behind the reality we know — without anticipating the next question of who or what determined that one. Further, the eternally created monads mean a predetermination that excludes causality as well as freedom. Leibniz had to subscribe to parallelism, virtually deny freedom of the will, and contradict his thesis that this is "the best of all possible worlds" by admitting equally eternal predetermination of the evils in it. Thus the most ambitious system added nothing but a miracle of infinitely many monads with human-like capacities. In spite of its sophistication Leibniz's great system represents an anthropomorphism of a naïve and fantastic kind.

No wonder the philosophies that we find at the next stage were critical of human capacities to know reality. British Empiricists, Locke, Berkeley and Hume, turned to the problems of cognition, and reached skeptical conclusions. In Germany there was a return to mysticism and romanticism after Leibniz and Wolff. Finally, an absolute **criticism,** denying the capacity of reason to know ultimate reality, was reached in the monumental philosophy of Kant — and has persisted ever since.

We have nothing much to add to such evidence of the impossibility of a philosophy of reason. But this then means the impossibility of all philosophy. For, as everybody knows, reason is the way to discover what is true. That is why philosophers themselves sought their truths by reasoning. To be sure, no proof of its impossibility can stop philosophizing. Striving for direct satisfaction, which philosophy is in the field of cognition, is never stopped by failures to attain it. The system of Kant himself is typical of philosophical criticism. After Kant discovered the impossibility of knowing transcendental reality, or things-in-themselves, he went on and discovered transcendental proofs in practical reason, which means the system of values. He could not have chosen a more delusory basis.

Philosophical **empiricism** and **skepticism** have followed the same pattern: the self-limitations of mind have been discovered, but the postulation of ultimate essences has not been abandoned. The more modern empiricists have either resorted to vaguer intuitive concepts or by implication recognized some ultimate transcendental reality, like things-in-themselves (Mill). The older empiricists and skeptics, e.g., Locke and Hume, sought for absolute certainties — after discovering their absence from empirical experiences — in such disciplines as mathematics and logic. Actually, these disciplines are as empirical and limited to their own terms as everything else. They are so universally certain only because we make them so. Here men have started with such simple terms as "one," "same," "different," "more" or "less," which cannot be different for any man as a material persistent and unified being. Since these terms can serve as precise, never-changing standards, we use them as universal terms for communicating, mentally recording and relating everything else. By practice, through the ages, complex systems have evolved which look even more miraculous than other adjustments under the philosophical method. By the way, Hume recognized the tautological nature of such systems when he spoke of mathematics as a system dealing with its own concepts.

Further, the empiricists and skeptics did not deal with the phenomena of mind as evolutionary endless processes but only as ready given "things." Ideas in themselves became the only realities — with all the actual irreality and confusion that this created. For instance, Locke found that we know only our own ideas, never reality itself. Consequently, Berkeley could argue that everything exists only in our mind, and that it is the grace of God which enables us to react so appropriately in every instance. The same method enabled Hume to prove that causality is delusory, that there is never any causal nexus between two things or events. Causation is a process, therefore it cannot be expressed in terms of a final knowledge of "things." It can be argued that Hume would have been closer to perceiving causal connections at work if he had gone down to submolecular forces instead of looking for the nexus at the last level, e.g., between fire and burning. But this does not exhaust Hume's argument. Even at the submolecular level one could continue going on endlessly into still more infinitesimal detail in search of the last causal nexus as a "thing." Zeno could prove the impossibility of movement by similar arguments.

These are only examples. Every philosophical empiricism or criticism means a similar search for implied ultimate essences and for understanding of final terms. Without this philosophical characteristic there would be no philosophical empiricism, but only plain scientific search for more facts and a scientific dealing in terms of continuous processes.

After Kant philosophy continued the same as before, though the truths that he demonstrated — and that were generally recognized — were sufficient to make all metaphysics and philosophizing proper futile. The certitude of reason and rational argumentation did decline, but value attitudes started replacing them. Soon all possible value concepts — we mentioned them before — were advanced in explanation. The postulation of ultimate essences continued, under various combinations of rational reasoning and emotional convictions. Of course, no two philosophers discovered

325

the same ultimate reality. Fitche postulated an ethical, freely self-determining Ego; Schelling, an Absolute with spirit and nature as its manifestations; Schleiermacher, God as a spaceless and timeless unity; Hegel, Idea as the only reality; Herbart, the plurality of Reals; Schopenhauer, the Will; Hartmann, the Unconscious; Nietzsche, the Will to Power; Lotze, Fechner and Wundt, the Soul; Green, Universal Consciousness; Bradley, the Absolute as the source of all experiences; Bosanquet, the Absolute as the concrete universal; Royce, the Logos as a supreme self; Renouvier, Presentations; Fouiller, Ideas-Forces; Boutroux, God as the embodiment of the highest freedom; Croce, the Spirit; Gentile, Self-Consciousness; Bergson, the *Elan Vital*; Alexander, Space-Time; and so on.

We discussed before what the essences originating in the notions of value or humanistic rationality amount to; and we hardly need to discuss further these or other philosophies. The examples from the different theories that we have already looked at may illustrate sufficiently the basic approaches that have been tried (we shall mention Hegelianism and the most modern approaches in a moment). Other individual systems represent rather recombinations of these main approaches. That is why all philosophies or their doctrines can be classified under such general theories as idealism, rationalism, empiricism, skepticism, realism and so on. Furthermore, as philosophy has advanced, the application of the philosophical method has become less characteristic. The increasing positivism has meant turning away from the philosophical and toward the scientific or common-sense methods. The founder of Positivism, Comte, was explicit about the merits of the scientific approach. Even more characteristic are such movements as Materialism, Utilitarianism, modern Empiricism, Pragmatism, Existentialism and the other modern movements emphasizing practical experiences.

Hegelianism represents the highest achievement in idealism and in philosophical system-building in general. Recombination of its ideas has given rise to Neo-Hegelianism and other systems. We saw the incomparable advantages gained by the idealistic method of substituting a system of thought for reality. In Hegel's philosophy such substitution is absolute. Idea as the quintessence of thought and reason is in Hegel's system the only and whole reality; it comprises everything, including nature and God. Under Hegel's Panlogism everything is only an expression of a logical idea.

As the philosophical method here reaches its extreme, the theory becomes also absurd to the extreme in terms of the scientific or common-sense knowledge of simple mortals. According to all reason, if the Idea is the whole of reality, then our thought, which is its richest depository, should have at least a minimum causal relation with everything else in nature. But nobody has yet seen thought move objects or have the slightest influence on them. Only because the philosophical method limits the view to the last as if ready given states of adjustment, can the philosopher remain blind to the fact that thought and ideas are produced and determined by material processes or nature, never the other way around.

To be sure, Hegel has explanations why his ideal reality has no causal connections with nature, which constitutes everything we simple mortals know. But Hegel's explanations can never be expressed in simple terms, or outside his "multidimensional" system. Considering that neither Hegel nor anybody else can think otherwise than in the same simple terms of matter, space and time, his explanations apparently rest on mere complexity.

But apart from the fact that Hegel's reality has nothing to do with the reality we know, his system is perfect and unattackable. The advantage of dealing with thought alone shows superbly under Hegel's dialectic method. This method of proceeding through the opposites of thesis and antithesis has proven to fit marvelously every imaginable human experience, discipline of thought, science or any form of knowledge. This is what can be expected considering that the rule of the opposites of need-satisfaction or value-disvalue governs all experience. We cannot discuss the perfect dialectic system into which Hegel fitted every science, even historical events. We can only point out that it is not reality that complies with the thesis-antithesis dialectic, but our way of seeing reality. An historical period does not realize itself exclusively as an opposition to the preceding period, but in our mind it does make sense only in its differences from or opposition to the preceding period. Hegel's dialectic method fits so well everything man can think of that his system came to be regarded as an example of perfect philosophy; and his dialectic method has been used to explain many varied things, including Communist doctrine.

When we turn to the last stage in Western philosophy — its **most modern movements** — we find that philosophy is reaching its own denial. The overt value approaches, ending with irrational emotionalism, mean direct rejection of the methods of reason, on which all true philosophy must rest. Existentialism, the most popular modern approach, is the most typical example. We have already explained the fallacy of the emotional or value approaches.

Even where abstract reasoning is relied on in modern philosophy, there are no claims of absolute certainties and no attempts to build exclusive systems. Thus, even those philosophers who have written major philosophical works — Russell, Dewey, Whitehead and Santayana — are rather eclectic and admit that their systems do not preclude other interpretations. Modern philosophers are more concerned with the limitations of human knowledge and the inherent difficulties of philosophy than with the promotion of settled philosophical systems. Philosophical reasoning is placed on the same level as artistic, literary or some general life experience; even practical success according to the pragmatists. In some works, like those of Santayana, philosophy merges with art, in others, like those of Dewey, James, Russell and Whitehead, it often merges with scientism, particularly psychology.

Further, the modern philosophers have not ventured beyond realism as opposed to the overt transcendentalism of idealism or rationalism. And the realists have not advanced much further than the epistemological problems bearing on the general capacity of man to know ultimate truths. Typically enough, while science has discovered much about human thinking, philosophy has led only to increased confusion. Considering what the philosophical method means, this is to be expected. Knowledge is a process, but the philosopher tries to formulate it in terms of "things" or essences. Between the object and the perceiver there can be imagined an infinite number of stages. Any one of them can be chosen by a philosopher as something that stands between the object and perceiver, therefore as excluding a *direct* perception or cognition

328

of the objects of reality. Hence the insurmountable difficulties of realism, and the numerous differing epistemological theories about objects, phenomena, sense data, "sensibles" (Moore), "sensations" (Russell), "initial data" vs. "objective datum" (Whitehead), "ideas" (Lovejoy) or "data of sense" (Santayana). Actually, any act can become a mystery under the philosophical method. If common sense did not prevail, philosopher could just as well argue that, for instance, sitting means merely receiving pressure from the seat cover, or from the sitter's own clothes, or skin and so on.

The difficulties inherent in the philosophical method cannot be avoided even by the most modern philosopher aware of every advance in science. The problem of universals is a good example. For instance, if the philosopher tries to find out what is the essence of the color "red," which means asking what "thing" it is, he must ascribe to it transcendental existence, since it certainly does not exist in time and space (as we saw, it is only a matter-to-matter relationship). Sure enough, we find color as a prominent illustration of universals in Russell's *Problems of Philosophy*; of "eternal objects" in Whiteheads' writings; and of "essences" in Santayana's *Realms of Being*. If viewed in the scientific, or ordinary way, the source of color sensation lies in the processes of our nervous system. But the philosophical method does not permit dealing with processes, or investigation of historical backgrounds.

The result is that the modern philosopher, with all his emphasis on practical experiences and on the equal revelation value of aesthetics or the sciences, cannot escape dealing with classical essences or universals. To use the previous example, the philosopher could just as well establish a metaphysical universal for the act of sitting. And if he forgot about the adjustment aspect completely, as a true philosopher should, he would have a proof of harmony and providence in the fact that there are chairs corresponding exactly to the function of sitting.

The most characteristic movements of modern philosophy, apart from Existentialism, are Pragmatism and Positivism, with their related systems of Instrumentalism, Conventionalism, Fictionalism, Phenomenalism and Contextualism. They all mean rejection of the possibility of metaphysics of reason and, therefore, of true

329

philosophy. In one form or another they recognize the relativity of knowledge. The conventionalists Mach and Poincaré have shown that knowledge consists of convenient definitions. Fictionalists see all concepts and theories of science and philosophy as merely useful fictions. The phenomenology of Husserl, or that of the pragmatist Peirce, draws its limits at the bracketing and description of phenomena, or their classification into categories.

Pragmatism, together with experimentalism, instrumentalism and contextualism, tends to identify truth with practical success, or with satisfactions depending upon motives and purposes. The limitation of knowledge to the need-satisfaction or question-answer mechanism is implicitly recognized. Actually, pragmatism means denial of philosophy and has no basis for continuing as a philosophy. But it suited well the half-scientism, half-philosophy practiced in the obscure fields of psychology by the great pragmatists William James and John Dewey.

Positivism as the last word in philosophy shows what philosophy has come to after everything has been tried. Positivism arrives at the conclusion that metaphysics and philosophy in its traditional sense are nonsensical. All we can know are either empirically verifiable statements of fact or tautological statements. The positivists have exposed logic and mathematics for what they are — systems of tautologies. The positivists have arrived at these conclusions after taking a wider view from other fields. The main positivists — the founders of the Vienna Circle with its outstanding members, Schlick and Carnap — were scientists, not professional philosophers. But positivism has become the leading philosophical movement of our times. It can be said that in positivism philosophy has found its evaluation in the light of all its previous endeavors as well as attainments in other areas — and has reached its own denial.

CONCLUSIONS

Philosophy is *a clearly specific* human endeavor. It represents the human striving for direct and pure satisfaction in the field of thought. From this follows the main characteristic of the philosophical method: absolute "explanations" by way of postulating some metaphysical essence behind reality. This amounts, in each case, to adding one more, equally incomprehensible anthropomorphic term — which is left unexplained. Due to the same striving for satisfaction, the *value approach* dominates philosophy. Thus every possible humanistic delusion here reaches its height, leading to more incongruities. We have shown these in the main philosophical movements. But the best proof of the failure of the philosophical method is the history of philosophy itself. There are as many contradictory theories as there are philosophers. The only "truths" that philosophers agree on are the superstitious value beliefs of the period they happen to live in. Whereas in other fields agreements have been reached and laws discovered as the science advanced, in philosophy the only agreement finally reached is that philosophy is impossible.

Philosophy has attained superiority over science and common sense only in one respect — complexity. Any philosophical theory if explained in simple terms appears rather a system of mere assertions or recombinations of old assertions, without much originality or really ingenious proofs. Only amidst the complexities of the system as a whole do the assertions acquire "depth" — or, one can rightly say, deepened confusion. As we saw, the simplest terms are sufficient as well as best suited to explain fundamental truths; but there is no limit to which a thing can be made complex if it is not understood. Only a multiplicity of factors may require complexity in explanation, but philosophy by its very nature is exempt from multiplicity.

Real solutions are unattainable in philosophy because satisfaction without needs, or value without disvalue, is impossible. Striving for such satisfaction can lead only to endless self-perpetuating complexes. Philosophy is in the field of thought what neurosis is in the emotional field. Of course, such an intellectual "neurosis" can only be beneficial, since it deepens fixations on intellectual interests. Also, the cult of philosophy — like religion and moral tradition — gives prominence to more refined and intellectual minds, since only those who have a rich intellectual life can become afflicted with this "neurosis."

Furthermore, philosophizing in the field of the sciences can open wider insights and lead to the discovery of more universal laws; philosophy has always claimed to be a science of "wholes." However, scientific philosophizing would have to reverse the present tendency to look for more acceptable, graceful or sensible explanations. Everything that seems acceptable and makes better sense corresponds more closely to some human value; and nowhere are human delusions stronger than in regard to values. Science grows to the extent that it is liberated from the humanly rich, graceful or "great" explanations. Scientists have long realized that the shortest or humanly poorest explanations are the right or most revealing ones for understanding nature.

Man can understand nature only the way he exists. Since nature *is* for man the way he *understands* it, the final terms of his existence become the final terms or universal laws of nature. Naturally, the final terms of his existence must appear to man himself, as the existing being, so absolutely simple or blank as to seem meaningless. They are never noticed by him because they are always with him. Further, they must appear absurd to man because of the ultimate contradiction of human and, consequently, all existence, deriving its reality from its own opposition. One consequence of this is that man aims at and sees only values or "sense," whereas in fact these derive from their opposites, disvalues and "nonsense." In short, the final terms or laws of the universe are absolutely simple but seem to man meaningless and absurd.

In this sense of scientific philosophizing we *can* give an ultimate explanation of everything. Ultimately man and everything exist by virtue of *persistence under opposition*. Anything that is not "capable" of thus persisting does not exist any more. We shall see in a moment how the physical world, which serves as the source of everything else, exists by virtue of two-sided opposition. Being itself cannot be without differentiation, which means opposition. We saw how on the level of living beings *persistence* in the form of the pleasure flow produces the complex living adjustment under the operation of *adversity* in the form of evolutionary difficulties. This complex interplay between pleasure and adversity, operating through the mechanism of need-satisfaction, further explains all adjustment, including the significance of value or meaning and the workings of the mind or soul—which constitute the main philosophical mysteries. We also saw how persistence in the face of adversity produces, by way of selection, seeming harmony, providence and reason in nature and the world of man—which constitute the rest of the philosophical mysteries. As final terms or laws, persistence and adversity, and with them inherently contradictory human existence, must remain a mystery—the only mystery. In human value terms it all seems nonsensical because it means mere *existence for the sake of existence*. Such self-explanatory simplicity, which may seem like a nonsensical tautology, is what we should expect from the ultimate law of nature.

Striving for existence as the only goal of life is the deeper reason why all philosophy searches for one essence, with Being as the central notion. In some modern systems we find such central essences as the will (Schopenhauer), the unconscious (Hartmann), vital force (Bergson), or primordial animal spirit (Santayana). But such concepts are still humanistic. They imply a deliberate willing or striving. A look further back shows that, for instance, the animal wills or strives only because it has evolved that way—because it *exists* that way. Thus we are back at the same rule of existence for the sake of existence.

Man will finally make breakthroughs leading to knowledge more "transcendental" than philosophers have ever imagined, and to ways of thinking as superior to ours as conscious thought is to the life of animals. Consciousness is a product of mechanistic but blind evolution. Man can do incomparably better by planning. But such mechanistic progress can be built only on a causal understanding which is the exact reverse of the value delusions, anthropomorphism and "neurotic" incongruities of philosophy striving to discover nonexistent transcendental wisdoms.

RELATIVITY OF KNOWLEDGE IN PHYSICS

In contrast to philosophy, our knowledge of the physical reality around us is the simplest but practically most important kind of knowledge. By showing how helplessly one-sided this knowledge is because of the paradox of relativity we can show the fullest range of the relativity of knowledge and the most obvious practical importance of understanding it.

Man as a creation of matter can get into relation with or know only matter. Objectively considered, however, matter is only a differentiation from nothingness. Matter and nothingness are two equal opposites. Whatever effects one of them has it derives through differentiation from the other. If absolutely everything were matter, there could be no concept of matter. Only human one-sidedness prevents us from attributing to nothingness an equal status with matter. An objective scientist, however, should be able to go beyond this one-sidedness. Moreover, he should be able to see that what is called nothingness is the more important, dominant, opposite. For it is clear that matter is only an exception in the universe — only an impurity, like bubbles, in the uniform universal continuum which means "nothingness" to us only because it is the opposite of matter. Occasionally physicists have used such terms for matter as "holes in the cheese"; apparently the truth seems too ridiculous here to be asserted in any other form than a joke.

It may seem really ridiculous to think that the empty space through which you see faraway objects or through which you move freely is full of something. The truth is that you do not see through a true nothingness. To see means to receive waves, and as Einstein has said, waves must be *in* something in order to exist. Wave is a form of the medium, therefore nonsensical without a medium. Nor do you move freely. If there is one certainty in physics, it is the law that nothing can happen or move unless there is an equal force applied to it. This force is the interaction between matter and "nothingness," which we shall call the Field from now on (field is the closest concept to space or emptiness as a reality in modern physics, especially in the Theory of Relativity). Actually, you do not move but are moved by the Field, the same as a deep-sea animal is moved by water pressures. To the minutest detail, the universe is ruled by this absolute compulsion. If there were the slightest chance of freedom, the laws of nature, and causality, would not be so absolutely strict. And if there were any other possibilities than an interaction between

334

two opposites, the world would not be limited to the inexorable polarity of positiveness and negativeness, force and counterforce, being and nonbeing, or simply "yes" and "no" in everything.

Because the Field is absolutely everywhere and participates in absolutely all effects, it cannot be known, felt or registered in any way. A deep-sea being could disprove beyond doubt and consider ridiculous the assertion that any pressure, or anything, exists around him. If physicists had realized that an omnipresent medium can be million times denser than any matter and still be less noticeable than the thinnest ether, they would long have discovered the ideal Ether or "field" that they have been searching for in order to explain their dilemmas.

We would like to make it clear here that we are not postulating any new substances or forces, or even any new hypothesis. *We are only explaining matter causally, and the insight of relativity permits us to see the reality of its negative causal background.* The Field is still a "nothingness," that is, nonmaterial, in every sense; it is opposite to matter. And we would not have much to say about it if it were not for scientific interest. In the same search for causal explanations, science, especially modern physics and the Relativity Theory, have come to recognize that the field around matter, or the empty space, is as real or concrete as any physical object. Our relative insight permits us to see that this opposite reality is truly and concretely there — serving as a causal source. Instead of the hundreds of unexplainable mysteries that scientists now have as physical laws, we can have one cause that is derived from nothing more mysterious than the properties of matter before our eyes. From the enormous compression of atoms we discover the pressure of the Field; from waves, its absolute fluidity; from uniform effects, its omnipresence and homogeneousness. But once these simple qualities are established, everything else can be understood as their derivative effects. Thus we discover a completely new causal world. And *no new postulates are required. The only requirement is that the scientist abandon the one-sidedness of the human outlook,* which is clear from everything else anyway.

As long as the unified causal source is not seen, physics has to remain a mystery. First, there is the unbelievable complexity of modern physics, as if the universe were ruled by a mathematical genius. The modern physicist can only describe the effects mathematically, never see the cause. Hence the enormous complexity, whereas the very fact that mathematics can be used here shows that the real causes are uniformly simple. Everybody knows that even the simplest phenomenon, like a turning propeller, can produce effects which can stagger the highest mathematics. Further, because physical effects are produced by a two-sided interaction and scientists see only one side, the basic physical effects become ghost phenomena. Modern physicists are used to saying that the fundamental physical processes cannot be humanly conceived. This is a pure mystification. Man as a material being exists along the same lines as everything else. Therefore no process, still less a basic process, can be beyond his grasp. Modern physics has dilemmas on every basic problem, because the main player in the two-sided causal game is never seen.

Difficulties would be even greater if modern physics ventured to face the really basic problems. For instance, what or who has created and is constantly creating the perfectly uniform particles throughout the universe? Who is operating them in their perfect ways, and maintaining them in perfect shape? Who is seeing that these inexorable uniform laws apply throughout the universe? What makes possible the uniform and miraculously effective interaction — as if by direct contact — between particles and bodies at enormous distances? What is the source of the universal forces of gravitation, electricity, transmission of energy, speed of light or of the cohesion of the atom? There is only "nothingness" or the Field throughout the universe. If the simple properties of the Field, which were mentioned above, are recognized, all these miracles become self-explanatory.

Naturally a scientist can expect ridicule if he proclaims nothingness to be equal to man's reality. And the ridicule here will be probably greater than that which was aroused by the truths of a moving earth or man's evolution from animals.

ETHER AND FIELD

All prominent physicists have recognized the existence of Ether, as soon as they have tried to explain physical effects causally. In modern physics only the name, not the reality, of the Ether has been abandoned, by treating it as an abstract field. Of course, only absurdities result from trying to imagine the Ether as a form of matter. Physicists recognized that Ether would have to be incomparably denser than any matter, but also unnoticeably thin.

We can mention only the most prominent theories on the Ether. Huygens construed light as waves in Ether. Newton sought to explain gravitation by assuming grosser and finer granules of Ether. Faraday had a very concrete but also complicated system of Ether, consisting of lines and tubes. Maxwell built his unified theory of electromagnetism on the concept of Ether similar in some respects to that of Faraday; Maxwell's equations are still basic in modern physics, especially in the Relativity Theory. Fresnel constructed Ether as a kind of elastic matter. Hertz recognized the necessity of Ether but denied to it mass or elasticity. Young postulated dense Ether but could not explain how it could exist. Stokes tried to find a solution by assuming that Ether could be something like sealing wax that remains rigid under rapid vibrations but melts under constant force. Lord Kelvin suggested that Ether may be a fluid in rapid motion.

Other scientists used ingenious experiments to discover Ether or its qualities. The most famous of such experiments were those of Fresnel, Fizeau, Michelson and Morley, Lodge, Miller and Kennedy. All these experiments failed. No drags or friction by Ether on moving bodies or any other effects were discovered. But there were equally strong proofs that a universal medium must exist. The conclusion was that physicists had encountered here a "conspiracy of natural laws." Now that physicists are discovering everything to exist or act as waves, the existence of Ether or field as reality has become even more evident.

Probably the best account of Ether has been given by the prominent physicist Sir Oliver Lodge in his book, *Ether and Reality*. According to him Ether is the universal connecting medium which fills space everywhere, even between atoms, "so completely that it is sometimes identified with space." It has to be "far more substantial than any form of matter," serve as a "universal storehouse of energy," "fritter no energy," transmit light "without waste or loss of any kind," and function as a "universal connecting link" in transmitting every kind of force. Lodge also points out that there can be no difficulty in having free movement in a completely filled space, just as there can be no difficulty for fish to move freely in the depths of the ocean. The three main functions that Lodge attributes to Ether are: the welding together of atoms by cohesion; the holding of the stars and planets together by gravitation; and the transmission of vibrations from one piece of matter to another. We shall discuss these functions in a moment.

The most revealing recognition of the reality of a universal medium we find in Einstein's Theory of Relativity. This theory began with the problem of Ether, namely, with the impossibility of discovering Ether in any way. The above experiments, especially those of Michelson and Morley, and theories so varied that we cannot discuss them here, showed that light moved with the same speed in and between moving systems whatever their movements or speeds. This would not be true if there were Ether as a kind of matter, necessarily exerting a drag on anything moving through it. On the other hand, if there were no Ether as a medium bearing the waves and if light were thrown out by moving bodies directly, its speed would be even less constant. Einstein had the audacity to proclaim the uniformity of the speed of light as the fundamental law and to disregard everything else. The above failures in the endeavor to discover differences in the speed of light were accounted for by a contraction postulated in the theory of Lorentz, according to which bodies in movement contract and clocks on moving systems slow down just enough to account for the Ether drag or differences arising from the movement of the systems.

After that Einstein omitted the notion of Ether completely. He used, instead, a purely abstract mathematical concept of field. This permitted him to deal with the empty space as a reality, without offending common sense. The results reached — spectacular

338

as they were — constituted, however, only a description of effects, not an explanation of the cause. Einstein continued searching for the causal reality behind the effects; and his remarks have been used by mystery-seekers as proofs of the unfathomable designs of the universe. His efforts were directed at an understanding of the field, as he continued working on his Unified Field Theory.

Under the Relativity Theory the field or empty space has always been recognized to be a reality as concrete as matter. In his book, *The Evolution of Physics,* Einstein says that the field has become more and more real, and is for the modern physicist as concrete as the chair he sits on. In another place he says that the electromagnetic field "once created exists, acts and changes according to Maxwell's laws"; and that there are two realities, matter and field. In conclusions, at the end of the book, the field is recognized as more significant or real than matter. There is a speculation about construing matter as a concentration of the field, thus explaining all physical phenomena by the structural laws or the field and eliminating the concept of matter. The book concludes: "The theory of relativity stresses the importance of the field in physics; but we have not yet succeeded in formulating a pure field physics."

The recognition of the reality of the universal field or medium is the great simple truth of the Relativity Theory. It derives from another simple truth that is the basis of the theory — the uniformity of the speed of light. As we shall see in a moment, the first follows from the second. But Einstein was able to speak in the highest mathematical language alone, thus avoiding the recognition of this truth, or of the field as a reality in terms of common speech, which would have appeared ridiculous. The point is that, ultimately, the Relativity Theory, like all great discoveries, rests on a *simple,* though seemingly impossible truth. The mystery woven around it stems from mystifications by secondhand interpreters.

Among these belong the speculations that if an astronaut traveled through space at speeds of light he would never get old or would become younger. Actually, the Relativity Theory does not warrant such assumptions. According to it, if an astronaut travels away from earth, it can be equally said that the earth travels away from him, at the same speed. Who then is becoming younger, the astronaut or the people on the earth? As we indicated above the assumption of the slowing down of clocks or natural processes in moving systems was made to counterbalance the other assumed effects. Since these were not there, the assumption was unnecessary; and factually no reality correspond to it. In any case, it is erroneous to apply that assumption here, out of its specific context.

The naïvest kind of speculations is the one based on time differences due to movement. It is true that a person traveling faster than light could meet an image of light that would not reach earth for a hundred years. But there is nothing miraculous about it. The same can be done on earth with sounds, by using fast planes. The pilots, however, do not become younger. Our experience of a given image or sound is only one tiny event or change amidst myriads of others. All these changes together constitute the continuous relationship that we know as time. If absolutely everything stopped changing in and around you, be it for a million years, you would not feel that even a second had passed. We can "become younger" in many respects by returning or changing back to some previous state. If one could change back every cell in himself, he would really become younger, but changing relationships in regard to one single tiny event — the experience of one image of light — cannot do it.

It is true that Einstein used illustrations of moving trains or coordinate systems to show the relativity of our notions of time; and to demonstrate how under every possible circumstance the assumed changes in the speed of light, due to the movement of the system, were counterbalanced by the assumed Lorentz contraction, so that uniform speed always resulted. As we said, neither of these assumptions was necessary; and as regards the final theory *their effects canceled out each other*. What remained was the always uniform speed of light — which inevitably implies a light-carrying medium. We all know that the speed of sound, carried by air, does not change with the movement of systems emitting or receiving it; and no assumptions about hypothetic

340

contractions are necessary. The *frequency* of sound waves changes with the movement of the emitting or receiving system, as can be easily observed by listening to a plane passing by. The same effect is often mentioned in confirmation of the Relativity Theory, especially with regard to light emitted by stars moving at great speeds. In any event, the results of the Relativity Theory are the same as those that follow from the assumption of a light-carrying medium. No mysterious effects are to be assumed or expected, with such a medium, as we see in regard to sound.

The Relativity Theory is a mathematical system built on the assumption of the uniform speed of light. Since the uniform speed of light is possible only when there is a light-carrying medium, the theory amounts to a recognition of this medium, in an indirect mathematical language. A mathematical genius — as Einstein apparently was — can start with one basic assumption about a phenomenon and discover its every aspect without ever realizing what the phenomenon really is. To the staggeringly complex mathematics of the Relativity Theory corresponds a simple reality, which, however, was never recognized because it would have offended common sense.

With this in mind we may look at the discoveries of Einstein, in order to see how real our concept of Field is in their light. The greatest discovery of Einstein was the prediction of the bending of a ray of light toward a strong gravitational field. In our non-mathematical language, the bending is due to differences in Field pressure. Gravitational field means the area around matter where the Field pressure is a little weaker or one-sided, because matter shields off some of the pressure coming from behind it (we will explain this in detail later). In other words, there is less pressure from the side where matter is. Since the ray of light is propagated by the same Field pressure from all sides, the ray bends to the side where the pressure is weaker.

The second greatest discovery of Einstein is known as the "Einstein effect." Since an atom is held together by the pressure of the Field, it naturally expands in a marked gravitational field where the pressure is less. As the layers in atoms, which emit the light waves, become longer and "softer," the waves lengthen. This produces the predicted shift in the spectra of light coming from heavy stars. The third greatest prediction of Einstein concerned the abnormal revolution of the perihelion of Mercury. It is generally recognized that this discovery was due to a replacement of Newtonian notions of force by concepts of the structural properties of the gravitational field. This means recognition as realities of the Field and its specific properties in the vicinity of matter, which we just indicated.

Equally, the clarifications in electromagnetism made possible by the Relativity Theory were due to the recognition of the structural properties of the field, especially by application of the equations of Maxwell, which were built on the assumption of the concrete structural reality of Ether. Even the famous energy equation of Einstein can be viewed as a formulation of the Field forces. The equation gives energy as the product of mass multiplied by the speed of light squared. Energy is equal to mass because energy is the capacity to counteract or oppose Field pressure; and matter exists as a concentrated opposition to that pressure. The speed of light as a factor brings out the actual potential of the energy hidden in mass, because that speed measures the degree of the pressure of the Field, and consequently of the equal resistance by matter. For the speed of light is determined by, and proportional to, the Field pressure. The squaring of the speed of light as a factor is necessary to express the spherical pressure of the Field on matter.

The increase of mass of an accelerated particle is another prediction of the Relativity Theory. This prediction is typical of the mathematical approach: it predicts effects but does not see the cause. The increase in mass of an accelerated particle is an effect of acceleration. The cause is lessened Field pressure, which is the only cause of every movement or acceleration. The cyclotron induces particles to accelerate by producing a strong electro-magnetic field, which means by lessening the Field pressure. Under the lessened pressure the particle expands and the frequencies of its vibrations become longer.

The most typical and most significant discovery, or rather a fundamental tenet, of the Relativity Theory is the curvature of space as a physical reality. Einstein himself compared it to concrete physical differences in the Field, like depressions in a ground for balls to roll into. Such concreteness, as well as the spherical structure of the space around matter, agrees exactly with the effects of the lessened Field pressure around matter, as we shall see more closely in discussing gravitation.

Naturally, if such a real curvature is to be assumed without anything real being there — if it is not understood what is curved and why — all kinds of mysteries arise. Hence the speculations about a new kind of geometry which would make a traveler going infinitely in space return to his starting point as a matter of new *geometric logic*. Actually, space is curved around our earth too, but we still can go away from it in a straight line. Human logic cannot change because of the discovery of realities that have always been there. The argument that five hundred years ago people equally did not realize that going straight ahead leads back to the starting point does not help here. Then people were in error about *facts*, not geometric *logic*. They did not know that the earth is round, but they knew that a line drawn on a round object circles back.

Finally, we may mention the mystification surrounding the "fourth dimension" of the space-time continuum. As Einstein himself has stated, the four-dimensional continuum is only a mathematical device, like the one used to indicate train or airplane stops on time schedules. These do not reveal any fourth dimension to their users. Actually, the four-dimensional time-space continuum was worked out by Minkowski before the Relativity Theory was established.

In conclusion, we can say that the theorists of physics have always been forced to recognize the nothingness that fills the universe as a reality more intense than matter itself. But Ether conceived as a kind of matter was clearly an impossibility. And the theories of an abstract field become mysteries. The concept of the Field as the omnipresent and therefore imperceptible opposite of matter removes all these difficulties, and does so without requiring any assumptions. All it requires is that the scientist abandon human nearsightedness.

THE MYSTERIES OF THE ATOM

The main property of the atom, as the universal form of all matter, is the tremendous force that holds it together. From this is to be deduced the main property of the Field — its tremendous pressure. As Lodge said, the main function of Ether is to weld atoms together by cohesion.

The atom is becoming increasingly complex in modern physics. It is assumed to consist of half a dozen particles — protons, neutrons, electrons, neutrinos. These supposedly harbor some thirty other kinds of particles and "antiparticles." All of them are supposed to observe definite ways of interaction — spin certain orbits, combine in certain shells, attract each other in certain ways though the charges otherwise attributed to them would push them apart with tremendous force, and so on — for unexplicable reasons. On the other hand, the reality of the particles is becoming questionable. All "particles" are found to have wave characteristics. The laws of indeterminacy and probability that modern physicists have been forced to admit show that some particles are never actually present at any spot; and that only average effects can be observed. The uniformity of mere "averages" indicates that more general higher forces are the determining realities. The substance of particles has always been found hazy. To account for this physicists have made impossible basic postulations, e.g., that the real mass of the atom is as small within it as a bee in a cathedral.

All these complexities and contradictions disappear if one sees matter as an opposite to the Field. The enormous pressure of the Field divides every larger mass of matter, to the limits where matter can oppose further division — to the limit of the primordial hydrogen atom. On the other hand, any bits of matter, or energy, smaller than such an atom, accumulate to the same limit permitted by the Field pressure, and form similar uniform atoms. Naturally, such a new creation cannot happen on earth, where every bit of surplus matter is absorbed immediately by impoverished matter. But in interstellar space such creation goes on, and hydrogen atoms are always found there.

The main point is that the universal Field pressure permits

344

explaining uniform atoms as the effects of a self-establishing balance. The uniform Field pressure also determines the uniform counterpressure of matter. Where the matter is weaker than the Field pressure, it is annihilated or compressed; where it is stronger, it expands until it reaches the same counterpressure. Thus matter can be viewed merely as an exception to the Field. By that we arrive at one medium and the principle of opposition as the ultimate explanations. No human understanding can be simpler than this, which means that we may have reached here the very first principle or law of nature.

More complex atoms are formed when two primary atoms are compressed by the same Field pressure, during cosmic disturbances that we shall mention later. The primary particle can be imagined as a fluid, therefore elastic, ball. It can be momentarily compressed by a certain margin, which can be fully regained by it at the next moment. When two such particles are joined, the margin of compression doubles, and one margin can be pressed off by the Field. This margin is not regained because the two joined particles still have one margin of elasticity, which now serves both of them. By similar further compressions more complex elements are created. The principle here is the same that permits the formation of chemical bonds through the "sharing" of electrons, except that here forces of cosmic proportions are required.

This process explains why all elements seem to consist of uniform primary units, and why there is a "packing" loss. It also explains why there are as many protons in an atom as there are electrons. Two compressed units may be regarded as consisting of one full and one compressed unit: one neutron and one proton. At the same time, where there has been compression there is a potential to expand again, at least temporarily and to some extent, under a special addition of surplus matter. This potential of temporary expansion — with subsequent retraction and the release of a matter quantum — constitutes all the effects that are known as the electron.

The permanence of the structure of the atom is insured by the permanence of the Field pressure. The atom may be in constant flux, may even disintegrate for a shortest instant. But if this

345

happens, the Field pressure instantly re-forms the particles and recompresses them — exactly in the same way as it did before. It cannot do differently because the same elements and forces are inexorably there.

Further, the permanence of equal mass units within the atom is maintained by the self-organization of its mass into spherical stationary waves. The peculiarity of stationary waves is that there can be only full and equal waves, but no fractional or different waves. Since the mass in the atom is like a fluid ball oscillating under the Field pressure, it automatically acquires the structure of stationary spheric waves which become like shells or layers of equal thickness. At first it may seem that the layers nearer the outside would have greater mass, since they are greater in the total due to their longer perimeters. But we have to remember that the whole system is the product of concentric pressure. The lines of pressure converge as they go toward the center. To the extent that the layers become smaller their mass increases in concentration. Thus the stationary wave system insures automatically that there be spherical waves of not only equal length but equal mass as well. Actually, it is not by accident that the particles acquire spherical form. This form permits the conservation of identity by the nucleons forming the particle — and thus offers the easiest attainable balance. Ultimately, the stationary waves in the atom coincide with nucleons or former atoms because both are determined by the same pressure of the Field.

Since modern physics is discovering that all "particles" have a wave nature, there have been increasing endeavors to conceive all matter as consisting of wave systems. De Broglie is the best-known theorist to do so. Einstein called his theory "new and courageous." Schroedinger developed a similar theory in mathematical form. But the difficulty is that unless forms of matter are seen as products of an omnipresent compressing medium, no circumstances can be imagined under which they could exist as spherical wave systems.

The **electron** as a quantum of matter results from the expansion and contraction of the compressed nucleons. In difference from radiation, the electron is the maximum accumulation of surplus before it is released. Therefore it can appear only under special circumstances and with special kinds of matter. Otherwise any surplus of matter is squeezed off the atom as soon as it reaches the tiny universal quantum of radiation, which we shall discuss later. Since all atoms have depressed nucleons (which can be thought of as protons), any surplus electron is immediately absorbed by some other atom. Thus electrons may serve the equalization of energy surpluses, inside specific kinds of matter, in the form of currents. Since the Field pressure as well as the forces of absorption and release of atoms are constant, electrons are uniform. Under specific circumstances an electron can be observed during its transition from one piece of matter to another. In such transition it may appear as a speck of matter, may even have spherical form under the Field pressure. Physicists observing this always uniform quantum have concluded that the electron must be an eternal uniform particle existing inside atoms. The experiments by Thomson and Millikan seemed to prove this conclusively.

The electron as the potential of the expansion and retraction of the atom represents the only change that the atom can have under ordinary circumstances. As a source of still further compressions electrons are responsible for the formation of all chemical bonds, which result from the "sharing" of electrons. In other words, the electron is the main source of all major properties of the atom. Consequently, the behavior of atoms or their place in the element table is determined by the number of their electrons. The existence of the corresponding *full* number of electrons for each element was demostrated by Moseley by use of X-ray spectra. Apparently, during the exceptionally energy-rich X-ray radiation *every* potentiality of expansion can show its impact, and *all* electrons appear.

The corpuscular nature of the electron can be considered as rejected in modern physics. Davisson and Germer discovered the wave properties of electrons. The equations of Schroedinger and Heisenberg showed the electrons to be harmonic vibrations of spherical waves. The evidence of the wave nature of electrons is too extensive to be discussed here. As Dr. Randall Caswell of the National Bureau of Standards has pointed out, the picture of the atom as a nucleus surrounded by electrons moving around it should have been discarded thirty years ago. Even such old authority as Jeans has stated that an electron has no definite position in space, as a particle would have; and that it is as meaningless to discuss how much room an electron would occupy as to discuss how much room a fear or anxiety would occupy. However, we have to mention three authoritative arguments for the corpuscular nature of the electron.

Einstein's interpretation of the photoelectric effect implies that photons are individual particles or grains of energy and that when they fall on metal surfaces they hit and release electrons. Barnett in his book, *The Universe and Dr. Einstein*, compares the process to an interaction by "two billiard balls." However, the mechanics of such interaction would be as puzzling as the "bullets" shooting out from "tissue paper" that we shall mention under Rutherford's experiment; and would require as involved assumptions as those we shall discuss under Bohr's model. What is more, the assumption that the photon also is a particle goes against everything known about it and against plain good sense. It is hard to believe that something like a ball travels all the way from faraway stars, and that it can have wave characteristics in such a shape. As Richmond says in his book, *The Dilemma of Modern Physics*, "It is doubtful whether Einstein took this hypothesis entirely seriously."

Another authoritative argument rests on the famous atom model worked out by Bohr. This model is a mathematical masterpiece. But its very complexity and ingenuity are the surest indication that this cannot be the way nature works. This model proves rather that even the best mind cannot construe an atom with electrons as particles. The assumptions that Bohr made are complex, contradictory and invented with no other foundation than the wish to render the model feasible. First, the electron is assumed to accelerate under centripetal attraction — but is not permitted to fall into the nucleus. Secondly, the energy and radiation are to be released by the electron not upon its acceleration or deceleration, as should naturally be expected, but only upon the jumping of the electron from one orbit to another — which is left unconnected with the receiving of energy or its

348

transmission from somewhere else. The very assumption that the electron follows exactly permitted orbits, with radii measuring in precise whole numbers, 1, 4, 9, 16, 25, and so on, without there being any cause for it, amounts to postulating miracles. Bohr had to make these assumptions in order to comply with the equations derived from light spectra.

Light spectra are a unique source of evidence that physicists have about the structure of atoms. The simplicity of relationships in light spectra has been long observed. Balmer as the first construed a simple formula for one series of hydrogen spectra; Lyman, Paschen, Bracket and Pfund, for other series. Rydberg derived a general equation; and a final simplification can be found in Ritz's Combination Principle, according to which any spectral line can be expressed as the difference between two values of the expression R/n^2 in which R is a universal constant, called Rydberg's constant, and n an integer. Practically, this means that we have to deal here only with a series of factors that measure in equal whole numbers squared. Only a system of stationary spherical waves can insure this. All waves in it are equal, and the squaring accounts for their spherical form. Apparently, light means shedding by the spherical waves of their surpluses or "crests" as soon as these reach the quantum that the Field can squeeze off; this quantum represents the universal "element of action" — actually, of interaction between matter and Field — known as Planck's constant.

The third main argument for the corpuscular nature of the electron, *and of radiation*, is derived from Compton's effect. In the scattering of X-rays Compton found a component of lengthened waves in the scattered radiation. This can be explained as a product of the collision of wave systems. Opposed waves are slowed down and lengthen. But Compton proceeded from the assumption that the X-ray photons were colliding with *corpuscular* electrons. Since the energy equations complied with those of colliding particles, *it was assumed that not only electron but also the photons were corpuscular.* Equally good equations could have been derived under the assumption that wave systems were colliding here. The slowing down of wave systems depends

349

equally upon the angle of collision or degree of opposition. Actually, it is such wave collision that is responsible for the collision effects of particles as well, for *ultimately all movement is the product of waves.* Here we may say more about motion in general. It has to be explained anyway; the physicist who takes motion for granted exhibits the blindness to what is most general.

Movement, like **radiation,** is the universal mechanism by which the Field tends to absorb any surplus matter around the particle. In radiation the surplus margin, when it reaches its tiny maximum limit, bursts off under the Field pressure (still holding together as much as possible). This means that the particle becomes smaller by a certain quantum, or that the Field thrusts in to occupy the place vacated. But as the Field thrusts in at one point, it loosens itself at the next, by the same quantum. Then this loosening is occupied by the Field further back, which creates still further loosening still further back, and so on. Thus a transversal wave is created, much as in all cases of waves. But it has to be remembered that the loosening in the Field always means matter. Thus for all practical purposes the wave means carrying a quantum of matter. The wave is absolutely straight because at each thrust-in by the Field none but the closest Field, that is, one straight behind, occupies the emptiness. The enormous pressure of the Field insures that there be not the slightest deviation.

In the case of movement the loosening or emptiness in the Field is occupied by the particle itself. As the Field presses in on one side, there is the same amount of loosening at the other, into which the particle then shifts, or moves in. As it does so, a further loosening behind, and a further thrust-in by the Field, follow. In other words, the repetition or the wave here hovers around the particle and "carries" it. Radiation starts only when the particle is prevented from occupying the ensuing emptiness itself. The movement goes in a straight line for the same reason that a wave does. Certain facts have to be kept in mind. First, any imbalance in the pressure from all sides has the effect that a slightly stronger push on one side makes all the excess pressure concentrate on the same side (and all the loosening on the other).

350

The simplest practical example of this is a slippery ball pressed between the fingers, which shoots off with *all* the impact under the *slightest* push from one side. Secondly, all effects here follow in quanta because we have to deal with oscillations between two uniform, opposed elastic media; and oscillations, by their very nature, involve definite quanta-like differences. Further, any quantum holds together because that offers the easiest balance, and because all particles of matter, however small, "gravitate" toward each other.

Anyway, movement and radiation are two forms of the same universal effect of the Field pressure. Every particle or piece of matter having surplus energy moves in this world; or radiates when colliding with other particles. The similarity of movement and radiation is known to quantum physics in several respects.

Returning to the nature of the electron, we may look at **chemical bonds** for further understanding. Besides light spectra, chemical bonds are the main practical source of evidence about the structure of the atom. Chemical bonds are formed by further compression by the Field of existing margins of compression, that is, electrons. The same Field that compresses primary atoms into more complex ones here makes the compression causally necessary. Modern chemistry recognizes that "sharing" of electrons is the basis of chemical bonds, but can give no explanation why the "sharing" should be causally necessary.

Chemical bonds show that under ordinary conditions there are only very few electrons present even in the heaviest elements. Otherwise the heavy elements would form incomparably stronger bonds, since they would have more electrons to share. The fact is that an element of 10, 18, or 54 electrons, for instance, is as inactive as one of only 2. Of course, scientists have worked out explanations for this—with complex assumptions, such as the exclusion principle of Pauli, or the minus and plus states of Dirac. The generally accepted assumption is that electrons form shells and that only those electrons, which are above the number needed for completion of certain shells can be shared. But no causal necessity for the existence of shells is given. The important thing is that such explanations recognize that for all practical purposes only few electrons are there to be "shared."

The reason why all electrons as completed potentials of expansion are not there in the atom, under ordinary energy conditions, is a further compression by the Field. Any surplus or filled margin, i.e., electron, is taken away by the Field by way of enforcing further compression of the margins inside the atom. Such compression naturally follows the simplest pattern of doubling up. The paired nucleons, or rather spherical waves, having one electron are further paired with similar pairs, then this new combination is paired with another, and so on. Hence the appearance of 2 and particularly 8 as preferred combinations of electrons in the "shells."

Chemical bonds and the periodic table are dominated by these combinations of pairs and octets. Atoms of larger size have preferred combinations or "shells" of 18 and 32, which can be viewed as further doublings up (plus the basic combination of 2 in the former case). Some theorists have pointed out that the number of electrons in shells increases in square proportions with the increase of size of atoms. This may be an average effect of the increase of pressure inside atoms in such square proportion due to their spherical structure. Anyway, the peculiar periodicity of the properties of elements, as brought out by the periodic table, is thus explained. The "shell" theory accounts for it in the same way, but there is no causal necessity or explanation for the existence of the "shells."

All in all, modern physics shows that the electron has wave properties and that it is only a potential, being physically present as little as "fear or anxiety" can be. But since the electron always appears there as a uniform, never-changing unit, when it can be observed, it is assumed to be an everlasting particle. Under such an assumption, only an act of a Creator could make an electron emerge, disappear or be transformed. The truth is that the Field acts as such a creator which can produce, change, transform and reproduce all the forms and effects of matter at any moment and at any distance.

THE PARTICLE-WAVE DILEMMA

This dilemma is best illustrated by the behavior of light. Physicists have ended with the saying that light behaves as particles on certain weekdays and as waves on others. By numerous experiments in diffraction, refraction, interference or polarization, it has been shown beyond doubt that light consists of waves. But other equally conclusive experiments show that light is created by particles leaving one place or piece of matter and reappearing at another. This is particularly clear in Eistein's interpretation of the photoelectric effect.

The wave-particle dilemma afflicts all physical phenomena. The experiments by Davisson and Germer with electrons and later experiments with diffraction of wave patterns from other particles, as well as the predictions and interpretations by De Broglie and Schroedinger, have shown that all forms of matter can behave as waves and as particles. Heisenberg and Born devised formulas that permit dealing with all quantum phenomena either in terms of waves or in terms of particles. The recognition of the dual wave-particle nature of all fundamental forms of energy and matter can now be considered as complete in physics. But since no models for a wave-particle can be imagined, mystery and a frankly admitted inability to conceive the basic phenomena reigns in modern physics.

Actually, there is no mystery and everything can be visualized if the Field as the opposite of matter is recognized. We saw how atoms, nucleons and electrons are formed by the Field pressure. Any surplus matter is absorbed by the Field and carried further as a wave of radiation. As we explained, *the wave here means a tiny bit of loosening or emptiness propagated through the Field, as in the case of all waves. But emptiness in the Field always means matter.* When such a bit of matter meets other matter it is absorbed by the latter; or produces any other effect that matter quantum or energy surplus has. Thus the transformation of particle into wave, or vice versa, is possible at every moment. What is more, due to the omnipresence and absolute density of the Field all this can be effected at any distance as easily as if there were no distance.

If this role of the Field with its enormous pressure and density is not seen, such transfers may seem miraculous. Sir William Bragg has said it is as if one dropped a plank into sea from a height of 100 feet and found that the spreading ripple was able, after traveling 1,000 miles, to act upon a wooden ship in such a way that a plank of that ship flew out of its place to a height of 100 feet. Such a miracle is possible because of the absolute density of the Field. If you push a mercury column at one end of a tube it pushes by exactly the same amount out at the other end, however long the column. Further, there is no loss of energy because matter as the opposite of the Field can never be absorbed by the Field for good. It can only be shifted by the Field from one place to another. The enormous speed in these shifts is insured by the same absolute density and pressure of the Field. Also, due to relativity, a speed that applies absolutely everywhere is the highest speed anyway, even if in itself it be slow.

The same density of the Field explains the form of the waves in energy radiations. Physicists have long recognized that transversal waves, which constitute all energy radiations, require an enormously dense medium. Of course, the "enormity" in the density, pressure or other properties of the Field is no more abnormal or miraculous than the tininess of human standards.

The mysteries of **Quantum Physics** can be equally accounted for. Because matter and Field are two opposed, *elastic* mediums in a state of balance their interaction can follow only in the form of *oscillations*. Since the elasticity as well as the force of opposition are constant, the oscillations can only be uniform. This means that matter yields to Field pressure only by way of uniform "quanta of action" in all energy transmissions. This explains the mysterious discontinuity of quantum physics. There the uniform "element of action" is known as Planck's Constant — generally recognized as the ultimate grain of the universe. The other peculiarities of quantum physics are due to the fact that all forms of matter are spherical wave systems. The outer waves are less compressed, therefore of less mass and greater volume. When squeezed

354

off by the field, as surpluses, they make longer radiation waves with smaller energy. Still further peculiarities of quantum physics are explainable by the rules of resonance between the harmonic wave systems which forms of matter are. The resonance here is absolute because due to the absolute density and omnipresence of the Field the wave systems interact as if there were no distance between them.

We may mention another mystery of forms of matter: **negative particles.** Since the constant interaction by the Field, producing various uniform effects, is not recognized, physicists can explain the various uniform quanta effects only by the assumption of as many never-changing permanent particles. Consequently, the number of distinct and miraculously intricate particles thus discovered is constantly increasing, and has reached already more than thirty, though it is beyond every scientific sense that nature could be so complex. This increase is particularly due to the discovery by physicists of negative particles. According to the famous antiproton physicist Segre, there must ultimately be as many kinds of negative particles as there are positive ones.

In fact, negative particles are only "holes" or negative countereffects appearing in matter at one place while particles or positive effects are produced at another. Such a transfer can occur only under extraordinary disturbances, because it means that matter must gain *as the first* an effect against the Field, which then produces, by transfer, the compensating negative effect in matter. Ordinarily, it is the Field as the dominant opposite which gains as the first all surpluses from matter, with the compensating subsequent effect then leading to a positive transfer, as we saw under radiation. But under extraordinary stresses during sudden cosmic interaction between Field and matter, or when a new particle springs into effect in outer space, secondary gains by matter against the Field may result. Since such gains, as if thrusts into the Field, are propagated through the Field further back, the same as in usual radiation, they become negative rays carrying negative "particles" or quanta having all the properties opposite to positive ones. The "pair production" — the appearance of a negative particle upon the emergence of a positive one — has been generally recognized. William A. Fowler wrote that physicists know only of this kind of creation; but that it could not account for the creation of matter because the opposite particles would also annihilate each other.

We cannot go into the details of negative radiation, which transfers the negative quanta, but one can imagine that it may travel through matter as a positive ray travels through the Field. Hence the enormous penetration power of cosmic rays and of other negative radiation. Such radiation must also be disorganizing for other matter, because its traveling through matter means the propagation of loosenings or "holes" in it, for which each particle tries to compensate by absorption from others.

Another source of misunderstandings is the capacity of a particle, as a wave system, to travel through other matter. The famous **experiments by Rutherford** showed that alpha particles could pass through metal foil; but that approximately one in twenty thousand was deflected and often doubled back on its course. Rutherford was astonished by this effect and said it was like shooting a bullet at a tissue paper and then seeing the bullet come back at you. Since explanations were sought in the collision of particles, atoms had to be assumed to consist of emptiness with tiny hard bits of matter in them. As Millikan said, the particle was seen as passing through more than a half-million atoms without suffering more than a couple of deflections. The nucleus of the atom was assumed to be as small in it as a fly in a house. The rest of the atom was assumed to be emptiness delimited by electron orbits.

Modern physics has built its theories and models on this clearly impossible assumption. If the atoms are empty, why do they not collapse into each other? The argument that electrons move so fast as to form a shield does not hold. Electrons of other atoms move equally fast and are small enough to penetrate such a shield. Stars exist as separate stars only where they can stay at enormous distances from each other. But modern physicists have found various other evidence of such atom structure. This is not surprising. They are viewing atoms in terms of particles, and average atomic effects can show only to a very small proportion what corresponds to solid particles.

In fact, the experiments on shooting particles through matter show something else. The alpha particles as well as the atoms through which they travel are wave systems. Therefore the alpha particles can be momentarily absorbed and re-emitted by the matter they pass through in the way electrons are. They may even be momentarily disintegrated and re-established in the process, because the Field that shapes them is always there. Since the whole process is dominated by the general impact of the shooting, the re-emissions follow the direction of the shooting, thus giving the impression that the particles are simply shot through. For the same reason the few stray re-emissions that bounce sideways agree in general with collision equations, since the stresses that cause them are also determined by the general impact of the shooting.

The hypothesis that these effects are created by the collision of particles is contradicted by the very nature of such effects. Rutherford had every reason to be astonished. A merely corpuscular dislocation of a particle can never have the effect of a bullet shooting back at you from a tissue paper. Only a radiation-like re-emission could have this effect. There are other indications which contradict the assumption that merely particles are interacting here. Physicists have pointed out that there is an unexplainable time lag between the supposed impact and rebounding of the particle. The event may take ten billion times longer than would be expected. Particles may continue bouncing back even after the shooting has ceased. The experiments, first performed by the Juliot-Curies, show that the same kind of shooting of alpha particles produces radiation which may continue for half an hour after the shooting is over. More modern experiments show that a particle in similar scatterings does not reflect in the way objects rebound. It may reflect from "all the atoms in the entire surface numbering many billions," in the words of Donald J. Hughes, who described such experiments.

If it seems incredible how a particle could be absorbed and re-emitted so many times, instead of just passing through, think of the passage of electrons through a conductor. It is absurd to assume that the electrons you are supplying at one end of the wire run the whole length of the wire to appear at the other end. And yet, as many electrons appear at the other end as you supply. It is equally absurd to assume that a photon runs all the way from the sun to the earth. The same applies to other "particles" traveling either in space or in matter. They all travel in the form of wave systems. Of course, the traveling of such wave systems in matter encounters difficulties. This is the reason why only specific particles that unfailingly recombine, like alpha particles, can travel through other matter. And only special elements, like the otherwise impenetrable metals, which do not have a tendency to absorb other matter permanently, permit such traveling.

To be sure, the series of absorptions and re-emissions may clearly appear like the path of a particle. Such paths, observed in the Wilson cloud chamber, and the later, improved bubble chambers, are assumed to be tracks of passing particles. Actually, something more than a mere passing of a particle is needed to form such tracks. For instance, it is known since the early work of Helmholtz and Richartz that tracks created in vapor are due to ionization, which means the absorption and re-emission of electrons. By its mere physical passage through a cloud no particle can form a trace-leaving track.

In conclusion, we may say that the unsolvable wave-particle dilemmas disappear as soon as the simple and scientifically inevitable universal medium, which we called the Field, is recognized. The simple properties of the Field make it possible for a particle to become a wave, be transferred as a wave system through distance, even through other matter, and be re-created again in exactly the same form as the particle.

THE MYSTERY OF GRAVITATION

The greatest mystery of gravitation is that it exists. How can two bodies attract each other without there being any bond between them? In his book, *Design of the Universe,* Fritz Kahn tells about a professor who started his course by showing a ball fall, and telling his students: "This is the greatest miracle I can show you in all my lectures." To say that gravitation is due to properties of field or to curvature of space does not explain anything. If there are properties, what is it that has them, what are they, and to what are they due? If there is a curvature, in what is it, and what produces it?

The concept of omnipresent Field pressure explains gravitation automatically. From the side of adjacent matter there comes no pressure. Therefore in the vicinity of matter the compression does not come from all sides equally. This means that the Field pressure is weaker and one-sided around matter. In other words, matter shelters off the Field pressure coming from behind it. Considering that the Field is perfectly fluid, and that all matter is floating in it, the sheltering effect can be only very weak. This explains why the gravitational force is so shadowy in comparison with the true cosmic forces that hold atoms together or make radiation travel with such enormous speeds. Naturally, this protective shadow decreases uniformly at a progressive rate as one goes further away from matter. This explains the spherical graduation of lines of gravitational force around matter, as if there were a spherical curvature of space around matter. From this curvature then follow the other observed effects of dependence of gravitation upon the shape of matter.

Since all matter and radiation are products of the same Field pressure, they are all attracted by gravitation. An atom, being pressed from all sides, gravitates into that direction from which pressure is less. The same applies to a ray of light, movement or any form of energy. Pieces of matter tend to hold together for the same reason. We can imagine that the force of attraction between particles hovering closely in each other's protective area may be considerable. These forces are responsible for the compactness and crystallization of matter as well as the other effects of intermolecular attraction. Since all matter is a product of Field pressure, all matter responds in the same way to gravitation. A light element falls to earth with the same speed as a heavy one; and a big body accelerates in its fall at the same rate as a small one, which is contrary to the ordinary laws of acceleration and inertia.

These curious effects, supposedly, induced Einstein to work out his theory of the equivalence of gravitation and inertia. He explained, by illustrations, that a body falling to earth performs in the same way as a body caught up by an accelerated elevator in a system without gravitation. There can be no doubt that gravitation and acceleration can be shown to be equivalent; they are both products of the same Field pressure. But it is difficult to see how Einstein's theory can help us understand gravitation causally. If the effects of gravitation are due to acceleration, we must be accelerating away from the center of the earth. This is not true either for earth or for any gravitational system.

ELECTROMAGNETISM

Modern physics has given up the endeavor to explain what electricity is and what causes it. With the understanding of the Field the explanation is almost self-suggesting. Electric current means the equalization of matter surplus. This equalization is effected by the universal Field pressure, as enriched atoms are more easily compressed and their surplus thus passed on. This property of equalization is an automatic function of the Field as an absolutely fluid, omnipresent and uniform force that compresses matter uniformly everywhere. In the case of electricity (in difference from radiation) the equalization can follow only through matter itself, serving as conductor, since the electrons cannot be absorbed by the Field.

That we have here to do with a surplus of matter is evidenced by thermionic emissions, the workings of thermoelectric couples, and the photoelectric effect, as well as the very nature of electricity as the flow of surplus electrons. The fact that all forms of energy, including electricity, can be converted into each other points to their common nature. All energy means shifts between matter and Field, evoked by irregularities or enrichments in matter. Universal equalization by the omnipresent Field explains not only the causal necessity of current, but also the attraction and repulsion at a distance of charges and magnets, as well as the electromagnetic fields and induction of current or movement by such fields.

But first let us make one thing clear. All the electromagnetic field effects are produced by "loosenings" in the Field, just as in case of radiation, movement or gravitation. But the "loosenings" in the case of electricity have a *specific grain* of their own. This grain is determined by the quantum of electron; every "loosening" corresponds to the electron that the Field shifts. That is why there is no direct transfer of effects, no resonance, between electricity and radiation or movement. Nor are there the usual gravitational effects, though generally loosening in the Field pressure means gravitation. In the case of electricity the quanta of loosening are too discontinuous, tiny, specific and weak to affect all matter gravitationally. But matter that is able to respond to the specific electron-quanta grain of these "loosenings" does show gravitational effects in the electric and magnetic fields. To participate in specific electromagnetic effects, the matter must have the specific properties of accepting, harboring and transmitting electrons freely.

The attraction between opposite charges is due to the same equalization function of the Field. Since direct equalization of electron enrichment, or impoverishment, is not possible at a distance, the Field pressure tends to produce the equalization by bringing the opposite charges together. This effect is automatic, due to the fact that the Field pressure is everywhere, and that everything is its product. The Field automatically equalizes any pressure differences in itself, as every fluid medium does, but electron-enriched matter means a higher compression potential, and electron-deprived matter a lower one, than universal pressure. The self-establishing equilibrium, or equality of pressures, in the Field therefore improves when opposite charges are approached, or equal charges pushed further apart. The process is no different here from the automatically self-establishing pressure equalization in any fluid medium, though it cannot be easily visualized because of the infinite multiplicity of pressures, or rather their directions, involved.

Perhaps one can understand the process better if he keeps in mind that, except for the factual equalization or discharge, the charged objects are in contact as if there were no distance between them, due to the omnipresence of the Field. One may picture an infinite number of rods or strings connecting each point or effect on one object with any point on the other. As opposite charges "push" and "pull" the "rods" in complementary ways, approaching results; and vice versa. This may also help to visualize why the same inverse-square rule applies here as it does in radiation, where we can picture the rays as dispersing themselves with distance.

Neutral or uncharged objects are attracted by charged ones because they offer at least a partial or half equalization.

The attraction of opposite charges, or rather the tendency of the Field to compensate for, or match, every inequality in itself by an opposite inequality or charge explains the induction of charge. The effects here can be easily visualized from the standard descriptions of induction of opposite charge in isolated conductors, Leyden jar, other capacitators and electrophorus or other electrostatic generators. What such descriptions do not explain is the cause of the process. Modern physics in general describes with great precision and complexity the effects of electricity or electromagnetic fields, but cannot explain what they are or what causes them. If one thinks of the universal, self-equalizing Field pressure, and the inequalities of compression potential of electron-enriched and impoverished matter, the causal explanation is clear. Wherever there is such inequality the self-equalization tends to match it by an opposite inequality. As long as such inequalities or charges are prevented from actually meeting, by distance or insulator, they simply accumulate on both sides of the separation as closely as possible.

An important phenomenon of electric charge is that it lies on the surface of the conductor. More correctly, electric effects take place always on the surface of a conductor, never inside it, even if it is hollow. Apparently it is not the conductor itself but its outer contact with space that produces the electrical effects. This shows clearly that the cause of such effects is the equalizing Field pressure which comes, in its overwhelming force, from the space all around. The standard descriptions of the density of charge in dependence upon the curvature of the body and of the assumed lines of force or equipotential lines in the electric field confirm this.

The most interesting phenomenon of electricity is the creation of an electromagnetic field, with its various effects, by the current. Here particularly physics has to resort to numerous rules, which are actually the effects of one unified cause. The field effects are due to the simple fact that, much as in radiation, "loosenings" in the Field follow as the Field presses into the conductor to produce the equalization. Naturally this pressure, and the direction of the "loosenings," is perpendicular to the wire. This explains the perpendicularity of the electromagnetic field to electric current in all their various reciprocal effects. But the pressure also has a secondary direction: it also goes along the wire in a peculiar whirl-like fashion (later showing around a magnet). For the final effect or "goal" of all the pressures is the propagation of electron inequalities along the wire. The process is not too different from what happens in ocean currents, hurricane whirls or the simple squeezing of a liquid along a tube.

Naturally, the "loosenings" in the Field have important effects on matter and energy. In a loosening Field matter expands and acquires electrons. This means a surging inequality in matter, and inequalities in matter always serve as a source of current. For the same reason matter passed through a strong static magnetic field can create current. Under the equalizing attraction that we explained above matter is deformed or polarized in such a field and the deformation or inequality when passed on is the current. Force is required here as well as in passing matter through an electromagnetic field because the polarization as well as the expansion by the matter means acquiring a balance with the changed Field pressure; and only an equal force can disrupt this balance. Exactly this disruption of the balance is what creates the current, by passing on the inequalities. These effects on matter by changes in the Field can causally explain electric generation, inductance, self-inductance or other phenomena of electromagnetic induction.

The motion of matter under the effects of an electromagnetic field is causally explained primarily by the simple fact that matter moves in the direction of the lesser pressure created by the "loosenings" in the Field. Further, when a stress in the Field, or a saturation opposite to the balances we mentioned above, is created by current in the magnetic field, the equalizing Field pressure moves the matter, the conductor of current, away from such surging imbalance. Also, the conflicting directions of the "whirls" of the Field around conductors carrying opposite currents make the conductors move away from each other. For the same reason conductors carrying parallel currents approach each other.

As we have already mentioned, the equalizing pressures of the Field do not follow in simple straight lines. Due to the fluid mechanics of the Field any pressure and loosening in one direction induces immediate displacement and compensation pressures in the form of cyclic streams. Hence the circular whirl-like lines of force around currents and magnets. It is to be understood that these lines of force should be thought of as three-dimensional movements in space, rather than two-dimensional lines in planes as usually depicted. Also, descriptions in terms of the North and South direction of magnets are misleading. Ferromagnetic bodies, like the compass needle, align themselves in this direction exactly because in this way they find more exposure to the determining lines of force, that go *perpendicularly* to it. For the same reason the strength of magnets depends upon their thickness, rather than their length in the direction of the North-South poles; and magnets retain their strength however thinly they are sliced along their thickness.

Because there are immediate subsequent compensating pressures in the Field, the induction of current by one straight conductor into another close by, as discovered by Faraday, takes place only during the short instants when the current is started or shut off. Coil formations of conductors have to be used in producing more continuous electromagnetic effects because only in that way can movements in the same direction be accumulated from the whirls around the conductors. Ferromagnetic metals, used as cores in the coils, aid in such accumulation.

Magnets are metals deformed by pressures and "loosenings" in the electric field. Naturally, these deformations are directional. That is why a section from either pole or any part of a magnet has both poles. The usual magnets are metals that retain the deformation by the field. What exactly the deformations are nobody knows. Modern physics seems to have established that they apply to submicroscopically small domains. This is sufficient to account for the various magnetic effects — provided an explanation is given why deformed matter can interact with other matter at a distance as if they were actually in contact. For it is clear that matter deformed in one direction would find a better balance, and therefore cling together, with matter oppositely deformed. Universal equalization by the omnipresent Field explains how this tendency becomes operative at a distance.

Electromagnetism, like gravitation, shows manifestly that the Field is a concrete reality. If the basically simple interaction between matter and the Field as the unified causal source is not seen here, electromagnetism becomes a system of rules so complex that only a supernatural anthropomorphic intelligence could account for their existence and maintenance.

COSMOGONIC CREATION

The clue to understanding the formation of stars is the chain-reaction effect of the concentration of matter. As some of the interstellar matter happens to come together, its force of gravitational attraction increases and leads to more concentration, which produces even greater attraction, and so forth. Of course, a slight stop in the process may produce a reversed chain reaction. The "pulsation" of stellar formations, also the phenomenon of novae, may be explained in this way. However, the general trend of the concentration of matter prevails in the end, and a spherical star is formed.

Planets are created by a similar concentration of matter that hovers, in spherical waves, around the star. The existence of such waves is inevitable because in fluid dynamics, which govern Field movements, any concentration is bound to create counter-concentration. In simple terms, movements toward the center produce secondary movements away from it. This can be easily observed in the dynamics of fluids. The matter moved away from the star becomes spherical wavelike concentrations due to the uniformity of pressures and the tendency of the displaced matter to concentrate on its own. Further concentration leads to the convergence of all matter of the spherical wave into one sphere by a process similar to that governing the formation of the star itself. This happens together with the universal tendency of matter to move.

As we explained before, the Field pressure makes all matter move sooner or later under the slightest enrichment. The illustration of a ball compressed between slippery fingers may serve here. The direction the ball shoots off depends upon the slightest push. This means that in an indecisively floating cloud of energy-rich matter any one movement may precipitate more movement in the same direction, which then creates even more such movement, and so on. The formation of cyclones, hurricanes or other currents is a good example. Of course, during the formation of a planet, conflicting currents may develop, but in the end there is bound to be one which prevails and therefore consolidates the whole mass and momentum or energy into one orbiting planet (a ring of matter may evolve as an incomplete concentration). Since planets represent consolidations of mass and momentum of spherical waves, the uniform Keplerian regularities become explainable. The spin of planets or stars derives from a similar consolidation of momentum of indecisively shifting loose matter within the ball itself.

The circular direction of the planetary movement is due to the spherical graduations of the Field pressure in the gravitational field of the sun. These graduations make every level or "line of force" of Field pressure spherically curved. Since the Field pressure determines all the effects of matter, every movement, originating in a gravitational field, goes in a curved line for the same reason that otherwise every movement goes in a straight line. In simplified terms, the parts of the planet on the outside move little faster because of the slightly higher Field pressure there, and thus curve the path of the planet. For the same reason a

366

planet travels faster while going through the farther ends of its elongated orbit — as predicted by Kepler's second law. The planet is thus kept in orbit with such perfection by the same Field pressure that keeps every movement, or radiation, in a perfectly straight line. Also, due to the fluidity dynamics of the Field, any movement "up" by any part in the planet creates an equal movement "down" by another part in it. This rule is equally inexorable because of the same enormous density of the Field. Explanations along these lines are sufficient to account for the "centrifugal" and "centripetal" as well as other effects of orbiting planets.

The existing hypotheses about the origin of planets have either been found untenable, like the nebular Kant-Laplace and the "binary-star" hypotheses, or imply that planets are due to extraordinary occurrences. According to the "close-encounter" hypothesis, only one star in a billion may happen to have planets. This is contradicted by the stark fact that in our solar system six out of nine planets have moons or planets of their own. Planetary systems, like spinning and orbiting, are universal phenomena owing their origin to the pressure mechanics of the Field. Man will have to learn once more that nothing about him is unique. But we can be sure that due to our humanly prejudiced notions we would not recognize life, not to speak of intelligence, in any different form even if we saw it.

Formation of heavier elements takes place during the condensation of a star. The *special higher* pressure needed for it derives from disequilibrium oscillations which are bound to occur during such condensation. Such oscillations are the only way a *special higher* effect can be produced between two equal opposites. In the simplest oscillations, a force added to produce a swing in one direction produces an equally great swing in the opposite direction. The typical thing in every oscillation is that each swing perpetuates itself to its highest possible limit, before the opposite swing starts and in its turn reaches the highest opposite limit. Since oscillation is the very nature of any interaction, or rather disturbance, between two balanced opposites, all interactions between matter and Field form opposite *chain reactions*, each one self-increasing to the highest limit and then giving rise to an equal opposite chain reaction. From the tiniest vibrations between matter and Field which create radiation to the expansion and contraction of galaxies, the oscillating chain reaction is the universal mechanism that makes them work.

During the condensation of a star, atoms deeper inside it find equilibrium at the lower Field pressure there and expand. Then if masses of such expanded matter happen to be pushed further outside and exposed to the higher Field pressure, the compression by the Field may acquire the opposite chain-reaction effect and the *special higher* force capable of producing higher nucleon compressions and heavier elements. The heavier elements then sink back into the interior, causing more displacement and more opportunity for further compressions. After billions of years of such turbulence a permanent equilibrium is found with a certain over-all density of matter. This density may depend upon length of concentration as well as the original amount of matter in the region where the concentration started.

The heavier elements are created under opposing tendencies. One is the tendency of the primary atoms emerging from the inside to cling together. The other is the force of the Field, which does not permit existence of too large or complex combinations but also tends to compress together as many as possible of the primary atoms. Where the tendencies reach their fullest impact a middle ground is met and greater equilibrium established. Hence the greater stability of elements in the middle of the element table. The lighter elements at the top can be increased by small additions, and the heaviest ones at the bottom can be split.

Such splitting permits new combinations and when these are formed the Field gets the opportunity of compressing the nucleons, which produces great amounts of energy. But here, just as during the natural creation of heavier elements, such splitting up requires an increased Field pressure, which can be brought about only through wider oscillations between the Field and matter. These can be started by enriching the matter even further, or by accumulating the more expanded heaviest elements; these had remained such because they escaped the full impact of the Field during their primordial creation. Thus the conditions, with the opportunity of greater oscillations, are reconstructed which governed during the natural creation of the elements.

Here we have to mention the general problem of creating chain reactions for the release of energy. In all cases where there is a latent enriched matter, the release of the enrichment can be brought about by making the Field pressure bear more forcibly on such matter. But there is no way of increasing the pressure of the Field directly; the universe would have to be changed for that. However, it is possible to bring about wider oscillations between matter and Field. This then can start chain-reaction effects of the dominant opposite, the Field. Such wider oscillations can be brought about by first enriching matter even further, or adding energy to it, which man can do.

This explains why in starting a chemical reaction, fire or nuclear "burning," extraordinary energy has to be added first, though in the end much more energy can be obtained. In the case of fissionable materials as well, these have first to be enriched or at least accumulated so that a more forcible compression and division by the Field of the heaviest atoms can start. The chain reaction when started goes on by itself, as disintegration of one fissionable atom exposes neighboring atoms to heavier Field pressure, which then disintegrate in their turn — not too differently from what happens in ordinary burning. The existing theory that shooting nucleons shatter nuclei is contradicted by the primary fact about fissions, namely, that slowed-down, not accelerated neutrons produce fissions; we saw how a shooting out of particles like "bullets," that could shatter the nuclei, can never result from their mere dislocation. Rather, the supply of neutrons and neutron-rich shielding here play the role of heightening the enrichment of matter and the chances of the opposite chain reaction to start. The same effect is achieved, in the case of fire or chemical reactions, by purifying the compounds and shielding or isolating the processes.

Before we conclude we may mention a curious **relativity of interdependent effects,** deriving from the universality of the Field as the source of all physical effects. For instance, when matter

369

is emitted in a volcanic eruption it is hot and liquid. Does this mean that matter below the thin surface layer of our earth is hot and liquid? If it were we would be boiling, and the earth would be expanding or contracting with tides. The same matter when it is deeper inside does not behave as hot and liquid because the particles there are less active under lesser Field pressure. The same equalizing "relativity" applies to all other properties of matter — density, weight, structure or energy levels — deeper inside the earth. To take another example, under the curious Avogadro law elements of big molecules occupy the same space, when in a gaseous state, as those of small molecules. Apparently, the same interaction between matter and Field that creates the bigger molecules equally affects their other properties — greater attraction. This "relativity" may help explain other curious phenomena — whether one thinks of the interaction of subatomic quanta or the expansion of the universe.

CONCLUSION

The realization of the relativity of our knowledge would enable scientists to see the other, causal, side of reality. Physicists then would discover the medium that they have always been looking for — the Ether or field that can be a million times denser than steel but also lighter than the thinnest air. Something that is absolutely everywhere and is absolutely essential to everything cannot be experienced or registered in any way.

We saw how the concept of such Ether, which we called the Field, removes dilemmas and supplies explanations where none can be given in modern physics. How precise the explanations are we gave is not the point; they surely can be improved. The point is that we are discovering here the reality of which modern physicists describe only the effects; and that this reality, though simple like everything in nature, reveals itself as *the unified causal source* of every phenomenon, including the fundamental mysteries not even faced by physicists, such as the creation of uniform particles and the maintenance of inexorable laws throughout the universe. And we cannot overemphasize that these explanations

370

do not require any hypothetic assumptions or new theories. *All that is required is that the physicist abandon a delusory human nearsightedness.*

We know that the main obstacle to accepting the concept of the Field will be the naïve but strong emotional prejudices of man. He will always ask how there can be such unthinkable "oppression" and density in the space in which he moves "freely" and which is so "empty" that he can see through it. We have already explained that scientifically these objections are silly, and every scientist knows it. Nontheless, these naïve prejudices will make the concept of the Field appear ridiculous so that even scientists will avoid using it. If it were not for such prejudices, a concept similar to that of the Field, as the universal causal background reality, would have been the first thing every scientist would have thought of.

X

THE PARADOX OF DISEASE AND CURE

The paradox of relative causation applies to physiology the same as it applies to psychology. The organism cannot be more or less than its normalcy, statically or dynamically. Therefore there can be no satisfaction without need, no release without restriction, and no excess increase without equal decrease in any function or its rate of performance. But since man as a conscious being plans and strives only for positive feelings or more release, overadjustment becomes the main source of human physiological maladjustments, which show as functional diseases. The danger increases as man's power and skill in improving his feeling of well-being or rate of living increase.

We saw that under overadjustment every improvement or "cure" becomes a source of worsening or "disease"; and that the vicious-circle effect can deepen any slight disorder into an abyss of negative reactions or gravest disease. As a person tries to derive satisfaction or release where no need or restriction pre-exists, there is an overexpenditure in physiological resources, or rather in the rate of living. Return to normalcy by restriction or by slowing down becomes necessary and shows as diseased reactions. These reactions can be overcome by removing the restrictions or increasing the stimulation so that still more release becomes available. Naturally, this means deepening even further the disease or exhaustion — and the need for even stronger means of release. Thus every "improvement" becomes a source of deeper worsening, in the same vicious-circle process that we explained under neuroses and psychoses. All that is needed to make this process self-perpetuating are means strong enough to remove the diseased reactions; and modern man is inventing them with alarming efficiency.

To understand the paradox here it is necessary to understand the causal contradiction or opposition inherent in all adjustment. Living being strives only for release, but release without a system of restrictions or accumulation of "reserves" would mean a formless dissipation and exhaustion. The higher the organic adjustment, the more extensive the system of restrictions. It is not by accident that life consists of as much dissatisfaction or restriction as satisfaction. If either side — the striving for pleasure or the system of restrictions — is removed, normal adjustment collapses. But man as a conscious being lives only by the rule of planning for more satisfactions. He pursues them with all his increasing might and skill, whereas he accepts restrictions only reluctantly by way of blind tradition or unintended learning. The two-sided play of adjustment thus gravitates towards one-sidedness and abnormalcy in the case of man. Let us look briefly at the two sides of our physiological adjustment.

On the side of restrictions biological and cultural conditioning persists, though consciously man strives to overcome them as hindrances in the feeling of well-being, or as superstitions. Also, there is some unconscious learning by way of general feeling or intuitive realization that in the case of certain overadjustment an aftermath will follow. If man did not have these protections, he would exhaust all his physiological reserves and would end with a state of complete immobility as well as negativism. This would mean every functional disease, or every negative reaction, the same as in neuroses. It would also mean further endeavors by the person to remove deeper biological restrictions in search of further release. The end result would be malignant growth, which is generally recognized as loss of restrictive controls over the more primitive tendency of every tissue to grow unrestrictedly.

On the side of satisfactions man has diverged a long way from his natural adjustment. He has used every means and every scientific achievement in planning his own well-being, or rather the feeling of well-being. The animal cannot plan such an increase in releases and can follow only the natural adjustment which has

373

evolved so that every release encounters a corresponding restriction or conditioning. Therefore the animal in its natural environment does not suffer from the functional diseases and malignant disorders that have become the scourge of modern man. If the animal were protected as well as man is against infectious diseases, and were left to its natural adjustment, it would never be ill, would survive even grave accidental inflictions and would reach its maximum age.

Generally it is not even suspected that man's capacity to plan his own well-being consciously is the greatest source of danger to his normalcy. Common man proceeds with an intuitive wisdom that life cannot be pleasure alone; and cultural tradition consists of restrictions more than anything else. But these wisdoms have no chance of standing up against man's conscious and scientific "improvements." Man does his best, in a hundred ways, to destroy the very basis, the two-sidedness of adjustment, on which his physiological normalcy rests. From the use of salt, started some twenty thousand years ago, to the energizers and tranquilizers of modern medicine, man is constantly trying to find ways for as unlimited releases as possible. This applies to every endeavor in every field, physical as well as psychological. Even such a lowly thing as bread means a great step toward increased enjoyment, though now only the peoples who do not bake bread know this. (Attila supposedly refused to eat bread because in his eyes such an enjoyment amounted to a sin.) Of course, the organism easily counteracts any such minor "improvements."

But the attack by modern man on the front of "improvements" is massive and intensively thorough. There is hardly any basic function that he has not tried to transform into a means of enjoyment. For instance, eating should normally consist of suffering hunger first, then finding satisfaction of it. For civilized man, however, eating means only a satisfaction. Likewise, the restrictive spirit of former morals is being rejected now as superstitious ignorance. The increased releases or enjoyments are not noticed because of the relativity of evaluations. Only opposite reactions are felt; and to silence them, stronger means are resorted to. In a word, overadjustment with all its vicious-circle effects is being perpetuated on a grand scale. The results show in the more than doubled rate of deaths from the major functional diseases and cancer.

Modern medicine, instead of seeing overadjustment as the main danger to human normalcy, fosters it. The erudition and resourcefulness of medicine are concentrated on making man feel better. There is hardly any drug or means of therapy that is not aimed at immediate relief. This amounts to helping overadjustment and deepening the vicious-circle effect. The very skillfulness of modern medicine becomes a source of danger. Usually, upon "improvements" by some drug or other means, the opposite reaction, or "side" effects follow as the organism tries to move back to its normalcy, or catch up with the "overexpenditure." But modern medicine does not leave things at that. It evolves increasingly subtle means of silencing such reactions. The removal of all kinds of "side" effects has become the main task of modern drug treatment, as drugs effecting immediate "cures" have been already discovered for almost every functional disease. The more "specific" means for removal of "side" effects are mostly those affecting the hormonal and nerve functions, which means exactly the more fundamental controls. Thus the restrictive side of adjustment may be gradually overcome at the deepest levels and nothing but the primordial tendency of uncontrolled growth or malignancy left.

Common sense is not of much help here because man understands his natural reactions only in the simplest cases. A person losing the sensation of pain in his frozen fingers would try to revive that pain. Or a person perspiring and feeling exhausted in heat would hesitate to use a drug that would stop the perspiration or make him feel ready for vigorous exertion. Also, a person feeling the aftermaths of previous intoxication or overenjoyment would rather accept them than seek new intoxication. Further, men know, at least with their reason, that the pleasant, reassuring well-being provided by such means as smoking, drinking, strong foods or other rich stimulation are dangerous to health. But when it comes to more involved reactions, like headache or fatigue, man is ready to overcome them by taking a drug, though this would certainly mean disorganizing even deeper central functions

—if he really succeeded. Fortunately, the reactions return. At least up to now medicine has not yet invented a means of silencing the demands of normalcy so easily.

One cannot blame here the attitude of the common man. Satisfaction of needs or removal of pain is the goal of life, from the point of view of man in the two-sided play. However, to conserve this two-sided normalcy, the pain has to be removed not by merely stopping it but by meeting the given disturbance in appropriate ways which may be extremely difficult to find and equally strenuous to follow. The stressful state of the organism under pain reflects this strenuous search. To be sure, only the organism itself can find and follow the ungraspably intricate ways in which it proceeds at millions of points in each instance and is guided by the all-integrating principle of pleasure under which myriads of the tiniest mechanisms act. No medical genius can understand, still less intervene in, this myriad world of complexity and purposefulness. To stop pain directly is like switching off an emergency system when it starts its complex operations.

Unfortunately, modern medicine does not have a causal theory on pleasure and pain as guides to adjustment; such a theory is unworkable without understanding the paradoxical logic of value reactions. Modern medicine follows the same "logical" rule that the common man does. He feels that he is improving in every respect as the pain or stress is being removed, or that he is deteriorating in every respect as the pain arises or continues. If anything, medicine in its formal scientific approach is more thorough in eliminating pain in all its forms of negative reactions or disease.

Here we have to make an important point. When a doctor makes extensive tests or technically involved analyses he is only finding out the *reactions* of separate organs and tissues. Just like the organism as a whole, separate organs or mechanisms perform more intensively under increased stimulation, whatever it may be, but suffer aftermaths during the return to normalcy following the over-stimulation. In other words, the same paradoxes of overadjustment or of worsening through "improvement" apply to all the functions that the doctor investigates, however complex his tests. He deals only with the reactions of organs and tissues, not with the causally underlying biochemical processes. As we have repeatedly indicated, no man can understand these processes directly. There are billions of them, each interacting with and depending upon billions of others, throughout the organism. Every one of them would have to be grasped at every infinitesimal instant, and the nature of the living process itself would have to be understood in the first place. Doctors simply cannot do differently than deal with the integrated wholes of these processes, which means with *reactions*.

That is why understanding the seemingly paradoxical logic of reactions is so important. This logic is just the reverse of ordinary and experimentally scientific logic. According to it, value in a feeling or reaction decreases as more of it is added, and vice versa, and the source of every value is its opposite or disvalue. We explained how this cannot be different in the life of the organism, limited to its normalcy and deriving all its satisfactions or releases only from previous needs or restrictions. We may only add that this paradoxical logic applies to every phase and every detail of organic reactions.

Naturally, if this logic is not understood, medicine can do more harm than good. In schematic terms, it may tend to increase releases or make "improvements," whereas those can lead only to exhaustion or opposite reactions and worsening. Or it may tend to remove restrictions or stresses and pains, whereas these alone can restore the normal reserves, or rather the potentials of growth and metabolism. This is the reason why modern medicine has not become a science but has remained an art, depending upon practical wisdom; and why any disorder can be causally interpreted by doctors in a number of conflicting ways. Even the first thing that the doctor starts with, namely, temperature, is not understood as to its cause and effect. It has been considered as an ill to be removed. But perhaps it is there for protection? The "plenty of liquids" treatment for colds, usually administered to keep temperature down, was reversed by Dr. Guy T. Vise and gave good results.

Doctors have become aware of the inconsistencies resulting from dealing with reactions of body. They are learning increasingly that removal of "symptoms" does not cure. But the whole theory about symptoms is defective. Symptoms are considered as something accidental. Nothing is accidental in organic adjustment. In fact, if the causal nature of symptoms were understood, treatment would aim at strengthening "symptoms" in most cases of functional disorders; and most disturbances would be found to be such "symptoms." A symptom is the feeling of pain and stress, which are there for the protection and restoration of normalcy.

What we have said so far does not apply to all fields of medicine. It applies only to diseases originating from overadjustments, or "improvements" in reactions. Here belong what we shall call the functional diseases: cardiovascular diseases, hypertension, arthritic conditions, diabetes, gastric disorders, combinations of these and other functional abnormalities and, above all, cancer. That a great misunderstanding rules on these diseases is evident from the most conspicuous truth about modern medicine: whereas impressive progress has been made in other fields of medicine, there has been an alarming increase in these diseases. Take the two most typical overadjustment disorders: heart disease and cancer. In the last fifty years the death rate from heart disease has increased by 129 percent and that from cancer by 127 percent. During the same period deaths from communicable diseases have decreased to one-eighth of what they were. The increase in functional diseases has been recognized as remarkable even by those who try to account for much of it by the increase in the average age of people.

Medicine, like every science, advances spectacularly as soon as basic causal understanding is reached. In the treatment of infectious diseases there are no difficulties in this respect. The cause, microbes, and the means of destroying them are understood. Typically enough, the paradoxical logic is applied here already: the disease is not avoided, but deliberately inflicted on the body by vaccination so that the body can establish a normal balance with it. We can be sure that progress in the treatment of functional diseases would be even greater if there was causal understanding of them. For it is easier for man to deal with his own reactions than with myriads of invisible microbes. It must be noted that the functional diseases, together with the infectious diseases, constitute almost all that man suffers from, and that the remaining difficulties with

378

infectious diseases are in the end mostly of a functional nature.

Equally spectacular progress has been made in surgery, as well as the technical means of diagnosis and treatment. Here as well no difficulty of causal understanding exists. Such achievements, and the unique effort that goes into medicine as the science that literally decides the life and death of men, have created a misleading attitude. It is assumed that medicine can improve, increase, change or add to any organic function if only the right means are found. This attitude is as wrong as it is general. It becomes a source of danger.

No medical effort can change or add to the slightest facet of the normalcy of the organism. Medicine cannot reproduce the tiniest tissue synthetically. How can it expect to alter constructively anything in an organism, in which even a minor modification involves every one of its millions of mechanisms? Medicine cannot change anything in the organism except by crippling its humanly ungraspable purposefulness, or by evoking reactions which are ultimately determined by this same normalcy of the body. Any improvements which intervention from outside seems to produce are due to the destruction or paralysis of the sensory mechanisms that evoke pain or maintain restrictions. An experienced doctor knows that his job is only to remove obstacles so that nature can do its work, though even this approach leads to error if the paradoxical nature of reactions is not understood.

Anybody who believes in the possibility of making changes or improvements in the organism should reflect on its quantitative complexities. The cells in the body number in the thousands of billions, and each one has specific relations to millions of others. Each cell consists of millions of molecules, and each molecule of thousands of atoms — each of them having as many specific relationships to the others. The virus, the simplest living component, may have ten million atoms in it. Proteins are incomparably more complex and there are hundred thousand different proteins in the human body. At the same time man is lucky if he can add a couple of atoms the way he wants in his products. But "molecular" psychology, "molecular" biology or "molecular" genetics proceeds exactly on the assumption that man can rebuild something in the living processes — though nobody even knows what a living process means causally. Scientists in these fields can always refer to such celebrities as Linus Carl Pauling in psychiatry and physiology, John Enders in biology or W. Eugene Knox in medicine and genetics. There can be no objection to such research, but the marked emphasis on it certainly indicates how modern medicine expects to solve its problems.

A typical illustration of the modern approach is offered by drug treatment, the main form of treatment in modern medicine.

Drugs are ridiculously simple products in comparison with organic compounds. At the same time, modern drugs may be spectacularly effective. Moreover, the same drug may be effective against a dozen most varied ills — from a psychological complex or allergy to heart disease. Repeated reports of these miraculous curing qualities have been written regarding cortisone, ACTH, steroids, estrogens, enzymes, sulfa drugs, antihistamines, meprobamates or drugs with such popular names as reserpine, thorazine, iproniazid, orinasse, lysine, luminal, prednisone, benemid, medrol or even aspirin in its various compounds. The explanation lies in the fact that a feeling of improvement is produced by release. In a normal way release comes following the meeting of a need. But release can be produced even better by destroying, or rather paralyzing normal restrictions. No complexity or precision is necessary to bring about the destruction of a tissue or of a certain component in it.

Such paralysis may either remove restrictions so that more release is obtained or it may eliminate the pressure of normal needs so that the existing releases can be enjoyed as a surplus. In the first case there is energization, in the second tranquilization. But the final goal is the same — more surplus release or what may be generally called "stimulation." Naturally, the return to normalcy involves opposite reactions, which show as the "disease," in both cases.

The argument that drugs can supply the stimulation which the body cannot produce itself is hardly tenable. First, there is the complexity that we just mentioned, which applies to the interaction of hormones with the organism, as well as with other hormones. Just to mention the most used cortical products, close to thirty hormones have been discovered as produced by the adrenal cortex alone, their exact interaction not being known.

Second, the hormones that the body needs and that could be supplied by organic compounds like cortisone or other sterols are used by the body in preposterously small amounts. The secretions of the pituitary gland, which seems to regulate other glands, can evoke physiological responses even if diluted to one part in hundred million. Adrenalin can act in a dilution of one part in 300 million. Thyroxin is used by the body in so minute amounts that only 3½ grains of it are produced annually. One-twentieth of a gram of hypertensin is sufficient to cause hypertension in 166,000 persons. The esterone produced by a woman in two hundred days weighs less than a postage stamp. Further, hormones are by far the simplest products of the body; many of them can now be produced or at least substituted synthetically. All this means that if the body really needed one hormone or another, it could produce it in more than the necessary amount. It also means that hormones, like nerves, play only the role of signaling devices; they sometimes have been called the "liquid nerves." Considering the enormous complexity of tissues, and of other hormones involved, it is sheer folly to try to interfere with the body's signaling system.

Another argument is that relief from pain removes the restlessness which may interfere with recovery. Actually, when the body or some part of it really needs rest, as in the case of injury, it will rest, or resist movement with acute pain or an incapacity far greater than necessary for actual safety; the organism always keeps large safety margins and reserves. But if there are restlessness, pain and stress, it means that the body needs them — that every function in it is being testesd and mobilized, in order to find a new organically integrated readjustment.

It is true that the body can function even while conscious feelings are shut out. But there are dangers in excluding consciousness from participation in important reactions. The nervous system is the organ of all learning and integrated adjustment for the whole body, and all its functions converge in consciousness as its highest control center. Man learns by conscious, though often unanalyzable feelings more than by factual realizations. This learning determines the over-all attitudes upon which everything else depends. If this central learning and coordinated integration are excluded, tendencies of release and disorganization may establish themselves unchecked. In this connection can be mentioned the Russian definition of malignant growth as a general illness depending upon the central nervous system.

However, in modern medicine it is simply unthinkable that a doctor would neglect any means which might help the patient avoid pain and stress. Actually, the relief by drugs is comparable to the relief that one obtains by getting drunk when a difficult performance lies ahead. If it were understood that there is never more pain or stress than satisfaction or relief, whatever man does, it might help. At present, when there are occasional reports about the beneficial influence of pain or stress, they seem improper in the medical profession, and pointless for practice. Dr. Wade O. Brinker reported that sick cats recovered better when kept in a stressful state — under threat by dogs. "Scaring" patients as a means of making them recover quicker was reported from Firland Sanatorium. But what doctor would wish to scare his patient or make him feel worse? The experimental logic of immediate relief or "improvement" is never doubted.

Naturally, "cures" by drugs only deepen most ills; and "side effects" have become the great problem of modern medicine. Miracle drugs for almost every functional disease have been discovered. Only the "side effects" have remained, and the drug industry is now concentrating on them. Though "side effects" always come back in one form or another, the modern doctor simply finds new separate "causes" to explain them. As we have repeatedly explained, the experimental approach never reveals the real organic cause, which lies one phase beyond observation. It reveals only the immediate causes, which are actually effects of an exactly opposite background cause. There many such immediate "causes" that the doctor can blame for the "side effects" — exhaustion of the organ, lack of response by a mechanism, ineffective dosage of the drug or some other concurrent effect.

At this point we may mention an attempt to introduce a new concept of disease in general, namely, the one that has emerged from the theory of Dr. Hans Selye. Modern medicine needs desperately a new general theory of disease, that would explain existing contradictions. Selye's theory has been hailed as a landmark in the theory of medicine. It has been accepted in explanation of blood pressure, asthma and peptic ulcer. Actually, his theory does recognize relative, or what we have called the vicious-circle, effects. But it misinterprets the causes. In his book, *The Stress of Life*, Selye tells of his experiments in which he fed corticoids to chicks and after ten days observed the curious effects. The chicks developed a kind of dropsy, with symptoms of Bright's disease. This he found surprising because logically such a diet should have produced just the opposite effects. He concluded that the body can have inconsistent reactions — too strong as well as too weak — under stressful conditions. Selye's theory implies that under stress even a wholly natural function may turn against the rest of the body, and the body may be poisoned by its own secretions. As we see, a conclusion is drawn that contradicts everything known about the truly miraculous purposefulness of the organism, because the paradoxical logic of overstimulation is not understood.

Among the numerous means of treatment there are, of course, some that give relief by remedying the ill itself rather than by removing the reactions. Such means of treatment are of no interest for our discussion here. But the problem arises how the physician can know whether the good reaction produced by his treatment is due to a real cure or merely to overadjustment — "improvement" that deepens the ill. Actually, this should be one of the main problems of medicine. And it is not unsolvable. Even the common man recognizes symptoms of overadjustment. By merely looking at the face of a person he can tell whether that person is living "fast" and above his normal level, which means overadjustment in general. Modern medicine can have means a thousand times more precise for eliciting such knowledge, once its importance is recognized.

We showed that overadjustment is the source of most of the

ills, apart from infectious diseases, that afflict man. Nature has given to the organism of animal or man all the reactions necessary to meet any emergency. The only exceptions may be some extraordinarily unfavorable and injurious influences — which modern man has long been able to keep off; or some microbes against which the race has not yet evolved defenses — which man now can meet by way of inoculations. As we said, if animals, which do not know how to overadjust, were cared for and protected against infectious diseases as man is, they would never be ill. Overadjustment should be the first thing for medicine to fight against. For there is no greater danger for man, advancing in power and skill, than his relentless striving to remove the negative or restrictive side of adjustment, which actually is more important for maintaining normalcy than the positive side, which comes of itself most easily. Instead, modern medicine fosters overadjustment with its endeavor to eliminate pain and stress and to improve feelings or reactions by all means.

The sick person more than anybody else should avoid means which make him *feel* better, or "improve" his well-being. An older person should avoid anything that makes him react younger than his natural state permits. Even a "normal" reaction induced in a person who is not in a normal condition means deepening such a condition into a real disease. We saw how in psychology excessive avoidance of unpleasantness or striving for better feeling leads to neuroses or psychoses. The same applies to man's physiological adjustment.

In fact, the problem here is more serious than in psychology. First, man is less capable of recognizing physiological overadjustment. In psychology, where the overadjustment is accessible at every moment, man learns intuitively and by cultural tradition to avoid overadjustment or living beyond reality. In physiology overadjustment is not easily recognized because only recently, with the availability of extraordinary artificial means, has it become possible to attain physiological overadjustment easily. Otherwise nature has strong protections against it. Further, overadjustment in physiology is more dangerous than in psychology. In the case of psychological overadjustment the physiological standards beneath remain intact and can curb the adjustment back to normalcy. But during long physiological overadjustment the very standards of normalcy may become effaced and nothing but the tendency of unlimited primitive growth may remain.

By the way, the increasing popularity of psychosomatic medicine and the numerous undeniable proofs it has brought forth confirm that overadjustment is the cause of the functional diseases we are discussing. This medicine has proved that all these diseases have emotional negativism or impoverishment as their deeper cause. Of course, the ways this negativism arises are the paradoxical ways in which overadjustment works. And they are exactly opposite to the logic under which psychosomatic medicine proceeds, the logic under which all modern human "sciences" proceed. But psychosomatics deals with organically more immediate and decisive factors. Consequently, psychosomatic medicine can only lead to more dangerous practical fallacies and an increase in the existing theoretical confusion.

Now we may consider individual functional diseases. But, first, we wish to make it clear that we do not intend to criticize the technical knowledge of the specialists in the field, or to add to such knowledge. We are concerned only with the simple causal principle of functional diseases, and its seemingly paradoxical logic. We derive our insight from the causal understanding of adjustment in general, psychological as well as physiological. As far as technical or professional aspects are concerned, our discussion is purely illustrative and has no value. But without understanding of the *causal*, seemingly paradoxical logic of disease and cure, technical skills can do as much harm as good. Further, it is the truly puzzling lack of understanding of the natural, therefore *simple, cause* of functional diseases, especially of cancer, that has kept medicine from making a breakthrough in their cure, as every doctor knows.

That a common, natural, therefore simple, principle governs the functional disorders is evident from the fact that they can all be "cured" by added stimulation, and that often the same simple stimulating drug can "cure" most of them. From what we have said already and from what we shall see as we go along, it is clear that the common cause of functional diseases is overadjustment which leads to all kinds of functional "negativism," not unlike psychotic negativism. The disability or exhaustion of a function shows in functional diseases exactly along the same lines as those from which the overadjustment was derived; and its development is characterized by the paradox of worsening through improvement, or the vicious-circle effect of all overadjustment. The causal similarity between neuroses or psychoses and the functional diseases is apparent. In both cases the symptoms may be a hundred, but the underlying cause is one.

HEART DISEASE

More people now die of heart disease than of any other disease. Considering that all releases and the feeling of well-being ultimately depend on the increased activity of the heart, it is not surprising that man drives his heart into an overadjustment with all its consequences. One should think here of man's resourcefulness and skill in improving his feeling of well-being, and the wide range of means that he uses to do so. The animal lacks these skills — and does not die of acute heart disease.

Though the connection between enjoyments or fast living and heart disorders is evident to everybody, when it comes to more involved reactions the common man as well as the doctor loses this insight. It is clear that the seemingly diseased feeling that slows down reactions is what can conserve the heart, whereas inducement of a feeling of well-being and vigor under conditions of overadjustment amounts to slow suicide. But what doctor would advise that feeling sick is good, and what man would resist the reassuring feeling of well-being? No wonder modern doctors are starting to see even alcohol as beneficial to the heart. Dr. John S. Davis found that alcohol can have good effect in cardiovascular cases as well as in gastroenterology, arthritis, even cirrhosis. In the "Symposium on Drinking" held at the University of California School of Medicine physiologists as well as psychiatrists extolled the beneficial effects of alcohol — and could amply prove them by experimental observation. It has to be kept in mind that a relaxant or tranquilizer does not induce a slowing down of body functions. If it did, it would be unpleasant. It only suppresses physiological needs, which later have to be met by increased effort; or be left unattended, which means deepening the abnormalcy.

An interesting controversy has arisen in regard to stress and work in their influence on the heart. Doctors have always accepted the seemingly logical view that burdens which clearly make a person feel a strain on the heart are damaging to it. Stair-climbing or running are typical examples. But now the greatest authorities, including Dr. White, are demonstrating that just the reverse is true. As researches are extended and cover longer periods of life, they start showing that work and stress are beneficial to the heart. As Lawrence Galton has pointed out, nowhere has there been a more marked reversal of opinion. Research by Becker, Kaufman and Vasey have shown that the normal pressures of work and competition are better in the long run than idleness. Equally, Dr. L. J. Goldwater has exposed idleness as a source of harm for cardiacs. Similar opinions have been expressed by Drs. E. Siminson, F. J. Stare, J. W. Walker and L. E. Hinkle.

The most extensive research here has probably been the one conducted by the British Medical Research Council in 1958. It showed that workers who seem to strain their hearts daily, who eat foods that offer no relieving stimulation, and have most worries in their lives are least affected by heart diseases. A comparative study by Dr. Groom on the primitive working and eating habits of Haitian Negroes and those of the comparatively better-off South Carolina Negroes led to similar conclusions. Apparently the things that seem to improve the activity of our heart are damaging it, but those that seem to burden it are conserving it. As Dr. Raab states with wonderment, it is not physical stress or hardships but relaxation or lack of exertion that strains the heart.

The greatest damage to the heart is done by overriding the natural feelings of uneasiness, pain and stress that press us to slow down. These are, certainly, unpleasant and give the feeling of disease. If a person artificially silences them for some time, by the use of energizers, relaxants, or hundreds of other means made available to modern man, he is bound to meet with strong accumulated pain in the end. Then modern medicine may give him stronger means to combat this reaction. The happiness pills, improved nitrites or other drugs may do the job. As Dr. Arthur M. Master has shown in regard to iproniazid — among its other miraculous improvements it relieves angina pectoris — the side effects appear and may lead to various disturbances, including coronary thrombosis. Of course, doctors consider the side effects only as unfortunate imperfections in the drug. Stronger or more subtle drugs, offering further "improvements," are seen as the solution.

HYPERTENSION

As in most cases of functional diseases, modern medicine does not know what causes hypertension. Dr. Irvine H. Page, the foremost authority on hypertension, says that the present trial-and-error method will be replaced by a causal understanding by 1967. Actually, there is no one cause like a mechanism to be discovered. Hypertension causally means a complex of opposite reactions to the easy, free and rich blood flow that we enjoy as the main source of higher vitality.

By striving for this enjoyment — by simply doing in a hundred ways what we find enjoyable — we overstimulate and exhaust the innumerable tissues and organs involved. When these tend to return to normalcy and slow down in their functioning or growth, all the opposite reactions result. There is a lack of vigor and a decrease of efficiency in circulation. These would slow the person down, if he did not find other means to overcome these incapacitating or diseased reactions. Thus a person continues at the previous rate of living but with an impaired circulatory system. Naturally, a higher pressure becomes necessary to carry out the normal body functions. One has always to keep in mind man's tendency toward relaxation and tranquilization, under which the organic needs are suppressed and releases used as surpluses. Since the needs have to be attended to sooner or later, that means later additional effort.

As can be expected, hypertension can be relieved by artificially increased stimulation and tranquilization. Further stimulation makes the circulatory mechanisms work with improved efficiency, and therefore with less pressure; naturally, the opposite reactions are only deepened. Tranquilizers delay the pressure of needs, and are responsible for various concurrent effects characterized by insufficient or distorted functioning of the basic mechanisms, mostly those serving the cleansing and nourishing functions. Probably for no other disease have there been discovered so many drugs that have been miraculously able to relieve it. The most often mentioned ones are: reserpine, protoveratrines, phenobarbital, hexamethonium, hydralazine, catron, ecolid, inversine and chlorothiazide, as well as the simpler potassium and thiocyanite compounds. Though these drugs have been miraculously effective, doctors know that we are as far as ever from having a drug against hypertension. The "side effects" have stubbornly persisted and reversed the "cures." Still doctors continue believing that a drug *could* be found which would relieve hypertension without "side effects." The modern doctor does not hesitate to advise other means that give immediate relief. Surgery of a kidney or of adrenals may have this effect. To be sure, kidneys and adrenals give the most trouble because they are most closely connected with the cleansing function.

The way to get permanent relief is adjustment at a lower normalcy. That is what the body is trying to do by its unpleasant and sickly reactions. These should be increased if anything. But the doctor proceeds in his experimentally logical way and tries to remove the unpleasant reactions by means that make patient feel better. Even such an authority as Dr. Page finds that coffee, tobacco and alcohol do no harm, but make the patient feel better. Actually, such means are the cause of hypertension, as the intuition of the common man rightly tells him.

The paradoxical logic characteristic of overadjustment is further evidenced by the fact that a real physiological emergency alleviates hypertension. Here we have a parallel to the relief produced by a real trouble or shock in psychotic disorders. As more imperative threats emerge, the overadjustment in regard to the functions overenjoyed all the time is interrupted. Doctors have used pyrogens to induce artificial fevers, which alleviate hypertension. A major surgery may have the same effect. This may explain why the removal of a kidney or adrenal operation may give a relief, at least for a while. Further, unpleasant treatments, like distasteful or restricted diets — sodium-free diet or even plain starvation — relieve hypertension. They are unpleasant because they are restrictive. Their effect is comparable to an emergency that interrupts the overenjoyments which the person has been cultivating.

ARTERIOSCLEROSIS

Medicine has as little causal explanation for the hardening and thickening of the arteries as it has for hypertension, with which they go together. Here again the causes may be a hundred. But unified causal insight sufficient to understand, predict and control the disease may be gained in terms of the opposite reactions of overadjustment. Because suppleness and vigor of the arteries gives man the enjoyment of vitality, he overadjusts exactly in these respects, by simply following what he finds more enjoyable. Then the opposite organic reactions with exactly the opposite effects of hardening and thickening of the arteries inevitably follow.

Everything in an organism is effected through growth. If there have been excesses in rate of growth, a slowdown has to follow and with it opposite effects. The tissues of the artery that have stopped growing lose their protoplasmic contents and become filled with less specialized metaplasmic material, as in all cases of exhaustion or aging of tissues. In this light one can understand the presence of the much discussed cholesterol in the walls of sclerotic arteries. Cholesterol has been blamed as the cause of arteriosclerosis. Actually, it may be there either as a brake or as the best arrangement that the body can make under the circumstances. This explains why the body itself may produce up to 90 percent of the cholesterol, while only the rest may come directly from diet. Apparently it is needed in the organic balance.

This is further confirmed by the fact that administration of cholesterol-like substances depresses the cholesterol level. Such experiments, though with a different interpretation, have been made by F. J. Stare and D. Steinberg. Apparently the body is quite capable of giving up the production of cholesterol and does so when a substitute, or what is accepted as a substitute, is provided. The same result would be obtained by administering real cholesterol: the body would decrease its own cholesterol production in conservation of the balance it is maintaining. That cholesterol may have the effect of "disease" is understandable under the paradoxical logic of overadjustment. The paradox explains the confusion. As Dr. A. M. Master has stated, the best doctors and scientists "have diametrically opposed views" on the matter of cholesterol.

Paradoxical logic as well as the other overadjustment characteristics here are illustrated by other observations. Experimenters have demonstrated spectacularly how an unpleasant emotion like depression, rage or anxiety increases the cholesterol level, while pleasant emotions decrease it. We can mention here the experiments of Dr. Stewart Wolf and his colleagues at the Oklahoma Medical Research Foundation. In psychotic complexes as well, an unpleasant emotion increases the symptoms distinctly, though the real cause of the complex is overenjoyment of pleasant emotions. We do not need to repeat here the explanation of this paradoxical logic.

Even if we assume that cholesterol only clogs up the tissues, as all body fats do, it still can perform a regulatory function, as the fats do. The fats in the body keep a person from overeating. If there were no hindrances from overclogging by fat, the person would increase his food intake and rate of metabolism unlimitedly, in complete disruption of normalcy. The natural obstacles that arouse unwanted feelings, or the "disease," force the body to maintain its normalcy. Such an obstacle is fats in body and in food. Pure fats and starches are the least stimulating foods. That is why they are least tasty and are never overeaten, especially if the body has too much of them stored up already. A person overeats the tasty and invigorating foods rich in proteins and highly saturated fats. The immediate effect of such foods is vigor and reduction in weight. But they mean overstimulation which inevitably leads to understimulation. Then overweight follows as

391

a person tries to derive enough stimulation from still more food. In brief, all the paradoxical and vicious-circle effects of over-adjustment follow. The paradox is best confirmed by the results of the Rockefeller Diet and by the fact that diets rich in plain tasteless, unsaturated fats keep the weight down. Any treatment with diets, drugs or other means that immediately decreases fats and cholesterol increases them in the long run. Modern life with its increased stimulations is the best example of this.

The existence of this paradox explains why there is such a confusion and controversy over the question of diet; this came to light curiously during the discussion of the best-seller, *Calories Don't Count*, by Taller. As the deeper cause is not understood, the fats in the diet are blamed for everything. The undue emphasis on diet in cardiovascular disorders has been pointed out by Dr. Stare, Dr. Master and others. But the de-emphasis on strict dieting often aims at making patients resume more "normal," pleasanter and more stimulating diets — which are exactly the cause of the trouble.

The existing views on diet are best represented by those of the great authority on dietary questions, Dr. Ancel Keys, the author of *Eat Well and Stay Well*. He upholds the general, seemingly logical belief that enjoying rich invigorating foods is the right thing to do, and that fats in the diet are the cause of our increasing troubles with fats in the body. But as Dr. Page explains, people in this country do not eat more fats now than they did forty years ago. A study by Dr. Reuben Straus shows that the Indians suffer less from cardiovascular disorders though they eat more fatty foods. This must apply in even a higher degree to Eskimos. Modern dieticians would have been horrified by the protein-poor diets that the people of Europe got during the war. But these people suffered from cardiovascular diseases less than at any other time, as several studies show. We can refer here to that of Dr. Herwig Hamperl.

We admit that a forcibly rich protein diet can also reduce overweight and cholesterol. The experiments of Dr. Alverly M. Nelson have shown this unmistakably. The explanation is that any expressly strict diet prevents overenjoyment and overadjustment. If there is a question of how a person could have over-adjusted without embarking on grand living, we have to remember that the means of overadjustment evolved by man are innumerable. Even salt is an unnatural stimulant; a linkage between salt and hypertension has been established in a study by Drs. L. K. Dahl and R. A. Love.

DIABETES

In the case of diabetes the characteristics of overadjustment are equally apparent. In terms of relative causation diabetes is due to man's exaggerated endeavor to increase his rate of metabolism — to stimulate the burning of food in the body. Over-stimulation leads to the opposite effects and the body's inability to burn those foods which offer less stimulation, namely, sugars and starches.

Of course, the capacity of the body to respond to stimulation is here, as in other cases, different for different people due to genetic differences. But this capacity may be lost or dulled by previous overstimulation. That is why diabetic disturbances increase with age. Even overstimulation in the previous generation counts. Dr. Daniel Brunner made a comparative study on Jews from Yemen who came recently to Israel. These Jews had a remarkably lower incidence of diabetes, as well as arteriosclerosis, due to their frugal diet. This low incidence extended to individuals in the second generation though these had changed their eating habits. The diet of the Yemen Jews was low in proteins and high in carbohydrates. Brunner concludes that these people are protected just because they do not follow the whims of medical fashion emphasizing high-protein diets and cutting down on starches. Brunner's conclusions — though contrary to the prevailing beliefs of modern medicine — are confirmed by general long-term observations.

People who live on a poor diet, which always means a preponderance of starches, suffer from diabetes less. Statistics from the two world wars show this conclusively. It can be said that the diabetes problem increases as foods become richer in proteins and stimulation, though precisely such foods have been proved to improve the state of diabetics. On the same grounds we can understand why the number of diabetics increases as more "effective" means of dealing with it are popularized.

One has only to start curing a mild stimulation deficiency, which can always be present under conditions of overstimulation, and the treatment will make the person dependent on increased stimulation to such an extent that he may become a regular patient. This can be easily observed in all cases of addiction to stimulation; of course, greater stimulation can be induced by many means, including a more "normal" diet. No wonder the Diabetes Association is discovering that another million Americans are suffering from diabetes "without knowing it." The increase in the number of such patients — who organically do not have the disease — explains why statistics may show a greater number of cases satisfactorily treated. Also, the death rate figured out in percentages from the increased number of such patients, naturally, goes down. Further, the "cure" of a diabetic disorder may deepen it into another, more basic disease, thus taking it out of the diabetes column.

Here we have to mention a general characteristic in the interpretation of the successes of certain "cures." Statistics may show lower death rates from a disease for which a "cure" has been found. But, in fact, the disease may be turned into a graver, deeper disorder which increases other columns in the statistics, especially those of heart disease and cancer.

In some cases the administration of insulin is necessary because the body may be unable to produce it in sufficient amounts, due to an innate deficiency. But even here, it has to be understood that such administration is inherently debilitating. The organism gives up its effort and the last chance to produce its own insulin. Moreover, the intricate balance of the body is never safe under the artificial interference with its reactions, especially as the person tends to increase the dosage of insulin to derive more stimulation. Dr. Harold Rifkin has pointed out that insulin therapy has raised "serious problems" and that its "overuse" impairs instead of improving the utilization of sugars.

394

That insulin acts rather as a stimulating or signaling device is confirmed by the fact that other, chemically unrelated compounds, like sulfa drugs, can substitute for it, as has been shown by Dr. J. A. Mirsky and Dr. H. Pollack. Even the common aspirin helps lower the blood sugar of diabetics, as Dr. Chauncey Leake has demonstrated. In most cases diabetics have their insulin-producing cells functioning. Dr. Henry Dolger has found this fact important. He explains that there will soon be some four million diabetics in this country, and argues that they could be treated by administration of orinasse which stimulates the insulin-producing cells, that are still there. Apparently, it all rests on stimulation of one kind or another. Considering how preposterously small amounts of relatively simple compounds the body uses for stimulation, it could itself produce all the stimulation it needs. If it does not do so, the reason may be that its over-all balance does not permit more intense metabolism. If we left the body alone, as the animal does, we would not have diabetes.

But modern man has many means of producing more "normal" reactions, especially when the body starts slowing down with age. Overadjustment with all it effects follows, as any overstimulation leads to understimulation. For instance, the stimulating effect of iron in medicinal preparations is well known and has been a fad in modern medicine. But a team of doctors at the University of Chicago, experimenting with hamsters, found that increased administration of iron may cause diabetes, as well as cirrhosis of the liver. Still, modern physicians, committed to their "scientism," cannot stop noticing the beneficial effects of stimulants. For instance, Dr. I. Phillips Frohman found that tea is a good all-round medicine.

ARTHRITIS

An overadjustment that continues without change may accumulate without the person noticing anything extraordinary. Stimulations that make the person enjoy vigor, suppleness and ease of physical movement may be accumulated all through his life. The corresponding physiological processes that make it all possible are evoked automatically as a person simply learns to concentrate on foods or other means that give him feeling of greater ease. When the opposite reactions follow, they are equally automatically accompanied by the exact opposite physiological processes. Nobody knows exactly how he evokes his physiological processes. But if there was overstimulation and exhaustion in them, the opposite processes follow equally without his knowledge.

It would be the role of the physician to discover the source of overadjustment in each case. It may be different for different individuals. Previous backgrounds and past overstimulation, even from the previous generation, may determine the predisposition toward overadjustment. The person himself may be unaware of it. Somebody used to abnormally spicy foods would notice abnormal reactions only when he was forced to eat normal food. Of course, the modern doctor, proceeding under experimental logic, would see the stimulation — the real cause of the disturbance — rather as a means of relief. Man suffers from arthritis, as he does from other functional disorders, because of his resourcefulness in obtaining increase in releases. An animal lacks this resourcefulness and is free of the disease, though organically an animal is capable of having arthritis, as has been shown in an experiment by Dr. G. M. Neher.

The nature of overadjustment in arthritis is evidenced by its miraculous "cures" under strong stimulation. When the use of ACTH and cortisone was introduced, patients miraculously improved within forty-eight hours. Even some of those who had been bed-ridden got up and walked with ease. But within two weeks there was complete relapse, and the dosage had to be increased to prevent the patients from becoming worse. There are a dozen other drugs, mostly stimulants and pain killers, that can "cure" arthritis. They range from aspirin and vitamin D to prednisone and dexamethasone, which is supposedly forty times stronger than cortisone. But they all have inevitable "side" effects. The end result is that arthritis is increasing along with improvements in treatment and living conditions. Supposedly thirty million people suffer from it in this country.

Just as with other overadjustment disorders, when a real

emergency arises in the organism, there is a relief from arthritis. A fever or a good bout of jaundice, as well as pregnancy in women, may bring recovery. For the same reason unpleasant therapies such as the injection of gold salts, streptococcus, vaccine, even milk or sea water are helpful. Gold salt therapy may help in two out of three cases, though nobody knows why it works. Characteristically enough, it provokes rather unpleasant reactions at the beginning. These therapies now rank above hormone therapy, according to a survey by William Kitay, who states that there has been a widespread disappointment with hormone therapy, though experimentally it is the most successful.

Interesting is a discovery made by Dr. Philip S. Hench. Physicians have been linking arthritis with a lack of cortisone or hydrocortisone, but the fact is that the cortisone level can be anywhere from below to above normal in the blood of arthritics. Ingenious theories have been advanced to explain the contradiction. Dr. Hench's discovery resulted from the observation of the treatment of rheumatic diseases with ACTH and cortisone-type drugs at the Mayo Clinic. He found that it was not the actual level of hydrocortisone that evoked the disease, but the change or transition from high to low levels. This seemed to be a strange new theory — so unorthodox that Dr. Hench did not expect other doctors to accept it. Actually, in every overadjustment all the symptoms of understimulation are present though the level of stimulation is much higher than normal. It is the transition or return from a higher to a lower level of stimulation that evokes the negative reaction in every overadjustment.

GASTRIC DISORDERS

It is almost a truism to say that stomach troubles increase as more attention is paid to them. This applies to the simplest indigestion as well as the most complex form of overadjustment — stomach ulcers. A study by Dr. Burrill B. Crohn shows that the people of Himalaya and India have the lowest incidence of stomach ulcers, but doctors the highest. Apparently, the more exquisite the care, the greater the trouble.

To illustrate the existing theory, we may mention a fairly representative example. Dr. Boris Sokoloff states with emphasis in his book, *Civilized Diseases*, that the acidity of the stomach is the best protection of good health and high vitality. With reference to previous researchers he shows that athletic, vigorous and healthy persons have the highest stomach acidity. He holds that every effort should be made to preserve the high level of stomach acidity, especially after the age of fifty when it starts to lower. We may agree that gastric acidity goes along with vigor. But a person may have to adjust on a lower level of vitality because of previous exhaustion, general state of health or age. If such a person tries to keep up his stomach acidity as a source of further vitality, he is bound to run into all the troubles of overadjustment of which the stomach ulcer is the surest symptom. Incidentally, Dr. Sokoloff notices himself that the "human organism works in a paradoxical manner," when he discusses the results of some previous researches showing that the administration of alkaline preparations raises instead of lowers gastric acidity. The body tends to preserve its coordinated normalcy and responds with opposite reactions to any change or "improvement" in it.

Stomach ulcers are a typical expression of the conflict between such "improvements" and the body's endeavor to regain its normalcy. By the way, the overstimulation of the stomach may have purely psychological causes; the response of the stomach to psychological excitement has been a subject of many interesting experiments. In any event, the conflict between the two tendencies explains the curious symptoms of stomach ulcers. Each increase in stimulation overcomes the resistance of the body and thus makes the conflict ineffective. Consequently the condition seems to improve. But as the stimulation wears off the conflict re-emerges. Finally, when the opposite understimulation sets in completely, the conflict again disappears.

This explains the typical recurrence of ulcer symptoms at various periods of day or night, year or occupational intensity. For instance, it is generally known that symptoms are strongest in March or April and September or October — just the intermediary periods between the most and least stimulative seasons.

The body's resistance to overadjustment in the case of peptic ulcers also explains why cancer does not occur as long as there are ulcers. For the same reason a person with an unopposed tendency toward overadjustment, such as a diabetic or an obese person, does not suffer from ulcers.

Naturally, without understanding the reversed logic of over-adjustment here doctors can only deepen the conflict — which they especially achieve in their own cases. By following the experimental logic of immediate improvement a doctor may favor such means as coffee, alcohol or a rich diet, which are intuitively suspected by the common man. Increasing "scientism" explains why doctors are becoming inclined toward greater permissiveness in this respect, as Dr. Richard Doll observes. Dr. Max A. Schneider could show in an experiment that adding spice to diet had no harmful effects. Remedies and drugs vary. They may produce immediate, often miraculous, relief, but the end result is very different.

Of course, the psychological experiences that may lie at the bottom of the conflict here are equally paradoxical. The Indian peasant seems to have less tensions because his life is one big tension. He cannot afford to indulge in excesses of release by the use of special means, as physicians or executives can. Therefore he suffers no excessive reverse reactions. His adjustment is more monotonous and no strong opposite reactions that would lead to conflict have a chance to accumulate.

We cannot go into a discussion of other functional gastric disorders. Various kinds of "improvements," sought as a means of increased release or feeling of well-being, are to blame for their increase. People who cannot afford to pay much attention to their digestive function do not suffer from peptic disturbances. As a typical example of what happens we can mention the use of laxatives. They undoubtedly give effective relief, but the end result is more trouble. Doctors have often condemned the use of laxatives, for here the cause-and-effect relationship is too evident to be missed. In a recent publication Dr. Charles W. Hock said that the public should be advised to leave their digestive and elimination system alone. Supposedly there are 100 million persons in this country using laxatives. Probably a greater number is using pills, or seeking prescriptions, for other digestive disturbances, arising from similar overadjustments.

CANCER

In no other disease is the nature of overadjustment so pronounced as in cancer. It almost could be called a physiological "psychosis" with its self-perpetuating, vicious-circle effect, except that in the case of cancer the limiting controls or standards may have been finally effaced at the deepest levels *irrevocably*. The paradoxical logic of overadjustment has prevented modern medicine from getting closer to understanding the cause of cancer. It has been often stated that the cure of cancer would become feasible if its cause were understood. Since there seems to be a single basic natural cause or principle of malignancy, it can only be simple. But in spite of the unique efforts in its study, it has remained a mystery. Apparently, it obeys a logic that is completely out of the question in modern medicine.

A typical evidence of overadjustment in cancer is the fact that the same substances that cause cancer have alleviating effect on it. Such substances are: the steroids, which include sex hormones, adrenal hormones, "wonder" hormones, or even vitamin D; carcinogenic tars and carbon compounds; enzymes; mineral-enriched preparations of potassium, sodium, magnesium, copper or cobalt; and the controversial folic acid. Also, X-rays, radium and ultraviolet rays have this ambivalent property. This curious fact that carcinogenic agents may arrest existing tumors has been insightfully described by Alexander Haddow. Such carcinogenic substances as estrogen, when they are used to induce tumors, are administered "long enough to permit reversion" of their effects. In an interesting experiment on human patients who were beyond hope of recovery, Dr. Charles Huggins used 3-methylcholanthrene and obtained temporary improvement. But this drug is the one used to induce cancer in mice. In explaining the treatment Dr. Huggins observes that almost every chemical used to alleviate cancer will itself cause the disease.

Modern medicine has no explanation for this paradox. It would seem that there is just a narrow difference — a very delicate balance, as Dr. James Ewing has termed it — between the normal and malignant growth. In fact, there is the difference of day and night between normal positivism and the self-perpetuating negativism that leads to malignancy. Under overadjustment the same factor that induces positive effects is bound to end with negative ones (the concept of exhaustion may help to visualize what happens).

Another fact points to overadjustment as the cause of cancer. Malignant growths originate mainly in the organs and tissues that serve more directly the releases or enjoyment. The strong hormonal involvement points to this. Hormone overproduction in the case of cancer has been evidenced by several studies. We can mention that of Dr. Sheldon C. Sommers, in which he proved a strong overgrowth of the adrenal glands and insulin-producing cells as well as an increase in the pituitary cells, in lung cancer cases. In experiments by Loeb and others, mice which usually developed breast cancers remained cancer-free when their ovaries were removed early. Similar effects are observed in the case of castration or removal of the prostate gland. By the method of castration Dr. Huggins obtained 22 percent cures even in advanced cases.

The criterion of enjoyment can help to eliminate wrong leads. In the controversial question of smoking, persistent efforts are made to discover and remove the carcinogenic agents, as if this could be done without removing the nicotine itself. Nicotine provides enjoyment through artificially increased releases, and thus becomes a typical means of overadjustment. Without such enjoyment nothing would happen. Mice induced to inhale tobacco smoke, in an experiment at the Roswell Park Memorial Institute, did not develop cancer. Smoke forced on an organism without enjoyment is coped with like any other intrusion. If something in the smoke as such, affecting the lungs, were the cause of cancer, how could the fact be explained that cigar smokers or women smokers, who usually do not inhale, develop cancer of the mouth? According to a report by Dr. Walter Dalitsch, mouth cancer, traceable to smoking, is increasing among women.

As with tobacco smoke, a food that gives high enjoyment, which means increase in metabolism, to man may be assimilated by a smaller, experiment animal with difficulty and have a completely different metabolism value. Thus conclusions from experiments about the influence of any food in itself on malignant growth may be misleading. The only correct criterion would be the enjoyment value of the food in each case. The enjoyment criterion may help, similarly, in other interpretations. For instance, sunshine is enjoyed because of its growth-stimulating influence. That is why it becomes a fad with modern man, ready to enjoy and "improve" his well-being, in rejection of old prejudices. The link between sun and cancer as well as aging of the skin has been conclusively shown in studies by Drs. J. M. Knox, J. B. Howell and A. C. Griffin. In an experiment by the Committee on Cosmetics of the A.M.A. repeated exposures to tanning rays produced cancer in 100 percent of the experimental animals. On the other hand, if the sun is not enjoyed but rejected, as in the case of the protectively pigmented skins of dark-skinned peoples *suffering* from sun, the cancer incidence is lower in spite of greater exposure.

But how to explain the fact that cancer often can be linked with an injury, irritation or disease? Incidentally, the belief that cancer may be caused by a single trauma is not founded, according to a study by Dr. Lionel S. Auster. We have to keep in mind that overenjoyment is relative, and is possible under any circumstance. There may be overstimulation even while it may seem that the person derives no enjoyment. For instance, eating poor food but trying to compensate for its lack of taste by the addition of stimulants means overadjustment. This may explain some puzzling incidences of stomach cancers among people of the poorest groups. Also, when there has been previous overstimulation (even in the previous generation) and therefore subsequent exhaustion, but the person succeeds in maintaining "normal" reactions by means of some specific stimulation, there is still overadjustment.

In every case where there is pain or disturbance, under which the organism should normally suffer but by some subtle arrangement avoids suffering, there is overenjoyment or avoidance of normal controls. Here modern drug medication and other "improve-

402

ments" may be the most important factor. Also, such arrangements may be facilitated by the capacity of some intruding agent or parasite in the body to induce insensitivity in surrounding tissue. The connection between some parasites and cancer has been brought out by some authors. In whatever way an avoidance is induced, it tends to perpetuate itself as every tissue lives with the same primordial tendency to avoid pain. Furthermore, an injury may merely *precipitate the appearance* of cancer, while the real disease, the overadjustment, might have been going on for a long time. We saw how in neuroses a difficulty precipitates the "disease" whereas previous overenjoyment is the real cause.

Here we come to another overadjustment characteristic in cancer. In every overadjustment the "disease" is either an endeavor by the organism to return to lesser, normal releases, or the incapacity finally of the organism to obtain any release, upon the exhaustion of the function. The actual disease, the overadjustment, goes on long before the "disease" appears. To mention the clearest, generally known instance, an organism exposed to carcinogenic substances or radiation develops cancer a long time after the exposure; the overadjustment may be purely physiological here.

In all diseases caused by overadjustment the person feels best while the real harm is being done, and starts feeling sick when the utter limit of overadjustment is reached. At that moment there may be an important difference between cancer and the other diseases arising from overadjustment. Other such diseases may bring about recovery if they are left alone, since the pressure by the deeper standards toward the return to normalcy may constitute the entire disease. But in the case of malignant growth the very standard itself — the fundamental, limiting differentiation of cells — may have been finally effaced.

Of course, the overenjoyment in many cases may be purely physiological, without clear conscious experience accompanying it. Particularly here science should help man — by revealing dangers that he cannot discern. But to do so the seemingly paradoxical logic of overadjustment must be understood. Further, it should be kept in mind that overadjustment really does not provide more enjoyment except at the initial stage. No continuous release without concurrent restriction is possible. Overadjustment, with its vicious-circle effect, means merely living around the last limit of the narrow margin of release potential and trying to overcome the limiting restrictions. The tendency toward overenjoyment, on the physiological as well as the psychological level, in the case of malignancy accords with other observations about it. Cancer attacks the vigorous, fast-living, excitement-seeking person rather than the weakling or person who lives at a low level.

As we explained under neuroses, the tendency toward over-enjoyment determines whether an influence becomes a source of better adjustment or of overadjustment, with its deepening negativism. Such a tendency is primarily innate. But it can be kept in check. Here conditioning and cultural tradition become important. But as we explained, these have not yet been evolved as regards the recognition of physiological overadjustment, made possible by the great modern "improvements." Here a scientific or planned restrictive intervention should be the primary goal of medicine. In any case, the inherent tendency of an organism toward overadjustment is decisive.

The inheritance factor in cancer has been sufficiently proved, especially through observation of malignancy in twins. The spectacular experiments of Dr. C. P. Rhoads with fourteen volunteers from the Ohio State Penitentiary showed that live cancer cells implanted in an organism are promptly rejected if there is no predisposition to cancer. Similarly, with regard to metastasis, millions of cells are liberated but only a few set up. Dr. George T. Pack shows that almost everyone has had low-grade cancer during his life. There is also the tendency of a cancer-prone organism to develop cancer in some other organ after it has been removed from one organ, just as in the case of neurosis the elimination of one trouble leads to the emergence of another. Anyway, as we said in mentioning the Russian defi-nition of cancer, its causes are to be sought in a general tendency depending upon the central nervous system rather than any accidental inflictions — as in all cases of overadjustment.

This does not contradict the virus theories. A virus is only a biochemical component that may be always present in the cell and may start an abnormal cycle only when the cell has loosened its restrictive controls. Many experiments — we may mention here those of Dr. André Lwoff, at the Pasteur Institute, with lysogenic bacteria — confirm the continuous presence of viruses in the cell. Even if it is assumed that the virus comes from outside, the loss of control by the cell may still be the precondition that makes it possible for these more primitive, less restricted forms of growth to take over. All kinds of viruses, the same as germs, are probably always in the human body, as René Dubos, of the Rockefeller Institute, explains.

By the way, the assumption of viruses as the cause of malignant growth has been used to explain reversals in the medication of cancer. Spectacular improvements followed by worse aftereffects has been the general pattern of cancer medication. Now it is argued that viruses become more vigorous because of the selection produced by the medication. Apparently, the real significance of the "improvement" is misunderstood.

The same misunderstanding underlies other theories. Researchers have observed that the administration of some compounds similar to natural growth materials sometimes produces relief in cancer cases. The theory has been advanced that counterfeit building materials can be supplied to the avidly growing malignant cells, thus disrupting their growth. A great amount of work has been invested in exploring these possibilities. The Sloan-Kettering Institute has done extensive research in creating such "counterfeit" building materials, especially nucleic acids. The success of such efforts is measured by the improvement that follows the administration of such materials. Actually, the criterion of immediate improvement here may be misleading, whatever the merits of the theory itself. Such improvement may mean instead a deepening of the ill. Supplying more concentrated materials for growth, even if they are "counterfeit," may actually induce more release in growth rate and produce this improvement — with the end result of further exhaustion of the function of normal growth. That these "counterfeit" materials are accepted by the organism shows that they may be good enough to stimulate accelerated metabolism.

Similar theorization has centered around another basic growth-

405

promoting substance — folic acid. The miraculous capacities of folic acid have been proven in various experiments; we can mention those by Lewisohn, Laszlo and Leuchtenberger. But other researchers have discovered just the opposite effects. The controversies appear in the theories of the Folic Acid Antagonists which have been the subject of several inconclusive conferences.

The perverse, self-perpetuating nature of malignant growth is due to the same paradoxical effect of worsening through improvement that constitutes the essence of every complex of overadjustment. At every step more release through growth becomes necessary as it is progressively exhausted. The self-perpetuating overadjustment is no longer felt after it has gone on for some time, as the margin of excess release becomes progressively narrower. But the accumulated excess rate of growth might have become considerable. Thus the overadjusting organism may end by living in an "orgy" of stimulation of growth, without it being felt. The increase, in the case of cancer, of amino acids, the main materials for growth, has been discovered by many researchers, particularly Dr. Richard W. Hendler, Dr. Fritz Lippman and Dr. Halvor N. Christensen. Various interpretations have been given to this evidence of the increased rate of growth.

Any interpretation of growth is misleading if the paradoxical logic of the effects of growth are not understood. Under this logic an increase of effect means its ultimate decrease. As there is excess of release in the rate of growth, exhaustion or at least a decrease in the function of growth becomes inevitable because of the general law of the unchangeable normalcy of the organism. The tendency of overadjustment — of continuous improvement — is therefore sufficient to deepen the exhaustion to a degree where nothing of the normal growth potential is available at the given stage, and the more primitive growth takes over. The paradox explains why the incidence of cancer increases with improved, i.e., *accelerated*, modern living, but at the same time reaches its peak with people of old age whose rate of living is *slowest*.

The self-perpetuation of overadjustment explains why malignant growth, once definitely established, continues by itself. Every cell in the body lives with the same primordial striving for more release. Once the cell or tissue is on the way to avoiding restrictions and increasing releases, it will continue doing so, especially if it is under stress. But the stress increases, as with the removal of restrictions abnormal conditions start prevailing. Here again, it has to be kept in mind that any overadjustment shows not so much in actual increase of releases as in a perverse procedure. Not much release can be obtained without concurrent restrictions. But under overadjustment the organism, or the cell, persists in the attempt to obtain releases without restriction. This means an inherently perverse organic adjustment. For, normally, release can be made available only upon the previous accumulation of "reserves" or previous restriction. In brief, under overadjustment an organically perverse process establishes itself, and spreads like a fire, in a chain-reaction fashion, due to the vicious-circle effect.

In view of the seemingly reversed logic of every growth and overadjustment, the present approaches in dealing with malignant growth should be rather reversed. The cell or tissue has to be forced to accept restrictions or stresses and pain. This means inducing negative effects, which are usually considered the disease. Antistimulation should be the main aim, and it should be enforced long before the malignancy appears as the disease. Insofar as the cancer has already appeared, the disease may have run its full course and there may be little left on which a cure can be based. Modern medicine has no methods of diagnosing overadjustment, though as we saw, the technical difficulties could be overcome.

Above all, modern medicine does not realize the dangers that follow from "improvements" through medication. Instead of warning the public against such "improvements" modern medicine favors them. The main thing to understand is that man can bring about destruction of the limited normalcy of his organism through his own increased skill and resourcefulness — by his very success in making constant improvements in his feeling of well-being. If he left his physiological self alone, as the animal does, he would not have puzzling malignant disorders. Perhaps methods aiming at the restoration of restrictions, stresses and pain would become more acceptable if it were realized that there is never more of negative than of positive feelings whatever man does.

Apart from antistimulation, and prevention of the "improvements" of overadjustment, something similar to the shock treatment in psychiatry might be thought of. However, the "shock" here should be deeply biological rather than psychological. Operations, which so far seem to be the only successful treatment of cancer, may have to some extent the concurrent effect of biological shock. Closer to biological shock, however, is an acute disease, and it has long been known that in many cases cancer disappears after the person has suffered an acute attack of infectious disease. The American Cancer Society reported that tuberculosis has been effective against cancer in rats.

Under proper causal understanding the possibilities here can be interesting. Dr. William B. Coley did considerable work on the influence of acute infection on cancer. Interest in this has been revived by Dr. Lloyd J. Old and associates at the Sloan-Kettering Institute. Naturally, scientists have looked here for more logical explanations. For instance, the beneficial influence of acute infection has been attributed to the stimulation of the reticulo-endothelic system. Actually, the shock effect here is as contrary to every logic as it is in psychiatry, where psychiatrists have also tried but finally given up any logical explanation of the only treatment in psychiatry that really works. The cure of cancer by acute infection has been hailed by some doctors as more concrete and definite than all the treatments, which usually do not provide much more than temporary remissions. Of course, progress in such paradoxical approaches depends on understanding and application of the paradoxical logic of adjustment at every step and in every detail.

Modern medicine may stumble blindly on some drug or treatment which has the effects of shock or antistimulation and to that extent offers a real cure, as has happened in psychiatry. It has to be kept in mind, however, that in an advanced cancer case the fundamental standards of normalcy themselves may have been lost, so that the restriction or shock may be too late to help. In general, however, modern medicine will continute with

408

the discovery of new wonder drugs that bring miraculous but only temporary remissions, and will praise itself for attaining at least some improvements. On the basis of such improvements during remissions doctors will draw further conclusions about the probable extension of the life of their patients, though nobody knows how long the patients would have lived without the improvements. On the other hand, any treatment that shows signs of evoking negative reactions will be excluded on that account alone. For instance, a filterable hemolitic agent that was found to protect animals against cancer — whatever its merits might be — was excluded from use on humans on the grounds that it induced symptoms of anemia.

Modern medicine has accumulated too great an erudition along the lines of experimentally logical approaches to be able to change its course. But only a change so radical that it may seem ridiculous at present could offer solutions. The cause of malignant growth, like all natural causes, can be only simple, though its understanding would mean the most far-reaching breakthrough. The reason why it has not been discovered, in spite of uniquely desperate efforts, is that it follows a logic contrary to everything modern medicine considers self-evident and scientific.

SOME OTHER PARADOXES

We can mention only briefly some other paradoxes of functional nature. **Hypothyroidism** is being discovered as a major disorder in this country, affecting now more than eight million people. Its symptoms are unexplained fatigue, understimulation and low metabolism. Apparently, the increasing availability in this country of all possible means for stimulation or improved well-being is showing here its inevitable effects — which may be genetically transmitted. All means of stimulation produce in the end effects opposite to those they show at the beginning.

A look at the most frequently used means of stimulation — the **popular drugs** — confirms this. We mentioned before the reversal effects of reserpine, the most popular modern drug. Next on the popularity list are the cortical hormones, cortisone, ACTH, or hydrocortisone. But these drugs have led to the most disappointing surprises and unresolved controversies. As Cooley explains in his *Science of Wonder Drugs*, the miraculous initial improvements may end with effects that can become disastrous; he mentions cases in which diabetes appeared, or even tuberculosis was "ignited." Antihistamines have become equally popular, and more than a dozen of them are now produced. But the effect is that antihistamines start increasing the amount of histamines in blood; a special theory has been advanced to explain this. On the other hand reactions evoked by histamines are more permanently cured by administration of small amounts of histamines. This method has been used in various desensitization treatments; we can refer here to Dr. Bayard T. Horton.

In the same connection we may mention the paradoxes of **allergies.** City dwellers, who are least exposed to pollen, suffer pollen alergies, while country people do not. Allergies to dust or to impurities of the air do not affect people who live with dust. Food allergies do not attach to foods that cannot be avoided. But foods like eggs, poultry or fish, which can be avoided, and which are encountered frequently enough to be repeatedly avoided, become objects of allergy. We explained under phobias that a frequent encounter with the avoided object is necessary to make the avoidance fixation reach its phobic intensity. In the case of allergies the avoidance fixation may be purely physiological; psychological realizations may only follow it. In this country, where the care of proper foods and pure air has reached the highest degree, the number of sufferers from allergies has increased to 17 million. As can be expected, allergies disappear in the case of acute infection or serious illness, as Feinberg states in his book on allergies.

Asthma is another, somewhat related, form of overadjustment. The tendency toward overadjustment here may be innate or induced by metabolic stimulations and "improvements." In simplest terms, asthma is due to the body's endeavor to improve the breathing function. By the very process of improving it the progressive worsening goes on. As Dr. Franklin D. Johnston explains, shortness of breath may be caused by overbreathing.

410

In simpler cases the deepening of an ill by **overtreatment** is too directly evident to be missed. Dr. George E. Morris tells of skin rashes that do not clear up because of overtreatment. The Council of Foods and Nutrition has warned against excessive use of vitamins A, D and folic acid, indicating that the symptoms may be worsened rather than improved as a result. Most doctors, however, let themselves be guided only by the favorable immediate effect. Here we may mention the increasingly popular enzyme treatments. Enzymes can be good for anything, from improving sleep to reducing swelling on a sprained ankle. Plain common sense tells us that the pain or swelling serves the purpose of preventing further harm. Removing these preventive measures by a means which certainly does not rebuild the ankle can only increase the harm.

Even the **water** we drink has become the subject of contradictions. Scientists always held that hard water hardens arteries. Dr. Henry A. Schroeder proceeded to prove this point by an extensive study of data from various states in this country. He ended by finding the opposite proof that hard water contributed less than soft water to the hardening of arteries. In regard to fluoridation scientists are taking a view of a little longer range. The hard, even slightly damaging influence of fluorine evokes greater vigor in the growth of teeth. But a view of still longer range would lead to a different conclusion. Exaggeration in any one direction is bound to lead to opposite exaggerations and exhaust the function sooner in the end.

The causal understanding of adjustment, with its laws of relativity of reactions and opposite causation, reveals as deleterious any excess, such as building up muscle, steeling the body against hardships, or cultivating grand-style athletics. Athletes, who usually start with a better than average physical constitution, end with health no better than average. A statistical study by Henry J. Montoye shows that athletes do not live longer than other people. The really favorable influences on the organism are of a different nature: they come from a gradual, unexciting and complex conditioning, like that resulting from continuous, boringly hard work.

Because of the relativity in physiological causation, only the relative factors matter. People catch **colds** as easily in very hot as in very cold weather. Statistically, this has been shown in an observation on students by Dr. John Summerskill. At the same time everybody knows that it is the cold as such that causes the ill. As long as the body maintains a response unexaggerated in one direction or another, even the hardest trial is met successfully. In another experiment with students, a deliberate attempt to make them catch cold, by exposing them to cold and humidity, failed.

Reversal rather than logical accumulation is the rule with all artificially induced effects. For instance, a relativistic reasoning would have foretold at once that the effort to restrict ovulation in **pregnancy control** by hormonal pills would lead to an opposite tendency. Sure enough, Dr. John Rock found the curious "rebound" effect, by which fertility was increased, and broke out in unexpectedly vigorous ovulation when the pills were discontinued. Now this procedure is being advised as a means for inducing fertility. A longer treatment with the pills will lead to such outbreaks even while the pills are being taken — unless pills of unusual and therefore inherently destructive potency are used. Any attempt to control or influence body reactions should take into account the seemingly paradoxical logic of relative causation or there are bound to be surprises and mystery.

Under relativistic logic the potential of a function is strengthened by its restriction and weakened by its increase. For instance, androgens stimulate hair growth, but eunuchs in whom the androgen production is suppressed are safest against baldness. A woman who wants her skin to look vital during the day should try to keep its vitality down during night, rather than the other way around. The cloggy creams applied during the night may have good effect — for reasons exactly opposite to those advertised. The quack rejuvenators of face skin by acid treatments have been popular because they could exploit this reversal effect, though such excess can be only harmful in the long run.

Many examples of the opposite effect are found in the field of **diet.** Numerous experiments have shown that a protein-rich diet produces greater physical well-being and mental vigor. But long-range studies show just the reverse to be true. A comparative study on the meat-eating Kirghiz and the more vegetarian Ukrainians is enlightening. A study by Dr. Morris H. Ross showed that extended low-protein diet increased the longevity of rats, made them behave brighter and look younger. We showed the paradoxical influence of poor and rich diets on most functional disorders.

Vitamins have become a fad, because of their stimulating effect. Actually, a vitamin has no value in separation from the food it goes with. Vitamins are only signaling devices that indicate the value and meaning of the given food. That is why the body does not store the most typical vitamins that serve nothing more than this function, and why vitamins perform this function in minute amounts. Also significant is the fact that there are as many vitamins or their combinations as there are foods. Some of these signals are unpleasant because they indicate the hard work of digestion and assimilation that the food will require. Miraculous as it may seem, the moment you taste a food you "know" what will happen to it during the long and incomprehensibly complex process of its assimilation. This is what the function of taste means. Anyway, because some of these signals are unpleasant men try to remove them — by cooking, rice polishing, grain milling and so on. There are many unconscious ways in which the body tries to avoid such unpleasantness, and often succeeds under unusual or artificial circumstances. Hence vitamin "deficiencies." Under normal circumstances the body can feed well, though suffering from unpleasantness of taste, on any food.

For the same reasons there are pleasant or physiologically stimulating vitamins. Their influence, as in all cases of stimulation, may be miraculous and may extend from improving IQ to removing horns. But as with all artificial stimulation, the final effects of the use of vitamins is the body's lessened capacity to respond to the normal amount of vitamins in food — and the increased danger of vitamin "deficiency." Every interference with the body's signaling system is dangerous and leads to reversed effects. That is why people who tinker with their foods or vitamins most also suffer most from vitamin "deficiencies."

The dependence of an illness, like **pellagra,** on stimulating nutrition is insightful. In his book, *You're the Doctor,* Heiser tells of the paradoxical increases and decreases of pellagra cases according to data from the Office of Public Health. The cases are fewest when diet stays at its *lowest level,* though in general the same data show that the cases decrease every time diet advances to a *higher level.* Sunshine has a similar paradoxical influence on pellagra.

INFECTIOUS DISEASES

The paradox of reversals extends even to the treatment of infectious diseases, though in general the causal understanding there has been correct, and progress spectacular. Paradoxical logic is already being applied in vaccination, which is the main cause of progress in this field — and about which we have nothing more to say.

But other means of fighting germs are used, and there the paradox of reversal applies to both main lines of attack. The one line is the strengthening of the body's resistance to germs, or rather raising its *general reactivity to germs.* Modern scientists are increasingly realizing that we live with all possible germs all the time but do not get infected by them. As René Dubos states, the idea that one "catches" an infection as soon as some germs get into the body is inherited from the nineteenth century. The proofs that the body reacts in some general way to all germs are too many to be discussed. They range from the self-injection of dreadful germs by experimenters to curious conditioning experiments in which a stimulus, like sound, accompanied by repeated injections of antibiotics finally evokes the same reactions without actual injection of the antibiotics.

It may be that even the most popular antibiotics, like penicillin or the other mycins, may act, to a great extent, by raising the general reactivity of the body. Scientists have proposed special theories to explain how some antibiotics protect the body without actually destroying the germs. Also, the antibiotics are used as stimulators of growth in animals; and may evoke other general reactions by the body, often showing as allergies to them. The strong protective reaction evoked by antibiotics may be due to the fact that they are products of extremely strong living particles which are able to destroy bacteria even in a test tube. But if antibiotics act by merely evoking a general reactivity, they may over-stimulate and thus make the body unable to respond, especially to less strong particles or their products. Doctors know the diminishing effect of antibiotics, but have tried to explain it mostly on the grounds of selection by germs.

Here we come to the second main line of attack in fighting germs: the direct *destruction of germs.* In its simple practical terms the paradoxical reversal shows here in the selection by germs: they become more virulent as stronger means are used against them. From time to time one may read reports about extremely virulent strains appearing in hospitals where the strongest means, internal or external, are used. There is no limit to which such virulence may be driven by merely using stronger means at each step. Thus the same vicious-circle effect may result here as in overstimulation, and the virulence of germs may be driven far above the range of the natural protective powers of man.

Thus, whether the means used evoke reactions or kill germs, excessive medical measures may become a source of danger. The capacity of man to react to germs may become dulled at the same time as their virulence increases at every step, each excessive measure in one direction evoking excessive opposite effects requiring even stronger measures. The similarity here to the paradoxical effects of miracle drugs or any overstimulation is typical: the search for stronger and stronger antibiotics in all corners of the world has become the main feature of antibiotic research. Of course, it would be plain madness to object to the use of antibiotics. They simply save lives. Their opposite aftereffects may accumulate only through generations of the human race; our protective capacities here are clearly a racial inheritance. In the meantime individuals cannot be allowed to die. But the reversal effect of antibiotics has to be understood even to conserve their present efficiency.

Such excessive methods that medicine uses are not the way nature works. By evolving just sufficient measures nature avoids extreme opposite effects and establishes a vast, delicate balance under which we are protected against the thousands of strains of germs with which we live. Even to such a clearly infectious disease as tuberculosis we may be becoming racially adapted. Dr. H. D. Chalke demonstrates that tuberculosis started to decline in the early nineteenth century when hygiene and sanitation were at their worst. Racial adaptation to all kinds of diseases, or lack of such adaptation, has been the deciding factor in the survival or decimation of many peoples, even in recent history. Of course, nature can only work blindly, by a selection that costs lives. But man could do a thousand times better, especially by methods utilizing the advantages of inner selection, which, as we saw, does not require the death of individuals in order to produce organic adaptation; vaccination is an excellent example of one such method.

In brief, the logical method of adding more immediate improvement in infection medication often leads to ultimate worsening. By use of excessive means modern medicine weakens the body's general reactivity as well as man's racial capacities to counteract infectious diseases. Any excess deviation from normalcy leads to an opposite effect; in the case of racial capacities we can speak of racial normalcy. Practically, with the use of the strongest means the body becomes incapable of reacting to any lesser infection; and the racial capacities become useless as the virulence of germs is driven above their range. This is manifestly dangerous because no artificial means can ever substitute for the myriad complexity of natural capacities. If the paradoxical effects of all medication are not understood, in the use of existing means or the development of new, even stronger ones, man may be losing a race against himself, especially in longer-range terms.

LONGEVITY

The paradox of relativity is apparent in the case of longevity from the simple general fact that all things which seem to make man younger only accelerate his rate of living and make him age faster.

The most extensive work on longevity is probably that of Raymond Pearl. In studying the lives of five thousand persons he came to the conclusion that two factors went together with longevity: having long-lived ancestors, and having a tranquil heart as well as a calm, serene disposition. People who are forced to live restricted lives because of restricting duties and continuous work — clergymen, dignitaries of the church, judges, high officials — live longer. Poverty helps, as overeating is one of the main causes of shortened lives. Eating little and keeping to diets with less meat prolong life; observations of immediate effects, of course, show that plenty of protein-rich foods make one feel young and vigorous. Nutrition is important because it constitutes the physical basis from which every other organic reaction arises.

Anything that slows down metabolism, which means interferes with our natural striving for accelerated living, helps longevity. The famous scientist Carrell tells how he discovered in his researches that, "strangely enough," deficiencies in diet, even the addition of harmful substances in food in small amounts, increased the longevity of animals. A physical handicap may prolong life in spite of its otherwise deleterious effects. Sir William Osler said that nothing promotes longevity so much as an early discovery of a trace of organic illness. The aging organism imposes its own restrictions as it discovers by continuous trial and error the best adjustment for its decreasing capacities.

The strong influence of inheritance on longevity is understandable in the light of relative causation. As we saw, the predetermined normalcy of each organism reverses every influence or interference. As a person tries to live faster than his normal rate, a slowing down automatically follows. The same happens with a deliberate attempt to slow down. However, this does not mean that nothing can be done to extend life. Man can oppose and change nature here as everywhere else. This has not been done up to now — thus leaving the rhythm set by inheritance to prevail — because man's efforts in this direction have been blind, helped only by inertial and intuitive tradition, and just as frequently counteracted by his deliberate striving for more vigorous living.

If man is to work for longevity scientifically, two main facts are to be understood. The first is the paradoxical logic of adjustment under which a higher, more elaborate and more extended life is attained through the imposition of more restrictions on the life flow. The second is the enormous multiplicity of mechanisms to which the restriction would have to be applied. Through a million-year evolution the restrictions have been imposed on so many and intricately interwoven mechanisms that no one of them can be suddenly slowed down without opposite effects from the others. To try to influence them all by some single effort is like trying to stop a river with the bare hands. But science could gradually develop equally extensive, watertight measures by working along the simple principle of general restriction. Science thus could amplify a thousandfold what evolution has done blindly. In a science-fiction fashion we can imagine that man will someday be capable to control and slow down the *rate* of his every function and correspondingly extend the *duration* of his life to any extent he wants. As we saw, restriction of physiological functions does not necessarily decrease the intellectual potential, can rather increase it. And there is never any loss, or gain, in pleasure and happiness whatever man does.

It may seem fairly obvious that the time of living can be extended only at the price of slowing it down. Simple common sense, as well as practical observation, tells us that this is so. However, where it really could make a difference, namely, in the sciences, the opposite attitude prevails. True to its experimental logic, modern science advocates intensified vigor and accelerated living in all their forms. Every book and article on longevity stresses the benefits of more vigorous living, more intense natural interests, and better ways of obtaining pleasurable satisfactions.

But have not the more pleasurable conditions and enjoyments of modern life increased life expectancy? The *average* extension of life looks really impressive, and is often brought out as one of the great benefits of modern life. But as life insurance statisticians and physiologists have repeatedly demonstrated, the increase is due entirely to the spectacular decrease in infant mortality and in deaths from infectious diseases. Everybody has a chance now to live to his last physiological capacities, but these capacities have not been increased. The diseases that specifically affect old age — cardio-vascular diseases, cancer, arthritis, diabetes and renal diseases — are on the increase. It also has to be kept in mind that modern man is still living by the tradition of the old biological and cultural standards even if he tries to overcome them. He does not show marked "success" in this effort because it takes ages before a new trend can establish itself and show its effects. The chronic stubbornness of the functional diseases bears witness to the persistence of the pre-established biological standards. In fact, those who live without modern improvements and medication for functional disorders suffer less from the old age diseases. As A. L. Visher states in his book on old age, a doctor may discover that the person of great age is one who has lived against every rule in the doctor's book.

The modern scientist studying longevity usually sees solutions in some one favorable natural factor or organic function, for which he then develops a pet theory. The famous Mecknikov saw the solution in keeping the alimentary tract healthy with a *bacillus bulgaricus*. Such approaches are futile. The longevity of species, as a product of long and complex conditioning in every organic function can be further extended only in the same way. Scientists can progressively intensify the same evolution, by working on all the innumerable functions, though using nothing more complex than the general method of restriction. But there is no single easy way or lucky formula. As a comparison, it can be mentioned that the only known instance of an endlessly prolonged living process is that of primitive plants which are cut down constantly. This is a crude form of restriction. In higher organic adjustment the same preclusion of physiological functions from reaching their goals directly is effected by way of innumerable and infinitesimal organic restrictions. Man has rightly been called a retarded or fetal ape. Incidentally, even the training of an animal contributes to its longevity.

Comparisons from the evolution of animals show that the imposition of restrictions and elaborations, as evidenced by the amount of nerve matter, is what makes organisms bigger, more complex and longer-living. As Nagornyi states in his *Starenie i prodolzhenie zhizni*, the longevity of animals goes along with increase of brain and retardation of maturing. Friedental, Buffon and Flourens, the older scientists to whom Nagornyi refers, have demonstrated the same correlation. Increase in brain means increase in restrictions. The very structure and physiological function of brain shows it to be a system of controls superimposed on several levels. The conditioning or learning that the brain produces as the universal method of higher evolution serves the purpose of making every function increasingly more circuitous under restriction, and consequently longer lasting.

REJUVENATION

Attempts at rejuvenation are typical of the "scientific" approch. Most of such attempts have centered on intensification of hormonal activity. Accordingly, stimulation of sexual function has been the main line of attack. To be sure, the immediate effects of such stimulation are always invigorating. A longer-range wisdom, however, shows unequivocally that it is exactly an intensified sexual life which is the surest way toward premature aging. The most famous rejuvenators — Lejeune, Claude Bernard, Brown-Sequard, Steinach and Voronoff — all tried to bring back youth by tampering with sexual hormones, either by injecting them or by grafting tissues of sexual glands. Immediate effects were sensational enough to attract great attention, but when the final results were in, there were no takers for such rejuvenation.

Steinach's method, based on ligature of the spermatic chord, is more controversial. Naturally, in such operations there was at first intensification of hormonal secretions, since the body always tries to compensate for imposed limitations. Probably, the favorable results were registered from this phase in the operations. Actually, the lasting improvements that the method of Steinach and Lichtenstein does seem to have produced must have come from the later decrease of hormonal activity, since a permanent

420

impediment imposed on the body leads in its later stages to corresponding restrictive limitations.

Some other rejuvenescent effects, like those produced by Bogomolets of Russia or Niehans of Switzerland, can be explained as the results of interference with body functions. An interference means restriction, and if it is accompanied by painful preparation, there is a feeling of relief as well as retarding or rejuvenating effects afterward. Any metabolic restriction can have similar effects. Antioxidants administrated to mice in experiments by Dr. Denham Harman increased their life span by 20 percent. A simple underfeeding of rats and other animals in experiments by Dr. C. M. McCay, of Cornell University, and Dr. G. E. Burch, of Tulane University, produced considerable extension of the life span of the animals, accompanied by their retarded maturation. Experiments by Drs. H. S. Simms and B. N. Berg, of Columbia University, also showed the beneficial effects of underfeeding on the longevity of rats.

Faster metabolism and maturation always mean a shorter life span. Dr. Stanley M. Garn found that fat children mature faster. The same can be said of fat men. But a longer waistline is the best indicator of a shorter life, as doctors and insurance men know. Shelby Gerking, of Indiana University, found in research on fish that the faster they grow, the earlier they die.

There have been all kinds of endeavors to regain the vigor of youth. Most of them have meant merely the intensification of releases, which always produces invigorating immediate effects. Dr. Anna Aslan of Rumania acquired international fame with her treatment — based on the administration of procaine, a pain killer and muscle relaxant used under various names for the last fifty years. But Dr. Aslan had all the proofs of the rejuvenating effects of her treatment. How could any doctor object to such proofs? Modern medicine lives by the same logic of immediate improvement. Our foremost geriatricians — we can refer here to Dr. Edward L. Bortz — are working at the promotion of the same reactions that procaine treatment produces: enjoyment of life, more "normal" metabolism, livelier interests, more pleasurable reactions and so on.

421

However subtle the means used, if the aim is the immediate increase of releases, such treatments as Dr. Aslan's are just the right thing. For the same reason, alcohol or the enjoyment of good eating, even if they make one fat, are not found to be harmful, as Dr. Andreas E. Laszlo explains. At the previously mentioned "Symposium on Drinking" the use of alcohol was praised as beneficial for aging people. In fact, the beneficial effects of alcohol have become one of the most popular discoveries of modern medicine.

INHERITANCE

Modern genetics is built on Mendel's law. According to this law, traits never change, and if intermixed revert back to the original type in the subsequent generation. This has given rise to the theory of never-changing genes.

When a white-flowering plant is crossed with a red-flowering one, the hybrid may be pink. But in the second generation pure reds again make up one-fourth; pure whites, one-fourth; and red-whites or pinks, two-fourths. The two-fourths of pinks segregate out again in the third generation as red and white, with the same proportion of pinks or red-whites. Apparently, the traits do not change but revert back. The same average of combinations would be obtained by drawing pairs of marbles from a bag that contained equal amounts of white and red marbles. When the combination of red and white in the plant gives externally a color so strongly pink that it cannot be distinguished from red, then there is, naturally, a segregation in the second generation of one white and three reds. Here then is the *dominant* trait, and the same relation of one to three goes on in all further segregations. In principle, this is all there is to the Mendelian rule. When more traits are combined, the resulting segregations are correspondingly more varied.

What does Mendel's law reveal? It reveals simply that every trait reverts back to its previous state. But is not the reversion to normalcy the general law of all organic adjustment? The principles of relative causation that causally explain all adjustment rest on just this law of reversion to normalcy. Therefore we can say that *in genetics we have to deal only with the same general principles that govern all organic adjustment. But under these principles permanent changes are not excluded, provided they are induced not by an external interference, as the pairing of traits is, but by the subtle process of conditioning that we encounter everywhere in evolution, and know best as learning.*

Modern genetics has discovered one-half of the truth, and is precluding the understanding of the other half. The reason for this is the experimental "scientism" of modern genetics. To understand conditioning geneticists would have to deal with processes so complex and involving the organism as a whole so intricately that they could be grasped only in terms of values, with pleasure in its widest sense as the central concept. All learning is extremely vague in its experimentally observable, material aspects; it always is seen as rather a "spiritual" thing. Moreover, conditioning is a contradictory or subtly "deceitful" process. Modern genetics has neither the methods nor causal understanding for dealing with such experimentally meaningless or contradictory effects. Further, while in ordinary learning the scientist can register at least its final results, in genetic learning the changes are so slow and intricately graded that no experiment can register them. On the contrary, *reversal as the resistance to conditioning is prominently registered.* In every learning resistance is primarily more evident than the subsequent permanent effect of learning which results in spite of the resistance. This applies in a much higher degree to genetic "learning," since the genetic self established through millions of years can only change equally gradually. In other words, it resists change or reverses with equal predominance.

Even for such change as could be induced — one can think here of the simplest organisms or mechanisms — the scientist would have to possess an intuitive genius for understanding what "pleases" the given mechanism, how it "evaluates" an influence under given conditions, or how it can be "deceived." Such understanding would go beyond science completely. But exerting an influence without it can produce only a reversal, as any interference with organic processes does. That is why a true modern scientist can produce and observe only the reversals predicted by Mendel's law, never anything else.

Since genetic traits reverse during segregation in a point-by-point fashion — as all normal reactions do upon interference — geneticists readily assumed that specific atoms of inheritance, or genes, are at work here. Thus "atomism" was established here just as it was in psychology. This is what experimental scientism requires — but is definitely absurd in terms of living organisms, where everything is interwoven with everything else and only "wholes" are causally decisive. Genes are very comfortable concepts. Since any number of genes can be assumed, anything that happens can be "explained" as being due to a specific gene. However, the perennial trouble with such easy explanations by separate monads arises. In order to explain the endless variety and fluidity of living processes, an endless number of such monads has to be assumed. At the present state of knowledge, geneticists have to postulate up to 100,000 genes for the reproductive cell of man, or up to 15,000 for that of a fly. Actually, as scientists learn about further new aspects of the organism they will have to postulate more genes. The final number is literally infinite. At present genes are discovered only where there are mutations of traits, or when Mendelian segregation takes place. The latter requires the existence of allelomorphs or different parallel traits in the two reproducing individuals. As T. Dobzhansky says in his *Evolution, Genetics, and Man*, if everybody in the world had brown eyes, no genes of the eye color would be assumed.

Actually, postulating the existence of even a dozen genes amounts to a scientific enormity or a miracle. Genes are assumed to contain codes for each organic trait. It cannot be overemphasized that organic traits are miraculously purposeful. As we have repeatedly explained, this miracle is attained by the long accumulation of evolutionary adaptation. But genes are not supposed to adapt or change in any way. That is the very essence of a gene. Therefore the miracle of organic purposefulness must be implanted in every gene at the moment of its creation as an eternal monad, all of which requires an anthropomorphically intelligent creator.

424

But what about evolutionary adapatation through gene mutations? The main source of such mutations is assumed to be *disruption* of the atom arrangements in genes by cosmic rays. Other secondary sources of mutation — such as other types of radiation, heat, and the dislocation or cross-over of gene contents — are of a similar disruptive nature. It has to be realized that every species has thousands of genes, each gene consisting of thousands of molecules, and each molecule of thousands of atoms. To obtain a harmonious change, any one of these factors must happen in exactly one certain fashion and no other. A purely disruptive factor, like a cosmic ray hitting the genes, could produce just as well any possible other arrangement. The average probability of obtaining the one harmonious arrangement therefore would be one in millions of millions of possibilities. It would not be even the one in ten million that Julian Huxley assumes in his book, *Evolution in Action.*

But even if the probability of one in ten million is accepted, it is sufficient to exclude any possibility of adaptive evolution. The *disruption* that governs such a mutation can produce a harmonious adaptation as little as shooting a machine gun into a china shop can make a better arrangement there. As long as the scientist directs his attention to the one improvement and forgets about the 9,999,999 deteriorations, he can speculate about a possible adaptation through the accumulation of such improvements. One bullet in the china shop may also turn a cup a little bit in the right direction. Then if one concentrates exclusively on the possibility that other lucky bullets may turn the same cup even more, he can argue about the possibility of a better arrangement. But the fact is that even the one improvement obtained is destroyed at the next stage with the probability of ten million to one.

Any species depending on such adaptation would deteriorate and perish in a few generations. As Sewall Wright has said, such mutation alone could produce an array of freaks but no evolution. No amount of sophistication about the unique effect of natural selection can help here. There is never any improvement left for the selection to start with. Huxley uses the argument of selection,

425

in the above book, but later states that he was surprised to realize how necessary it is to reduce the rate of such mutations. Does not this amount to the recognition that mutation is a factor of deterioration rather than evolution?

That is what it is. The main thing in the evolution of a species is that it be absolutely protected against such disruptive mutations, while the adaptation goes on in very different ways. *Living evolution can be characterized as an imperceptibly gradual but constant shaping of organisms by the environment.* The whale has the same genetic makeup as all mammals, but it has become like a fish because it lives in water. The wings of a bird, a bat and a butterfly are similar, but there is no affinity in their genetic makeup. Such cases of homology and analogy are encountered at each step in nature. The *gradualness* of evolution is evidenced in all the imperceptible changes in organs, through millions of years, and in their dwindling into rudimentary remains under the purposefully shaping hand of environment. Also, the biogenetic recapitulation, by the embryo, of previous stages of evolution indicates that gradual transition, not sudden disruptions, is the way evolution works. All this gradualness and purposefulness of change, so evident everywhere, are completely incompatible with the concept of unchanging genes or their disruptive mutations.

Actually, the gene is a fiction that permits geneticists to continue with their "scientific" methods. Nobody has seen genes and nobody ventures to say what exactly they consist of. The more cautious geneticists, even such authorities as Muller and Goldschmidt, have expressed doubts about their existence. In his *Physiological Genetics* Goldschmidt shows how the effects of the "genes" can be explained by chromosome rearrangements. This means attributing genetic effects to wider genetic wholes. Goldschmidt says that Muller and the workers on the famous drosophila fly experiments drew similar conclusions, though "shrinking from the last step — the abolition of the gene concept."

Of course, there is genetic material that controls traits. The greater part of such material for a certain trait may, naturally, be located around one spot in the chromosome. Further, such material

426

conserves itself as the traits reverse or separate out through generations. All this is sufficient to explain what geneticists have discovered about the substance, location, maps or cross-over frequencies of "genes." But it does not warrant the existence of genes as separate monads or atoms. Man has legs, eyes and organs, but to treat the organism as a combination of them would mean replacing scientism with an Empedoclean mystery. It is certainly difficult to deal with the organism as a whole in the experimental, atomistic fashion, but unless this is done no understanding of organic life can be gained. If geneticists have to divide, in order to proceed with their methods, they should not go beyond the chromosomes; nature itself indicates that these are the last divisible sub-wholes.

The gene theory can show itself wise, *after the fact*, by postulating unlimited new genes or their mutations to account for any traits or changes in them. But even so, difficulties have arisen, and geneticists have postulated a dozen other mechanisms at work: multiple allelomorphs, multiple factors, gene modifiers, complementary factors, supplementary factors, cummulative factors, multiple effects of genes, correlated responses and so on. And there is always the excuse that the gene was recessive, or that there might have been chromosomal deficiencies, inversions or translocations. Still there is the disturbing plasmogenic or cytoplasmic inheritance; unexplainable mutation back, observed especially in bacterial reaction to antibiotics; change of gene functions; dependence between mutants; Mendelian behavior in asexual organisms; the clearly proved mutation of bacteria corresponding to changes in the environment, and so on.

The gene theory has become a complex doctrine that never offers anything new, but only lags behind facts in seeking explanations for its own assumptions. Insofar as predictions are made they are self-explanatory as effects of the preservation of organic identity, which is the general law of adjustment. On this law relative causation rests, which can account for the Mendelian law or reversals — but also can explain much more about genetic identity in reproduction, as well as all the other important effects of organic causation.

The genetic self may be considered as continuing from one

generation into another. The influences, especially the overadjustments, in one generation do not remain without effect for the next generation; the "sins" of one generation are visited upon the next. We know this from intuition, common-sense observation, tradition and even experiment. The genetic self lives uninterruptedly through generations, following all the laws of adjustment, including conditioning or learning and paradoxical opposite reactions. Of course, without understanding the logic of these laws the scientist discovers only Mendelian reversals even where deeper, permanent, though slight changes are being conditioned, as we saw already.

Life and evolution contradict the doctrine of never-changing genes. Practical breeders have always worked with a view to producing changes. Naturally, they use the method of cross-breeding that gives quick immediate results — which primarily comply with the Mendelian law. Actually, even cross-breeding may produce deeper gradual changes under hybrid interaction; such interaction is witnessed in a more obvious form in hybrid vigor. Whatever the curbing influences, the breeders as well as evolution in general, must have brought about the endlessly rich improvements in ways other than mere Mendelian cross-breeding. Mere combinations of never changing and always returning inferior traits cannot account for all the incomparably superior permanent traits obtained. Nor could these result from the supposed disruptive mutation of genes. Even in absolutely controlled and endlessly repeated experiments no really viable or harmonious change has ever been produced by such mutations in a single tiny trait. But modern genetics is tied down by its experimental discovery of Mendel's law. Theories holding more practically tenable views exist, but cannot prevail against the "scientific" proofs of experiment.

Now we come to the most difficult question, namely, the inheritance of acquired traits. It is easily observable that an animal adapts to some extent even physiologically to the requirements of its environment during its life, by way of a constant trial-and-error search for better satisfactions at every level. The question is how such adaptation can become inheritable. Actually, this question has become so difficult only with the discovery by modern genetics of seemingly unchanging traits. Otherwise, the transfer by an organism to its reproductive cell of acquired qualities would appear much more feasible than the miraculous reproduction of the whole organism, with its endless details, from the tiny reproductive cell. It is clear that genetically the animal continues from one generation to another.

In any case, the problem here involves understanding the mechanisms of the living process itself. This is a problem clearly beyond our reach. We are not competent to understand it and we can only make a conjecture — which we think worthwhile for the following reasons. Present speculations on the nature and origins of life are not only equally incompetent but have never advanced beyond mere repetitions of the same unimaginative theme. One finds here only endless conjectures on how elements could have accidentally combined, and continued adding to the combination, until complex living compounds emerged. No new distinct principle has ever been advanced, though the first thing about the living process is its completely distinct nature from nonliving processes. Even a wild speculation here could be more fruitful than such repetitions.

We venture a new principle. And we do not need to invent anything new or postulate any hypotheses. The principle follows automatically from our previously explained causal understanding of all phenomena of matter and energy, which applies everywhere — to the existence of atoms, the yes-or-no structure of everything that exists, as well as the laws of gravitation and electricity. Further, our principle agrees with the newest discoveries of science about living processes. Therefore, even if the conjecture be wrong in detail, it will point at least in the right general direction. Our causal understanding of all phenomena of matter requires the acceptance of the seemingly strange concept of the Field as an opposing counterpart of matter. But, as we saw, this followed automatically from the abandonment of man's delusory one-sidedness of outlook. The Field is scientifically not only acceptable but has been always recognized by physicists as a reality in one form or another.

Now we may try to show how the opposition between the Field and matter explains the phenomena of life, and how this agrees with the newest findings of science.

In the light of this opposition *living process is explainable as a chain reaction — like fire, though opposite in nature — sparked by the presence of an unusually large molecule.* A giant molecule, once created, has around it an area or field protected against Field pressure. In this protective field or area atoms accumulate into increasing formations, under the operation of Field pressure, as we explained under gravitation. These atoms are also able to accumulate energy. Atoms always absorb energy but immediately have to release it under Field pressure. In the protective field of a giant molecule, however, the absorbed energy can be kept by the atoms. The incomparably greater number of atoms, and their higher energy states, accumulated around the original giant molecule and now forming a new unit, permit the formation of new bonds or "crystals" with other such units (supplied by reproduction) with extraordinarily rich and far-reaching effects. Thus can the principle of growth and self-organization of living matter be schematically explained.

The second main property of living matter, division or reproduction, follows from the same opposition between matter and Field. The matter around the giant molecule is bound to accumulate to the limit where it becomes unstable under Field pressure. Since its breaking up by the Field meets with an equal tendency of the matter to continue with its accumulation, division into two gradually separating and accruing parts is an inevitable outcome. The two parts become quantitatively equal because if one part were smaller, it would automatically attract matter from the other part. Since mere quantity determines all the qualitative properties of the accumulated matter, two exactly similar new formations result with the same potential to accumulate other matter around them until each again reaches the breaking point. The total of such divisions, on the level of the strung-up spirals of nucleic molecules, then results in the division of whole cells.

Modern science is beginning to recognize that living processes are induced by the field forces of giant molecules. It recognizes

430

that enzymes and their catalytic action are the organizers of all living processes. But enzymes are giant molecules, and the catalysis means the inducing of biological processes by the mere presence of field forces of such giant molecules. Borek explains in his book, *Man the Chemical Machine*, how catalytic enzyme action can account for all life functions, including genes, and how every protein has this enzyme property. In his book, *Life, its Nature and Origin*, Jerome Alexander shows how catalysts functioning by virtue of their fields of force may explain the self-creation and self-organization of living matter in ways similar to crystallization. Causally, crystallization is due to the same opposition between Field and matter, which creates the protective or "gravitational" field around every piece of matter.

Many scientists have seen living growth as a more complex crystallization. Since living molecules may be thousands of times greater than nonliving ones, the crystals they form must be richer in variations of forms and in their far-reaching capacity to interlock by an astronomical number. The more primitive forms of living matter, such as viruses, even look like crystals. The more complex or larger forms are more rounded because of their multiplicity of axes. The same field forces or catalytic effects can account for the equally rich dissolution, or changes among living molecules.

Of course, the forms of life are ungraspably miraculous in their purposefulness and harmony. But, as we saw, selection in the wider sense, especially inner selection, explains this miracle as the result of adverse interaction. This is easier to understand if one abandons the naïve humanistic view that man and his world *had* to be or were *intended* to be created the way they are. Actually, they *happen* to be the way they are. Man and his world may be incongruity itself from any other point of view. Man as the most complex phenomenon is clearly the most incompatible one even in the terms of his own world. Anything that conforms with man and his notions of harmony or intelligence conforms only with that incompatibility.

Anyway, the endless power of life, its incessant surging forth, like a fire spreading through every opening and connection, is explainable by the same never-ceasing opposition between matter and Field, which lies at the bottom of all physical phenomena with their perpetual motion, vibrations and interactions. In the chain reaction released by the spark of the giant molecule, matter brings this incessant opposition into fuller realization from its side. All this explains how nonliving matter can emerge so intensively alive in the living process, and how this process incessantly provides new forms for selection to work on.

After that there is only one more thing to be explained: the miraculous regularity, or innumerable laws, that every living process follows. This is again explainable by the same inexorable opposition between Field and matter. If you take two perfect card players and distribute to them certain cards, in an open game, you determine by that every move that will follow for as long as the play lasts. In the play between Field and matter the "cards" mean quantitative variations of several factors (which is the same with playing cards), such as the size of the initial molecule, other elements accumulated, their energy potentials, interaction with other molecules and so on. The "cards" here are innumerable, but once they are given, the play can go on in only one, and no other way, for millions and millions of moves ahead — as long as the living process continues.

Under what exact circumstances the first giant molecule could have sprung into existence is difficult even to conjecture. One cannot create such a giant molecule on earth now, just as one cannot strike a spark under water. The Field immediately takes away the slightest surplus. A molecule of overpowering size could arise only in the absence of Field pressure, be it for the shortest moment and at the tiniest spot. This requires upheavals of cosmic proportions. But upheavals of such a nature are possible during the evolution of a planet. For instance, during a period of cooling off on a universal scale, radiation, which always means loosenings in the Field, may become so universally saturated and locked in that all kinds of unusual concentration of such loosenings in the Field may occur. At present the closest thing to distinctive loosenings in the Field can be created by a strong electric flow, as we saw in discussing electricity. It is not surprising, therefore, that all experimenters who have been able to produce something approaching living compounds, have done so by the use of electric discharges. That is why scientists often mention lightning in their speculations on the origins of life.

However living matter originated, it could not result merely from an extremely lucky combination of ordinary lifeless elements happening to come together. It must have been something simpler as well as more fundamental: a reversal in the usual processes of nature, like a reversed fire, in which matter, for once, accrues instead of being dissolved, in a chain-reaction fashion. The theory of the lucky combination does not agree with the fact that life extends to all possible combinations of matter, and that the simplest elements, abundant everywhere, are the staple materials of living formations.

Now we may return to the primary question of the inheritance of acquired traits — of how the influences of life experience can be impressed on the reproductive cells. The main argument of Weissmannism is that such a mechanism, which would work "backward," is not even conceivable. Darwin assumed such a mechanism. He thought that all organs, even the cells of the body, produce gemmules, which are transferred to the sex glands, where they form the sex cells. Darwin's theory of evolution is the greatest discovery in human history. He must have known that this theory required and pointed to the inheritance of acquired traits. But the pangenetic mechanism was described by Darwin in terms of mechanisms conceived by man. It cannot be overemphasized that nature does not work the way man does or thinks. Nature works with inconceivable multiplicity and intricacy as far as its "mechanisms" are concerned, whereas the principles by which it works are as simple and easily understandable as the principle of selection itself.

The inconceivability of natural mechanisms is evidenced first in the fact that the single reproductive cell reproduces the whole organism in its myriad of tiniest details. It is clear that the core of the organism is the genetic self contained in the reproductive cell that starts the organism, and is reproduced again in millions of new reproductive cells. The persistence and reproduction of

433

this self is the primary biological purpose. The organism that is evolved around this genetic self is only a shell of subordinate significance. The important thing to understand is that this core or genetic self does not need to be there like a real, topographical center. It can be dispersed throughout the organism, be endlessly represented in every cell — and still act as a real center, from which everything emanates, to which everything reflects back, and which can precisely reproduce itself at every moment in the reproductive cells.

With this we come to the decisive point. The genetic self as the center produces the organism by its field forces; the organism constitutes the realized field. But as we saw in discussing the causal effects of matter, a center or matter and the field work both ways. The center determines the field, but the field can also determine the matter. In other words, the genetic self shapes the organism, but the organism can shape the genetic self in virtue of the changes that the organism undergoes. These changes further depend upon the environment as the outermost field. Thus environment can shape the reproducing genetic self. Since the organism is developed through long evolution along precise and purposeful lines in regard to the environment, the influences backward from the environment, along the same lines, are just as precise and purposeful. For the same reason, the influences are as slow and gradual as was the adaptation to the environment during the evolution. Actually, any short-lasting influence produces a temporary opposite rather than a permanent direct effect.

Let us visualize the whole evolutionary adaptation as represented by innumerable superimposed layers around the genetic center. When there is an influence, let us say a hindrance, exerted on an outer layer, then the normal pressure from the layer below will evolve additional, compensative pathways. Consequently, there will be temporarily, at the next phase, an increased rather than diminished performance. In truth, there will also be a very slight *permanent* diminishing effect because of the influence of the field toward the center, but this effect will be further reversed, with an even slighter direct permanent effect left, on the next level, and so on. That is why an influence may require uncounted

434

generations before its direct permanent effects, rather than the temporary reversals, become noticeable in the case of more complex organisms. On the other hand, absolutely every influence, even the tiniest one, has this direct permanent effect, however infinitesimally slight, in this humanly inconceivable process of myriads of submicroscopic interactions at innumerable points at every instant. By the way, the above reversals and permanent effects are not different from those we observed in all conditioning.

This working backward of environmental influences in an exactly corresponding, purposeful and gradual way is what explains the genetic shaping of the species by the environment. To illustrate what happens in humanly comprehensible terms of wholes, rather than of multiplicity, let us use the concept of pleasure. As we saw, pleasure is only another term for living itself, consequently for the realization of the genetic self through its field forces. And the two-way interaction is illustrated here, in humanly comprehensible terms, by the relation between pleasure, as an over-all integrated realization of life, and the environment. The pleasure drive determines how the environment is used, but the environment, also determines how the pleasure pathways are conditioned — how the organism learns, in the widest sense of the term.

Let us imagine an animal which obtains better food from higher branches and therefore constantly stretches its neck. At first the animal would suffer pain and aftereffects that would force it to desist from stretching the neck muscles. Even if the animal continues doing so, in spite of discomfort, and thus grows stronger neck muscles, the reversal effects would show in the next generation, with only slight direct effect. But if under the over-all pleasure economy the animal continues obtaining its food from upper branches for generations and even develops a fixation on that food, then deeper and deeper, slight changes will take place. To avoid pain or discomfort in the muscle the organism will automatically, through thousands of physiological trials and errors, gravitate toward less disturbing deeper readjustments. Such readjustments will be enhanced as will diminish the pain. For instance, blood flow to the muscle would have to be increased.

But to do that the deeper mechanism that determines the blood flow has to be correspondingly changed; and to change that a still deeper mechanism has to be changed, and so on. Finally, readjustments would be reached which would enhance the growth of a longer neck from the deepest mechanisms up. This, then, would mean an organism changed to its very center of organization — its genetic core, which then would reproduce itself in the new form. Thus nothing more than the all-integrated striving for pleasure brings purposeful genetic changes about. We have explained repeatedly the significance of pleasure as the all-integrated self-realization of the living process itself.

XI

THE PARADOX IN ECONOMICS, POLITICS
AND HISTORY

The paradoxes of relative causation apply to social phenomena as well because these are equally determined by human motivations and values. A people as a whole may suffer from neurotic negativism as a result of striving exaggeratedly for positive motivations. They may land into an economic slump because of exaggerations in confidence during the boom. They may start a war or a witch hunt without actually wanting it, because of exaggerations in motivation or "love" for their own nation, people or belief. Further, as we saw, a highly civilized people living in an atmosphere of the strongest conditioned restrictions may extol the belief that freedoms are the essence of their life, while other people actually living in high freedom may rise in a fierce revolt because of deep resentment against limitations in their freedoms. This applies to every social value, as every value actually derives from its opposite or disvalue — from an essential lack of the given value.

We also saw how everybody strives for and praises only positive values and motivations while it is actually their opposite, the negative backgrounds, which are their real causal source. This makes every motivation in social life contradictory, and every success blind or contrary to avowed intentions, just as in individual emotional adjustment.

The humanist or social scientist is as unaware as anybody else of these paradoxes which govern the causation of all social events. Explanations of contradictions are sought in complex theories — as many as there are theorists — postulating specific sociological, technically elaborate, often almost metaphysical concepts, or seeking reassurance in classical unquestioned truths about spiritual goals, natural rights or eternal human values. As a typical example we can mention the theories, in the vein of Lévy-Bruhl or Durkheim, of a social will or of a specific social psychology as being different from that of individuals. In fact, there is no reason to believe, when men collectively as a society want something, that they end by wanting something else. There are plenty of distortions, but they are due to the paradoxes which originate on the level of individual psychology. Social psychology can be treated quite adequately as a mere total of individual psychologies. A social reaction may be slower or less articulate — but only because it represents an average compromise of innumerable individual reactions.

Insofar as social scientists avoid such mystifications they seek explanations in logical insights, in the way psychologists seek explanations of individual behavior. We saw how this leads either to the postulation of a world of ghosts, or to inane conclusions which blame lack of learning or faulty habits. Hundreds of explanations are offered by social theorists in terms of fortunate or unfortunate coincidences, the emergence of new ideas, great leaders and their teachings, political constitutions, policies, exceptional events and so on.

In fact, none of these factors is causally decisive. They may lead to completely opposite reactions depending upon the availability, or unavailability, of the simplest of things: positive emotion or positive motivation — just as in individual psychology. The best reasons and wisest policies are worthless in practice if positive motivation is lacking, or when emotional negativism takes over. The neurotic knows perfectly well what is right, and may have every reason to feel well, but he doesn't. In the same way a society may strangle itself and head for disaster or turn the wisest program into a travesty, if that simplest of things, positive emotion, is missing. Conversely, any constitution, policy or program works if the positive emotion is there.

The nature of this emotion — the scarcest and most valuable thing in the world — is the capacity to experience enough satisfaction in following through the difficulties that every social

438

endeavor requires. The greatest difficulty is the overcoming of egotistic interests or distrust, and bearing sacrifice for others. The attainment of such satisfaction potential is paradoxical, as in the case of every satisfaction. The humanist, social theorist, and especially the practical leader see what is lacking, just as the common man does. They all try to promote positive emotion — either with or without sophistication — in the various, *direct, easy* ways that we shall discuss in a moment. But this amounts to positive emotional exaggeration. The result is *emotional negativism*, which can plunge a society into a neurosis, just as in individual psychology.

Since altruism and trust are the feelings that are most strived for — in easy, exaggerated ways without real conditioning — hate and fear are the central emotions of the resulting emotional negativism. When such negativism takes over, a nation may go to war, its economy may collapse in a slump, or a witch hunt may engulf the people, without apparent reason or cause. Then everybody, including the humanistic theorist, may wonder how men can be so irrational or bestial. Actually, people do not crave to kill a neighboring people, or to torture dissidents among themselves; nor do they panic by design. They simply cannot help it, just as the neurotic cannot help his feeling of persecution or of anxiety.

Conditioning alone can produce unreversing positive reactions. But as we saw, conditioning is a contradictory, inherently "deceitful" process. And it depends on the general omnipresent social atmosphere. These are the reasons why it is not understood, or even noticed, by the humanist or social theorist. We saw how this atmosphere depends upon all the people in the society rather than on any exceptional individuals or teachings. The real sources of social progress, which ultimately determine technical progress as well, are deeper and more general than any great ideas, lucky coincidences or revolutionary discoveries. America would have been discovered perhaps fifty years later if there had been no Columbus, but the same things would have happened to it in all other respects. We cannot imagine how the twentieth century could be without engines or electricity; and we can understand

439

why Hero's steam engine, invented three centuries before Christ, remained an insignificant speculation.

ECONOMICS

The paradox of relative causation, evidently, does not apply to the physical growth of economics. That growth is not limited by any predetermined normalcy. But the paradox applies where human motivations and values come in. These ultimately determine everything in economics. Take the business cycles — the central problem of all difficulties in modern economics. A simple loss of confidence leads to the collapse of the economy. The cause is a simple emotion, but the consequences are colossal, and so involved that economists can write volumes about them. It is clear to everybody that the economic potential is even higher when the slump starts than when the recovery begins. It is also clear that the boom could go on and on if people only continued to feel in the same way. This would mean that everybody would be employed to the limit he wants; and that every project would grow at a progressively increasing rate, reaching stupendous proportions in few decades. In a word, it would mean attaining everything man decides he wants. But boom is followed by slump under the same inexorable law under which the bliss of a drug addict or of a maniac is followed by depression. No reasons and no means in the world can help it. When science begins to understand why this is so, economics will have at least theoretical explanations and an insight into the direction in which the solutions are to be looked for.

We may divide our discussion under two headings: the contradictions of economic life as a form of adjustment, due to the general paradox of human adjustment; and the fallacies of economic theory, due to the lack of insight into the paradoxical logic of psychological causation.

I. Human adjustment is paradoxical because improvement in it is attained through seeming worsening. Enrichment and elaboration of release are attained through its restriction. Almost anything man strives for in his economic adjustment — unlimited

440

resources, unrestricted consumption, removal of difficulties, elimination of inequalities and competition — if reached fully would degrade his economy to a hand-to-mouth level in the end. Striving for material enjoyments directly is not the way to attain them. This explains why people who are highly materialistic never attain a higher economic development. Primitive man has no economy to speak of because he strives for his economic enjoyments in the most direct way, and has no patience or time for the seemingly useless accumulation of capital or learning. On the other hand, spiritually minded people who have learned to sacrifice their materialistic enjoyments reach the highest economic adjustment. As Toynbee has pointed out, the industrial revolution started — of all places — in Puritan England.

A deep misunderstanding about the opposition between spirituality and materialism has arisen because of this paradox. Spirituality or morals is only the embodiment of immemorial wisdoms which serve better adjustment. Ultimately, the only goal of this adjustment is material benefits. But to attain them man has to live in society, become culturally conditioned and observe restrictive tradition, as well as accumulate economic means and skills by saving and learning. All this means denial of immediate material enjoyments; and since man does not understand the paradox involved he accepts these wisdoms as religious dictates aimed against materialism. The modern humanist has retained the same attitude and sees moral values as being at least independent of materialistic benefits. Actually, these benefits are the only thing that remains after everything is said and done. Morals without them is worth so much words and hot air. The thousand-year moral tradition represents an intuitive compliance with the paradox of adjustment, but the meaning of it all has still not been understood.

We do not realize how much economic development depends on spirituality because we live in its atmosphere and cannot think of anything different. Imagine a different economic community — one in which honesty and diligence were not recognized as values. Then the most ambitious efforts would be consecrated, understandably, to learning how to steal and avoid work. We can imagine how primitive such a community would be. But we do not see how similar tendencies persisting in our society keep our economy on primitive levels. We showed how social cooperation based on true altruism would bring material benefits for everybody to an extent we at present cannot dream of. Even as it is, Western civilization has achieved an unprecedented progress because it has its roots in an equally unprecedented era of moral fervor, namely, the Middle Ages in Europe. As J. S. Gambs and S. Wertimer explain in their *Economics and Man*, the European countries started on their course of higher civilization about five hundred years ago. Up to that time European civilization did not differ essentially from others. Apparently, something happened in Europe at the height of the spirituality of the Middle Ages. We still live by the tradition of this spirituality, though the improved conditions that it has made possible are permitting us to lapse into increasing indifference to it.

By the way, the fact that the real purpose of morals is misunderstood matters little. It does not matter under what pretext a restriction is imposed. Once the background of restrictions is accumulated, it can serve as a source of motivation for any purpose; and man never lacks good, reasonable purposes.

The main paradox of adjustment is the beneficial effect of difficulties. Man strives to make his adjustment more comfortable and free of difficulties. But it is exactly the difficulties which are the factors that bring about progress with its higher benefits in the end. One of the greatest problems for man has been overpopulation. There man has met a difficulty that can really force him to change — a threat imposed by other, equally skillful beings. But the conflicts of increasing populations have brought about the social organization that is the basis for all cultural and economic development. Today economists see doom in overpopulation, as Malthus saw it in a population increase that we have long surpassed. Actually, overpopulation will make necessary scientific intervention in human eugenics, which is the next greatest breakthrough awaiting man. It will also bring men closer to the beehive integration toward which we are slowly but inevitably advancing.

The other main difficulty that economists have worried about

442

is the exhaustion of natural resources. In fact, every time there has been an exhaustion of some natural or "normal" resource, greater technical progress has resulted. The earth we live on is a ball of energy, and the energy deriving from the sun in various forms — from simple heat to waterfalls — is enormous. The sooner the resources which man knows how to use as a child of nature are exhausted, the sooner the era will arrive when incomparably greater artificial resources will be opened up. Of course, any difficulty or shortage has to be interspersed with opposite, favorable, conditions, for otherwise a shortage may become a "normalcy."

Inequality of wealth is another difficulty that economists have seen as an obstacle to more "normal" economic development. Actually, the abnormalcy — the difference in standards — that the inequality brings about is a primary source of progress (it also helps the accumulation of capital, as we shall see in a moment). If people could live in the undisturbed, competitionless peace of equality, they would continue on abominable levels and accept them as normal. All human evaluations are relative. In a few hundred years from now our own "normal" standards will be found unthinkably primitive. We know this will be so, but such knowledge does not help us much, because we cannot derive motivation from abstract conclusions. We have to live side by side with real examples of inequality that keep our feelings of inadequacy and need alive every day, before a motivation can accumulate. The same applies to countries. The most advanced country could continue expanding at the same pioneer rate it had during its early stages of development, if it had the example of a still more advanced country.

The mere realization that different standards are possible is sufficient to sustain progress at any pace, provided such a realization is established as an emotional reality. Civilized people placed on a primitive island would not cease struggling until they had attained the level of civilization they knew to be possible. Countries devastated by war, like Germany or Japan, could count the devastation as a blessing as far as the rebuilding of their economies was concerned. Wars in general are the greatest source of economic progress because they create difficulties that can be overcome only by going beyond what is "normal." Economists expected unemployment and recession after the last war, but an expansion took place instead.

Inequality of wealth between individuals or countries as well as differences in economic conditions of the same people at different times is the main source of the differences in standards that nurture progress. The American higher economy originated from the circumstance that the Europeans who came here had lived under more restricted conditions and intensive exploitation. When they found here richer resources, they could not think of leaving them unexploited even if that meant producing beyond what they "normally" needed. Feudal systems have been decried, but they performed the function of providing centers of higher and different standards. At present we see similar influences between countries. In the underdeveloped countries people had lived without change for millenniums — even after they had theoretically learned about higher standards elsewhere. Now these countries have awakened because these different standards have come closer to them as a reality. Still, if the people in these countries had things their way, they would rather see the higher standards disappear — insofar as they are not available to them.

All higher adjustment is governed by the rule of greater resourcefulness through greater restriction. In economics this manifests itself primarily in *saving* as restriction on the use of resources, and in learning as restriction on the immediate exercise of the productive function. Actually, it is saving that makes the learning and research possible and necessary within its ultimate function of the *creation of capital* as the source of all economic resourcefulness. Man's economic adjustment is a struggle with opposing natural forces. The first rule in such a struggle is that the side which has accumulated overwhelming power goes on winning in a chain-reaction fashion without much further effort. From the origins of life to the nuclear "burning" of elements that will finally open up unlimited sources of energy to man, *concentration of superior power* is what produces the stunning effect. Man can rule the universe without effort once he has accumulated such power. Accumulation of capital is the beginning of it. Specialization,

444

organization and learning serve the same goal. They enable man to apply power in a concentrated way, at precise points. When the ape-man used a sharpened stone, he attained the same concentration of his force on one point.

It is important to understand the principle of accumulation of superior power. All the phenomena of our technological age are expressions of it. The gigantic concentration of capital through investments, the increasing social integration, the teeming city, machines, extreme specialization, extension of research and life-long learning, are realizations of the same principle of greater resourcefulness, attainable through greater restraint. As the famous Austrian economist Boehm-Bawerk explains in his theory of "roundabout" production, the higher the form of production, the more it implies restraint on the *direct* exercise of activities aiming at production. Instead of attacking a layer of coal with the first tool at hand, man has first to organize society, accumulate capital, build machines and learn many other things; only then he can start the mining.

Of course, once the economic system with all the enormous capital investment and need for learning is established, economists accept it all as normal and never think of the basic paradox that it implies. But this lack of understanding what it all means is fundamentally important. It spells the difference between purposefully planned progress and the mere acceptance as normal of what has already been attained.

An "economist" from a more primitive system would argue that savings or restriction of consumption, as well as the waste of long years in unproductive learning, would ruin his economy by disrupting its normal consumption and production. We know how short-sighted such arguments are. But our wisdom is only one step higher. Our future generations will wonder how we could have been so primitive as to rush into spending or full living before accumulating the investment and learning which they will consider as the minimum requirements of a normal economy. Our economists argue exactly as the primitive "economist" does. For them also a decrease in consumption means disruption of our "normal" economy; and any additional, "unnecessary" learning, basic research, or investment in "human capital" appear under strict economic analysis as irrelevant, or even undesirable if they interfere with consumption. Even such mild criticism of the existing emphasis on indiscriminate consumption as was expressed in Galbraith's *Affluent Society* was considered unorthodox. Increased consumption, as a means of sustaining a "normal" rate of economic advance, is what the modern economist strives to promote.

Of course, it can be argued that the accumulation of capital, through restricted consumption, may only paralyze the economy if there are no enterprisers to invest it or no new inventions to use it for. This argument is valid in a theory which only follows, or lags behind, economic development instead of engineering it. It is clear, in practice, that if people have great economic resources and free time to learn, they will develop the skills and make the discoveries necessary for a better use of resources. This means discovery by plan, rather than by luck. Such a method is the mark of a higher economy. As to enterprising spirit, it is always there, in every man. And a carefully planned entrepreneurship rather than adventurousness is necessary to sustain consistent progress. Luck in discovery and adventure in enterprise are typical of blind, unplanned progress. There man happens to come upon a new possibility first and then starts accumulating the capital for its realization. Under a planned progress the process should be reversed.

There can be instances where capital is accumulated but finds no investment. The most important instance is the lack of investment of capital during regularly recurring periods of recessions. Modern views about underconsumption — about the evils of too much saving and the benefits of greater consumption, even dissaving — originate from observations of such depressions. In fact, depressions are due to the lack of accumulation of capital sufficient to sustain a real potential as the basis for the boom to continue. Then, as the boom breaks down and turns into a depression, everything collapses, including consumption and investment.

Naturally, the intellectual and moral capacities of people determine how intensively the available capital is invested. These factors cannot be affected directly by the mere accumulation of capital. But the availability of capital makes it possible for whatever capacities there are to be brought to fruition. Actually, it is not so much intellectual or technical difficulties as the inertial economic attitude that holds back progress. There is nothing technically difficult or fortuitous about economic progress. As long as people are determined to find better ways in the use of their accumulated resources for increased productivity, the rest follows automatically. They can start simply by building more machines, more schools, more roads or more extensive institutions for social cooperation. The improvements and discoveries come by themselves as the effort is continued; one can learn only by learning. The capacities of people are not so different either. In a capital-rich, highly developed economy even a person from an underdeveloped country performs satisfactorily.

In the last analysis it is waste in economic means and time that destroys the possibilities of progress. If a country does not progress in spite of the riches accumulated by some people, it is because those riches are wasted on personal enjoyments, the production of luxury goods, the cultivation of leisure or other wasteful goals. Waste is the greatest sin, and should be considered despicable in its every form. Only because morals evolve slowly and blindly, has waste not yet been recognized as the most loathsome of sins—and a stupidity. It is a stupidity because any capital that is accumulated now brings much greater advantages later.

But modern economists see increased consumption as the goal, and saving as an outright danger. Keynes is recognized as the greatest economic theorist of our time, but he is the prophet of those who blame saving or underconsumption as the cause of all economic ills and advocate dissaving as the remedy. Here we have a repetition in economic theory of the general fallacy of "scientism" in the human sciences, according to which more release is considered the source of higher motivation. Consumption in economics corresponds to release in psychology. To be sure, consumption supplies outwardly, in terms of experimental logic,

447

the vigor of economic expansion. But actually it is saving or restriction on consumption that supplies the capital necessary to save expansion from exhaustion and a lapse into recession. The paradox of release and restriction — as contrary to "scientism" as ever — is paralleled here. No wonder the best minds in this country cannot decide who is right: the economic scientists advocating increased spending and deficit budgets, or their conservative opponents.

Modern economists are so concerned with consumption that they interpret any kind of consumption, even absolutely unproductive luxury and entertainment goods and services, as sign of economic expansion. The car industry is the most important instance. Plain common sense tells us that unproductive consumption is a factor of economic regression rather than progress. A community which derived all its spendings and income from nothing more than unproductive services by its members to each other — let us say entertainment — would end with inflationary ruin, starvation and economic primitivism.

The result is that modern economics, not unlike psychology, has reached enormous heights of learning, but has not discovered much more than contradictions as regards the fundamental causes of economic progress. The more orthodox economists, in a parallel with experimental psychologists, have ended by rejecting all theories and simply following the economic facts, mostly statistical data. This deepens even more the attitude of lagging behind the economy instead of understanding its deeper causes and leading it. Actually, the truths that such statistical or factual study reveals — the trends that it discovers — are the worst possible basis for predicting or understanding anything.

If there is one striking feature in economic development, it is the reversal of a trend when it is strongest. Opposites, the boom and the slump, inherently generate each other, as most economists know. In other words, the paradoxical logic of opposite causation is there, and unless it is applied to every aspect and detail in the economic investigation, the results will be wrong. This explains why predictions by economists, vague and controversial as they are come true in hardly more than half of the cases — the average

448

of plain guessing. Actually, as regards the most important developments, namely, the reversing turns in the trends of expansion and depression, predictions by economists come out mostly wrong.

Economics has not yet become a science, but has remained an art, depending on the practical experience and intuitive intelligence of economists. In practice, skill in this art is often as important as theoretical understanding, much as it is in education. In economics, as in psychology, the release, which in economics means consumption, often has to be used to attain restrictions, which in economics means the accumulation of capital. As more goods are consumed, and mass production intensified, more capital investment is accumulated. This is a blind and unplanned progress. Moreover, insofar as the economist proceeds as a "scientist" rather than a wise practical man, he finds himself favoring increased consumption at the cost of savings, as a means of sustaining "normal" demand and "normal" economic advance.

By the way, it is pointless to try to stimulate consumption. People would work like crazy and consume like crazy if given the opportunity of unlimited employment. But to provide this, there must be a steady expansion, resting on an increase in economic potential through the accumulation of capital, not on its decrease through consumption.

The plain practical facts tell us that capital is a unique ingredient of progress. Capital is what enables man to produce with less effort; and once accumulated, it works for him forever. Practical life has evaluated this truth correctly. If one wants to achieve more with less work, he must have capital. The interest paid for capital represents the evaluation of this advantage by the practical man. And if one has plenty of capital, he can live without work. The argument that the capitalist can live without work only because he exploits others is not valid. The others, too, could live without working if they had saved enough. Then, who would be working? Machines. Capital means machines. Man's function in the universe is to organize and direct forces by the use of his brain alone. But, as we have said, man can do so only to the extent that he gains an overwhelming superiority in resourcefulness. In its primary form this means accumulated capital, best thought of

449

as machines. Practical sense tells us that the production of "machines that make more machines" is the way the highest progress will be attained.

But economic theory has no place for such simple truths. They are known to economists as commonplace facts but do not fit into a logical "scientific" system. How can saving or the restriction of consumption help if everything begins with demand or consumption. It seems senseless to produce machines for which there is no demand. The paradox of initial restriction for greater resourcefulness is strange here in every aspect. The more learned an economist is, the more he purifies the theory of all such illogic — and moves farther away from understanding the real source of economic progress. The high learning of modern economics is rather a handicap, as all high learning without causal understanding has been throughout history. Of course, a great part of economics means the technical training of professionals in the art of running existing business, and is fully valid.

Economics can never be simple, but the real problems lie in a completely different direction. They lie in man's difficulty in bearing restriction of the immediate enjoyments. That is why progress is so slow — even if men know well enough how it can be attained. If we could condition ourselves so that we all lived for what in simple terms means savings or the accumulation of capital, and its use in "production for the sake of production" or "machines for more machines," a utopian prosperity could be reached in a few generations. This may sound like a truism, but that is exactly the point. Simple practical knowledge shows what is right — but too difficult to follow. As in psychology, no theoretical maneuvering or know-how can help here. But the scientist tries to find advantageous "scientific" ways, different from the common-sense truisms which he considers not worthy of his learned interest. As in alchemy or modern psychology, such "scientism" rests, however, on pretension rather than understanding. All sciences have advanced by coming down to earth.

By the way, one should not think that a central regimentation is necessary for conscious or planned progress. As long as everybody, individually, saves and invests, he can attain prosperity with less

450

effort. A few generations of misers can accumulate so much that the next generations can begin living in prosperity and ease. This could apply to everybody and to the economic community as a whole. Further, as long as everybody thought only in terms of endless production ahead, with the idea of continuous investment, there would be a continuous, fully sustained boom with unlimited employment and exponential rate of growth.

It is through such simple but hard to obey truths that economics can become a science capable of leading instead of merely lagging behind economic progress. Perhaps in our age of scientism a true science can do much — even influence human attitudes and thus supply what tardily advancing morals has not yet evolved, this being ultimately the most important factor. As it is, economics, like all human sciences, has reached, side by side with an incredible amount of learning, an impasse to the point of mystery in causal understanding of its fundamental phenomena. This shows best in the fact that the cyclic convulsions of modern economy have remained its pivotal problem, but also a complete mystery. At the same time, the principles of all human adjustment as a product of man's nature and his position in the universe can be only simple. These principles are embodied in our commonplace attitudes. These, however, are found neither interesting nor causally revealing by the scientist.

In all fields, attitudes or changes in attitudes contribute more than anything else in reaching scientific breakthroughs. In economics as a science of the total results of behavior, attitude is all-important. Think of the industrial revolution. It could have been started a thousand years earlier by a simple change of attitude. All that was needed was a dogged determination to continue concentrating, by planned vast research, for generations, on the discovery of better tools and materials. No deep insight would have been necessary to see that this is the right way. But anybody who insisted on such an idea would have been deemed a crank. Especially would highly learned men have considered such an idea below their dignity and standards of learning.

It is inherent in man's adjustment that progress comes in spite of his intentions and sense of values, which includes his sense

451

of scientism. Man's adjustment, like his sciences, are inertial. Man learns the deeper wisdoms through blind intuitive tradition, but finds them unacceptable in his theoretical reasoning. The cultural tradition stresses economic *restriction* in the forms of thrift, rejection of materialistic enjoyments and a predilection for spirituality; and the practical sense recognizes the primary importance of capital attainable through savings. But economics as a logical and inventively "scientific" learning rejects such simple wisdoms and advocates increased consumption or economic *release* instead.

We cannot discuss the various doctrines of modern economic theory, but we can mention the most persistent one: that of underconsumption. It has been the main thesis of Marxism, which in the form of various socialisms dominates the modern political and economic scene. The same attitude, permitting the natural tendencies of people to prevail, has led to the dominant patterns of modern economy, as illustrated by inflationary wages, consumption promotion, advertising, living on credit and modern affluent spending. Decrease in consumption is seen as an outright danger. According to the Marxian thesis, depressions are inevitable because capitalists underpay the workers so that these become unable to purchase what they have produced. This view has been held by the most famous economists, including Malthus, Hobson and Keynes, and is logically almost unattackable. But life shows that just the reverse is true. In countries where capital accumulation is highest, which means where capitalists have consistently and really grossly underpaid the workers, employment is highest and the economy most progressive. Apparently, the capitalists here have behaved in the economically illogical way of investing where it was economically absurd to invest, where no demand, theoretically, could exist — and have raised the economy to a new, higher, "normalcy."

The history of Marxism and socialism is revealing. Socialistic economists, whose well-meant humanitarian ideas dominate modern economic theory, have laid more stress on the equalization of wealth than the accumulation of capital. Actually, distribution of wealth among the spending-prone masses means the destruction

452

of capital and of the means of production on which employment of the masses depends. The highest expression of socialism, Communism, derived its power from the revolutionary masses who wanted to get the wealth of the rich. They got very little of it, but destroyed the capital on which their own livelihood depended. Communist dictators had to sweat that capital out of the masses by slave-driving, turning into a travesty the ideals of human freedom, dignity or even equality.

However the problem is examined, capital is the exceptional source of economic progress. The primary practical facts about the underdeveloped countries are increasingly showing this. And there is no other way to accumulate capital than by saving and underpayment of the masses, who usually tend to overspend rather than save. The hated, greedy capitalist perfoms the highest social service. He accumulates capital and invests it with the utmost care and skill for the best possible production. He leaves it for the next generation, who does the same. The capital ultimately serves everybody, in the form of cumulatively expanding and improving means of production, since in the end each capitalist would have used only a small portion of it for his own personal spending. Capitalists are usually thrifty. The very stinginess that everybody hates in a capitalist — and which often makes him one — is the greatest bonanza for the economic community.

Even if the capitalist hoards his money — modern economists, especially Keynesians, blame hoarding as the main evil — he contributes to economic expansion. Money hoarded means capital given to others, as every economist should know. It thus becomes an interest-free loan to other producers. In the end, no institution could perform such an extremely careful and skillful service to the community at so little expense. The good-intentioned socialist, who wants to give more to the workers, would reduce the economy to primitive levels where the workers would have to scratch for their living with bare hands, — if he had his wishes fulfilled.

Of all economic factors — labor, management or resources — capital is the only one that works for man automatically by itself once it is accumulated, like a robot created by man, as is clearly evident in machines, the most typical form of capital. This fact harbors a deep causal truth about man's adjustment, which economic theorists have not yet understood.

II. Now we may look at the fallacies of economic theory which originate from the lack of understanding of the paradox of psychological relativity. It should be clear that *economic theories and laws rest on certain basic psychological assumptions.* It is assumed that people, in pursuit of their interests, evaluate advantages, act according to certain sets of values, have expectations, fears, value preferences and so on, in definite predictable ways. Since all these reactions are psychological and therefore subject to the reversals of relative causation, the conclusions of economists often make appear as true the exact opposite of what is causally true; or they are at least incomplete. To take recessions, which are so important, their cause is a loss of confidence originating in a previous exaggeration of confidence. This is a paradox that the economist as an experimental scientist can never accept. Further, the paradox induces him to reject the causal relevance of the confidence factor in the first place. For he observes that the slump occurs at the moment when confidence has reached its highest accumulation.

Psychological values as dealt with by economists are absolute, unchanging values. This means dealing with an ever "normal," logically consistent world. In view of the paradoxical logic of motivation and adjustment, such a "normal" world of the economists represents a world of mere hypotheses to which nothing in real life corresponds. Apart from the main fact that exceptions to the "normalcy" are the cause of progress and of every *significant* development in economic life, even a static economy could not persist under "normal" conditions. For instance, in the absolutely normal world of the economists, supply and demand are balanced. There needs to be only as much production as there is consumption. But in real life man must constantly aim to produce more than he consumes, even if he is only to hold his own. Otherwise, the hundreds of adversities of life would drive his standards imperceptibly down toward a hand-to-mouth economy. Man has this tendency to produce more because he never finds sufficient what he has, due to the relativity or inconsistency of values. Thus an "abnormalcy" or constant lopsidedness is what sustains normalcy, though the theorist suspects neither the underlying adversity nor the "abnormal" aspirations of real life.

In the static, ever "normal" world of the economists, great economic progress with a hundredfold accumulation of capital investment amounts to an aberration from the balanced interplay of demand and supply on which economic theory rests. We saw how higher economic standards, like those of America, have resulted from "erroneous" lopsidedness in that interplay. But to the modern economic theorist this means the disbalance of underconsumption as the main danger of economic recession. Actually, every advance results from such economically abnormal or illogical human reactions. During periods of expansion people are crazy enough not to realize that there is no real demand for what they are producing. But as they proceed, demand increases, a different normalcy emerges and it all ends with success. Capitalists do this all the time by withholding capital from consumption, producing absurdly for the mere sake of production—and finally dragging the economy into a new normalcy.

Naturally, in the static, ever "normal" world of the economists, an economic factor has meaning only as it exists. But anything significant in economic development originates from a disregard of the *existing* state of a factor. If the law of diminishing returns were right, there would be no advances in production. Disregard of this law leads to progress. Somebody is illogical enough to continue beyond the existing normal return and succeeds in discovering a new method of production, or in opening up a new kind of resource. We saw how the realization that things are not normal the way they are is the source of economic progress with different standards of return and ways of production.

The fallacy of absolute or "normal" causal factors shows best in the various theories or laws of value. To take the most popular theory—that of marginal utility, established by Jevons, Menger and Clark, which predominates in modern economy—it does not correspond to reality, because of the relativity of values and utility. The margin of "utility" may extend endlessly, as the value of "better," "more" or any other secondary value may become as important as the primary utility value. Due to the relativity of evaluations no value has a logical effect. A need may persist though it may seem to have been fully met; or satisfaction may never be complete in spite of every logical evidence to the contrary.

People may also behave like neurotic perfectionists in regard to their economic avoidances and enjoyments. This applies to every economic motivation. Even competition—one of the main factors of economic life—which is clearly dominated by cold reason, cannot be gauged in the logical terms that seem unmistakably to apply to it at any given moment. Due to relativity of motivation, competition resurges on secondary levels after it seems to have been basically removed. One economist explains how Chevrolet competes with Pontiac and Buick inside General Motors. Even where a monopoly position is gained, people and subdivisions within it may start competing in unsuspected ways. Economists are noticing that competition is resurging in weird illogical ways in modern economy, and have expounded various theories to explain it.

Actually, none of the supposed economic laws works in reality. The economically determining factors are value factors. Dealing with them in any "normal" or logical terms is delusory, because of the reversals, fixations and irrational perfectionism in all value behavior. No wonder the institutional economics that oppose the logical classical approaches are gaining followers. But institutionalism is equally misleading in the absence of an understanding of relative causation, especially the mechanisms of fixation and reversals.

Like the classical economic theories and laws, new ones are postulated on the same basis: psychological or motivational truths newly discovered by the theorist. For instance, the central idea of the most important modern economic theory, namely that of Keynes, was built on a new psychological assumption. He assumed as a "fundamental psychological law" that an increase in earnings causes an increase in savings and a relative decrease in spending. In fact, the psychological effect of wage increases and saving is as relative as anything else. A person used to wage increases has a greater rather than a smaller propensity to spend.

We cannot go into a discussion of all the instances of theoretical fallacies due to the paradox of the relativity of values and motivations. We shall limit ourselves to the most important instance: the one which concerns the expectations and fears that determine the over-all economic motivation. With this we come to the central problem of modern economy, namely, cyclic depressions.

BUSINESS CYCLES

The alternating recurrence of economic expansions and recessions has come to be recognized as an inevitability. Kiekhofer says in his *Economic Principles, Problems and Policies* that there may be a "quality of the human mind that finds expression in alternative states of optimism and pessimism." Economists know that there is a direct relation between expansion and recession, as if they automatically generated each other. Mitchell, the foremost authority on business cycles, and Schumpeter have advised that a recession should be left alone to work itself into an expansion. They have explained that otherwise the interference "leaves part of the work of the depression undone."

We cannot discuss in detail all the forms of expectations and fears, or of confidence and loss of confidence, in economic life. These forms are as many as there are business activities. From the small shopkeeper to the great banker, all business is governed by expectation of gain — by an emotional value. Every one of the millions of varied transactions are supported by this feeling. But all feelings are subject to the simple law of relative causation.

The optimistic confidence that supports economic expansion is pleasant as well as highly profitable for all. Therefore it is exaggerated to extremes. The inevitable opposite reaction then brings about the loss of confidence, and a depression, in an equally exaggerated form. Keynes, in his *General Theory*, speaks of the "contrary error of pessimism" as the cause of depressions. He points out that bankers and businessmen are right in emphasizing the factor of confidence, while economists underestimate it. Confidence was recognized as an important economic factor by Marshall, in his classical work, *Principles of Economics*. Everybody knows that there is nothing wrong with an economy during a depression; that it can produce at full capacity, but that some mysterious force keeps it from doing so. This mysterious force is the same that makes a neurotic behave irrationally even while he knows it. A recession breaks out *suddenly* because the opposite background, optimism, is unremittingly upheld to its utmost limit. Recovery comes *slowly* because its opposite background, pessimism, is resisted and its acceptance drawn out.

Why the confidence or loss of it has this kind of effect is understandable from the *interdependence* of destinies of people in a highly specialized economy. For instance, when the masses become cautious and slow down in their purchase of cars, the car industry orders less steel, which induces the steel industry to curtail its production and cut employment. This makes the masses even more cautious — and a chain reaction may be on its way. In practice the interdependence is much wider and more intricate. The important fact is the realization by everybody that he is exposing himself to ruin to the extent that he expands or spends when a general depression is about to start. Consequently, everybody tries to recede first, before it is too late — and a general panic results. The strongest army can be defeated if it loses confidence. As every soldier tries to flee before the others do, all of them may perish, though with confidence they could have won easily.

The decisive factor, in starting the chain-reaction panic of economic recession, is a general emotional saturation — a general propensity toward negativism in evaluations, arising from an equally general opposite exaggeration. Actually such exaggeration in confidence is what makes during a period of boom, every business expand in expectation of gain, and succeed. The ensuing opposite emotions have exactly corresponding opposite effects in every respect and in every form of business activity.

Does this mean that there must always be as great depression as there was expansion? Rather not. Economic growth is not relative in itself. The economy can grow endlessly. All that men would have to do is to exclude emotions as business motivation and act according to the rational conviction that the economy can grow unlimitedly, even if it has to go through temporary shortages or difficulties. Keynes has pointed out the disastrous influence of the emotionally minded masses on the stock market. Unfortunately, we cannot exclude emotion from business. There is no substitute for interest. If interest is missing, everything goes to pieces. The interest can only be conditioned. The main aim of such conditioning should be the creation of a moral atmosphere in which people would not act like scared and confused strangers distrusting everybody and everything. Also, the more serene emotional attitudes that come with restrictive cultural conditioning can make people act more consistently with rational beliefs in a never-ending progress. All this may seem more like a spiritual development, but its effects are not less real than the money it causes business to lose or win. And it is going on imperceptibly all the time.

Another, causally similar, but presently more tangible possibility of preventing the exaggeration in the "contrary error" lies in *the creation of a really existing basis for continuous expansion. The opposite reaction that causes a depression is due to exaggerations in evaluating reality. To the extent that real possibilities of expansion do exist and therefore no real exaggerations are incurred, the opposite reversal has no cause to arise.* The evaluations as to these real possibilities are complex and imperceptible. They go on at every moment in the heads of millions of people and slowly result in a common feeling. All psychological evaluations are complex in detail beyond our grasp, but nevertheless precise and compelling. What those real possibilities for expansion are we have already showed. They all can be traced back to one thing: the accumulation of capital, which means more savings and less consumption.

But modern economists advise dissaving and increase in consumption as the means of avoiding depressions. As Kiekhofer says in his book, this view is held by the most naïve as well as the most sophisticated people and has been made respectable by the Keynesian theory. We are witnessing here an example of the paradox of overadjustment — improvement that brings about worsening in the end — on the economic level. An initial release produces a spurt of vigor but precludes the development of a basis for real expansion. The underconsumptionist view has become very popular and dominates economic theory. All kinds of promotions of consumption are favored by economists. Thus we find ourselves financing our own depression. Installment buying and credit plans, that are wasteful and costly, as well as the fabulously expensive advertising, add tens of billions of dollars on top of consumption itself. People steeped in cultural tradition feel that this is all wrong. But economic "science" is more convincing in our age of scientism, though when a depression comes economists are as puzzled as everybody else.

Keynes derived his theory on depressions from observations during a depression — as is logical for experimental scientism. Naturally, during a depression savings find no investment, consumption decreases and everything works out wrong, because of the panic. Keynes himself recognized, under his multiplier concept, that investment is what multiplies the possibilities of employment. He advised more savings *and* more consumption. This is like giving the advice: behave as you did during expansion and everything will be all right. Everybody knows it would be all right — but nobody can help it. Any stimulation — the assurances of the economists, the cry of the politician that there is nothing to fear but fear itself, or an increase in advertising — is helpless because there was already overstimulation. But the logic of experimental scientism never reveals the deeper opposite cause.

By the way, advertising can establish silly fixations on certain often less valuable and most unproductive goods and services, but cannot increase consumption as a whole, because its effects wear out and reverse as it continues. Everybody has to shout louder and louder just to keep from being drowned out by others; the "shouting" may become very subtle, but that only increases the cost. Advertising is a waste that decreases economic potential, raises prices and handicaps the more serious, morally better businessman, who is more valuable for a sound economy because as a rule he is also more capable intellectually. The same reversal of effect applies to all endeavors aiming at the promotion of consumption.

460

Overproduction is blamed by other economists as the cause of depressions. The very fact that people are eager to work and earn during a depression shows that not enough has been produced. The mysterious paralysis during a depression is purely psychological. It is like the emotional negativism in neurosis. It can neither be helped by reasoning nor explained by the usual logic. The statistics on inventories or the durability periods of goods are handy to economists for "explaining" after the fact what happened, or "predicting" a trend while it continues. When the depression is on, everything and everybody can be blamed. For instance, the producers can say that if consumers bought more, a revival would start; the consumers can say that if the producers did not slow down, there would be enough money to buy; the bankers can say that if business were more aggressive, credits could be extended; but businessmen can say that if credits were easier to get, business would pick up.

This explains why there are half a dozen fully convincing theories, each blaming some one factor as the cause of depressions: unavailability of money and credit, inflexibility of prices, fluctuations in the rate of investment or output of durable goods. The most inclusive is the theory, expounded by Mitchell, of the behavior of profit margins. Profits undoubtedly play the central role in business cycles, since they are the goal of all business. But in this theory as well, only the immediate "causes," which are actually effects of deeper opposite causes, are recognized. It is not the decline of profits due to the business slowdown that causes the slump, but the slump due to overoptimism, that causes the collapse of profits. The economy can go on expanding forever in spite of temporary slowdowns provided there is a realistic confidence in the possibilities of expansion, which means that these possibilities must be there as accumulated capital and skills.

The innovation theory, worked out by Schumpeter, shows how booms have depended on inventions: the railroad, automobile, telephone and radio. We can only agree with this. Anything that inspires hopes of profit, or offers new possibilities, can start economic expansion. But if the expansion is not supported by

461

real economic potential, that is, availability of capital, a depression will follow. Moreover, inventions reach their full exploitation only when the accumulation of capital, especially in the form of machines and advanced skills in their production, has reached the corresponding level.

Most economists, especially the more orthodoxly "scientific" ones, have given up unified theories and are inclined to accept the view that many varied factors are the causes of business cycles. This is manifestly wrong. Business cycles are so characteristically uniform and regular in their general effects that only one uniform cause can account for their existence.

What can be done to prevent depressions? In our emotionally motivated and incompletely integrated society only the avoidance of booms can prevent the occurrence of slumps. Such an avoidance establishes itself as a matter of psychological adjustment, if the business is left to itself. A big crash like that of the thirties can keep businessmen cautious for decades. Then no great booms or slumps occur. But is such a state of moderation preferable? Rather not. Men learn by being exposed to difficulties, especially if the periods of difficulties are interspersed with periods of high advance. In fact, a period of slump is more productive of new ways of thinking, hard learning, innovations and social reform than a period of boom. Selection also has opportunity to work during difficulties. During the big recession of the thirties some highly viable enterprises, in plastics and electronics, survived unscathed.

Periods of depression are appallingly destructive. National income dropped from $87.2 billion in 1929 to $42.2 billion in 1932. No calamity, except a major war, can destroy so much. But gains during booms are equally spectacular. Enterprises that otherwise would have remained only dreams become realities. Because everybody believes in everybody else, like soldiers in battle, impossible or "abnormal" projects are attacked and new levels of normalcy established.

All the efforts that are usually made to prevent or alleviate a depression mean also slowing down the preceding or succeeding boom. A government can make loans easier only if it has built up previous reserves, which means withdrawing capital from investments during the boom. The reserve systems now functioning in most countries act on this principle. If the government reduces taxes, it must levy more later or must have levied more previously. If it intervenes as enterpriser, it takes business away from the private sector. There is no doubt that government could proceed without being exposed to depressions. Government does not need emotions for motivation, therefore it suffers no emotional reversals, which cause depressions. That is why recessions do not exist in government-controlled economies. But by taking emotion out of economy, its most valuable force, private initiative, is also destroyed. Absence of economic organic unity, which the state has politically, is the reason for the economic convulsions. But such unity cannot be created by decree. It should be evolved by conditioning private interests into common interests and reciprocal trust.

To the extent that government already has control of some section of the economy, it should exercise reason rather than yield to pressures. For instance, two governments having control of foreign trade could lessen a depression by increasing trade between themselves by simple rational agreement, even if this seemed absurd in terms of the immediate interests of each. Increased exports would mean increased production by each country for the other. To the same extent people in both countries would be kept working and earning — and finally buying. However, it oftener happens that governments also get panicky and restrict trade, thus deepening the depression.

In brief, periods of depression neither can nor should be avoided in our present, emotionally nurtured economic system striving for expansion. The background accumulated during a depression is precisely the source of the optimism and confidence that bring about the boom. Here the psychological cause of booms and slumps shows clearly. The economy is incomparably weaker and more disrupted when the recovery starts, after a long slump, than it was when the recession started, after a long boom. Economic shortages or disturbances in themselves never cause recessions, as is again evident in government-controlled economies. Recession is a necessary counterpart of expansion. That is

463

why they inevitably follow each other, and must be allowed to run their full course, just as experts on business cycles suggest. Only a psychological, never an economic, causation can explain why this is so. To predict or control this causation, economists should understand its paradoxical logic, which at present is the last thing they recognize.

POLITICS

In the theory of political sciences there are two main series of misunderstandings arising because of the paradox of relative causation. The first is due to the emotional negativism growing out of exaggerations of positive emotions. The second is due to the deceit underlying social conditioning, and to the delusionism inherent in value beliefs.

As to the first, nations may go to wars or engage in the persecution of minorities and "witch hunts" without ever wanting to — as if driven by an evil destiny. As we have repeatedly explained, there can be no emotion without an opposite background. To exalt something as good without hating something else, that is different, as bad is an impossibility. An emotional recognition by people of themselves as "we" is nonsensical if there are no "others" — external enemies or internal minorities.

No country can exist without an emotional readiness of its people to bear sacrifice. The love of one's own country or people is the underlying force in any national endeavor. If the nation has a particularly difficult task to complete, the people work themselves into a frenzy of self-love and self-justification. Then an equal hate for the "others" and the feeling of being wronged or not sufficiently recognized become compulsive. The process is the same as in the case of a person who has to perform a difficult task, derives his motivation from self-indulgence, and ends by hating everybody and everything. In all such cases the feeling is characterized mostly by hate and fear or mistrust because the positive exaggeration mostly centers on love and the sense of security. The "love" here is the primitive source of all motivation, or self-love, which in the case of a nation means the love of

464

one's "own" country, "own" beliefs or "own" people. Patriotism is always an extended egotism.

The only alternative to such a "neurosis" is age-long social conditioning, enabling people to bear sacrifice and personal restrictions for the common good without special emotional appeals, or feelings that something special has been done. The readiness to obey laws and to cooperate with political opponents are the main concrete expressions of such social conditioning. They depend to a great degree upon the general moral conditioning of the people. As we saw, any conditioned restriction constitutes an emotional capital that can be used for any motivation, and man never lacks reasonable intentions. Greater conditioning is required if the national tasks aimed at are more difficult but its people feel less close to each other. Consequently, ambitious but culturally less integrated nations of more varied peoples or larger territories suffer from complexes more. Good and logically correct intentions to build big new nations therefore often shatter in practice, as has been the case in Latin America and in Africa. If such difficulties are overriden, internal political factions build up on the obsessive feelings of "we" and the "others." Political cooperation becomes impossible and only a dictatorship can do.

The main point is that a nation may want the war and persecution or internal strife and dictatorship as little as a neurotic wants his hate, emotional negativism or obsession. Even the best intentions turn out wrong to the extent that a nation suffers from its "neurosis." The famous publicist, Norman Angell, explains in his book, *The Unseen Assassin,* that nations do not desire wars and other evils, but unfortunately apply policies with unforeseen vile implications which become the unseen assassins of their peace and welfare.

The complexes of opposite emotions explain why otherwise reasonable people may engage in witch hunts of various kinds. In the countries under Communist regimes one finds repeated persecutions of saboteurs and counterrevolutionaries, though in these countries of totalitarian terror few even think of sabotage. In our country as well we sometimes live through unexplainable excesses. McCarthyism was obviously due to a specific kind of opposite

465

exaggeration. The friendly emotional attitude that was cultivated toward Communism, especially during the war, reversed into its opposite upon the discovery of the true face of Communism. The medieval witch hunts, Crusades and Inquisitions were due to similar exaggerations, as the public emotions oscillated between Christian fervor and strong lingering heathen beliefs. The people who burned witches were as intelligent as we are, but they could not help doing absurd things because the emotional compulsion was there. When there is an emotional need, completely plausible justifications are always found. At present, the most typical of all is the need of a nation in difficulties to hate some other nation. The nation hated is one that the people know more about: a neighbor, a nation with which it has had the longest relations, or simply a prominent nation. The "hate Americans" outbursts in countries suffering the aftereffects of great ambitions are typical of this complex.

All this has to remain a mystery, especially as to its exact causal process, to political scientists who do not even suspect the paradox of opposite causation. The causal connection between the exaggerated cultivation of love of one's own people or country and the hate of others, for instance, is never understood. Patriotism as the expression of high positive feelings and love would be the last thing blamed if it were not for the unmistakable observation that strong nationalisms do lead to wars and persecutions. Numerous explanations for this are sought in logical deductions about ideologies, political incidents or factual conditions. Equally numerous recommendations and solutions based on logical reasons are offered. Actually, logical reasons and justifications are always found, by all concerned, but have nothing to do with the real cause — the paradoxical complex.

Some theorists blame wrong understanding of legal concepts, such as sovereignty. They hope to promote order in the world by teaching the right understanding of these concepts. Understanding can help here as little as in the case of a neurosis. Sovereignty is mainly used as an excuse by a nation in difficulty. The very idea of sovereignty and the national state arose from the need to engage people more intensively in political cooperation.

Legalistic notions are only expressions of psychological realities and grow out of them, not the other way around.

As long as high ambitions are to be fulfilled by people who are not conditioned up to them, hate between nations and internal groups or political blocs is inevitable. Men can only try to turn hate into competition for more worthwhile goals. Such goals can be moral prestige, economic progress, scientific advance, foreign aid or conquest of space. Well-meant endeavors to replace cold war by friendship may lead to equally exaggerated aftereffects in the other direction — hysterical hostility and the outbreak of conflict. A reactionary policy cultivating "brinkmanship" may be less dangerous than one aimed at cultivating friendship.

All this does not mean that patriotism and nationalism are wrong. Even in their neurotic forms they are beneficial, just as the sufferings of the neurotic are beneficial. Nationalism means an endeavor to make individuals transform their narrow egotistic interests into somewhat wider interests. The very fact that "neurotic" reactions arise here shows that the endeavor of transformation is strong — actually too fast in relation to the existing general moral conditioning. But while the nation suffers under its "neurosis" it accepts the new transformation gradually. The only wrong patriotism is the one from which the people try to derive pleasure or the gratification of self-pride. Such patriotism, like any enjoyment, degrades conditioning and deepens the chauvinistic fixations which are a great obstacle to wider integration between nations with its incomparable benefits.

On the other hand, a patriotism of higher quality means learning to bear sacrifice for more and more remote groups. Such patriotism is a necessary intermediary step on the way to gradual regional and world-wide integrations. Nations which are internally so deeply patriotic that they do not need nationalistic appeals are the ones that cooperate among themselves more fruitfully. Of course, the internationalists see nationalism as leading away from world government and as an obstacle to be removed. Internationalists suggest various logically convincing legal forms, constitutions and procedures. This is a waste of effort. Political cooperation grows out of age-long conditioning and slowly

467

evolving motivations. When these are there any legal form or constitution can do.

The only other way toward world government is conquest. People, if forced to integrate as one nation, gradually acquiesce. As they continue bearing sacrifice for the unified country it becomes "their" achievement, "their" common good. The unification of the score of German states into one Reich is a good example. The number of deeper common ties, harmony of interests, even new common successes may determine how well such integration succeeds. Germany held up well as long as new successes were reached or fervently anticipated by the people. The defeat in the First World War, however, made all its difficulties rebounce. The new exaggerated effort then led to the Nazi regime and a new war.

Now we may turn to the second series of misunderstandings — those arising from the self-deceit underlying social conditioning, and from the delusions inherent in value beliefs. As we saw, the conditioning to be successful has to be so general and thorough that it is not felt or noticed. This explains why conditioning does not exist for humanists and social scientists, though it certainly is the main source of social cooperation. We also explained that conditioning is a contradictory process, in which a natural drive is transformed and gradually turned against itself by its own operation. Altruism grows from the conditioning of egotism. That is why religious conditioning, based on the promise of rewards, and traditional moral conditioning, based on the sense of one's own worth, security or superiority, are the best methods of social education. It is not by accident that the same inherently contradictory religious and moral methods evolve in all societies. Even Communism returns to them, though it starts out with their rejection.

In political life, freedom has become the main value in the name of which political conditioning is imposed. The freedom derives its increasing value from the intense general level of restrictions in higher societies. All social movements and revolutions of modern times have risen under the slogans of freedom, though people have immediately, if unwillingly, learned the necessity of restrictions. In brief, we find freedoms as the persisting highest social goals, often written into constitutions, in the more advanced societies actually living under the highest restrictions. Then it looks as if such societies have advanced because of their struggles for freedom, and the freedoms seem to be the main source of social progress. In other words, we have here a simple case of the general delusionism of the value outlook. Unfortunately, humanists and social theorists build most of their theories on the salient belief that freedoms are the sources of social progress. Actually, freedom derives its meaning and value only from its opposite. The same applies to all other values, such as individual worth, self-expression, natural human rights and so on.

The misconceptions arising from this delusionism have permeated all modern political thinking, often with unfortunate consequences. For instance, the more primitive peoples, like the young nations of Africa, learn from Western theorists that freedoms and personal rights are what make nations great. A travesty of political life results. Those peoples need a tradition of subordination and abdication of personal rights more than anything else. Western peoples lived for a thousand years in the spirit of unquestioned subordination before they became sufficiently socially conditioned so that they could afford the slogans and theories of freedom. The primitive peoples could have continued advancing at a progressive rate under Western colonization as they have done in Africa during the past decades. In the last fifty years many African peoples have been brought up from the stone age to half-civilization. Fifty years more, and they might really be able to become civilized nations.

But how can any modern man support colonialism? We all speak only of freedoms and human rights. We extol them and teach them to everybody, including the few educated Africans. These then drive their people into nationalistic frenzies. Naturally, the primitive people who listen to such leaders feel the cultural restrictions imposed by their masters very hard indeed, and expect that the promised freedoms will give them everything the masters have.

469

The final result is that such peoples get their freedom, by violence, but find it meaningless — as in itself it is. Soon they land under the dictatorship of their own leaders, which is more primitive and less beneficial culturally than colonialism was. Whatever cultural influence these people continue receiving comes from the same Western peoples. Names change and enthusiasms flare up, but the cultural realities remain the same. In fact, there is not much loss either, at least in the beginning. The new free nations are emotionally aroused to show their best. After the first misunderstandings, confusions and emotional upheavals, often costly in lives and suffering, the people learn, under the pressure of their own-created difficulties and ambitions, the need for subordination and restrictions, which they so hated to accept under their old masters. In the long run there may be some loss, as the progressive influences of former colonizers become less direct. But with modern means of communication and the struggle for world-wide influence, no people can remain remote for long.

What we have said here about new nations fighting for freedom applies to the "internal proletariats" fighting for more liberal policies. The intelligentsia is usually the more articulate element of this proletariat — probably because of its absorption of political theories. This proletariat usually becomes the breeding ground for a more liberal political party. While such a party grows, in opposition to the more reactionary party, it advocates all kinds of political freedoms and economic socialism. But when it starts participating in political life, it learns the hard realities and soon reverts to the same old "reactionary" policies. Then another still more leftist party grows into power, but with time turns reactionary too. This has been the general pattern in the history of political parties, though in some cases the party retains its old name while adopting more leftist platform.

There is some irony in those cases where power is gained alternately by the reactionary and the liberal blocs in a country. The reactionary party builds on what we could generally designate economic and social restrictions. This means building up a background for a greater future potential. The immediate results may

470

seem like a slowing down — especially to a theorist dealing "scientifically" with statistics and immediate effects. Then the more liberal party, when it gets in power, starts policies of freer spending and social concessions. The result is comparable to the spectacular successes attained by the progressive educator or the doctor using miracle drugs. If the "reactionary" party manages to get back into power, it again has the ungrateful task of building a new background of economic and social potential.

In practice the misunderstandings of humanists and theorists of political sciences matter little. As in education, in political conditioning the delusory value beliefs serve as inducements. The only objection is that the present humanistic delusionism will make it difficult for a causal understanding of political problems ever to prevail. Such understanding is the basis on which man could turn his own adjustment into a science that in the end could transform our life more spectacularly than technical sciences have done in their area. Of course, with the present lack of causal understanding only more confusion can result from scientific intervention into social adjustment. Probably, this is the reason why serious sociologists have remained skeptical at present. William F. Ogburn, one of the founders of modern sociology, says in his *Sociology*: "The idea that a tremendous development like the superorganic can be controlled or even directed is a fantasy."

Now we may look at the main types of modern governments. **Democracy** is the modern ideal. Technological progress has made life so much easier that people can afford to choose freer governments. The general atmosphere of liberties finds its expression in the democratic forms of government. Since the more liberal forms of government thus come with progress, they are often assumed as the cause of progress. Actually, democracy *is* better than totalitarianism or Communism — but not because of the democratic principles it is supposed to realize. *Democracy can work successfully only to the extent that it denies its principles in practice*, whatever way, conscious or unconscious, this compromise is attained.

Everybody knows that democracy could not work if the politi-

471

cians cultivated separationist tendencies, disregard of common interests and favoritism for local or factional interests. But if democratic representation were carried out as it is supposed to be, then exactly these factional interests would be the goal to be sought by the elected representatives. The politician bargaining only for the benefits and deals that his voters expect from him would be the ideal politician. The representation of interests may sound logical in theory, but only chaos would result if in fact the interests that every voter really feels important were to be "represented" or heard. The politicians who get elected on particular promises rather than capacity to serve the nation as a whole in full independence are the curse of democracy. The success of a democratic or any government depends on its ability to act for common national goals and to provide expertness in government rather than on the opportunity for politicians to bargain their voting power. But this can be insured only to the extent that government gravitates toward methods which exactly oppose what a truly representative democracy should stand for.

The same can be said about the other democratic ideals. Personal freedoms and individualism are good only so far as they permit reciprocal restrictions. Freedom if attained would lead to anarchy; and true individualism is inherently incompatible with social cooperation. Equality, too, if brought about literally would annihilate competition, which is the main advantage of democracy. Of course, the defenders of democracy can find every imaginable rationalization, under the delusionism about values, which are here rich and many. The arguments are as noble and emotionally convincing as they are naïve. Everybody feels it his duty to defend the Great Truths, though characteristically enough, everybody also admits that these truths are to be taken with many qualifications. The paradoxes of democracy are recognized even by its most ardent defenders. Mark H. Heald, who in his book, *A Free Society*, extols democratic ideals as much as any man can, consecrates a special section to the "Paradoxical Aspects of Democracy." Sidney Hook wrote an interesting book on *The Paradoxes of Freedom*.

The practical success of democracy is explainable by the general contradiction of social coexistence. Egotism is the only force through which "altruistic" social cooperation can be brought about. By giving the greatest possible freedom to individuals and their opposed egotistic interests the most extensive reciprocal restrictions are attained. Nothing can restrict man so well as other men. Since men find themselves in constant cooperation because of the advantages it offers, their opposed interests become an inexhaustible source of subtle, reciprocally imposed and self-accepted, restrictive social conditioning. The masters of political science have construed this system of reciprocal restrictions as a "social contract." This seems to be the only satisfactory concept in explaining logically society at work. Actually, such explanation is as unreal as the factual existence of any contract. It took the idealism of Rousseau to believe in such a contract — or in the logical and noble conduct of men in their free natural state. The very different mechanism of social conditioning through recip-rocal restriction is the real explanation. Democracy is the best system because it produces in the deepest and subtlest ways this restrictive conditioning. Religion and morals, which best induce the individual to accept such conditioning — again for egotistic reasons — are therefore important in democracy.

Communism and **socialism** are built on the general humanistic delusion that the social qualities of men are ready given. The humanistic attitude here reaches its most logical, naïve and intense realization — without being mitigated or compromised by the practical humanistic tradition, which in practice denies the humanistic ideals and rationalizations. The Communist doctrine rests on the belief that by insuring real freedom to men — by making them equal and independent — the best human coopera-tion can be achieved.

Communism is a living illustration of how an ideal turns into a nightmare if the driving force, egotism, is not used for motivation or in the transformation of human nature. Those who have not lived under a Communist regime never really know the amount of suffering, confusion and lies that this nightmare brings. There is not only economic misery, as everything sags because of lack of incentives, but also rule by the unethical,

473

lower-grade element over the higher. As Hayek says in his book, *The Road to Serfdom*, under the Communist system the worst people get on top. This is understandable considering that everything in the system is unnatural and distorted. Communism gains its fierce and reckless followers among the rejects of life who expect to get on top through forcible equalization. As a rule, such rejects are the intellectually and morally lower individuals. They rise to power, become a torture to others, but also are brutally cashiered, because of their failures, by equally reckless new henchmen. The resulting continuous convulsions have the same deeper cause that makes all idealistic revolutions "devour their own children." In any event, the intellectually and morally higher individual neither can be enthusiastic about the forcible equalization nor is fooled by the distortion and lie that go with it.

Communism in practice becomes very different from its idealistic theory. Its inherent errors have led to disasters rarely exceeded in history. Only confusion and strife result from the expected altruism and harmony of men made free and equal. At first, everybody accuses everybody else, without noticing his own egotism. Then, by trial and error the system gravitates toward the only possible form of government — dictatorship. Where inner driving force is missing it has to be supplied by the whip.

The most important change in Communism takes place when the necessity of moral conditioning is recognized, and enforced in the form of "brain-washing." The deceit and hypocrisy of morals that the Communist idealists rose to destroy return in a more primitive form. Brain-washing lacks the effectiveness and subtlety of our religious and moral conditioning, but in essence it is the same. It is not by accident that we find in Communism all the elements of religion — in primitive form. Communism has become a cult with its personified "gods," sanctity of dogma, ceremonials in which the adoration of the "gods" becomes quite effusive, hierarchy of "priests" and hypocrisy of established orthodox "church."

Here it may be interesting to reflect how all cultural endeavors by men end with adoption of the same methods, serving the same basic goals. In simple terms these methods are: conditioning, serving closer social integration; and accumulation of capital and skills, serving man's physical superiority in the struggle with the adversities of nature. From every trial and error men learn how closer social integration brings higher benefits. But such integration requires abdication of immediate egotistic interests. These, however, are the only force that lies behind motivation. Consequently, the use of egotism and its transformation into altruism is the only possible method. Hence the universality of the same contradictory and deceitful conditioning in all cultures. Children everywhere are persuaded to do the things they do not like by promises that something they like will come from it; and are conditioned to feel fear or "conscience" upon disobeying authority. The same method, in subtler ways, is used on grownups.

Closer integration and conditioning are the unconscious goals of our more subtle morals, just as they are of the more direct and clumsy Communist morals. The humanist or social scientist decrying "brain-washing" or the "anthill" society misses the point. But the rationalized formulations of the beliefs matter here as little as everywhere else. As far as the lofty ideas about human nature and the brotherhood of men are concerned, anything our humanists can say the Communists can say better. That is why Communism spreads like cancer, for which humanists prepare the ground. What really matters is the way of life, and there the humanist tradition offers methods embodying age-long wisdoms, whereas Communism can only use force in trying to make men comply with its ideals. Communism can be exposed as the torture method that it is only through understanding the inherent contradiction of human adjustment and conditioning, under which delusory value beliefs have to be used in order to attain something completely different. The present struggle against Communism is comparable to the old religious wars in which people died combating religious beliefs that were essentially the same as their own, but did not see the real causes or the important meaning of their struggle.

As to the economic sources of human progress, the story of

Communism illustrates blatantly the general fallacy prevailing in all existing theorization. Communistic theorists did not understand the ultimate significance of capital. They were as little aware as anybody else of human adjustment as a product of adversity in which man has to overreach nature — by capital accumulation through restraint — in order to win. Communists noticed the significance of capital only after they had destroyed it. Millions died during the misery and chaos before capital was restored. The promised equality and liberation from servitude to capital ended in a virtual serfdom. At the same time, in the countries of highest capitalism the factual equality and material independence of everybody have become so great that it is almost impossible to obtain servants.

It cannot be overemphasized that the ownership of capital does not matter, and that the more capitalistic a system is, the more benefit it brings to the general public. As we explained before, the capitalists only fulfill the role of most effective accumulators and administrators of capital. However, far one goes, there is only accumulated capital left after the capitalist leaves. Ultimately, the general public profits and determines what the capital as increased production potential is used for, since the capitalists ultimately have to produce for somebody, as they themselves consume relatively little. In contrast to the useless consumption of the enjoyment-seeking masses, the serious capitalist reinvests almost everything. Even his personal spending goes mostly into things that remain for posterity or have cultural impact. Of course, there are useless, lower-grade individuals among the rich as well, who are not capable of anything else in life but pointless consumption. The new materialistic morals has not evolved far enough to brand them as the dregs of society that they are; all morals are difficult and sinful things look more attractive, due to the general contradiction of human adjustment.

But generally there has been great progress even in this respect in the capitalistic countries, and it is precisely the accumulation of capital that brought it about. This accumulation cannot help producing with accelerated plenty, which has to devolve on everybody in one form or another, especially as the portion consumed by the "capitalists" decreases. As material things become available to everybody, wealth loses its power and its status meaning. The value of property is disappearing in various ways. Schumpeter has described interesting characteristics of the process of the "Evaporation of the Substance of Property" in his book, *Capitalism, Socialism and Democracy*. Other, immaterial values become the objects of social competition or value fixations. The millionaire now often prefers to live as simply as anybody else if that permits him to fulfill ambitions of high public office or other worthy service, recognized as such by the general public.

Finally, we may look at **totalitarianism.** United authority working for common goals is the essence of every government. In democracy it is attained by compromising the representation principle. In Communism and Fascism it means the rule of one person. Such rule can be spectacularly efficient in comparison with democratic governments. United plan and purpose, through every phase of government, as well as coordination without interference from always diverging individual interests, can be achieved only by one-man rule. It was not any miracles of soul but plain sense that made European countries accept dictators before the Second World War. Unfortunately, the field was left to fanatics and adventurers. If wise dictators could be put in power, totalitarian regimes would be the most efficient in all respects. Even social conditioning can be best achieved in a totalitarian state.

But in our world of democratic ideas no dictator can command moral authority. Anybody who is dissatisfied with existing conditions feels morally authorized to turn against the dictator. Therefore dictators can stay in power only by brutal oppressions, by buying the favors of his collaborators or by exaggerated appeal to national passions, which then leads to wars and persecutions. Under these circumstances only a cruel adventurer or demagogue can rise to dictatorial power; and the worst happens after he gets in power. Human beings remain normal only so long as they have to live under restrictions. The great advantage of democracy is that the men in government are kept under constant pressure. Dictators are bound to become corrupt. When one reads the life stories of Roman emperors he gets an impression of a mysteriously vicious force like a curse of degeneration hanging over them. Equally grave is the problem of insuring succession under a dictatorship. Even if such institutions as party or a ruling clique can take care of it, they degenerate into stagnation while continuing without real pressures from outside.

Aristocracy is ineffective for the same reason. It degenerates. The laws of adjustment tell us that giving man everything good — everything he wants — turns him bad in every respect. This is the reason why humanity can never evolve true class societies. Because of his intelligence man, unlike the ant, takes his place in society according to his over-all superiority, but this superiority generally goes down as the given individual, family or class climbs up. Men have a strong tendency to establish classes, especially upon conquest; and the need for specialization is conductive to class structure. But wherever classes established themselves they have shifted and changed, or lost their real power.

THEORY OF HISTORY

In the study of history the fallacies due to the paradox of relative causation arise mainly from two sources: the relativity of evaluations, and the general paradox of adjustment under which "maladjustments" lead to enrichment and "improvements" to impoverishment of adjustment.

Historical sources, if interpreted with the usual logic, may tell the historian exactly what is *not* causally fundamental to a given people or period. The ever-present fundamental backgrounds which determine values and motivations are never noticed by the people or their historians. Rather are the exceptions to such backgrounds saliently noticed and considered as characteristic. Further, the disvalues, which are the real causal sources of positive values and motivations, are never suspected as having anything to do with them, and are seen as being opposed to them. The same applies to the emergence of feelings of disvalue, with their corresponding motivations, from their opposites — values.

Future historians looking at the literary and artistic sources left by our period would find it as characterized by insecurity

478

and absence of enjoyments. Actually, overprotection and over-enjoyments are the causal realities of our time. Similarly, people living amidst few treasures may leave rich legends about them, whereas other people living amidst general riches would not notice them as anything particular. This becomes interesting in regard to artistic and cultural treasures or ambitions, as we shall see in a moment. We have already explained how the main social values, the freedoms, are seen as the essence of their social life by peoples who live under the highest restrictions, and vice versa. The same relativity and value delusionism apply to every feeling, motivation or value notion. For instance, if we listened to Roman sources, or their interpretation by Wells, we would assume that Romans were effeminate, since effeminacy was repeatedly decried by Roman writers. Of course, in simple instances like these any historian with a good intuition perceives the underlying truth. But historical sources are by no means simple.

Religions, customs, folklore, beliefs, social movements, as well as humanistic interpretations in every field, serve as sources of history. But all of them are subject to the same paradox of relative causation and the delusionism of the value outlook. Historians may notice the contradictions where these become too apparent. For instance, the rise and fall of the Roman Empire has been so much studied that historians now agree on placing the beginning of its decay at the height of its prosperity, the post-Augustian period. But generally historians never suspect that every success or improvement, great or small, like any value experience, from the moment it starts becomes the cause of its own reversal in the end.

The reversals that the historians could not miss observing on a grand scale, they have tried to explain by the theory of historic cycles which, accordingly, has become the only theory great historians have repeatedly recognized. But on a smaller scale and in details the reversals are neither noticed nor explained. Rather, more logically sounding explanations are sought. The result is a confusion and endless variety of explanations. The more sober historians have ended by limiting themselves to descriptions. Apparently, history tells nothing if one looks at it without an insight into its paradoxical logic. Not one law or general truth, apart from the metaphysical cycle theory, has been learned yet by human scientists from the richest source of learning—the past record of the repeated successes and failures of man.

Relative causation in history is as subtle as it is in all adjustment, on which history rests. An effect may seem to have a logical immediate cause, while in fact the cause is an exactly opposite background. To take a simple example, it is true that immediate difficulties or oppressions make people rise in revolutions. But the real cause of revolutions generally is a previous background of freedoms. The great French Revolution started at the time when new burdens became necessary. But the real cause was the previous freedoms enjoyed by the French people. In no other country in continental Europe had serfdom been loosened or the people given representation to the same extent. The very Estates General that started the whole trouble could not be thought of in other countries.

In history, as in individual adjustment, accumulation of enjoyment or value causes dissatisfaction or a feeling of disvalue. In other words, the paradoxical logic of relativity applies to all reactions of peoples in history. It makes the behavior of peoples appear inconsistent and irrational, and historical events neither explainable nor predictable in logical terms. Though value in motivation springs from disvalue, as satisfaction springs from needs, nobody looks for the negative background of needs or restrictions in order to attain the positive values or motivations everybody strives for. That is why progress is so blind, and why history becomes a story of contradictions: peoples seem to resist their own progress and to rush eagerly into their own disasters. In the light of later advance they seem to have been blind to the clearest advantages right before their eyes. Naturally, disturbance or change, which is the quintessence of every need or disvalue, is resisted most. That is why cultural inertia as resistance to change has ruled and continues to rule the destinies of peoples with an unbelievable supremacy, perpetuating their every stupidity.

There are many ways in which the paradox of the relativity of reactions makes peoples in history appear the exact opposite of what they actually were. To take one of the most important examples, Christianity may seem to have originated as a religion of refined, peace-loving, satisfied and materialistically indifferent people. In fact, early Christians were the aggressive, dissatisfied and crude barbarians who brought about the destruction of the Roman Empire from inside, as Gibbon has rightly explained. The traditional view here is naïve indeed. How could the lowest masses of Rome who rose in anger, much like our Communists, have the refined qualities attributed to them? We shall explain later how the misunderstanding arises here. Actually, the non-Christian Romans were the refined, satisfied and materialistically resigned people. They were the bearers of the civilization that we have learned through Christianity. But to them this civilization was the atmosphere they lived in. On the other hand, for the barbarian masses who lacked it, but saw it all around them, it was a revelation of fascinating brilliance. *Christianity was a reflection of the Roman civilization in the minds of barbarians who lacked it.*

To take another important example, historians usually see periods of rich elaborations in art and in forms of living as cultural peaks. In fact, such cultural exhibitionism means either a lack or exhaustion of real cultural treasures and aspirations. Peoples who are exposed to a really superior culture, as Europeans were during the Middle Ages — during the period of the assimilation of Roman culture — feel that they have nothing worthy to say or show. On the other hand, peoples who are narrowly limited to a few cultural treasures, or have exhausted their cultural ambitions and are unmotivated by any higher standards, find high value in endless elaborations of their own arts, forms of living or products of thought. The post-Periclean period in Greece is probably the most typical example of such a seemingly superior culture. But history shows what such periods really are. They are fraught with impoverishment and decay. Collapse usually follows them. And the historian is left with a mystery for which he seeks an explanation in the metaphysical cycles of civilizations.

481

Historians could not miss noticing the fact that hardships make people strong and satisfactions lead to their decline. Overcoming difficulties is also the underlying idea of Toynbee's "challenge" — the central concept of the most important historical theory today. In fact, any difficulty as well as challenge is subject to the same seemingly paradoxical logic. To feel difficulty there must be a previous opposite background. Adding difficulty means decreasing the feeling for it. Equally, to feel a challenge or see an advantage man must have an opposite background in order to experience it. We may be living right now amidst the most interesting challenges or greatest abnormalcies — without being able to respond to them just because they are all around us.

Explanations of how a people progressed because it responded to a challenge make nice descriptions, but explain nothing. One could as well "explain" how a people progressed because they had a progressive attitude. Actually, the historian has to explain why the people had such attitude — why they responded to one out of innumerable other "challenges" that are always there. But to explain that the historian has to understand the paradox of opposite causation — or he will never even suspect the real cause.

Actually, there is never a conscious or logical response to a challenge — advancing above what people are used to and find "normal." The people who respond to a "challenge" are those who had been forced to live under more difficult circumstances and therefore have evolved higher capacities. Then when they come to new opportunities where their capacities can be used with greater advantage they build on beyond all previous "normal" needs. This explains the contradiction about hardy peoples and the births of civilizations. Historians agree that hardy peoples are more capable culturally. But historians also know that the cradles of civilizations lie in the fertile river valleys of the Tigris and Euphrates, Nile, Yellow River or Indus. There must be an opposite background before a reaction or response to a "challenge" can result.

The same relativity of reactions explains other attitudes of peoples toward civilization. It is generally held that the back-

482

ward peoples, like the Eskimos or tropical aborigines, have not advanced because they suffer under the hardships of nature. It is said that nature oppresses the Eskimo, and makes lazy the tropical man. This is a rather naïve imputation by the historian or anthropologist of his own feelings to such peoples. The truth is that these peoples have adjusted too well to their environment — so well that any change for them means nothing but harassment. It is true that nature in its extremes has influenced these people more. One could say that they have "suffered" more. But here as everywhere else the "suffering" precludes itself after a long continuation, and leaves these peoples with the feeling of perfect adjustment to their conditions.

Man has to be forced to move constantly from harder conditions to better ones, and back, if he is to progress. He should not be permitted either to adjust completely to the hard conditions or to continue under favorable ones for long. The seasonal contrasts of what we call the temperate zone make people work hard in order to preserve during winter the adjustment they eagerly espouse during summer. Such achievements as keeping reserves, intensifying food production or building houses are the beginnings of all higher civilizations. There has to be an abnormalcy, either felt as maladjustment or responded to as an unusual opportunity, if progress is to result.

The white race is in general more productive culturally because the white man "feels" himself permanently maladjusted. He is like a plant deprived of light — pale, drawn, ever tense and lacking in sustained temperament — in comparison with the norm of the human species. Human intelligence itself apparently evolved during the ice ages — the hardest period that the species had to live through. But as we saw, this same intelligence conferred on man such an advantage that he ceased to progress until he again met with a formidable difficulty — threat by other men. The higher civilization has emerged during the last few thousand years at the same explosive rate that populations have grown.

Biologically and culturally built-in difficulties confer advantages, therefore establish themselves by way of selection. Consciousness

483

in general is a biologically built-in difficulty, since it presents to man potential threats and future needs. Also, due to conscious realizations the relativity of values, which leaves man always dissatisfied with his achievements, becomes another built-in difficulty. However, the relativity of values is also responsible for the various forms of cultural fixation, which lead to the greatest hindrance to progress: cultural inertia, with its limitations of aims and bigoted blindness.

The culturally built-in difficulties assume, predictably, a religious character, since they are unexplainable otherwise. Such difficulties we find in curious obsessions that appear in various religions and customs, sometimes as characteristic means of keeping the society working together, concentrating on some common task or continuing on a footing of war. To mention a couple, the Egyptians built crazy-size pyramids. Most peoples of the East built "towers of Babel." The Aztecs on the other side of the ocean did the same. The Aztecs excelled in another self-imposed calamity that has kept peoples under strain, often in a continuous war with neighbors — human sacrifice. They required hundreds of enemy victims for a single occasion. Actually, other peoples did equally well. The Carthagians ended by sacrificing their own children, two hundred of them on one occasion. The Kwakiutl Indians burned piles of blankets in their intertribal competitions. Such clearly absurd excesses may not be too general. But the far more important irrational restrictions in religions or moral systems, and the tortured solemnity or seemingly senseless despotism in relations between rulers and the ruled, are fairly general. People seem to torture themselves or invent hard religions for the sole purpose of making life difficult.

The general effect of the paradox of adjustment is that races, nations or groups constantly reverse themselves in their successes and failures. Whatever the challenge that motivates the people, it disappears if satisfaction is attained directly or in the way it was wanted without new difficulties or challenges. People struggling for security may establish an empire, but after attaining everything they wanted may lose it all, succumbing to a harder people, because of the disappearance of the needs that brought the empire about. Other people struggling for specific material improvements may sink into stagnation and inertial fixations on a given level of unproductive materialism to the extent that they were lucky in reaching their goals exactly in the way they wanted them. Degeneration as a consequence of abundance is a well-known truth. All reactions are determined by values and the feeling of value decreases while it is being added.

We admit that these reversals of effect apply only to the psychological factor. But in the average this factor determines everything else. Studying factual events and physical factors in logical terms of cause and effect may lead to more confusion than causal understanding. Any one factor may be the cause of success or of defeat, depending upon an exactly opposite background. A person suffering from lack of motivation may blame unfortunate circumstances and may really seem to be their victim, whereas the real cause of his failures may be the too fortunate past which permitted overenjoyments leading to emotional negativism.

We can take as example the causes of decline of the Roman Empire, which have been exhaustively studied. The following factors have been blamed: extension of the money economy; the rise of big land ownership in Italy; the decrease in the number of slaves and labor force; attacks by barbarians and their gradual penetration inside the Empire; an archaic administrative organization; the decline of older political institutions; rule by army-elected emperors; increased taxation; even plagues, malaria and mosquitoes. If you look at any one of these factors, you can see that it might just as well have served as a great challenge, and the cause of progress, even as an immediate advantage. But they all became causes of failure because there was no motivation left, and the challenges went unnoticed. The various strivings and forces that had created the Empire the way it was were gone, because they had met with full satisfaction.

In view of the universality of reversals it is not surprising to find that **cyclic theories** dominate the more advanced study of history searching for final causes. The best-known cyclic theories are those of Spengler, Toynbee, Danilevsky, Chapin, Sorokin,

Adams and the older theorist Vico. It may be sufficient for us to look at the theories of Spengler and Toynbee, since they are more extensive ones — and probably the most influential of all theories on history.

Spengler viewed civilizations as individual entities which are born, flourish, ripen and decay, during their periods of spring, summer, autumn and winter. They evolve like plants of different species. All of them pass through the same phases, but each has its own strictly distinct nature. To the phase of Pericles and Alexander the Great in the Apollonian culture corresponds exactly the phase of Louis XIV and Napoleon in the Faustian culture. But the products of Apollonian culture, like geometry, are completely incomprehensible to a man from the Faustian culture; he may learn or teach geometry but never believe in it. Incidentally, individuals in each culture pass through the same phases as their culture. Each culture has its prime symbol or characteristic of its soul. The Egyptian soul sees itself as moving through a narrow passage; the Chinese soul, as wandering through a garden; the Magian, as dwelling in the unearthly light of a cave.

According to Spengler, whatever a culture produces is the expression of its soul. Perspective painting, printing, credit, long-range artillery, calculus and contemporary music are expressions of the Faustian soul, whereas the city-state, nude statue, Euclidean geometry and Greek coin are expressions of the Apollonian soul. Columbus, apparently, discovered America not because of the development of shipping and science, but because search in space is a quality of the Faustian soul. Every science is a product of a specific inner vision. "There is Stoicism and there is Socialism of atom," and "every atomic theory is a myth, not an experience."

After Spengler set out the thousand-year periods of his civilizations, he arrived at the eleventh century as the beginning of our Faustian culture. Therefore Christianity or any cultural institution of the tenth century was to be considered as a completely different thing from that of the eleventh century. Spengler has other such mysterious differences, where other historians rather see similarities; for instance, between classical and Renaissance art. Actually, we do not need to go into the absurdities of Spengler. The metaphysical nature of his theory is evident from every bit of it. If one has any doubts, he may reflect about the basic assumption of Spengler that destiny not causality determines history. The point is, however, that Spengler is one of the greatest historians. His main work, the *Untergang des Abendlandes*, is admired as much by historians as by seekers of mystery. Spengler did reveal the universal cyclic pattern in history. Only he did not see its simple, though seemingly illogical cause. He had no choice but to accept metaphysical causes. Spengler's system is a good example of how even the greatest erudition leads to mere mystifications if the causal seemingly paradoxical laws of human adjustment in history are not understood.

Toynbee is, certainly, the greatest historian of our time. He took up the Spenglerian cyclic theory, but tried to interpret the cyclic destinies of civilizations in terms of moral values. The important thing is that Toynbee as the greatest historian we have recognizes cyclic reversals as the basic pattern of history. Here as everywhere else, we do not intend to criticize the technical erudition of a professional in his field. We are concerned here with the causal laws of history. As far as such laws exist they can rest only on the general laws of adjustment, which as natural laws can be only simple and universal. As such they must be evident from everything — the tiniest common event or the thousand-year fate of peoples, generally known to every student of history. There is no need for sophistication or complexity. If such laws cannot be established in simple ways, they cannot be established at all.

Actually, the very complexity and humanistic sophistication of Toynbee's theory are the best indicators that it cannot be scientifically true. Toynbee's superhuman historical beings following their own subtle laws and fulfilling religious missions may be humanistically convincing and interesting. But what is interesting in human terms and resembles human purposes is anthropomorphic rather than scientific. Nature works by the simplest, seemingly meaningless principles, which may appear absurd in human value terms. The humanistic truths of Toynbee's theory cannot be reduced to simple natural principles.

487

Toynbee's historical beings are superhuman: civilizations, societies, minorities, proletariats. They live according to their own laws. Civilization, the main being, is almost as specific as Spengler's civilization, except that organic analogies are avoided. Toynbee's civilizations obey a regular pattern and go through definite phases of development. According to Toynbee, each civilization is born out of a particular challenge, and once born it follows the prescribed phases. If the prescribed pattern is not followed, this constitutes an exceptional instance. Thus Toynbee has identified twenty-six civilizations as having been born alive, four as having miscarried, five as having been arrested, and sixteen as being already dead. Once a civilization has reached a certain phase of its development nothing can change it, though hundreds of years filled with important historical events may follow. As one critic has said, the last seven hundred years since the fatal emergence of Frederick II are according to Toynbee's theory a mere aberration. Once a civilization is doomed, it follows a three and half beat rhythm of rout and rally, and dies leaving a religion as the chrysalis for a new civilization. This bearing of a new religion is the fulfillment of the mandate of every civilization.

Even within the main phases of development there are definite, more detailed patterns or laws that civilizations follow, which are not reducible to any simpler principles. The Failure of Self-Determination has several specific and irreversible causes: mechanicalness of mimesis, delayed mimesis, nemesis of idolization of an ephemeral self, institution or technique, or intoxication of victory. Schism in the Body Social follows a definite pattern with the appearance of a dominant minority as well as internal and external proletariats, which follow their specific patterns. Schism in the Soul has its specific and irreversible causes: sense of sin, disunity, or detachment and so on.

All these reactions, resembling psychological complexes, are supposed to arise from predetermined inner debilities of the soul rather than from influences of correspondingly great or lasting impact. Here we have a parallel to the alchemistic spirit of modern psychology, according to which a great disturbance can arise

488

from an insignificant incident. It is characteristic that Toynbee has called Jung his guide; he could not have chosen a more alchemistic psychologist. Toynbee, not unlike Jung, likes to discover the characteristics of the social soul from striking bits of legend, folklore or art, though in fact what is striking here is causally least essential. It is equally alchemistic, psychologically, to regard all such reactions, like "intoxication" or the "sense of sin," as irreversible or fatal once they happen to arise. Actually, every reaction extinguishes itself and reverses as it continues.

In any case, the basic causal principles in Toynbee's theory are too complex and humanistic to be reduced to simple natural causes. Even such concepts as challenge or creative minority, which come closer to natural fundamental factors, are not treated as such in Toynbee's system. Each challenge is specific for the given civilization; it must meet with successful etherialization of forces and specific further challenges. Also, there must be a golden mean of conditions. The creative minority and its functions are equally specific and follow a prescribed course with equal uniformity depending upon multiple factors. All this would mean extraordinary coincidence or luck. But luck or chance is the last thing to go with the absolutely normative, uniform destinies of civilizations in Toynbee's theory. Consequently, a metaphysical predetermination is the only possible explanation.

Here we come to the most important part of Toynbee's system: the implied acceptance of metaphysical causes of history. Toynbee's civilizations are here for a mission. A universal religion as a chrysalis for a new civilization is born in each civilization. This is a pathetic view, worthy of any civilized mind. That is why Toynbee's history appeals to so many. But such an approach is unscientific. It is worth as much as any belief or emotion. Actually, it rests on value convictions, which, as we saw, point to what is causally least true. But Toynbee did the only sensible thing he could do. If natural causal explanation of the cyclic destinies of civilizations is not available, acceptance of truths inherent in general human beliefs offers at least the certitude of being right in a very general sense.

If a less exalted view of religion is adopted, the historian can see that religion is only a reflection of a civilization which finds through it formal unity and identification. Naturally, the external forms here — the crystallized dogmas and teachings — become sacrosanct due to fixation. Whatever the process, universal religions appeared after more universal societies had evolved. Christianity was a reflection of Roman civilization, elevated into a religion by barbarians who were impressed by it. Later, other barbarians accepted it, also because it came with a higher, respect-inspiring civilization. In the Middle Ages to be religious meant to be civilized. This was the reason why Christianity expanded; it was not because of any mysterious revelations or uniqueness of its teachings. Christianity was amazingly similar to other religions, especially Mithraism, that arose on Roman soil. The similarity was so glaring that Christians blamed it on the perverse ingenuity of Satan, as Lynn Thorndike tells in his *Short History of Civilization.*

If Toynbee had seen religions for what they are, he would have agreed with the greatest truth of all history, namely, that there is only one strikingly continuous civilization. It has grown at a continuous progressive rate during the last few thousand years, though the *names* and *labels* of its bearers have changed. Here we meet with another general truth noticed by most historians. A civilized nation or empire may be conquered by another people, but it continues, by transforming or conquering the conquerors culturally. Roman civilization continued, after the fall of Rome, as Christianity. Even outwardly Rome continued as the center of the civilized world. Characteristically enough, it continued also in name, as the Holy Roman Empire, up to the nineteenth century. But names do not matter. Nor do political organizations, though the theories of cyclic civilizations are built on observation of the growth and decline of political empires.

Cyclic flourishing and decline rest on the universal rule of reversals in the adjustment of men, and can be treated as a general pattern or law of history. But it applies equally to individuals, families, institutions, classes, states, even races. Only a coincidence in the total adjustments of all these may produce a decline of the given political empire. Under different coincidences it may continue, as the Eastern Roman Empire did. What is not accidental is that the same civilization continues, under changed names and the general pattern of reversals in adjustment of its bearers. If this is not understood, the historian is bound to reach completely distorted conclusions.

Here we have to say more about the fallacy of names and labels. In the case of conquerors who become continuators of the civilization of their conquered opponents, the discrepancies in names and labels are clear. But more often an empire or state is conquered not from outside but from inside, and in endless phases. The constant surging of lower classes from below, getting on top, then declining in their own turn is the most important historical reality. Of course, in many cases this comes about by an assimilation so slow and gradual that outwardly there are no distinctive movements to be perceived. But in those cases where distinctive revolutionary or reformatory movements appear, they reveal a story that is fraught with the same paradox. We explained before the deeper cause of this paradox. The movement which grows to oppose everything of the old order ends by cultivating what the old order represented, though such a movement continues bearing its own, very different slogans and names. In most cases, the masses in such movements are led under slogans or teachings of liberation and release. But once established the movement becomes reactionary and restrictive, as this remains the only way to sustain the civilization that has been learned in the meantime. The slogans and teachings, however, remain and may become sacrosanct through fixation.

The end result is that historians searching to illuminate the origins of a historical movement in the light of its essence as it appears later are bound to reach conclusions exactly opposite to what was true; or historians trying to elicit the nature of a later movement from its continued original ideologies and teachings may reach equally wrong conclusions. The essence of historical movements reverses while the names and labels remain; or the same civilization is continued by peoples and movements that seem to be its exact opponents.

491

To use the same example of Christianity, there is hardly an institution that is more conservative, morally restrictive, immaterialistic and nonaggressive than the present-day church. But Christianity started as a revolutionary, morally irreverent and aggressive movement of dissatisfied classes. It was very much like modern Communism. The antireligiousness and moral irreverence of Christians was the main reason they were persecuted. Romans were extremely tolerant in religious matters. They revered Greek and Oriental deities, and sometimes made offerings to the deities of an enemy before they attacked it. The early Christians, however, were completely different, and religiously as well as morally offensive. They were preoccupied with their new Kingdom and the equality for all people, just as Communists are now. They were so unconcerned about religious matters that they had no elaborate rituals or multiple gods which as lowest-class people they would have otherwise inevitably had. Above all, they were revolutionaries with all their crudity, deep-seated hatred, and irreverence for conventional, existing morals. A group of early Christians, if it appeared today, would be branded by our churches as enemy number one.

But once Christianity established itself, its ideals became "corrupt," and the Roman civilization that the Christians set out to destroy became its real soul. One should not be deceived by the proclaimed Christian ideals. There never are bad ideals, whether they be of the early Christians, French Revolution or Chinese Communism; and the physically weaker opponent always invokes nonviolence. The very idea of Christ as their martyred god reveals impotent hatred and injured self-righteousness as the emotions that nurtured their movement. Anyway, a historian unaware of the reversals involved would see the Romans who persecuted the Christians as religiously and morally callous uncultured brutes, while just the reverse was true. Gibbon shows his exceptionally deep understanding of Roman history by perceiving this truth.

Praise and blame often go to the wrong sides in history. The reason is the contradiction of adjustment and conditioning, just as in the education and adjustment of individuals. Those who restrict and build reap little immediate praise or success. Those who work by release and spending get all the praise and immediate miraculous results. Of course, collapse and disasters then invariably follow — but are readily blamed on something else. Alexander the Great and Attila are praised as great warriors though they only spent what their fathers, Philip and Munzuk, had laboriously built and accumulated.

CONCLUSION

The same complete lack of causal understanding that prevents psychology from advancing beyond its alchemistic stage governs the modern social sciences. For, ultimately, social adjustment is determined by psychological adjustment. The success or failure of social adjustment in every instance depends on the availability of positive emotions or motivations, whatever their forms, just as in the case of individuals, of which society consists. But the "scientism" of social theorists would hinder rather than help the causal understanding or promotion of such positive emotions or motivations. Social theorists suspect as little as ordinary man that the real causal source of a positive emotion or satisfaction is an exactly opposite negative emotion or need. In fact, the more thoroughly scientific approach of the social theorists makes them more consequentially averse to such seeming paradox. The experimental methods of modern "scientism" show release to be the source of motivation in all its forms, individual or social, though, as we saw, only a previous restriction can make that release possible.

Modern social sciences have grown into tremendous systems of learning. But more learning can only confuse more if the very logic on which it is based is completely wrong. No wonder social scientists themselves recognize that present science cannot determine social events, nor even has rules for predicting them. Actually, the social sciences could transform — probably very slowly at the beginning — human adjustment much more spectacularly than the technical sciences have. But for that the laws of causation of human reactions and adjustment would have to be understood.

INDEX

A

Adjustment, 176ff., 478, 484
  theories and treatises on, 218ff.
Adler, A., 166-167
Aesthetics, 296ff.
  and cultural progress, 232, 298
  laws of, 56, 296
Alchemy:
  in modern psychology, 63, 64, 138
  in psychoanalysis, 157, 175,
Alexander, F., 158, 171
Analysis as therapy, 133
Angell, N., 465
Animals, feelings by, 255-56
Anxiety, 104-105
Art:
  appreciation of, by critics, 304
  modern abstract, 299
  sources of its superiority, 302
  styles of, 300ff.
Aslan, A., 421
Atheism, 272
Atom, the mysteries of, 344ff.

B

Background causation, 15, 191, 335
  (*see also* Negative experience)
Beauty as value, 228-232
Bergson, H., 44
Bohr, N., 348
Brunner, D., 393
Business cycles, 457ff.

C

Cancer, 400-409
Capital and progress, 449, 453, 476
Causal law, psychological 2-3
  (*see also* Relative causation)
Cholesterol, 390-391
Christianity, 481, 490, 492
Coleman, L. L., 220
Coley, W. B., 408
Collection of books, antiques, etc., 307
Common sense, superiority of, over:
  "high learning," 23, 450
  moral rationalizations, 270
  philosophical mysteries, 295
Communism, 473ff.
Compton, A. H., 349
Conditioning, 4, 29-33, 186, 468
  perfectionism and refinement in, 179
Conscience:
  loss by increase of feeling of, 209
  nature and origin, 32, 186
Consciousness, nature of, 44-45
Contrast, 55, 298, 302
Cultural inertia, 307-309
Culture, causal sources of, 259ff.
  (*see also* Progress, cultural)
Cyclic reversals, in history, 479-484
  and the Cyclic theories, 485ff.

D

Darwin, C. R., 28, 433
Daydreaming, 213
Death, 256-258
  belief in life after, 273-274
Defense:
  in neuroses, 99
  in psychoanalytic theory, 158
Dewey, J., 93
Discoveries, scientific, source of, 15

495

Diseases:
   mental, 120ff.
   physical, 372ff.
   (*see also* Paradoxical logic of)
Disvalues, 252-257
Dreams:
   accidental nature of, 37, 155
   in psychoanalysis, 155ff.
Drinking, 201
Drug treatment:
   of neuroses and psychoses, 128
   of physical diseases, 380ff.
Drugs:
   addiction to, 4, 34
   use of, 202
Dubos, R., 405, 414

E

Economics, 440ff.
Education, 177-189
Egotism importance of, 269, 473-5
Einstein's Relativity Theory, 339
   and reality of the Field, 338
Electromagnetism, 360
Environment, importance of, 17, 184
Equivalence:
   of emotions, 46-52
   and modern "alchemy," 12, 50,
      63, 138
   in mental disorders, 99, 130, 140
   of satisfaction and need, 3, 220
Existence:
   and basic universal laws, 237
   and terms of knowledge, 293, 333
Experiment:
   examples in psychology, 65ff.
   misunderstood role of, 24, 70

F

Ferenczi, S., 103
Field, the, in physics: 334ff.
   and the Ether or field, 337
Fixation, 53, 211, 297
Free education, 62, 178, 182, 185

Freedom, as value notion, 249
   political, 468-470
Freud, S., 135, 146, 164-166

G

Games and sports, 210, 308
   cultural inertia and, 307
   fixation on, 211, 308
Genetics, 422ff.
God:
   source of belief in, 13, 271
   proofs of existence of, 281, 290
Golden rule, the, 266
Goldschmidt, R. B., 426
Gravitation, 358-360
Guilt, complex of, 111

H

Haddow, A., 400
Happiness:
   and higher interests, 51, 227
   nature and causal origin of, 224ff.
Harmony as value, 233ff.
   and evolution, 235, 286
   humanistic fallacies about, 239
Hayek, F. A., 474
Headaches, 203
Hench, P. S., 397
Hope and faith, 248
Horney, K., 102
Huggins, C., 400, 401
Human nature:
   belief in the sanctity of, 269
   "crippling" by conditioning,
      29-30, 179
Humanistic delusion, 14, 20, 234,
   238, 270
Humor, sense of, 251
Huxley, J., 425
Hypochondria, 124

I

Illusions, perceptual, 79ff.
Immortality, belief in, 242, 272-274
Infectious diseases, 414-416

496

Inferiority complex, 114, 167
Interests:
   natural, 178, 196
   spiritual, 50-51, 224
Instincts:
   and hormic theories, 92-93
   superiority of, over intellect, 44
Intellectual potential, unlimited, 61
Introspection, 70

J

James, W., 68, 93
Jones, E., 170
Juvenile delinquency, 194-196
Jung, C. G., 168

K

Keynes, J. M., 447, 457, 460
Keys, A., 392
Koehler, W., 87, 88
Koffka, K., 88

L

Language and thought, 278ff.
Laws of nature:
   simplicity of, 1-2, 22
   ultimate explanation of, 237, 332
Learning, abstract, 189-194
   and negative background, 191
Lewin, K., 90
Life, nature and origin of, 429ff.
Literature, 304-307
Lobotomy, 139
Lodge, O., 337
Longevity, 416-419
Love, 243-248
   in education, 182ff.

M

Maladjustment:
   paradox of, 176, 189
   sexual, 196-199
Malraux, A., 304
McDougall, W., 92
Marriage, sexual compatibility in, 198

Master, A. M., 388, 392
Medicine, modern, fallacies of, 375ff.
Memories, the paradox of, 51, 67
Menninger, K., 137, 158, 199
Mental health:
   increasing problem, 128, 139
   modern approach on, 136-140
Miracle and mystery:
   as requirement in beliefs, 277
   in philosophy, 295
Mitchell, W. C., 457
Morals, nature and origins of, 265ff.
Motivation:
   difficulty to increase, 16-17
   the paradox of, 8, 493
   (see also Negative experience)
Movement, causal explanation, 350
Muller, H. J., 426

N

Needs, conditioning of, 31ff.
Negative experience, importance of:
   in adjustment, 176, 221
   in education, 181
   in learning, 191, 193
   in motivation, 15, 176, 480
   (see also Background causation)
Neuroses, main types, 104ff.
   Retirement, Sunday, a. o., 103
Nuclear fission and "burning," 369

O

Oedipus complex, 147, 149
Old, L. J., 408
Old age, 215-16
Opposite causation, 57-61
Overadjustment:
   definition of, 4, 99, 372
   in disease and cure, 372ff., 384ff.
   in neuroses and psychoses, 99, 120
Overstreet, H. and B., 219
Overweight, 199-201, 392

P

Page, I. H., 388, 389

Pain, 254, 376
Paradoxical logic of:
  disease and cure, 99, 372
  historical causation, 478ff.
  psychological causation, 3, 5, 9, 10
  social causation, 437, 480
Particle-wave dilemma, 353-358
Patriotism, 265, 467
Peale, N. V., 46, 218
Philosophy:
  as source of beliefs, 282, 295
  failure of, 286ff., 331
  nature of its method, 312-314
  schools and theories of, 314ff.
Physical care in adjustment, 211
Physics:
  and the background reality, 334
  and human one-sidedness, 371
  dilemmas and mysteries of, 335ff.
  relativity of knowledge, and, 333ff.
Pitkin, W. B., 225
Planets, creation and orbits of, 366
Play, 210
  fixation on, 211
  (see also Games and sports)
Pleasure, 25-27
  as source of motivation, 5, 8, 25
  measurement of, 35-38
  nature of, 26ff.
  paradox of, 8, 258, 493
  (see also Equivalence of emotions)
Politics and political systems, 464ff.
Progress:
  cultural, 221, 310
  economic, 440ff.
  future, 309-310
  social, 471, 493
Projection, a. o. mechanisms, 115-16
Psychoanalysis, 142ff.
  examples of theorization, 172-174
  masters of, 164-172
  most harmful errors of, 175
  success of, 160-162

Psychology:
  modern theory of, 19, 64ff., 96-97
  schools of, 74ff.
Psychosomatic medicine, 385
Psychoses, 120-127

Q

Quantum physics, 354

R

Radiation, causal explanation of, 350
Rank, O., 169
Ray, M. R., 219
Reason and truth, delusion of,
  240, 287
Rejuvenation, 420-422
Redl, F., 180
Relative causation, 3, 5, 10-12
  reversed logic of, 9, 39, 191, 222,
  439, 479
  (see also Paradoxical logic of)
Relativity:
  in some philosophies, 7, 8, 294, 330
  of cognition, 42-45
  of knowledge in philosophy, 312;
  in physics, 333ff., 369
  of sensations, 39-41,
  unacceptability of, to man, 3, 5, 61,
  103, 222
Religion, 271ff.
  dogmas, sanctity of, 275
  in history, 276, 490
Repression,
  in neuroses, 99, 132, 139,
  in psychoanalysis, 159-160
Restriction:
  and cultural tradition, 8, 120, 198
  and intelligence, 34, 62, 192
  and release, paradox of, 27, 96, 493
  during infancy, 188
  importance of, 11, 120, 141, 181
Russell, B., 224
Rutherford, E., 356

498

S

Satisfaction:
  and need equivalence, 3, 5, 222
  in learning, 189ff.
  in motivation, 176, 186, 493
  paradox of, 5, 42, 140, 221
Schindler, J. A., 137
Schumpeter, J. A., 457, 461, 477
Scientism of modern psychology:
  and cultural tradition, 270, 310
  as an imitation, 64ff.
  fallacies of, 97-98
Selection, natural, 16, 28
  Inner, 28
Self-punishment, 158
Selye, H., 383
Sexual drive, 151, 197
  cultural restrictions on, 8, 198
  importance of, 152, 197
  in psychoanalysis, 150ff.
Shock treatment, 131, 408
Shyness, compulsive, 111-113
Sleeplessness, 204
Smoking, 201
Social adjustment, 213-215
Social cooperation political, 464ff.
  and social "neuroses," 464-66
  sources of, 473, 474-5
  ultimate goals of, 475-76
Social integration:
  utopian advantages of, 268
  as the ultimate goal, 475
Social nature of man, 262, 269
Societies:
  exponential growth of, 263
  forces of creation, 261, 264
Sokoloff, B., 398
Spengler's theory, 486
Stare, F. J., 387, 391, 392
Steckle L. C., 220
Stress and mental disorders, 100, 132, 140

Suicide, 216-218
Sullivan, H. S., 138

T

Thorndike, L., 490
Thorpe, L. P., 220
Toynbee's theory, 487
  the "challenge" in, 482
Tradition, cultural:
  and rationalism, 241, 310
  decline with scientism, 141, 258, 270
  importance of, 17, 179, 196, 261
  restrictive wisdom of, 8, 63, 140, 176, 198

V

Value concepts, 69, 78, 87, 255, 377
Value delusions:
  causal explanation of, 12, 223
  cultural, 259ff
  everyday, 222ff
Value outlook, 12-15, 55, 238, 314
Vicious-circle effect:
  in mental disorders, 99ff.
  in physical diseases, 22, 372
Vitamins, 413

W

Wars:
  as source of social progress, 263-64
  prevention of, 264
Watson, J. B., 76
Weber-Fechner law, 39, 254
Wolff H. G., 204
Work:
  in adjustment and therapy, 206ff.
  pleasure as motivation in, 16-17, 49, 207
Worries, shelving of, 209-10
Worsening through improvement, 99, 101, 372ff.
  (see also Vicious-circle effect)
Wundt, W., 39, 93